Since the time of the Second World War, there has been a marked rise in all sorts of psychosocial problems in young people – criminal activities, suicidal behavior, alcohol and drug abuse, depression, and eating disorders. The rise has been striking because during this same time period, the physical health of people and their living conditions have improved in most developed countries. Why have psychosocial disorders in adolescents increased and what can be done to prevent the disorders or at least reduce their adverse impact?

In *Psychosocial Disturbances in Young People: Challenges for Prevention*, top experts provide an overview of adolescent problems, ranging from delinquency to depression, addressing these key questions: To what extent is the problem meaningfully separate from other disorders occurring in the same age group? What are the respective influences of individual, family, and societal factors in the etiology of such problems? To what extent are there similarities or differences in the presentation and cause of these problems in childhood, adolescence, and adulthood? To what extent are there continuities between childhood and adulthood, and what are the risk factors and protective factors?

The contributors examine ways that problems might be prevented through schools, youth organizations, and other mechanisms for coping with stress. The volume successfully integrates various perspectives, with a summary chapter framing the issue of psychosocial problems in adolescence.

Psychosocial Disturbances in Young People

Psychosocial disturbances in young people

Challenges for prevention

Edited by
Michael Rutter
Institute of Psychiatry
University of London

CAMBRIDGE
UNIVERSITY PRESS

PUBLISHED BY THE PRESS SYNDICATE OF THE UNIVERSITY OF CAMBRIDGE
The Pitt Building, Trumpington Street, Cambridge CB2 1RP, United Kingdom

CAMBRIDGE UNIVERSITY PRESS
The Edinburgh Building, Cambridge CB2 2RU, United Kingdom
40 West 20th Street, New York, NY 10011-4211, USA
10 Stamford Road, Oakleigh, Melbourne 3166, Australia

First published 1995
First paperback edition 1997

Printed in the United States of America

Typeset in Palatino

A catalogue record for this book is available from the British Library

Library of Congress Cataloguing-in-Publication Data is available

ISBN 0-521-46187-1 hardback
ISBN 0-521-59873-7 paperback

Contents

Foreword

This volume is the second in a series of books sponsored by the Johann Jacobs Foundation as part of its remit to build bridges between the scientific community and the practitioners, policymakers, business leaders, educationalists, and other field-workers who can incorporate useful research findings into their everyday work. The Foundation is devoted to the encouragement and support of research, program development, and professional activities designed to improve our understanding of human development, with a particular focus on adolescents and young people. Extensive social, demographic, economic, technological, and cultural change is taking place all over the world. Some of these changes are clearly for the good, but others are not. In many countries, there is a regrettable disjunction between the conditions needed for the optimal development of young people and conditions provided by society and its various organizations and institutions. The Foundation's goals are to increase knowledge of what is needed to improve this situation and to ensure that such knowledge is made available to those in a position to act upon it.

This volume is part of that basic endeavor. It had its origins in a conference held at the Foundation's Communication Centre, Marbach Castle (Germany) on November 5–7, 1992, with the participation of over forty scientists and young scholars from many parts of the world, especially Europe and North America. The meeting contributed greatly to our understanding of the biological, cultural, psychological, historical, economic, and educational contexts in which young people face adolescence. This crucially formative second decade of life is an age period not only of great risks but also of tremendous opportunities. The chapters in this book reflect that better understanding of the challenges of adolescence and how they may be met more successfully. The particular focus of the book is on why psychosocial disorders in young people are increasing in frequency and what can be done to prevent such disorders or reduce their adverse impact. The book should be of interest to all people concerned with the well-being of youth and especially to those involved in services for this age group – whether in schools, youth organizations, community planning, clinics, or counseling.

The Johann Jacobs Foundation hopes that the knowledge disseminated by this volume will result in improved policies and practices and contribute to the development of better, research-informed strategies to foster the development and well-being of adolescents – those in special risk or need groups and those in the population as a whole.

Klaus Jacobs
Founder and Chairman of the Board
The Johann Jacobs Foundation

Preface

Up until some twenty or thirty years ago, many people viewed adolescence as an age period necessarily characterized by emotional turmoil and disturbance. Supposedly, it was "normal" during adolescence to behave in ways that would be indicative of psychosocial disorder if they occurred later in life. Systematic general population studies clearly showed that this view was mistaken. Most young people went through the teenage years without marked problems of any kind. This is not to say that parent-child disagreements over matters of dress, hair length, autonomy, and the time to be home at night are not quite common. These *are* a normal part of the growing up process for many young people. But the evidence was clear cut that such disagreements were associated with disorder in only a minority of cases.

Paradoxically, just as it was being appreciated that most adolescents did *not* manifest psychosocial disorders, the evidence began to accumulate that, since the Second World War, there has been a marked rise in psychosocial problems in young people – criminal activities, suicidal behavior, alcohol and drug abuse, depression, and eating disorders. The rise was particularly striking because, over this same time period, the *physical* health of people had shown a marked improvement. Infant mortality rates continued to fall and life expectancy increased. Also, living conditions were improving in most developed countries, and the 1950s and 1960s were years of particularly low unemployment in most countries. Why were psychosocial disorders in young people increasing and what might be done to prevent such disorders or reduce their adverse impact? Those questions concern the backdrop to this volume.

The book starts with a consideration of the changes involved in adolescence, moves to a review of the major challenges provided by antisocial behavior and depression (two forms of disturbance that increase in frequency over the teenage years), and then considers crime and suicidal behaviors in greater detail. The next four chapters discuss possible modes of preventive intervention and the final chapter pulls together the various themes considered throughout the book.

Anne Petersen and Nancy Leffert discuss changes that have taken place over time and the meaning of adolescence. The prolongation of education, changes in public attitudes, and the development of a mass youth market in music and clothes have all played a part in making adolescence a much more distinctive phase of life than it has been in past centuries. During puberty the physical alterations are more rapid and more major than at any other time after infancy. There are also momentous psychological transitions and striking individual variations in reactions to puberty. Young people become better able to engage in abstract reasoning and show an increased capacity to consider future perspectives. They are more psychological in their self-descriptions, and their self-identity becomes more distinctive. There is an increasing expectancy that young people function autonomously and there are changes in the pattern and quality of their individual relationships. All young people undergo these various physical and psychological changes, but they vary greatly in how they cope with the transitions. The teenage years are also an age period in which there is a marked increase in the rate of many types of psychosocial disturbance and disorder.

In considering the changes over time that have taken place in rates of disorder, attention is drawn to the parallel changes over time in family patterns, with an increase in divorce rate and in the number of single parent families. Traditionally, emphasis has been placed on the family as the major influence on the psychological development of young people, but there is good evidence that peer groups, schools, and neighborhoods also make a considerable impact.

At one time, psychological development tended to be viewed as largely established during the preschool years, and became increasingly fixed after that. We now know this view greatly underestimates the degree of developmental fluidity. Experiences during the teenage years can make a decisive impact and there is a complex pattern of continuities and discontinuities with respect to the sequelae of changes for the worse or for the better during adolescence. Some experiences tend to accentuate preexisting characteristics and others lead to changes in psychological functioning. But psychological development does not come to a halt in the teens. Getting "back on track" is still possible for troubled youngsters in early adult life provided they have the right experiences.

The physical changes of puberty and their psychological consequences are considered in greater detail by François Alsaker. She notes that psychosocial problems that become prominent during adolescence may nevertheless have begun well before that time. A distinction needs to be drawn between disorders that start *de novo* during the teenage years and those that began in much earlier childhood but which become accentuated during adolescence. There are very marked hormonal changes associated with puberty; these begin in middle childhood before the physical changes are apparent externally. As is well known, puberty begins a couple of years earlier in girls than in boys and there are huge individual differences in the timing of puberty.

It is a mistake to consider the psychological consequences of puberty primarily in terms of hormones and sexuality. These are important but the psychological impact of the physical changes of puberty varies with social context and the reactions of others to young people's growing physical maturity. Nowadays the mass media have a much greater role in shaping attitudes and behavior than they did earlier in the century. There is generally a decrease during adolescence in the extent to which parents monitor their children's behavior but, again, there are marked individual variations. Puberty is usually welcomed by boys but tends to be a source of dissatisfaction in girls. Hormones have both direct and indirect effects on behavior but the importance of such effects in relation to the changes in behavior during the teenage years, especially in relation to psychosocial disturbances, remains quite uncertain. The chapter ends with a discussion of the implications of research findings and an emphasis on the need to prevent the negative effect of reactions to early puberty.

David Farrington discusses the major challenge presented by antisocial behavior, which most people particularly associate with adolescence. He notes that teenage antisocial behavior ranges greatly in seriousness. Minor transient antisocial behavior is almost universal in boys and also quite common in girls, but conduct *disorders* are much less frequent – arising in perhaps 9 percent of males and 2 percent of females. There is considerable continuity in antisocial behavior, between both early childhood and adolescence and adolescence and adult life. There is a general tendency, however, for offending to peak in the teenage years and decrease in the twenties. Thus, if we are to understand the factors influencing antisocial behavior, we must consider those associated with the general increase in offending during adolescence and the general tendency for desistance in delinquent behavior during early adult life, as well as the factors influencing individual differences in the degree of antisocial behavior.

We know a good deal about the variables that are statistically associated with antisocial behavior but we know less about the mechanisms involved. The important risk factors for antisocial behavior include the temperamental characteristic of impulsivity, low intelligence, poor parental supervision and adverse parenting, parental criminality, memberships of the delinquent peer group, large family size and low family income, and opportunities for crime. It is interesting that social isolation seems to be a protective factor with respect to offending, although not with respect to social dysfunction more generally. The chapter ends with a consideration of possibilities for intervening to prevent antisocial behavior. The promising interventions include cognitive-behavioral interpersonal skills training, good schooling, enhancing parenting skills, positive influences on the peer group, possibly income maintenance (although evidence suggests this is not very effective), and situational manipulations to reduce crime opportunities.

The other major psychosocial disorder that becomes much more frequent during the teenage years is depressive disorder. Kathleen Merikangas and Jules Angst consider the different meanings of depression as an emotion and depression as a disorder. The experience of misery and unhappiness is extremely common during the teenage years but episodes of major depressive disorder are much less frequent, probably arising in less than 5 percent of the population. Major depressive disorders in adolescence are associated with a greatly increased risk of similar disorders in adult life, and need to be taken seriously. Depressive disorders are about equally frequent in males and females during childhood, but become much more frequent in women than men after the teenage period. The reasons for the change in sex ratio are not as yet understood. Parental depressive disorder is associated with a marked increased risk of depressive disorders in the children, but the mechanisms involved are by no means entirely clear. The risk probably stems from both genetic predisposition and psychosocial adversities, the admixture stemming in part from the fact that parental depression tends to be accompanied by a range of family difficulties. Attention is drawn to the high frequency with which depressive problems co-occur with supposedly separate types of disorder – especially anxiety states and conduct disturbances. It is important that we gain a greater understanding of how this co-occurrence comes about.

David Smith, in his chapter, focuses on patterns in crime, taking up some of the key issues raised by David Farrington. He notes the need to account for mechanisms underlying the striking age-crime curve. It is equally important to understand what is involved in the heterogeneity of antisocial behavior and the individual differences in continuities over time. Psychologists have traditionally tended to consider developmental continuities in terms of individual behavioral traits and characteristics. Thus, there has often been a focus on continuities over time in aggression. Smith cites findings from the Stockholm longitudinal study that the main continuities over time in aggression come about because of a subgroup of young people who show a combination of aggression, hyperactivity, and poor peer relationships. The most important adult outcome of antisocial problems in the teenage years is antisocial personality disorder. Epidemiological studies show, however, that this disorder is present in only 3 percent of adults and hence that the great majority of juvenile delinquents do not show this adverse progression. The range of individual factors that may play a part in the predisposition to delinquency are discussed and attention is drawn to the marked sex difference in the rate of delinquency. Although this has diminished somewhat over time, it is still very strong. There is a strong association between delinquent behavior and abuse of alcohol and illicit drugs.

David Smith notes particularly the trends over time in crime rates. Important methodological problems must be taken into account when considering such secular trends, but a careful consideration of the evidence indicates a marked rise in the crime rate since World War II. There are important cross-national differences in crime rates as well, but their meaning remains uncertain. The various theoretical explanations put forward to account for crime, and for its variations over time, are critically considered. The chapter ends with a discussion of situational crime prevention, the impact of changes over time in family functioning, and the probable decline in the effectiveness of informal social controls.

Suicidal behavior is distinctly uncommon during childhood but becomes much more frequent during the teenage period. The general public tends to think of suicide as a more severe form of attempted suicide. René Diekstra points out that, although the two are related, they are far from synonymous. Most young people who engage in suicidal behavior do not go on to kill themselves and the factors associated with parasuicide are not identical with those associated with completed suicide. As with crime, there are important measurement issues to be considered when asking whether there have been changes over time in rates of parasuicide and completed suicide. It is clear, however, that there has been an increase in suicidal risk among adolescents and young adults over the past two decades in many countries. There is also evidence that depressive disorders in young people have probably increased. It is unlikely that there is a single explanation for this change in suicide rates.

It is suggested, however, that the lowering of the age of puberty, together with a prolongation in education and changes in the meaning of adolescence, may have caused a disjunction between biological development on the one hand and psychosocial development on the other. The increased availability of models of suicide (as in the mass media) and an increase in the use of drugs and alcohol is likely to have played a part as well.

The second half of the book considers how some of the most important preventive interventions may be applied. Bruce Compas discusses concepts of stress and coping and prevention at the individual level. Jane Quinn, by contrast, focuses on the positive role of youth organizations, Albert Reiss discusses community influences on adolescent behavior, and Peter Mortimore discusses the role of schools.

Bruce Compas notes the challenge to help young people develop effective ways of coping with the stresses they face and avoiding maladaptive responses. Stress is a very broad concept and it includes a quite diverse range of experiences. Thus, there are various normative stresses that are part of the growing up process: starting and leaving school, the negotiation of puberty, and leaving home. But there are also acute stresses: parental divorce, bereavement, rebuffs from friends, or broken relationships. Although these are indeed "acute" happenings, they often represent drawn out processes. In considering the effects of divorce, for instance, it is necessary to recognize that the breakup of the marriage may well have been preceded by discord over many years and may bring with it all sorts of sequelae. There are as well severe chronic stresses of various kinds: poverty, chronic family discord, and prolonged parental illness.

Coping with these various forms of stress involves both the practical steps taken to deal with the situation and the emotional response. Both may well be influenced by the ways in which young people think about what happens to them. Effective coping seems to involve matching one's own appraisal of the circumstances with the use of active problem-focused coping strategies. Ineffective coping seems to be characterized at least in part by unhelpfully focusing attention on negative feelings, rather than on what could be done to improve the situation.

Bruce Compas reviews the evidence from studies examining the effectiveness of programs designed to facilitate and promote successful coping. Generic programs have focused on the development of a set of attitudes and behaviors that foster positive feelings about oneself, mutually adaptive relationships with other people, and skills to solve life problems and to cope with life stressors. Evaluations indicate that the results of these forms of intervention are quite promising. A second, rather different, set of interventions seeks to address specific problems or types of psychopathology and a third group focuses on coping with severe acute stresses such as divorce and bereavement. In spite of the known importance of chronic stressors, there has been little work on the development of interventions to help adolescents cope with these. Interventions in this field are beginning to be studied, however, and clearly it is a priority for the future.

Adults have long appreciated that organizations that bring young people together in constructive pursuits have the potential for harnessing the many idealistic and prosocial elements at least as characteristic of the teenage period as the psychosocial difficulties that give rise to concern. Jane Quinn considers the extent to which youth organizations achieve their aims, relying particularly on the findings of a three-year study of American youth organizations conducted by the Carnegie Council on Adolescent Development. Youth organizations rank second only to schools in the number of young people reached by their services each year, yet there has been surprisingly little research into their impact. It is important to note that many youth organizations find it quite difficult to retain the interest of teenagers. There tends to be a precipitous decline in attendance beginning around the age of twelve or thirteen. It has also proved more difficult to attract young people from socially disadvantaged areas than teenagers from more affluent backgrounds. The empirical evidence from systematic evaluative studies remains patchy and somewhat inconclusive. There is nevertheless an important handful of promising studies that document the beneficial effects on young people of participation in youth organizations. For this conclusion to be of value in planning for the future, it is essential to know the characteristics of effective programs. Jane Quinn provides a thoughtful and helpful review of these characteristics.

The general public tends to assume that there are important community influences on the behavior of young people. Most parents thus seek homes in areas that they think will provide not only a safe environment in which to grow up but also one most likely to foster positive attitudes and behavior. Albert Reiss reviews what is known about community influences, focusing mainly on the research findings on antisocial behavior. He notes the several different meanings of communities and neighborhoods and emphasizes that these are not just a matter of geography. Social groups with which people identify, and whose activities they participate in, may or may not be coterminous with the streets surrounding their home. From a practical point of view, it is difficult to differentiate between the effects of school and community because so many schools serve particular geographical areas. From a policy point of view, however, this differentiation is important. Reiss also notes that the effects of poverty are probably different when they are concentrated in urban ghettos that create social isolation than when the poor are not cut off from the opportunities provided by society. There is consistent evidence from many different studies of important area differences in antisocial behavior and also many indications that broader social circumstances do make an impact on individual behavior. It is more difficult, however, to disentangle the key mechanisms involved. It is obviously not just a matter of living in a city because cities vary so markedly in their rates of psychosocial problems. Even within a single city there are variations between different neighborhoods and, within each neighborhood, subtle and important differences according to streets. There have been few efforts so far to use the findings on community influences to devise prevention strategies, partly due to our lack of understanding of the key community features that are beneficial or disadvantageous. Nevertheless, as Albert Reiss points out, the findings do provide a potential for prevention that it is important to build on.

Peter Mortimore provides a succinct summary of the evidence from studies that have systematically examined school effectiveness. He notes the crucial methodological issues to be taken into account in determining whether schools do indeed have a truly causal impact. Consistent findings from well conducted studies clearly show, however, that schools have an important influence on children's behavior and educational progress. Moreover, these effects are not dependent on the school receiving an unusually favored population. Mortimore discusses the mechanisms most likely associated with more effective schooling. Knowing what characterizes a good school, and knowing what needs to be done to change a badly functioning school into a well functioning one are two different things. There is limited evidence on how best to improve particular schools, let alone whole educational systems. Nevertheless, there are a variety of useful leads on what may be needed to bring about improvement and these are discussed with an eye to the future.

The final chapter by Lee Robins brings together the main themes considered throughout the book. She notes that researchers have tended to focus more on the problems of adolescence than on its successes. Although it is important to correct that balance, one must be concerned about the increase of psychosocial problems in young people over the last half century. This rise is probably not due to any single factor. It is suggested that it may be due to the decline of occupational opportunities, to a rising level of material "needs," to a decline in some aspects of adolescents' health, to factors associated with the urbanization of society, to changing family structures, to the drug epidemic, to the lowering of the age of puberty, and to ambiguity in the expectations of and responsibilities placed on young people. It is important to note that there are marked individual variations in the extent to which young people are at risk. The warning signs lie not only in early personal characteristics, but also in the peer group, in the family, in schools, and in neighborhoods. All these provide opportunities for worthwhile preventive interventions. Experiments designed to reduce or remove precursors of adolescent problems have had only mixed success. There are examples of interventions, however, that, although initially unsuccessful, have shown evidence of benefits when examined more broadly. It is also crucial to recognize that interventions are a way of testing causal hypotheses. The systematic study of the effects of interventions can be most helpful in pinpointing the social circumstances that represent the most important risk mechanisms. Interventions need to be concerned as much with avoiding the continuation of problems as with preventing their onset. Many psychosocial difficulties in young people are, by their nature, recurrent, and much would be gained if we could reduce the rate of recurrence, although the rate of onset might remain the same.

No one has effective answers to all the problems of young people. There is no neat package of actions that are bound to improve their lot. However, we do know a lot about the difficulties experienced by adolescents, the factors that create risks for disorder and factors that seem protective. We know about interventions that carry promise of improving young people's circumstances, enabling them to cope better with the challenges they encounter and reducing the risks of disorder. It is clear from the findings reviewed in this book that we all have a responsibility in this regard. Some of the steps recommended involve interaction with individuals, but many require actions at the level of youth organizations, schools, and the community as a whole.

Contributors

François Alsaker, Universitet I Bergen, Institutt for Samfunnspsykologi, Bergen, Norway

Bruce E. Compas, Department of Psychology, University of Vermont, Burlington, VT, U.S.A.

René Diekstra, Studierichting Psychologie, Rijksuniversiteit te Leiden, Faculteit der Sociale Wetenschappen, Leiden, The Netherlands

David Farrington, Institute of Criminology, University of Cambridge, Cambridge, England

Peter Mortimore, Institute of Education, University of London, London, England

Anne Petersen, University of Minnesota, Minneapolis, MN, U.S.A.

Jane Quinn, DeWitt Wallace–Reader's Digest Fund, New York, NY, U.S.A.

Albert Reiss, Jr., Department of Sociology, Yale University, New Haven, CT, U.S.A.

Lee Robins, Department of Psychiatry, Washington University School of Medicine, St. Louis, MO, U.S.A.

Michael Rutter, Department of Child and Adolescent Pyschiatry, Institute of Psychiatry, London, England

David Smith, Policy Studies Institute, London, England

Contributors

I. Adolescence: Developmental trends and psychosocial disorders

1. What is special about adolescence?

ANNE C. PETERSEN & NANCY LEFFERT

What *is* special about adolescence? Although some features of modern adolescence such as the biological changes of puberty are fairly universal across historical time and across nations, most other features are distinctively flavored by the historical period and social context in which adolescence takes place (Elder, 1985). In earlier or even current agrarian societies, adolescence consists primarily of puberty, with the transitions to adult work and family roles beginning in childhood through observational and participatory learning. Adolescence is distinctly different in modern technological society. Preparation for adult work roles now requires years of schooling, and preparation for adult family roles is more difficult for some to acquire through observation. In some communities, children and especially adolescents spend most of their daily lives isolated from the work world of adults. Our increasingly complex societies have made it even more difficult for adolescents to understand what kinds of adults they are to become and how they are to accomplish this.

It is interesting to juxtapose the current complexity of society, with its implications for adolescent development, with traditional views of adolescence. Since about 1900, in both Europe and the United States, adolescence has been thought to be characterized by "storm and stress" (Hall, 1904). Many have assumed that a tumultuous adolescence is normal individual development (e.g., Blos, 1970; A. Freud, 1958). This chapter argues that adolescence is characterized by change, and is challenging, but it need not be tumultuous and problematic unless societal conditions prompt it. Children who enter adolescence already vulnerable psychologically or socially are likely to experience a more difficult adolescent decade under challenging social circumstances. Unfortunately, most of our societies have failed to recognize the increased challenge of our complex societies to developing adolescents and have increased the likelihood that adolescence will be a difficult period.

To frame our central argument, this chapter will review research on normal adolescent development, as well as cross-national evidence for problems during adolescence. The chapter concludes with a proposal for ways to enhance the opportunities and minimize the problems of adolescent development.

Adolescent development

In most developed countries, adolescence is a long enough period – roughly a decade – that it can be considered a phase of life in and of itself and not merely a transitional phase between childhood and adulthood. At the same time, the movement from childhood to adulthood characterizes the period, flavoring adolescence with transitional issues. Many scholars of adolescence find it useful to consider the adolescent decade as having three phases: early, middle, and late, each distinctive from the others. Picture an eleven-year-old standing next to a nineteen-year-old, and you will quickly realize the extent of change over this period, as well as some of the distinctions from one period to the next.

Early adolescence, roughly the period from age ten to thirteen, is dominated by pubertal change. The appearance of the biological changes of puberty mark the passage from childhood into adolescence. Most adolescents finish, go through, or at least start puberty during these years. Many other changes occur during early adolescence, with variations in the extent of their relationship to puberty. Some changes appear to be linked to pubertal change; for example, an increased interest in other-sex peers appears to be stimulated by the development of secondary sex characteristics. Some changes occur at about the same time but have not yet been directly linked to pubertal change; for example, cognitive change. Other changes occurring at about this time are not caused by pubertal change. In the United States, for example, most young adolescents change from neighborhood elementary schools to larger, community-wide middle or junior high schools; in at least some school districts, pubertal change at this age is used as a rationale for housing further developed youngsters in different buildings from elementary school children. In some fashion, change occurs during early adolescence in every aspect of individual development and in every important social context (e.g., Petersen, 1987). The hallmark of this period, then, is change.

Middle adolescence, roughly the years from fourteen to sixteen, may be considered the phase most think of as adolescence. In many societies, young people in this phase dress distinctively, have special musical preferences, and adopt particular hair styles. These distinctive features of appearance and lifestyle have been termed the "youth culture" (Coleman, 1961). In contrast to the changes of early adolescence, over which the young person has little control, in middle adolescence the adolescents themselves bring about the changes. They cannot be considered as behaving individualistically, however, as most of the appearance and lifestyle preferences are exhibited *en masse* or at least in peer subgroups.

Late adolescence, roughly the years from seventeen to twenty, is the phase most explicitly looking toward young adulthood. Many young people in this age group have completed formal schooling and may already be in the work force. Those continuing in education are typically beginning to at least think about, and perhaps plan for, future work roles. Some are anticipating family roles, with a minority of adolescents in most developed countries already beginning families. The extent of change in this phase thus depends on the route taken to adulthood and the adolescent's timing of entry into adult work and family roles.

Developmental transitions

Developmental transitions are periods in the life course characterized by significant change in biological or social spheres of life, or both (e.g., Emde & Harmon, 1984; Maughan & Champion, 1988). Periods characterized by rapid biological changes are infancy, puberty, pregnancy, and menopause. Significant social normative changes include school entry, college or military entry, job entry, marriage, becoming a parent, and retirement. A developmental transition can provide challenge and new opportunity or it can become overwhelming and stressful. The individual trajectory following a developmental transition depends on the timing of the transition, whether it is normative or nonnormative, the social context for the transition, and the individual's response. Nonnormative changes – such as the death of a family member or a divorce – constitute an additional source of stress at any age (e.g., Kessler, Price, & Wortman, 1985) and may have amplified effects when they occur simultaneously with a developmental transition.

Adolescence obviously fits the definition of a developmental transition, with significant change in both the biological and social spheres of life. There is evidence that the sheer number of changes experienced simultaneously is related to worse outcomes for the adolescent (Simmons &

Blyth, 1987), supporting Coleman's (1978) focal theory that developmental tasks can be managed if experienced sequentially, or without too many changes at once. In particular, going through puberty before or during a change from a small, neighborhood elementary school to a larger, middle or junior high school is related to poorer self-image in both boys and girls (Crockett et al., 1989). It appears to be better to move to a new school still looking like a child, perhaps because an increasingly mature appearance brings expectations for experimentation with new behaviors, including such problem behaviors as delinquency and substance use.

Especially important to development in adolescence is the high degree of inter- and intraindividual variability. Although there is evidence of typical patterns for aspects of change, individuals do not experience all these typical patterns in the same way. Within the individual, different changes may proceed at different rates and times, with different patterns for different changes. For example, one child may grow tall at a relatively early age in adolescence but not develop secondary sex characteristics or more mature social skills for a few years. This child fits a stereotype of the gangly, awkward young adolescent.

Developmental change in adolescence

Adolescence is a period in the life cycle characterized by change and transition. Of particular interest are primary changes in the biological, cognitive, and psychosocial domains. These changes are affected, both directly and indirectly, by important contexts, including family, school, and peers. As we will describe, most of the changes are in a positive direction, giving the adolescent more capacity for individual functioning.

Biological development

Biological development involves perhaps the most dramatic change in adolescence, both for an outsider to witness and for the adolescent to experience (Petersen & Taylor, 1980). Basically, adolescents grow a new body. They experience changes in height, skin, muscle to fat body composition, body hair, voice, and secondary sex characteristics such as menarche and breast development for girls and penis and scrotum development in boys. These somatic changes are driven by complex hormonal feedback loops. What sets these changes in motion is not completely understood, but researchers have made much progress during the past two decades in advancing our understanding of the process (cf. Brooks-Gunn & Reiter, 1990).

These inevitable pubertal changes have wide variation in both their timing and tempo (Eichorn, 1975). Normal puberty may begin any time between eight and thirteen years of age in girls and nine to fourteen years of age in boys (Tanner, 1972). The onset of puberty has gotten earlier over the past century (Wyshak & Frisch, 1982), a trend most scholars attribute to better health and nutrition (Chumlea, 1982). The changes of puberty may take from one and a half to six years; the average is four years. Factors influencing the rate of pubertal change have not received much attention from researchers. Because of the large variations in timing and tempo (or rate), youngsters will begin puberty with different levels of preparation, a factor found to influence responses to pubertal change (Ruble & Brooks-Gunn, 1982). Moreover, among those in early adolescence, the entire spectrum of physical maturation from childlike to adultlike is seen among age cohorts (e.g., thirteen-year-olds).

Pubertal change has been found to affect body image and self-esteem, the nature of the effects varying by gender and culture. Increased maturation is viewed positively by boys but more negatively by girls (e.g., Dorn, Crockett, & Petersen, 1988). These findings are usually explained in terms of cultural ideals for body shape (e.g., Faust, 1983), the ideal for girls being unrealistically slim relative to normal changes in weight and fat deposition (e.g., Frisch, 1983). Early maturing girls are most likely to have a negative body image, because they develop mature bodies while their peers still have slim, prepubertal shapes more consistent with the slender ideal (e.g., Alsaker, this volume; Magnusson, 1987; Petersen, Kennedy, & Sullivan, 1991). Early maturation appears to be a risk factor for girls in most samples in the United States and Europe but at least one study suggests that it may be culturally dependent. A study with an urban German sample (Silbereisen et al., 1989) found that early maturing girls had *more* positive body images and good outcomes than later maturers. These authors speculated that in Berlin more mature body shapes may be valued rather than feared.

A recent area for research related to puberty is that of brain growth (e.g., Holland et al., 1986; Graber & Petersen, 1991). There is evidence that brain growth continues into adolescence, not in terms of increasing numbers of neurons but in proliferation of the support cells which nourish the neurons, and in myelination, which permits faster neural processing (e.g., Epstein, H. T., 1986; Yakovlev & Lecours, 1967). The number of neural interconnections decreases in the second decade of life (Feinberg, 1987), presumably reflecting "pruning" or reduction of redundant or unused neural connections.

Cognitive development

In addition to biological changes during adolescence, there are changes in cognition. The changes in the brain may stimulate cognitive advances and these primary changes in the biological and cognitive domains may greatly impact one another, with effects on self-image. Cognitive changes, for instance, enable the adolescent to think differently about his or her body; conversely, changes in one's body may themselves stimulate more complex cognition, especially self-cognition.

Cognitive change during the adolescent period involves increases in the capacity for abstract reasoning (Inhelder & Piaget, 1958; Keating, 1980). Between eleven and fourteen years of age, most adolescents become increasingly capable of thinking hypothetically, applying formal logic, and using abstract concepts (Inhelder & Piaget, 1958). Thinking becomes more relative, less absolute, and more self-reflective (e.g., Turiel, 1989). Adolescents also become capable of considering future time perspective rather than being tied to the present (Greene, 1986). Laboratory studies of cognitive capacity may, however, overestimate what adolescents are able to do in real life because everyday situations are usually more time-pressured and may be personally stressful (Keating & Clark, 1980; Keating, 1990), producing thinking that is less systematic and reflective, and more dependent on prior knowledge (Eylon & Linn, 1988). Studies (e.g., Lalo, 1989) show that societies in which there is no need for abstract thinking are less likely to show the developmental pattern we describe; schooling in these societies, however, produces increases in abstract reasoning (e.g., Greenfield, 1976).

Decision-making ability also increases over the adolescent decade (Weithorn & Campbell, 1982). Awareness of possible risks, consideration of future consequences, and the tendency to consult with experts all show age-related increases through middle adolescence (Lewis, 1981). By this age, adolescents are able to reason as well as adults, with similar reasoning flaws (Kuhn, Amsel, & O'Loughlin, 1988). Effective decision-making can be taught to adolescents as young as twelve years of age (Mann et al., 1988). Although decision-making in the abstract, as measured in laboratory tests, shows developmental increases and teachability, real life decision-making requires consideration of emotions, beliefs, experience, and cognitions in order to be effective (e.g., Adler et al., 1990), attributes perhaps less available to the relatively immature adolescent.

Three theories are posited for the change in reasoning and decision-making ability during adolescence: brain growth (Epstein, 1978), pubertal change (Petersen, 1983), and changes in socialization (Graber & Petersen,

1991). The first two propose that biological change drives the changes occurring in cognition during this period of time. Most of the research testing these hypotheses has focused on gender differences in the timing of pubertal change as explanations of gender differences in cognition (e.g., Maccoby & Jacklin, 1974). With at least one aspect of cognition, spatial ability, prepubertal rather than pubertal biological influences appear to be implicated (e.g., Linn & Petersen, 1985). There is also evidence that a wide variety of socialization experiences, including school and extracurricular activities, enhance the special nature of cognitive change during this period (Graber & Petersen, 1991). This may be especially important if the focus is not only on changes in the ability to reason and perform more complex academic tasks, but also on the ability to think about oneself and one's situation.

Psychosocial development

The other primary change during this period of adolescent development is that occurring in psychosocial development. Changes in conceptions of self, self-esteem, identity, and autonomy all occur over the adolescent decade. These changes, in turn, affect how the adolescent relates to others. Relationships with others further influence the development of the individual.

Conceptions of self. The cognitive changes described earlier permit more abstract understandings of the self in adolescence. Compared to children, adolescents are more psychological in their self-descriptions, focusing on personal and interpersonal characteristics, beliefs, and emotional states, with recognition of variations related to differentiation of setting and yielding the capacity to create a biography (cf. Crockett & Petersen, 1993). This brings advantages in the capacity to categorize and summarize complex behaviors and feelings but also brings disadvantages in that abstractions are more vulnerable to distortions related to emotions or inadequate reasoning (Harter, 1990).

Self-esteem. Self-esteem increases slightly over the second decade of life (e.g., Alsaker & Olweus, 1989; McCarthy & Hoge, 1982; O'Malley & Bachman, 1983), although the increases may follow an initial decline in self-esteem in early adolescence, particularly among girls (Simmons & Rosenberg, 1975). This increase is especially noteworthy in view of popular beliefs about adolescents falling apart psychologically.

In addition to global assessments, self-esteem is frequently assessed in domains such as physical attractiveness, peer acceptance, academic competence, athletic ability, and conduct (Harter, 1990). Although self-esteem is typically correlated among domains, developmental trends may vary for an individual across domains (e.g., Fend & Schröer, 1985). For example, one adolescent could perceive increasing peer acceptance and decreasing academic competence over the second decade of life. One study found different longitudinal trends across domains in the same group of individuals (Abramowitz, Petersen, & Schulenberg, 1984) .

Identity. Identity formation is considered the most important developmental task of adolescence, involving a selective narrowing of and commitment to choices regarding sexual, occupational, and social roles (Erikson, 1968). Research on identity achievement considers progress in the domains of occupational, social, and ideological identity with four statuses possible at any one time: achievement, moratorium, foreclosure, and diffusion (Bosma, 1992; Marcia, 1966; 1980). Research demonstrates that the most common age-based progression toward achievement by late adolescence begins from diffusion through moratorium; some adolescents proceed from diffusion to foreclosure, with regressions seen occasionally (Waterman, 1985). Moreover, different progressions occur in the same individuals across domains. Reliable gender differences exist in developmental trends and salience of domains (Archer, 1985; Camarena, Stemmler & Petersen, 1994).

Both the content of and progression toward identity achievement are affected by experiences and opportunities (Ianni, 1989). For example, Spencer and Markstrom-Adams (1990) cite several barriers to identity formation in minority youth in the United States: conflicting values between the minority reference group and the broader society, lack of adult role models who exemplify positive ethnic identity, and inadequate preparation to counter the stereotyping and prejudice they experience. A similar effect may be operating among German students in the lowest school track, who are disproportionately classified as having foreclosed identities (Fend, 1994).

Autonomy. Most societies expect that adolescents will learn how to function autonomously. Self-reliance, self-control, and the capacity for independent decision-making all show improvement over the adolescent decade (cf. Crockett & Petersen, 1993; Steinberg & Silverberg, 1986). Conformity to parental opinion decreases steadily over the adolescent decade whereas conformity to peers increases in early adolescence, with a peak around the age of thirteen or fourteen, then declining over the rest of the decade (Berndt, 1979). Truly autonomous decision-making thus begins only in middle adolescence.

Autonomy is another area with sensitivity to cultural variations (e.g., Feldman & Rosenthal, 1991). The extent to which a society emphasizes individualism versus collectivism, for example, will affect the manifestation of autonomy in adolescence as seen clearly in a comparative study of West Berlin and Warsaw youth (Silbereisen, Noack, & Schönpflug, 1994a). The German adolescents appeared to be more oriented toward the self than the Polish adolescents, although the authors note that this could be explained by different timing of changes in the two groups.

Relationships. Adolescents also increase their capacity to form meaningful relationships with others over the second decade of life. The number of close interpersonal relationships and the degree of intimacy in these relationships (e.g., Savin-Williams & Berndt, 1990) increase over adolescence. Relationship change is facilitated by cognitive development and by other aspects of psychosocial development (e.g., Palmonari, Kirchler, & Pombeni, 1991), although relatively little research thus far has examined linkage between these developmental changes.

Recent research has greatly enhanced our knowledge of the changes over adolescence in family relationships (e.g., Steinberg, 1981; 1990). The popular media, at least in the United States, have portrayed parent-child relationships during adolescence as fraught with conflict and intensity of emotion. Recent research finds, however, that although adolescence is a time of special change in family relationships, the changes are neither necessarily stormy nor particularly stressful (Petersen, 1988; Steinberg, 1990). Adolescence *is* a time in which the parent-child relationship is transformed, but, contrary to early psychoanalytic writing, the relationship is maintained *and* the child develops autonomy (Hill & Holmbeck, 1986; Maccoby, 1984). Adolescents continue to feel close to their parents (Youniss & Smollar, 1985), to respect them, and to feel they can rely on them (Offer, Ostrov, & Howard, 1981). This comes about by a gradual shifting of regulation of children's activities and responsibilities from the earlier period of parent control to a time of co-regulation, and finally in late adolescence or early adulthood, to self-regulation (Maccoby, 1984). Except during the period of peak pubertal change, adolescents continue to see their parents as important people in their lives, with whom they spend time and by whom they are influenced (Kandel & Lesser, 1972; Rutter et al., 1976).

Parent-child conflict does increase in adolescence, however. It first appears in early adolescence and peaks with pubertal change (Hill et al., 1985; Steinberg, 1981), reaches a plateau in mid-adolescence, and declines when the adolescent leaves the parental home (Montemayor, 1983). Conflict usually focuses on mundane topics (e.g., chores or schoolwork) and is severe in only about 15 percent of families (Montemayer, 1983).

Peer relationships also change during adolescence. In early and middle childhood, peer relationships are based on shared activities. In adolescence, friendships are formed on the mutual sharing of ideas, feelings, and experiences, and this new intimacy is the first evidence we have of true adultlike relationships (Berndt, 1982; Camarena, Sarigiani, & Petersen, 1990; Hartup, 1983; Meeus, 1989; Youniss & Smollar, 1985). Both stability and reciprocity of friendships increase over the adolescent decade, more for girls than for boys (Epstein & Karweit, 1983). Friends tend to become more similar over adolescence, especially in long-term, reciprocated friendships (Epstein, J. L., 1986; 1989). Adolescents with satisfying and harmonious friendships tend to be more popular with classmates and to be socially skillful (Savin-Williams & Berndt, 1990).

Although Hall (1904) portrayed adolescence as a special period characterized by "storm and stress" and Freudian portrayals proposed that adolescence was a time in which the loosening of parental bonds must be accompanied by conflict to accomplish the adult goal of autonomy (A. Freud, 1958), researchers have concluded that the developmental changes in relationships that occur during adolescence are basically positive in nature (e.g., Savin-Williams & Berndt, 1990; Steinberg, 1990).

Summary

In all aspects of individual development there is change over the adolescent decade, largely in a positive direction. Puberty brings increasing size, strength, and reproductive potential. Cognitive change permits abstract reasoning and increased cognitive potential. Psychosocial change involves increased self-understanding, improved self-esteem, identity development, increased autonomy, and expanded as well as higher quality interpersonal relationships. The second decade of life concludes with a young person ready to take on adult responsibilities. At least, this is the potential afforded by developmental change; but changes in individual development are not the only changes over adolescence.

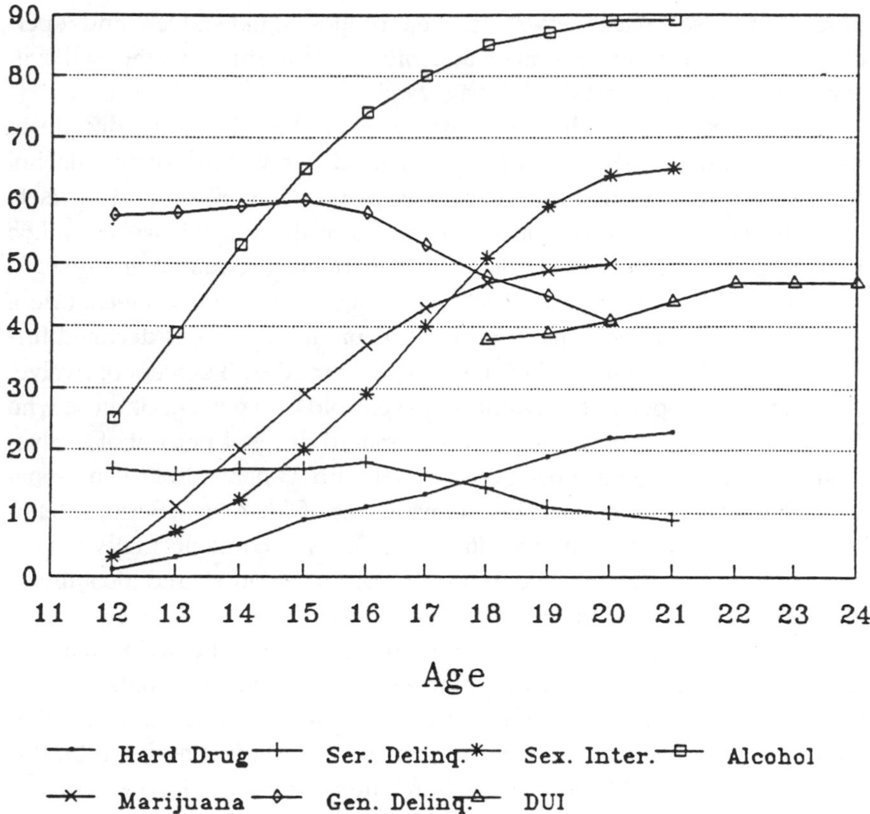

Figure 1.1. Developmental change in problem behavior. (Elliott, in press; reprinted with permission from Oxford University Press.)

Developmental trajectories in problem behavior

Although development changes tend to take positive directions over the adolescent years in all aspects of biological, cognitive, and psychosocial change, rates of problem behaviors also increase during this time (see Diekstra, this volume; Farrington, this volume; Merikangas, Ries, & Angst, this volume). Elliott (1993) has charted the developmental change in problem behavior (see Figure 1.1). Delinquency is the only behavior that peaks and then declines during the adolescent decade (in these U.S. data adolescence is described as covering ages eleven to twenty-one). Rates of general delinquency (including milder offenses such as shoplifting) are 57 percent at age thirteen, 60 percent at age fifteen, declining to 40 percent at age twenty. Serious delinquency in these samples occurs in 17 percent of those aged twelve, 18 percent of those aged sixteen, and 9 percent of those aged twenty-one years. Fifty percent of those who will ever commit a delinquent act do so by age twelve.

All other problem behaviors increase over the adolescent decade in these U.S. data. Fifteen percent of youth aged twelve have drunk alcohol whereas 90 percent of those aged twenty-one have; 50 percent of users begin by age fourteen. As for sex, 3 percent of those aged twelve and 65 percent of those aged twenty-one have experienced sexual intercourse; 50 percent of youth initiate sexual activity by age the age of seventeen. (More recent U.S. data suggest that the age of sexual initiation has declined further [e.g., Dryfoos, 1990].) Marijuana has been tried by 3 percent of twelve-year-olds and 50 percent of twenty-one-year-olds; 50 percent of those who use marijuana do so by age sixteen. As for hard drugs, 1 percent of twelve-year-olds have used hard drugs compared with 23 percent of twenty-one-year-olds; 50 percent of users began by the age of seventeen. Serious delinquency, hard drug use, and marijuana use never become normative in the population; by the age of twenty-one, sexual intercourse and alcohol use are behaviors engaged in by the majority of youth.

These developmental trends in rates of problem behavior may be slightly different in European countries, but the available data suggest that U.S. trends are more similar to than different from those in other countries (e.g., Diekstra, in press; Silbereisen, et al., in press; Smith, this volume). There are some notable differences, however, in the forms of problem behaviors as manifested in different countries.

It is worth noting that all the behaviors discussed in Figure 1.1 are highly correlated in early adolescence and to some extent in middle adolescence (Elliott, 1993). The link of alcohol use and sex to other problem behaviors diminishes significantly once these two behaviors become normative in the population (i.e., engaged in by more than half of young people). Thus, only early involvement in sex and alcohol co-vary with other problem behaviors. Late onset of hard drug use is only infrequently associated with delinquency or crime.

There is less change over time in overall levels of behavior with sex and drugs than with delinquency. Eighty percent of delinquents terminate this behavior by age seventeen, whereas only 13 percent of alcohol users and 30 percent of marijuana users terminate these behaviors by age seventeen. There are also demographic variations in continuity of behaviors. More females than males terminate delinquent behavior, marijuana use, and polydrug use, for instance. More blacks than whites terminate minor delinquent behaviors, but they are less likely to terminate serious delinquent behaviors. More middle- than low-income youth terminate serious delinquent behaviors. More urban than rural youth terminate alcohol and marijuana use, but they are less likely to terminate serious delinquency (Elliott, 1993).

A subgroup of adolescents engages in a health-compromising lifestyle that involves sex, substance use, and crime earlier than other youth (Elliott, 1993). Approximately 20 to 25 percent of youth engage in mild forms of all three. The percentage engaging in serious and problematic forms of all three types of behaviors is small but this group carries a disproportionate burden of mortality and morbidity of many kinds into adulthood. Thus, a small percent of youth are responsible for increases in serious problem behaviors but one-fifth to one-fourth are surely at risk for other problems in adulthood.

Integrating problem behavior and developmental trends

How can we reconcile the patterns of increasing problem behaviors with the ones cited earlier showing increasing capacity in aspects of individual development in adolescence? These two trends – change in aspects of individual development and rates of problem behavior over adolescence – may seem contradictory: How can adolescents increase simultaneously in opposite directions – increasing problems *and* increasing positive development? Although definitive research is lacking, we can pose logical explanations.

To some extent, the different patterns represent different individuals. Most studies of normal adolescent development have been conducted with middle- to upper-middle-class samples, whereas problem behaviors increase most dramatically among lower income groups. To the extent that lower income groups are included in studies of developmental change, those experiencing less positive development would decrease the observed differences in the two patterns, but as just discussed, those with seriously problematic development are a minority of youth.

Another factor that could produce these apparently paradoxical trends is that an adolescent can both develop positively and engage in some level of problem behavior. For example, research demonstrates that those engaging in mild delinquent behavior may also have high self-esteem (Silbereisen & Noack, 1988). Another example is that of heroin use among soldiers in Vietnam, most of whom quit the habit on returning to the United States (Robins, 1974). Depending on the social context, some problem behaviors represent adaptations to context rather than a lack of strength.

What causes an adolescent to engage in problem behavior that would appear to compromise his or her potential strengths for positive development? Income, usually assessed in terms of social class, is one gross variable that appears to have an effect. In Elliott's (1993) studies of problem behavior he concluded that middle and lower income youth experiment with problem behaviors at the same rates and at the same ages. The major difference is that middle income youth move on to more positive pursuits whereas lower income youth are more likely to become stuck in a life-style focused around problem behavior. Most of us believe that lack of opportunity during adolescence and into adulthood constitutes the major barrier to positive development in lower income youth.

But income is not the whole story. Several very interesting studies have demonstrated that neighborhoods at similar income levels can provide very different resources to young people, the more positive neighborhoods facilitating development and the more negative neighborhoods suppressing it (e.g., Hurrelmann, 1989; Ianni, 1989; also see Reiss, this volume). Boehnke, Silbereisen, and Noack (1992) have found that neighborhood effects on alcohol use are different for adolescent boys and girls, presumably because girls tend to be more restricted geographically. In our own research, we have found that the community has an effect even when social class is controlled (Petersen et al., 1991).

Cross-national differences in problem behaviors tell a similar story. Among developed countries, the United States has the highest rates of adolescent pregnancy and childbearing, and of violent behavior (Department of International Economic and Social Affairs, 1988). The United States also has the highest mortality rate among adolescents, a factor surely related to the prevalence of violence in this society (Carnegie Council on Adolescent Development, 1990). Cross-national similarities such as suicide rates (Diekstra, in press) and substance use (Silbereisen et al., in press-b) suggest that national variations in contexts have specific, not general, effects on adolescent outcomes. The examination of social contexts for their effect on adolescent development and behavior should further illuminate the processes involved.

Social contexts for adolescent development

As we have seen, there are individual variations in how adolescence is negotiated; for some, it involves the development of serious problem behaviors necessitating treatment of some kind. The individual variations observed in the development of problem behaviors are numerous. Recent research has examined aspects of developmental continuity (e.g., Elliott, 1993; Crockett & Petersen, 1993) and the impact of the social context on the initiation into and maintenance of problem behaviors such as substance use, delinquency, and inappropriate sexual habits (e.g., Elliott, 1993; Petersen, 1991).

Increasing attention has also focused on how social contexts influence the course of individual development (e.g., Bronfenbrenner, 1979; Feldman & Elliott, 1990). The family, the peer group, the neighborhood, school and work, and the broader society all have impact on adolescent development. The study of family factors is not of recent origin, but recent behavior genetics research has shifted attention from between-family factors to within-family factors (Daniels et al., 1985; Plomin & Daniels, 1987). The peer group has been of interest, although until recently the research has been largely descriptive. As mentioned earlier, one of the most interesting areas considered recently is that of neighborhood effects. School is also an important context in most societies, replaced by work for some youth in late adolescence. The entire society can have a clear influence on the course of adolescent development, through policies and the resultant social arrangements, as well as the values shared by the majority in a society. Each of these social contexts has influence on positive versus negative development.

Family influences

The family has long been assumed to have a major influence on the development of children (e.g., Maccoby & Martin, 1983). How this influence occurs, however, has been more difficult to document. Moreover, the family itself has been changing significantly in the United States (Furstenberg, 1990) and much of Europe (Hess, in press). Divorce rates have increased in most countries, increasing the likelihood that adolescents will grow up with a single parent, or with a "reconstituted" family, adding a stepparent and perhaps stepsiblings. In the United States and some European countries, women have entered the labor force in large numbers, especially when their children become adolescents (Hess, in press). The style of parenting is another important factor.

Family structure. Both family structure and parenting style have been found to have an influence on adolescent outcomes. In general, children in two-parent families tend to have more positive outcomes than those in single-parent families (Maccoby & Martin, 1983), although the simple inference that the difference reflects a risk from single parenthood may be simplistic and misleading (Barber & Eccles, 1992). In addition, a great deal of work suggests that family changes, such as the death of a parent or parental divorce, is disruptive for adolescent development, at least for the short term (e.g., Hetherington, 1991; Hetherington & Camara, 1984). Again, there is controversy about this conclusion (e.g., Barber & Eccles, 1992). Some research suggests that whereas boys appear to be more affected by divorce in childhood, girls appear to have more negative outcomes when a divorce occurs during their adolescence (Sarigiani, 1990).

Maternal employment. Most researchers have concluded that mothers' employment has no powerful or uniform direct effect on children (Galambos, 1985; Hayes & Kamerman, 1983; Lamb, 1982). There is some evidence that maternal employment may have positive effects on the development of daughters but possibly negative effects in some areas of development for adolescent sons (Hoffman, 1979; Lerner & Galambos, 1985).

Parenting style. The way in which parents behave toward their children has an independent influence beyond any structural effects of parental composition (Steinberg, 1990). Maccoby and Martin (1983) defined four parenting styles: authoritative, authoritarian, indulgent, and indifferent. Authoritative parents exert both control and warmth and, during adolescence, tend to support their children's need for increasing autonomy while giving them increasing responsibility (Baumrind, 1971). Authoritarian (or autocratic) parents tend to provide strict discipline (or demandingness) without much warmth or psychological autonomy. Indulgent parents express love but little control and practice laissez-faire decision-making. Indifferent parents are deficient in all areas; their offspring have the worst outcomes. Authoritarian and laissez-faire parenting tend to produce poorer outcomes than authoritative parenting.

Much of this research has been done with middle-class families (Steinberg, 1990). In general, authoritative parenting appears to be best for promoting good academic performance; this is found across age, gender, socioeconomic groups, and family structures (Dornbusch et al., 1987; Steinberg et al., 1992). There is some evidence that the effect is less strong among African-American families (Steinberg, 1992) than among other ethnic groups. The pattern is not related to socioeconomic status. Steinberg and colleagues (Steinberg, Dornbusch, & Brown, 1992; Steinberg et al.,

1992) suggest that school performance among African-American students, and to some extent among Asian-American and Hispanic students, is particularly influenced by peers, which may interfere with the otherwise positive influence of authoritarian parental practices on school performance and achievement. An intervention that teaches parents demandingness has proved to be effective in improving behaviors of the target child and siblings (Loeber & Stouthamer-Loeber, 1986; Patterson, 1986). But more research is needed on diverse populations.

Within-family variations. Behavior genetic analyses have found that within-family variations are more important than between-family variations for adolescent outcomes (Daniels et al., 1985; Plomin & Daniels, 1987). Between-family variations include traditional family variables such as social class and family composition (e.g., number of adults, relationships, numbers of children). Within-family variables include differential treatment of siblings and children's different experience of the family depending on birth order. Observational studies have charted the different behavior of parents toward each child, and what factors seem to influence these differences (Dunn, Plomin, & Daniels, 1986). More research is needed on these family processes relative to adolescent outcomes.

Peer groups

The structure of the peer network also changes over adolescence (Crockett & Petersen, 1993). Beginning in early adolescence at least in the United States, young people move from small groups of friends (usually from the neighborhood) to larger groups, frequently based in the school (cf. Brown, 1990). Large peer groups ("crowds") become more prevalent by middle adolescence; research identifies several kinds of peer groups with distinctive characteristics (e.g., jocks, nerds). Recent research in the United States has begun to document the role these different peer groups play in influencing developmental trajectories (e.g., Brown, 1989). For example, athletes in some U.S. schools are given high status by other students and accorded privileged treatment by the teachers and other adults (e.g., Eckert, 1989).

Although evidence suggests that these peer groups influence the appearance and preferences of adolescents in regard to popular culture, there is no evidence that they dramatically divert young people from family values on broader issues of religion, politics, or life goals (e.g., Lerner et al., 1975; Kandel & Lesser, 1972). The influence of peer groups on behavior, especially problem behavior can, however, have an effect on the developmental trajectory (e.g., Brown, 1989). Perceived peer pressure for problem behavior appears to increase over the adolescent decade (Brown, Clasen, & Eicher, 1986). Some youth may be more at risk for negative peer influence, such as youth with weak family ties or early maturing girls (Magnusson, 1987). Minority youth may turn to their peers, aware of their parents' lack of power in society (Spencer & Dornbusch, 1990). These subgroups may be more influenced by peers in negative, developmental trajectory-altering ways.

Peers may also have positive influences on adolescent development (e.g., Brown et al., 1986; Hill & Holmbeck, 1986). Occasionally in middle adolescence but especially by later adolescence, peers, now operating more as individuals, may have positive influence on youth through social support. There is evidence that by this age good peer relationships can even buffer negative parental or other influences (Klepp, Halper, & Perry, 1986; Sarigiani, 1990).

Neighborhoods

There is an emerging body of research in the United States and Europe indicating the role that neighborhoods can play in adolescent development (e.g., Hurrelmann, 1989; Ianni, 1989; see also Reiss, this volume). Some neighborhoods have almost no resources, in social services or in local businesses. Other neighborhoods provide a rich context for adolescent development. A neighborhood can function like a small town, providing significant opportunities for children and adolescents to grow up understanding what adults do, having access to adults other than parents, and having opportunities for exploration in a safe environment (Barker & Gump, 1964). One study (Brooks-Gunn et al., 1993) shows that controlling for indicators of familial social class, neighborhood resources are related to more positive outcomes among youth. Some neighborhoods are extremely high risk, with high rates of violence, drug use, and other problems that threaten the very survival of young people as well as increase the likelihood that they will be drawn into problem behavior life-styles. This research shows promise of beginning to understand the neighborhood factors that set, maintain, and offset a developmental course.

School and work

Schools. Schooling has become increasingly important in preparing young people for adult work roles. In addition to knowledge imparted by traditional education, current jobs increasingly require both technical and communication skills (Mark, 1987). Schooling is probably the social context with the greatest variation among the countries of Europe and the United States. When indicators of achievement and retention are compared, the United States fares badly. Many factors differentiate schools in Europe and the United States, including organization, tracking and selection, and integration with the workplace (e.g., Petersen, Hurrelmann, & Leffert, 1993). Apprentice systems are particularly effective in providing workplace integration (e.g., Hamilton, 1987; 1990) but any system that provides "transparency" linking school to work has similar effects (Hamilton, 1990). Note that there are longer term disadvantages to transparency, particularly on "permeability," or the ease of shifting from these initial work positions in response to changes in the economy or personal interests.

Another factor that appears to disrupt development in U.S. studies is the transition to larger schools, particularly from small, neighborhood elementary schools to larger, more anonymous secondary schools (e.g., Eccles & Midgley, 1989). Academic performance drops with each school transition, relative to achievement levels of same-aged peers not making a transition (Blyth, Simmons, & Carlton-Ford, 1983), with stronger negative effects for adolescents making earlier or multiple, closely spaced transitions (Crockett et al., 1989). There also may be negative effects on self-esteem, although these have been found only for urban girls (Simmons & Blyth, 1987) and not in other populations (Crockett, et al., 1989; Fenzel & Blyth, 1986). Process analyses reveal that these transitions involve constriction of choice, less participation in decision-making, less small group work, more frequent evaluations, and less positive relationships with teachers (Feldlaufer, Midgley, & Eccles, 1988; Gullickson, 1985; Hawkins & Berndt, 1985). European school systems are generally more uniform, perhaps giving adolescents clearer expectations about school. Some German research shows effects of track changes (Silbereisen, 1990).

Several studies (Bryk & Thum, 1989; Rutter et al., 1979) have identified practices and conditions that lead to better student outcomes for adolescents: an orderly social environment, high faculty interest and involvement, high emphasis on academic pursuits, and fewer differences among student courses of study (see Mortimore, this volume). A sense of anonymity appears to be highly destructive (Arhar, Johnson, & Markle, 1989).

Work. By mid-adolescence, work is an increasingly important setting in both Europe and the United States. In the United States, half of all high school sophomores (fifteen to sixteen years of age) and two-thirds of all seniors (seventeen to eighteen years of age) hold part-time jobs while going to school (Lewin-Epstein, 1981). In many countries of Europe, adolescents combine school with work through more structured programs such as apprenticeships (Hamilton, 1990; Petersen et al., in press). The U.S. pattern has some positive outcomes, such as the development of a work orientation and, among girls, the development of self-reliance (Greenberger & Steinberg, 1986; Mortimer, 1994). But part-time work has also been linked with negative outcomes such as poorer performance in school and more problem behavior (e.g., Greenberger, Steinberg, & Vaux, 1981; Steinberg et al., 1982; Steinberg & Dornbusch, 1991).

Unemployment among youth shows significant negative outcomes (e.g., Mortimer, 1994). Although a poor economy is the single biggest factor in producing youth unemployment, several approaches are effective in stabilizing youth employment levels and minimizing negative effects. Most notable are programs directly linked to employment such as apprenticeship or internship (e.g., Hamilton, 1994).

Broader society

Although much more distal than social contexts, the broader society may nevertheless have some influence on adolescent development through the organization of social institutions, the economy, the media, and social policy. Policies adopted by the society will determine educational opportunities and access to jobs. Youth policies also determine social responsibilities (e.g., voting), and define adult status (e.g., drinking or driving laws). The media condoned and supported by the society can influence young people in negative or in positive directions by promoting unhealthy versus healthy behavior (Wartella, in press). Media also carry messages about norms related to violence and sex. Societal values and expectations concerning adolescent behavior and development are also transmitted through local institutions and the adolescent's social network.

Models of influence on development

There has not yet been much research on developmental trajectories (or paths, or routes for development), or on factors that influence particular trajectories. There is enough evidence, however, to begin to propose how key parameters of development are affected. Effects on the developmental course may be temporary or long lasting. They may appear immediately or have a "sleeper" effect. Assuming that development is a linear function, key parameters that could be affected are rate and slope of the growth curve. Timing of key events or subprocesses, such as puberty, is also important. Those issues for which there is even minimal evidence provide the focus for the next discussion. Unfortunately, some issues, such as sleeper effects and rate of development, have thus far received scant attention.

Timing effects

Most of the developmental process research in adolescence has focused on pubertal development. We have fairly good evidence for the nature of growth in height, for example, so we can model variations in that growth (e.g., Bock et al., 1973). Starvation curtails growth but growth catches up once adequate feeding resumes (Galler et al., 1987; Kulin et al., 1982). It is interesting that restriction of nutritional intake (though not starvation), together with high demands on the body through exercise, delays the onset of puberty (Frisch, Wyshak, & Vincent, 1980). For example, although the timing of puberty is highly heritable (Brooks-Gunn & Reiter, 1990), adolescent girls who are dancers begin menstruation later than their mothers and sisters; they also ultimately develop a different body shape, with longer limbs, presumably because of the longer period of prepubertal growth (Warren, 1980). Thus, pubertal timing can be delayed with control of eating and exercise, and can affect body shape.

There is also evidence that prepubertal sexual abuse can stimulate earlier onset of puberty (Trickett & Putnam, 1993). This abuse apparently stimulates the endocrine system that turns on puberty. Early puberty also appears to have largely negative effects in girls, over both the short and long terms (Dubas, Graber, & Petersen, 1991; Petersen et al., 1991; Stattin & Magnusson, 1990). For example, Stattin and Magnusson (1990) found that early maturing girls manifested more problem behavior in adolescence and had lower educational and occupational attainments in adulthood (by their mid thirties). Their research and that of others suggests that perhaps early developing girls are recruited into problem behavior (e.g., early sex and substance use) by older boys; this is especially likely without the protective factor of parental supervision. Psychosocially immature but physically mature girls are likely to be flattered by the attention shown them by older boys, and lack the interpersonal skills to resist pressures. The involvement of girls in problem behavior may preclude the sort of engagement with schooling that would permit higher educational and occupational attainments. In addition, early unprotected sex is likely to lead to earlier childbearing, another factor that may limit educational and occupational attainments (e.g., Jones et al., 1986). Thus, early puberty appears to have long lasting and negative effects on girls, especially girls who lack compensatory protective factors. Note, however, that timing of puberty may not be the beginning of the causal chain. Sex abuse, mentioned earlier, could be a causal factor. Moffitt and colleagues (Moffitt et al., 1992) also found that early maturing girls showed behavioral differences prepubertally, supporting the importance of identifying the onset of the developmental process involved.

Effects of the timing of puberty are also seen with boys, over both the short and long term. For example, early maturing boys evidence more self-confidence and popularity (Simmons & Blyth, 1987) than later maturing boys (Alsaker, this volume; Brack, Orr, & Ingersoll, 1988). They also have more positive body images and higher levels of self-esteem (Blyth et al., 1981). Late maturing boys tend to have more traffic accidents and other problem behaviors in adulthood, presumably related to attention-seeking behavior associated with late development in adolescence (Andersson & Magnusson, 1986; Pulkkinen, 1990).

Slope effects

Contexts may constrain or enhance development relative to some otherwise "natural" course. These effects alter the slope of the developmental curve, and perhaps even the shape of the curve. For example, girls whose families suffered from economic hardship showed lower occupational aspirations (Galambos & Silbereisen, 1987). The effect of economic hardship presumably lowers the trajectory of economic aspirations. Another example of this effect may be Elliott's (1993) speculation that lower income youth become stuck in a problem behavior life-style; they get on a developmental trajectory that precludes advancement in positive domains but propels them forward in more negative ones. This kind of life trajectory may be adaptive even if it not normative or socially acceptable to mainstream society (e.g., Ogbu, 1974).

The positive analogue to these more negative trajectories may be seen in lives in which the right level of challenge, especially favorable contexts, or special individual characteristics could stimulate some individuals to develop more positively than would otherwise be expected. Suomi's (e.g., 1987) research with monkeys provides some examples of development that turn out better than expected. For example, he finds that anxious monkeys reared by especially supportive but autonomy-producing mothers (perhaps analogous to authoritative parents) become social leaders demonstrating a balance of sensitivity and self-confidence.

Some research has identified the factor of resilience that permits an individual to develop more positively than would be expected given adverse circumstances (Garmezy, 1985; Garmezy & Rutter, 1983). The best predictor of a steeper developmental trajectory appears to be a level of challenge involving an optimal fit between individual characteristics and the context.

Changes in the slope of the developmental trajectory are described in recent research identifying "accentuating" effects. For example, Caspi et al. (1993) found that early developers engaged in more delinquent behavior, but that they showed more evidence of problems prior to the early adolescent transition. Experiencing the transition to adolescence earlier than other young people amplified prior differences. Similarly, both Block (1991) and Sarigiani (1990) found that adolescents who had trouble after a parental divorce were different prior to the divorce; divorce only accentuated prior status.

Clear conceptualization about developmental processes, and especially developmental trajectories, will enhance our understanding of causal sequences. Longitudinal data are needed to test hypotheses about causal effects over development in order to identify factors that set, maintain, and offset a developmental course. Such information will also provide important information for the design of effective interventions (Rutter, in press).

Adolescence is special but so what?

There are many special features of adolescence but do they matter for development? Is this simply an odd period in development with no implications for what happens later? The existing evidence suggests that what happens in adolescence *is* important for subsequent development. Trajectories are real in that they represent tracks into adulthood that are difficult to reverse. Getting offtrack in adolescence is significant because of the altered trajectory itself and because of the aspects of development missed while being offtrack. For example, an adolescent hospitalized for a clinical depression will miss important developmental opportunities during this period. It is easier to catch up on some aspects of development than others, for example, academic achievement as compared to interpersonal relationships. An adolescent who is incarcerated has multiple areas in which development may be suppressed or retarded while he or she is out of mainstream society. Both these versions of being offtrack could be compensated for upon release, but programs do not typically attend to developmental disadvantages incurred through hospitalization or incarceration.

Another example of getting offtrack may be seen in the adolescent who copes with overwhelming challenges by substance abuse. This adolescent is missing important developmental opportunities difficult to acquire later in life. Young people who have missed learning how to form close relationships may need to start over in this process. It is much more difficult once one is physically mature and others assume the learning has already taken place. And, as with treatment for mental illness or incarceration, drug treatments seldom recognize the particular developmental needs of one who missed key parts of adolescence. Programs that consider deficits in prior development have shown good results (e.g., Uchtenhagen & Zimmer-Hoefler, 1985).

Although it is difficult to remedy these developmental gaps, there is reason to be optimistic about the possibility of intervention. Without intervention, mothers who were abused as children tend to perpetuate the cycle of abuse. Fortunately, both psychotherapeutic treatment and a healthy marital relationship appear to decrease the likelihood that the mother will abuse her own children (Egeland, Jacobvitz, & Sroufe, 1988). It seems important to apply the nutrition analogue to "catch-up growth" for other developmental trajectory-altering processes.

The evidence that all aspects of individual development are basically positive suggests that all youth could enter adulthood ready to take on responsible adult roles as long as their social contexts supported or even stimulated positive development. We know little as yet about the minimum required to produce positive development. Like covariation in manifestations of problem behavior, poor contexts tend to covary. The adolescent in a less favorable family environment is more likely to encounter negative peer environments, a poor neighborhood, inadequate schools, poor work opportunities, and negative messages from the broader society. But how many contexts need to be improved for sufficiently positive development to occur? Will an adolescent develop positively if at least one context is supportive? Or does it take more? Understanding the interactions among contexts and their effects on development is important for knowing where to place priorities for policies and programs (e.g., Bronfenbrenner & Weiss, 1983).

We know much more about adolescence now than we did even a decade ago. We can begin to identify ways to increase the likelihood that young people will reach adulthood ready to contribute to society.

Although there are individual contributions to both positive and negative development, it is quite clear that the contexts in which development takes place can enhance, inhibit, or otherwise alter the development that could occur. It would seem to be in the interest of society to create environments that have the greatest likelihood of facilitating positive development. Our research knowledge should be addressed to this challenge on behalf of society.

References

Abramowitz, R. H., Petersen, A. C., & Schulenberg, J. E. (1984). Changes in self-image during early adolescence. In *Patterns of Adolescent Self-Image*, ed. D. Offer, E. Ostrov, & K. Howard, pp. 19–28. San Francisco: Jossey-Bass.

Adler, N. E., Kegelis, S. M., Irwin, C. E., & Wibbelsman, C. (1990). Adolescent contraceptive behavior: An assessment of decision processes. *Journal of Pediatrics*, 116, 463–71.

Alsaker, F., & Olweus, D. (1989). *Stability of Self-Esteem in Early Adolescence: Review of the Literature and Results from a Cohort Longitudinal Study*. Paper presented at the International Society for the Study of Behavioral Development, Jyväskylä, Finland.

Andersson, T., & Magnusson, D. (1986). Drinking habits and alcohol abuse from 15–25 years of age. Unpublished manuscript, Department of Psychology, University of Stockholm.

Archer, S. L. (1985). Identity and the choice of social roles. In *Identity in Adolescence: Processes and Contents*, ed. A. S. Waterman, pp. 79–100. San Francisco: Jossey-Bass.

Arhar, J. M., Johnson, J. H., & Markle, G. C. (1989). The effects of teaming on students. *Middle School Journal*, 20, 24–7.

Barber, B. L., & Eccles, J. S. (1992). Long-term influence of divorce and single-parenting on adolescent family- and work-related values, behaviors and aspirations. *Psychological Bulletin*, 11, 108–26.

Barker, R., & Gump, P. (1964). *Big School, Small School*. Stanford, CA: Stanford University Press.

Baumrind, D. (1971). Current patterns of parental authority. *Developmental Psychology Monographs*, 1, 1–103.

Berndt, T. (1979). Developmental changes in conformity to peers and parents. *Developmental Psychology*, 15, 608–16.

(1982). The features and effects of friendship in early adolescence. *Child Development*, 53, 1447–60.

Block, J. (1991, April). *Self-Esteem Through Time: Gender Similarities and Differences*. Paper presented at the 1991 biennial meeting of the Society for Research in Child Development, Seattle, WA.

Blos, P. (1970). *The Adolescent Passage*. New York: International Universities Press.

Blyth, D. A., Simmons, R. G., Bulcroft, R., Felt, D., VanCleave, E. F., & Bush, D. M. (1981). The effects of physical development on self-image and satisfaction with body image for early adolescent males. In *Research in Community and Mental Health*, 2, ed. R.G. Simmons, pp. 43–73. Greenwich, CT: JAI Press.

Blyth, D. A., Simmons, R. G., & Carlton-Ford, S. (1983). The adjustment of early adolescents to school transitions. *Journal of Early Adolescence*, 3, 105–20.

Bock, R. D., Wainer, H., Petersen, A., Thissen, D., Murray, J., & Roche, A. (1973). A parameterization for individual human growth curves. *Human Biology*, 45, 63–80.

Boehnke, K., Silbereisen, R. K., & Noack, P. (1992). Experiencing urban environment in adolescence: A study on the perception and evaluation of environmental characteristics and their impact on substance use. In H. Dettenborn, ed., *Berichte aus der Arbeit des Instituts fuer Paedagogische Psychologie am Fachbereich Erziehungswissenschaften der Humboldt-Universitait zu Berlin*, Vol. 4. Berlin: Humboldt University.

Bosma, H. A. (1992). Identity in adolescence: Managing commitments. In *Identity Formation During Adolescence*, ed. G. R. Adams, T. Gullotta, & R. Montemayor, pp. 91–121. Newbury Park, CA: Sage.

Brack, C. J., Orr, D. P., & Ingersoll, G. (1988). Pubertal maturation and adolescent self-esteem. *Journal of Adolescent Health Care*, 9, 280–5.

Bronfenbrenner, U. (1979). *The Ecology of Human Development: Experiments by Nature and Design*. Cambridge, MA: Harvard University Press.

Bronfenbrenner, U., & Weiss, H. B. (1983). Beyond policies without people: An ecological perspective on child and family policy. In *Social Policy for Children and Their Families: A Primer*, ed. E. Zigler, S. L. Kagan, & E. Kleigman. Cambridge, England: Cambridge University Press.

Brooks-Gunn, J., Duncan, G. J., Klebanov, P., & Sealand, N. (1993). Do neighborhoods influence child and adolescent development?, *American Journal of Sociology*, 99, 353–95.

Brooks-Gunn, J., & Reiter, E. O. (1990). The role of pubertal process. In *At the Threshold: The Developing Adolescent*, ed. S. S. Feldman & G. R. Elliott, pp. 16–53. Cambridge, MA: Harvard University Press.

Brown, B. (1989). The role of peer groups in adolescents' adjustment to secondary school. In *Peer Relationships in Child Development*, ed. T. J. Berndt & G. W. Ladd, pp. 188–216. New York: Wiley.

(1990). Peer groups and peer cultures. In *At the Threshold: The Developing Adolescent*, ed. S. S. Feldman & G. R. Elliott, pp. 171–96. Cambridge, MA: Harvard University Press.

Brown, B., Clasen, D., & Eicher, S. (1986). Perceptions of peer pressure, peer conformity dispositions, and self-reported behavior among adolescents. *Developmental Psychology*, 22, 521–30.

Bryk, A. S., & Thum, Y. M. (1989). The effects of high school organization on dropping out: An exploratory investigation. *American Educational Research Journal*, 26, 353–83.

Camarena, P. M., Sarigiani, P. A., & Petersen, A. C. (1990). Gender-specific pathways to intimacy in early adolescence. *Journal of Youth and Adolescence*, 19, 19–32.

Camarena, P. M., Stemmler, M., & Petersen, A. C. (1994). The gender differential significance of work and family: An exploration of adolescent experience and expectation. In *Adolescence in Context: The Interplay of Family, School, Peers, and Work in Adjustment*, ed. R. K. Silbereisen & E. Todt, pp. 201–21. New York: Springer.

Carnegie Council on Adolescent Development (1990). *Prevention of Adolescent Injury*. New York: Carnegie Corporation of New York.

Caspi, A., Lynam, D., Moffitt, T. E., & Silva, P. A. (1993). Unraveling girls' delinquency: Biological, dispositional, and contextual contributions to adolescent misbehavior. *Developmental Psychology*, 29, 19–30.

Chumlea, W. C. (1982). Physical growth at adolescence. In *Handbook of Developmental Psychology*, ed. B. B. Wolman, G. Stricker, S. J. Ellman, P. Keith-Spiegel, & D. S. Palermo, pp. 471–85. Englewood Cliffs, NJ: Prentice-Hall.

Coleman, J. (1961). *The Adolescent Society*. Glencoe, IL: Free Press.

Coleman, J. C. (1978). Current contradictions in adolescent theory. *Journal of Youth and Adolescence*, 7, 1–11.

Crockett, L. J., & Petersen, A. C. (1993). Adolescent development: Health risks and opportunities for health promotion. In *Promoting the Health of Adolescents: New Directions for the Twenty-First Century*, ed. S. G. Millstein, A. C. Petersen, & E. O. Nightingale, pp. 13–37. New York: Oxford University Press.

Crockett, L. J., Petersen, A. C., Graber, J. A., Schulenberg, J. E., & Ebata, A. T. (1989). School transitions and adjustment during early adolescence. *Journal of Early Adolescence*, 9, 181–210.

Daniels, D., Dunn, J., Furstenberg, F. F., Jr., & Plomin, R. (1985). Environmental differences within the family and adjustment differences within pairs of adolescent siblings. *Child Development*, 56, 764–74.

Department of International Economic and Social Affairs, United Nations (1988). Adolescent reproductive behavior: Evidence from developed countries. *Population Studies*, 109.

Diekstra, R. (in press). Suicide and parasuicide among youth. In *Psychosocial Disorders in Young People: Time Trends and Their Origins*, ed. M. Rutter & D. Smith. Chichester: Wiley.

Dorn, L. D., Crockett, L. J., & Petersen, A. C. (1988). The relations of pubertal status to intrapersonal changes in young adolescents. *Journal of Early Adolescence*, 8, 405–19.

Dornbusch, S., Ritter, P., Leiderman, P., Roberts, D., & Fraleigh, M. (1987). The relation of parenting style to adolescent school performance. *Child Development*, 58, 1244–57.

Dryfoos, J. G. (1990). *Adolescents at Risk*. New York: Oxford University Press.

Dubas, J. S., Graber, J. A., & Petersen, A. C. (1991). A longitudinal investigation of adolescents' changing perceptions of pubertal timing. *Developmental Psychology*, 27, 580–6.

Dunn, J. F., Plomin, R., & Daniels, D. (1986). Consistency and change in mothers' behavior toward young siblings. *Child Development*, 57, 348–56.

Eccles, J. S., & Midgley, C. (1989). Stage/environment fit: Developmentally appropriate classrooms for early adolescents. In *Research on Motivation in Education Vol. 3. Goals and Cognition*, ed. R. E. Ames & C. Ames. New York: Academic Press.

Eckert, P. (1989). *Jocks and Burnouts: Social Categories and Identity in the High School*. New York: Teachers College Press.

Egeland, B., Jacobvitz, D., & Sroufe, L. A. (1988). Breaking the cycle of abuse. *Child Development*, 59, 1080–8.

Eichorn, D. H. (1975). Asynchronization in adolescent development. In *Adolescence in the Life Cycle: Psychological Change and Social Context*, ed. S. E. Dragastin & G. H. Elder, Jr., pp. 81–96. Washington, DC: Hemisphere.

Elder, G. (1985). *Life Course Dynamics*. Ithaca, NY: Cornell University Press.

Elliott, D. S. (in press). Health enhancing and health compromising lifestyles. In *Promoting the Health of Adolescents: New Directions for the Twenty-First Century*, ed. S. G. Millstein, A. C. Petersen, & E. O. Nightingale, pp. 119–45. New York: Oxford University Press.

Emde, R. N., & Harmon, R. J. (Eds.) (1984). *Continuities and Discontinuities in Development*. New York: Plenum Press.

Epstein, H. T. (1978). Growth spurts during brain development: Implications for educational policy and practice. In *Education and the Brain*, ed. J. S. Chall & A. F. Mirsky, pp. 345–70. Chicago: Society for the Study of Education.

(1986). Stages in human brain development. *Developments in Brain Research*, 30, 114–9.

Epstein, J. L. (1986). Friendship selection: Developmental and environmental influences. In *Process and outcome in peer relationships*, ed. R. C. Mueller & C. R. Cooper, pp. 129–60. New York: Academic Press.

(1989). The selection of friends: Changes across the grades and in different school communities. In *Peer relationships and child development*, ed. T. J. Berndt & G. W. Ladd, pp. 158–87. New York: Wiley.

Epstein, J. L., & Karweit, N. L. (Eds.) (1983). *Friends in School*. New York: Academic Press.

Erikson, E. H. (1968). *Identity: Youth and Crisis*. New York: W. W. Norton.

Eylon, B., & Lynn, M. C. (1988). Learning and instruction: An examination of four research perspectives in science education. *Review of Educational Research*, 58, 251–301.

Faust, M. S. (1983). Alternative constructions of adolescent growth. In *Girls at Puberty: Biological and Psychosocial Perspectives*, ed. J. Brooks-Gunn & A. C. Petersen, pp. 105–25. New York: Plenum.

Feinberg, J. (1987). Adolescence and mental illness [letter]. *Science*, 236, 507–8.

Feldlaufer, H., Midgley, C., & Eccles, J. S. (1988). Student, teacher, and observer perceptions of the classroom environment before and after the transition to junior high school. *Journal of Early Adolescence*, 8, 133–56.

Feldman, S. S., & Elliott, G. R. (Eds.) (1990). *At the Threshold: The Developing Adolescent*, Cambridge, MA: Harvard University Press.

Feldman, S. S., & Rosenthal, D. A. (1991). Age expectations of behavioural autonomy in Hong Kong, Australian and American youth: The influence of family variables and adolescents' values. *International Journal of Psychology*, 26, 1–23.

Fend, H. (1994). The historical context of transition to work and youth unemployment. In *Youth Unemployment and Society*, ed. A. C. Petersen & J. Mortimer, pp. 77–94. New York: Cambridge University Press.

Fend, H., & Schröer, S. (1985). The formation of self-concepts in the context of educational systems. *International Journal of Behavioral Development*, 8, 423–44.

Fenzel, L. M., & Blyth, D. A. (1986). Individual adjustment to school transitions: An exploration of the role of supportive peer relations. *Journal of Early Adolescence*, 6, 315–29.

Freud, A. (1958). Adolescence. *Psychoanalytic Study of the Child*, 13, 255–78.

Frisch, R. (1983). Fatness, puberty, and fertility: The effect of nutrition and physical training on menarche and ovulation. In *Girls at Puberty: Biological and Psychosocial Perspectives*, ed. J. Brooks-Gunn & A. C. Petersen, pp. 29–49. New York: Plenum.

Frisch, R. E., Wyshak, G., & Vincent, L. (1980). Delayed menarche and amenorrhea in ballet dancers. *New England Journal of Medicine*, 303, 17–9.

Furstenberg, F. (1990). Coming of age in a changing family system. In *At the Threshold: The Developing Adolescent*, ed. S. S. Feldman & G. R. Elliott, pp. 147–70. Cambridge, MA: Harvard University Press.

Galambos, N. L. (1985). *Maternal Role Satisfaction, Mother–Adolescent Relations, and Sex-Typing in Early Adolescent Boys and Girls*. Unpublished doctoral dissertation, Pennsylvania State University, University Park, PA.

Galambos, N., & Silbereisen, R. K. (1987). Income change, parental life outlook and adolescent expectations for job success. *Journal of Marriage and the Family*, 49, 141–9.

Galler, J. R., Ramsey, F. C., Salt, P., & Archer, E. (1987). Long-term effects of early kwashiorkor compared with marasmus. I. Physical growth and sexual maturation. *Journal of Pediatric Gastroenterology and Nutrition*, 6, 841–6.

Garmezy, N. (1985). Stress-resistant children: The search for protective factors. In *Recent Research in Developmental Psychopathology*, ed. J. E. Stevenson, pp. 213–33. Oxford: Pergamon Press.

Garmezy, N., & Rutter, M. (Eds.) (1983). *Stress, Coping, and Development in Children*. New York: McGraw-Hill.

Graber, J. A., & Petersen, A. C. (1991). Cognitive changes at adolescence: Biological perspectives. In *Brain Maturation and Cognitive Development: Comparative and Cross-Cultural Perspectives*, ed. K. R. Gibson & A. C. Petersen, pp. 253–79. New York: Aldine de Gruyter.

Greenberger, E., & Steinberg, L. (1986). *When Teenagers Work: The Psychological and Social Costs of Adolescent Employment*. New York: Basic Books.

Greenberger, E., Steinberg, L., & Vaux, A. (1981). Adolescents who work: Health and behavioral consequences of job stress. *Developmental Psychology*, 17, 691–703.

Greene, A. L. (1986). Future time-perspective in adolescence: The present of things future revisited. *Journal of Youth and Adolescence*, 15, 99–113.

Greenfield, P. (1976). Cross-cultural research and Piagetian theory: Paradox and progress. In Riegel & J. Meacham (Eds.), *The Developing Individual in a Changing World* pp. 322–33. The Hague: Mouton.

Gullickson, A. R. (1985). Student evaluation techniques and their relationship to grade and curriculum. *Journal of Educational Research*, 79, 96–100.

Hall, G. S. (1904). *Adolescence: Its Psychology and Its Relations to Physiology, Anthropology, Sociology, Sex, Crime, Religion, and Education*. New York: Appleton.

Hamilton, S. F. (1987). Adolescent problem behavior in the United States and the Federal Republic of Germany: Implications for prevention. In *Social Intervention: Potential and Constraints*, ed. K. Hurrelmann, F. Kaufmann, & F. Lösel, pp. 185–204. Berlin: Walter de Gruyter.

(1990). *Apprenticeship for Adulthood: Preparing Youth for the Future*. New York: Free Press.

(1994). Social roles for youth: Interventions in unemployment. In *Youth Unemployment and Society*, ed. A. C. Petersen & J. Mortimer, pp. 248–69. New York: Cambridge.

Harter, S. (1990). Self and identity development. In *At the Threshold: The Developing Adolescent*, ed. S. S. Feldman & G. R. Elliott, pp. 352–87. Cambridge, MA: Harvard University Press.

Hartup, W. W. (1983). Peer relations. In *Handbook of Child Psychology*, Vol. 4, ed. P. H. Mussen, pp. 103–96. New York: Wiley.

Hawkins, J., & Berndt, T. J. (1985, April). *Adjustment Following the Transition to Junior High School*. Paper presented at the biennial meeting of the Society for Research in Child Development, Toronto, Canada.

Hayes, C. D., & Kamerman, S. B. (Eds.) (1983). *Children of Working Parents: Experiences and Outcomes*. Washington, DC: National Academy Press.

Hess, L. E. (in press). Changing family patterns in Europe: Opportunity and risk factors for adolescent development. In *Psychosocial Disorders in Young People: Time Trends and Their Origins*, ed. M. Rutter & D. Smith. Chichester: Wiley.

Hetherington, E. M. (1991). Presidential address: Families, lies, and videotapes. *Journal of Research on Adolescence*, 1, 323–48.

Hetherington, E. M., & Camara, K. (1984). Families in transition: The processes of dissolution and reconstitution. In *Review of Child Development Research*, Vol. 7, ed. R. D. Parke, pp. 398–439. Chicago: University of Chicago Press.

Hill, J., & Holmbeck, G. (1986). Attachment and autonomy during adolescence. In *Annals of Child Development*, ed. G. Whitehurst. Greenwich, CT: JAI Press.

Hill, J., Holmbeck, G., Marlow, L., Green, T., & Lynch, M. (1985). Menarcheal status and parent-child relations in families of seventh-grade girls. *Journal of Youth and Adolescence*, 14, 301–16.

Hoffman, L. W. (1979). Maternal employment. *American Psychologist*, 34, 859–65.

Holland, B. A., Haas, D. K., Norman, D., Brandt-Zawadski, M., & Newton, T. H. (1986). MRI of normal brain maturation. *American Journal of Neuroradiology*, 7, 201–8.

Hurrelmann, K. (1989). Adolescents as productive processors of reality: Methodological perspectives. In *The Social World of Adolescents: International Perspectives*, ed. K. Hurrelmann & U. Engel, pp. 107–18. New York: Walter de Gruyter.

Ianni, F. (1989). *The Search for Structure: A Report on American Youth Today*. New York: Free Press.

Inhelder, B., & Piaget, J. (1958). *The Growth of Logical Thinking from Childhood to Adolescence*. New York: Basic Books.

Jones, E. F., Forrest, J. D., Goldman, N., Henshaw, S., Lincoln, R., Rosoff, J. I., Westoff, C. F., & Wulf, D. (1986). *Teenage Pregnancy in Industrialized Countries: A Study Sponsored by the Alan Guttmacher Institute*. New Haven, CT: Yale University Press.

Kandel, D., & Lesser, G. (1972). *Youth in Two Worlds*. San Francisco: Jossey-Bass.

Keating, D. P. (1980). Thinking processes in adolescence. In *Handbook of Adolescent Psychology*, ed. J. Adelson, pp. 211–46. New York: Wiley.

(1990). Adolescent thinking. In *At the Threshold: The Developing Adolescent*, ed. S. S. Feldman & G. R. Elliott, pp. 54–89. Cambridge, MA: Harvard University Press.

Keating, D. P., & Clark, L. V. (1980). Development of physical and social reasoning in adolescence. *Developmental Psychology*, 16, 23–30.

Kessler, R. C., Price, R. H., & Wortman, C. B. (1985). Social factors in psychopathology: Stress, social support and coping processes. *Annual Review of Psychology*, 36, 351–72.

Klepp, K. I., Halper, A., & Perry, C. L. (1986). The efficacy of peer leaders in drug abuse prevention. *Journal of School Health*, 56, 407–11.

Kuhn, D., Amsel, E., & O'Loughlin, M. (1988). *The Development of Scientific Thinking Skills*. San Diego, CA: Academic Press.

Kulin, H. E., Bwibo, N., Mutie, D., & Santner, S. J. (1982). The effect of chronic childhood malnutrition on pubertal growth and development. *The American Journal of Clinical Nutrition*, 36, 527–36.

Lalo, A. (1989). Social change and equilibration of cognitive structures: The role of schooling and urbanisation. *International Journal of Behavioral Development*, 12, 321–45.

Lamb, M. (Ed.) (1982). *Nontraditional Families: Parenting and Child Development*, Hillsdale, NJ: Erlbaum.

Lerner, J. V., & Galambos, N. L. (1985). Maternal role satisfaction, mother-child interaction, and child temperament: A process model. *Developmental Psychology*, 21, 1157–64.

Lerner, R. M., Karson, M., Meidels, M., & Knapp, J. R. (1975). Actual and perceived attitudes of late adolescents and their parents: The phenomenon of the generation gaps. *Journal of Genetic Psychology*, 126, 195–207.

Lewin-Epstein, N. (1981). *Youth Employment During High School*. Washington, DC: National Center for Education Statistics.

Lewis, C. (1981). How adolescents approach decisions: Changes over grades seven to twelve and policy implications. *Child Development*, 52, 538–44.

Linn, M. C., & Petersen, A. C. (1985). Emergence and characterization of sex differences in spatial ability. *Child Development*, 56, 1479–98.

Loeber, R., & Stouthamer-Loeber, M. (1986). Family factors as correlates and predictors of juvenile conduct problems and delinquency. In *Crime and Justice*, Vol. 7, ed. M. Tonry & N. Morris. Chicago: University of Chicago Press.

Maccoby, E. E. (1984). Middle childhood in the context of the family. In *Development During Middle Childhood: The Years from Six to Twelve*, ed. W. A. Collins, pp. 184–239. Washington, DC: National Academy of Sciences Press.

Maccoby, E. E., & Jacklin, C. N. (1974). *The Psychology of Sex Differences*. Stanford, CA: Stanford University Press.

Maccoby, E., & Martin, J. (1983). Socialization in the context of the family: Parent-child interaction. In *Handbook of Child Psychology Vol. 4, Socialization, Personality, and Social Development*, ed. E. M. Hetherington, pp. 103–96. New York: Wiley.

Magnusson, D. (1987). *Individual Development in an Interactional Perspective*, Vol. 1, *Paths through Life*, ed. D. Magnusson. Hillsdale, NJ: Erlbaum.

Mann, L., Harmoni, R., Power, C., Beswick, G., & Ormond, C. (1988). Effectiveness of GOFOR course in decision-making for high school students. *Journal of Behavioral Decision-Making*, 1, 159–68.

Marcia, J. E. (1966). Development and validation of ego-identity status. *Journal of Personality and Social Psychology*, 3, 551–8.

(1980). Identity in adolescence. In *Handbook of Adolescent Psychology*, ed. J. Adelson, New York: Wiley.

Mark, J. A. (1987). Technological change and employment: Some results from BLS research. *Monthly Labor Review*, 110, 26–9.

Maughan, B., & Champion, L. (1988). *Risk and Protective Factors in the Transition to Young Adulthood*. Paper presented at the European Science Foundation Workshop. Longitudinal Research and the Study of Successful Aging, Castle Ringber, Federal Republic of Germany.

McCarthy, J. D., & Hoge, D. R. (1982). Analysis of age effects in longitudinal studies of adolescent self-esteem. *Developmental Psychology*, 18, 372–9.

Meeus, W. (1989). Parental and peer support in adolescence. In *The Social World of Adolescents: International Perspectives*, ed. K. Hurrelmann & U. Engel, pp. 167–84. Berlin: Walter de Gruyter.

Moffitt, T. E., Caspi, A., Belsky, J., & Silva, P. (1991). Childhood experience and the onset of menarche: A test of a sociobiological model. *Child Development*, 63, 47–58.

Montemayor, R. (1983). Parents and adolescents in conflict: All families some of the time and some families most of the time. *Journal of Early Adolescence*, 3, 83–103.

Mortimer, J. (1994). Individual differences and precursors of unemployment. In *Youth Unemployment and Society*, ed. A. C. Petersen & J. Mortimer. New York: Cambridge.

Offer, D., Ostrov, E., & Howard, K. I. (1981). The mental health professional's concept of the normal adolescent. *Archives of General Psychiatry*, 38, 149–52.

Ogbu, J. (1974). *The Next Generation: An Ethnography of Education in an Urban Neighborhood*. New York: Academic Press.

O'Malley, P. M., & Bachman, J. G. (1983). Self-esteem: Change and stability between ages 13 and 23. *Developmental Psychology*, 19, 257–68.

Palmonari, A., Kirchler, E., & Pombeni, M. L. (1991). Differential effects of identification with family and peers on coping and developmental tasks in adolescents. *European Journal of Social Psychology*, 21, 381–402.

Patterson, G. (1986). Performance models for antisocial boys. *American Psychologist*, 41, 432–44.

Petersen, A. C. (1983). Pubertal change and cognition. In *Girls at Puberty: Biological and Psychosocial Perspectives*, ed. J. Brooks-Gunn & A. C. Petersen, pp. 179–98. New York: Plenum.

(1987). The nature of biological-psychosocial interactions. In *Early Adolescent Transitions*, ed. M. Levine & E. McAnarney, pp. 123–37. Lexington, MA: D. C. Heath.

(1988). Adolescent development. *Annual Review of Psychology*, 39, 583–607.

(1991, April). *Adolescence in America: Effects on Girls*. The 1991 Gisela Konopka Lecture, University of Minnesota, Minneapolis, MN.

Petersen, A. C., Bingham, C. R., Stemmler, M., & Crockett, L. J. (1991, July). *Subcultural Variation in Developmental Processes: The Development of Depressed Affect*. Poster presented at the biennial meeting of the International Society for the Study of Behavioral Development, Minneapolis, MN.

Petersen, A. C., Hurrelmann, K., & Leffert, N. (1993). Adolescence and schooling in Germany and the United States: A comparison of societal socialization to adulthood. *Teachers College Record*, 94(3), 611–28.

Petersen, A. C., Kennedy, R. E., & Sullivan, P. (1991). Coping with adolescence. In *Adolescent Stress: Causes and Consequences*, ed. M. E. Colten & S. Gore, pp. 93–110. Hawthorne, NY: Aldine de Gruyter.

Petersen, A. C., Sarigiani, P. A., & Kennedy, R. E. (1991). Adolescent depression: Why more girls? *Journal of Youth and Adolescence*, 20, 247–71.

Petersen, A. C., & Taylor, B. (1980). The biological approach to adolescence: Biological change and psychosocial adaptation. In *Handbook of Adolescent Psychology*, ed. J. Adelson, pp. 117–55. New York: Wiley.

Plomin, R., & Daniels, D. (1987). Why are children in the same family so different from each other? *Behavioral and Brain Sciences*, 10, 1–16.

Pulkkinen, L. (1990). Young adults' health and its antecedents in evolving lifestyles. In *Health Hazards in Adolescence*, ed. K. Hurrelmann & F. Lösel, pp. 67–90. New York: Walter de Gruyter.

Robins, L. N. (1974, May). The Vietnam drug user returns. *Special Action Office Monograph* (Series A, No. 2). Washington, DC: U.S. Government Printing Office.

Ruble, D. N., & Brooks-Gunn, J. (1982). The experience of menarche. *Child Development*, 53, 1557–666.

Rutter, M. (in press). Causal concepts and their testing. In *Psychosocial Disorders in Young People: Time Trends and Their Origins*, ed. M. Rutter & D. Smith. Chichester: Wiley.

Rutter, M., Graham, P., Chadwick, O., & Yule, W. (1976). Adolescent turmoil: Fact or fiction? *Journal of Child Psychology and Psychiatry*, 17, 35–56.

Rutter, M., Maughan, B., Mortimore, P., Ouston, J., & Smith, A. (1979). *Fifteen Thousands Hours: Secondary Schools and Their Effects on Children*. Cambridge, MA: Harvard University Press.

Sarigiani, P. (1990). *A Longitudinal Study of Relationship Adjustment of Young Adults from Divorced and Nondivorced Families*. Unpublished doctoral dissertation, Pennsylvania State University, University Park, PA.

Savin-Williams, R. C., & Berndt, T. J. (1990). Friendship and peer relations. In *At the Threshold: The Developing Adolescent*, ed. S. S. Feldman & G. R. Elliott, pp. 277–307. Cambridge, MA: Harvard University Press.

Silbereisen, R. K. (1990). Smoking and drinking: Prospective analyses in German and Polish adolescents. In *Health Hazards in Adolescence*, ed. K. Hurrelmann & F. Lösel, 167–90. Berlin: Walter de Gruyter.

Silbereisen, R. K., & Noack, P. (1988). On the constructive role of problem behavior in adolescence. In *Person in Conflict: Developmental Processes*, ed. N. Bolger, A. Caspi, G. Downey, & M. Moorehouse, pp. 152–80. Cambridge, MA: Cambridge University Press.

Silbereisen, R. K., Noack, P., & Schönpflug, U. (1994). Comparative analyses of beliefs, leisure contexts, and substance abuse in West Berlin and Warsaw. In *Adolescence in Context: The Interplay of Family, School, Peers, and Work in Adjustment*, ed. R. K. Silbereisen & E. Todt, pp. 176–98. New York: Springer.

Silbereisen, R. K., Petersen, A. C., Albrecht, H. T., & Kracke, B. (1989). Maturational timing and the development of problem behavior: Longitudinal studies in adolescence. *Journal of Early Adolescence*, 9, 247–68.

Silbereisen, R. K., Robins, L., & Rutter, M. (in press). Secular trends in substance use: Concepts and data on the impact of social change on alcohol and drug use. In *Psychosocial Disorders in Young People: Time Trends and Their Origins*, ed. M. Rutter & D. Smith. Chichester: Wiley.

Simmons, R. G., & Blyth, D. A. (1987). *Moving into Adolescence: The Impact of Pubertal Change and School Context*. Hawthorne, NY: Aldine de Gruyter.

Simmons, R. G., & Rosenberg, F. (1975). Sex, sex roles, and self-image. *Journal of Youth and Adolescence*, 4, 229–58.

Spencer, M., & Dornbusch, S. (1990). Challenges in studying minority youth. In *At the Threshold: The Developing Adolescent*, ed. S. S. Feldman & G. R. Elliott, pp. 123–46. Cambridge, MA: Harvard University Press.

Spencer, M., & Markstrom-Adams, C. (1990). Identity processes among racial and ethnic minority children in America. *Child Development*, 61, 290–310.

Stattin, H., & Magnusson, D. (1990). *Pubertal Maturation in Female Development, Vol. 2, Paths Through Life*. Hillsdale, NJ: Erlbaum.

Steinberg, L. D. (1981). Transformations in family relations at puberty. *Developmental Psychology*, 17, 833–40.

(1990). Autonomy, conflict and harmony in the family relationship. In *At the Threshold: The Developing Adolescent*, ed. S. S. Feldman & G. R. Elliott, pp. 255–76. Cambridge, MA: Harvard University Press.

(1992, March). Discussant's comments. In *Psychosocial Antecedents of the Timing of Puberty*, chair R. K. Silbereisen. Symposium conducted at the biennial meeting of the Society for Research on Adolescence, Washington, D.C.

Steinberg, L., & Dornbusch, S. M. (1991). Negative correlates of part-time employment during adolescence: Replication and elaboration. *Developmental Psychology*, 27, 304–13.

Steinberg, L., Dornbusch, S., & Brown, B. B. (1992). Ethnic differences in adolescent achievement: An ecological perspective. *American Psychologist*, 47, 723–9.

Steinberg, L. D., Greenberger, E., Garduque, L., Ruggiero, M., & Vaux, A. (1982). Effects of working on adolescent development. *Developmental Psychology*, 18, 385–95.

Steinberg, L., Lamborn, S. D., Dornbusch, S. M., & Darling, N. (1992). Impact of parenting practices on adolescent achievement: Authoritative parenting, school involvement, and encouragement to succeed. *Child Development*, 63, 1266–81.

Steinberg, L., & Silverberg, S. (1986). The vicissitudes of autonomy in early adolescence. *Child Development*, 57, 841–51.

Suomi, S. (1987). *Individual Differences in Rhesus Monkey Behavioral and Adrenocortical Responses to Social Challenge: Correlations with Measures of Heart Rate Variability*. Paper presented at the biennial meeting of the Society for Research in Child Development, Baltimore, MD.

Tanner, J. M. (1972). Sequence, tempo, and individual variation in growth and development of boys and girls aged twelve to sixteen. In *Twelve to Sixteen: Early Adolescence*, ed. J. Kagan & R. Coles, pp. 1–24. New York: Norton.

Trickett, P. K., & Putnam, F. W. (in press). The impact of child sexual abuse on females: Toward a developmental, psychobiological integration. *Psychological Science*, 4, 81–7.

Turiel, E. (1989). Domain-specific social judgements and domain ambiguities. *Merrill-Palmer Quarterly*, 35, 89–114.

Uchtenhagen, A., & Zimmer-Hoefler, D. (1985). *Heroinabhaengige und ihre "Normalen" Altersgenossen*. Bern: Verlag Paul Haupt.

Warren, M. (1980). The effects of exercise on pubertal progression and reproductive function in girls. *Journal of Clinical Endocrinology and Metabolism*, 51, 1150–7.

Wartella, E. (in press). Media and the problem behaviors of adolescents. In *Psychosocial Disorders in Young People: Time Trends and Their Origins*, ed. M. Rutter & D. Smith. Chichester: Wiley.

Waterman, A. S. (1985). Identity in the context of adolescent psychology. In *Identity in Adolescence: Processes and Contents*, ed. A. S. Waterman, pp. 5–24. San Francisco: Jossey-Bass.

Weithorn, L. A., & Campbell, S. B. (1982). The competency of children and adolescents to make informed treatment decisions. *Child Development*, 53, 1589–98.

Wyshak, G. L., & Frisch, R. E. (1982). Evidence for a secular change in age of menarche. *New England Journal of Medicine*, 306, 1033–5.

Yakovlev, P. I., & Lecours, A. R. (1967). The myelogenetic cycles of regional maturation in the brain. In *Regional Development of the Brain in Early Life*, ed. A. Minkowski, pp. 3–70. Oxford: Blackwell.

Youniss, J., & Smollar, J. (1985). *Adolescents' Relations with Mothers, Fathers, and Friends*. Chicago: University of Chicago Press.

2. Timing of puberty and reactions to pubertal changes

FRANÇOISE D. ALSAKER

The period around puberty has generally been characterized as a period of rapid and dramatic changes (e.g., Brooks-Gunn & Petersen, 1984; Cairns & Cairns, 1988; Dorn, Crockett & Petersen, 1988). Pubertal maturation signifies sexual maturity and hence also the transition to the reproductive phase of life and eventual responsibility for offspring. Puberty is unique in combining rapid biological with essential social changes.

In many societies, the importance of the transition is emphasized at some point by rites of passage. Such ceremonies usually help the adolescent and others to redefine their roles and to make expectations of the new roles clear. In most Western societies the transition is considered a private event. Given the conspicuous changes that take place, however, pubertal maturation cannot remain a private event. Therefore, the physical changes of puberty challenge the young adolescent's view of her- or himself as well as the view other people have of her or him and require at least some redefinition of roles. Nonetheless, because of the semiprivacy of pubertal events, the ways the adolescent and others will cope with the transition and redefine their roles will vary and depend on individual, relational, and contextual factors.

Early adolescence is also marked by cognitive and social changes. Relations to others (parents and peers) are often in transition, and most young adolescents experience changes in their school environment (e.g., moving from elementary school to junior high school). Hence, pubertal development typically occurs at the same time as changes in other areas. Although

This review was written while I was a visiting professor at the University of Bern. I am deeply indebted to the Johann Jacobs Foundation which supported my stay and to Professor August Flammer who invited me to the department for child and youth psychology in Bern. I am also grateful to all colleagues at the same department for valuable discussions and an inspiring and pleasant atmosphere. I wish to thank Aida Huber-Ghanim who has been language consultant for this chapter. Comments from Terje G. Alsaker, August Flammer, Alexander Grob, and Bärbel Kracke on an earlier draft are greatly appreciated.

co-occurrence does not mean causality, it may suggest it, especially when large individual differences are observed in biological and behavioral variables. Consequently, a wide array of social, behavioral, cognitive, and psychological variables have been examined as to their possible dependence on pubertal maturation.

It should be noted, however, that the co-occurrence of biological and psychosocial variables has also been suggestive of causality in the opposite direction. For example, social factors such as socioeconomic status, size of the family, and birth order have been seen as predictors of onset of puberty (Adams, 1981). Some hypotheses have been proposed that postulate an accelerating effect of stress through *positive* stimulation (Adams, 1981) or through *negative* effects, that is, internalizing problems leading to lower metabolism and higher storage of fat, leading in turn to an acceleration of the biological maturation (Belsky, Steinberg & Draper, 1991). Aversive family environments, however, have been demonstrated to have dramatic retarding effects on growth and pubertal maturation (Money & Wolff, 1974). As demonstrated by these three contradictory positions, the possible influence of social factors on biological maturation remains equivocal. We ought to bear in mind that co-occurrence of events may also indicate the effect of some other factors on the co-occurring events. For example, Campbell and Udry (1992) have demonstrated a clear association between mothers' and daughters' age at menarche. A genetic factor may explain the association between early menarche in daughters and divorce in the family. Early maturing girls are more likely to marry at an earlier age and hence also to divorce. Being also more likely to have daughters who will mature earlier, their daughters will more often grow up in the context of a divorced family. In other words, the relation between early onset of puberty and divorce is spurious, and should not be interpreted as support for an accelerating hypothesis. A recent study including 1,888 pairs of monozygotic and dizygotic twins (Meyer et al., 1991) has also demonstrated clear genetic effects on the timing of menarche.

The co-occurrence of developmental events is one of the most intricate problems, or challenges, in research on pubertal maturation. All developmental events are supposed to influence the behavior of the adolescent and reactions from others, regardless of the possible interdependence of development in different areas. It may, therefore, be hard to say whether individual differences appearing during pubertal maturation are reactions to pubertal changes or not. For example, when young adolescents are referred to counseling services, it is not unusual to find that their problems have been of a long-lasting character, but that the manifestation of the problems may have been different and less disruptive to others in childhood (Saucier & Marquette, 1985). In other words, symptoms may be found in relation to pubertal maturation, but their appearance may be due to factors that co-occur with puberty (such as cognitive development) rather than to pubertal maturation in itself. Studies concurrently addressing several areas of influence are sparse. Hence, this chapter will be based primarily on studies that have addressed the issue of possible effects of pubertal maturation on behavior and psychosocial adjustment. Although the term "effect" is usually reserved for causal relationships, it has commonly been used in the literature on puberty, even when data have been clearly correlational ones. Therefore, although the term is used in the following as a matter of convenience, it should not be given any strict causal interpretation.

The role of pubertal maturation in psychological adjustment has attracted much research interest as early as the thirties. Results from studies conducted in the late thirties and forties have been presented by Jones and Mussen (1958); Petersen and Taylor (1980) have given a detailed review of findings in the fifties through seventies, and Greif and Ulman (1982) have also provided an exhaustive review of studies on menarche. The present review will, therefore, focus on more recent literature, especially reports published during the last decade.[1]

Before the findings from the literature can be presented, we will present a short description of the major biological events occurring during pubertal maturation and discuss concepts used in the literature. Thereafter, factors that may influence the reactions of adolescents to pubertal changes and models pertaining to different positions will be presented.

Pubertal changes

Biological development

The endocrine systems responsible for the typical pubertal changes are active long before changes are observable. The maturation of the adrenal glands starts between the ages of six and eight, and the maturation of the gonads begins at around nine or ten years (Susman et al, 1987). The hormones that contribute to sexual maturation can be divided roughly into three main groups: gonadal hormones (steroids), including testosterone

1. Marginal results ($p < 0.10$) have been included in summaries of results without any argumentation or reference to their marginality. Since large numbers of variables are often used in the studies, only significant results ($p < 0.05$) are included in the present review. Furthermore, among the number of isolated findings reported in papers, only those that can be integrated with other results will be presented.

and estradiol, adrenal androgens, and gonadotropins. The last named include luteinizing hormones (LH) and follicle stimulating hormones (FSH). Testosterone may increase eighteen-fold in males in the course of pubertal development. A corresponding eight-fold increase of estradiol is usually observed in females (Nottelmann et al., 1987). Testosterone levels have been shown to be strongly correlated with pubertal maturation in boys, but correlations are often of a more moderate character for other hormones, and for all hormones in girls (see Brooks-Gunn & Warren, 1989; Nottelmann et al., 1987). This fits well with observations of large individual differences in hormonal levels (e.g., Bierich, 1975, Figure 4); the differences are probably related to factors present prior to pubertal maturation (Susman, Dorn & Chrousos, 1991). Moreover, hormones are not only produced by the glands, but may also be produced in other body tissues (Petersen & Taylor, 1980) where some hormones may be transformed into other hormones.

The major hormonal changes involve the hypothalamic-pituitary-gonadal axis. The secretion of gonadotropin-releasing hormones (GnRH), which occurs in the hypothalamus, is suppressed during childhood (Mansfield & Emans, 1989); the hypothalamus has to mature before pubertal changes can start (Tanner, 1972).

It is not possible to deal with the full complexity of the biological maturation in this chapter. Only a brief presentation will be given, based on a subdivision proposed by Finkelstein (1980). Pubertal development may be divided into five phases characterized by endocrinological and physical changes. *Late prepuberty* (or onset of puberty) is characterized by some activity of the hypothalamic-pituitary-gonadal axis, growth rate is at its lowest point, and no physical changes are observed. In a second phase, called *very early puberty*, increased releases of GnRH, FSH, LH, and sex steroids are detectable (only during sleep), but there are still no observable physical changes. At *early puberty*, the concentration of hormones augments, and primary and secondary sexual maturation starts, that is, the first physical changes are observable. In addition to continued growth of secondary sexual characteristics, *mid-puberty* is characterized by the onset of voice change and increased muscularity in boys and peak height velocity and changes in distribution of fat in girls. By that time some enlargement of the breasts may also occur in boys. By the time of *late puberty* genitals, pubic hair, axillary hair, breasts, and so forth continue to develop, facial hair appears, and peak height velocity is reached in boys. Changes in fat distribution in girls and muscularity in boys are obvious, and it is usually the time of menarche in girls. It may take up to five years, however, until the majority of menstrual cycles become ovulatory.

In sum, pubertal maturation is characterized by large increases of sex hormones and rather dramatic changes in physical appearance. In addition to the redistribution of fat in girls, there is also evidence of increases in weight and body fat (Garn & Clark, 1976) in boys and girls. The increase often starts before other morphological changes. However, whereas there is a loss of fat in boys with the development of muscles (Slap, 1986; Tanner, 1972), the growth spurt in girls is not sufficient to produce a similar effect. Girls come out of puberty with a clear gain in fat (Slap, 1986) and, if the growth spurt is delayed, it may result in some degree of overweight (Warren, 1983).

Although the mechanisms that trigger the onset of menarche are still unknown, the increase in fat tissue is thought to play some role in the process (Slap, 1986). Fat tissues may be an important source of estrogen, as conversion of adrenal androgens into estrogens occurs there. Strenuous physical activity and leanness from early childhood have been observed to be associated with delayed menarche (Behrman et al., 1992). Moderate weight loss has been found to lead to secondary amenorrhea (Hagenfeldt, 1985; Warren, 1983) and early pubertal onset may occur in obese children (Warren, 1983). It should also be noted that girls who mature earlier than same-age peers have been found to be less lean and somewhat shorter than others (e.g., Brooks-Gunn, 1988) and to have a broad and stocky build (Jones & Mussen, 1958) when pubertal maturation is completed.

Pubertal status, pubertal timing and measurement issues

Pubertal status Pubertal status usually refers to the level of development reached by an individual in terms of physical changes. The physical changes that have been assessed vary considerably across studies. Since pubertal maturation has been found to be highly related to ossification (e.g., Behrman et al., 1992), X-rays of the wrist have sometimes (in early studies) been employed to determine the young adolescents' level of maturation. When a medical examination has been available, assessments of changes in secondary sexual characteristics have been used (genital, breast, and pubic hair development), following the criteria proposed by Tanner. When such examinations have not been practicable, parents' reports and self-reports have often been used. Such reports have varied to a large extent in the specificity of the items used, ranging from drawings of breasts, genitals, and pubic hair to relatively global statements. Self-report of menarcheal status and age has been adopted by many researchers in this context. Being a usually late pubertal event, however, menarche remains a rather rough indication of pubertal maturation and excludes the early changes of puberty. In general, given the wide variation in the sequence of pubertal changes, and the possible independence of some of the changes, measures considering only one single aspect of pubertal maturation should be avoided when the general pubertal development is assessed. A self-report instrument that has shown good validity without being too intrusive is the Pubertal Development Scale (PDS) developed by Petersen and colleagues (Petersen et al., 1988).

Asynchronies Despite the universal nature of puberty there are great individual differences with regard to onset of pubertal changes and their sequence within individuals (Eichorn, 1975; Finkelstein, 1980). Puberty is thus characterized rather by interindividual and intraindividual asynchronies than by uniformity. In girls, the time elapsed between the first signs of pubertal maturation and complete maturity may vary from one and a half to six years (Tanner, 1972). Corresponding variation in rate and order of changes is also observed in boys (Nottelmann et al., 1987). Furthermore, there is evidence for a relative independence of adrenarche which is associated with the development of pubic hair, and other endocrinological processes associated with genital and breast development (Nadler et al., 1987).

Pubertal timing Pubertal timing may be conceived of as a measure of an individual's relative development in comparison with expected pubertal maturation at a given age or within some reference group (criterion based; see Brooks-Gunn, Petersen, & Eichorn, 1985). Whether timing should be calculated on the basis of some age norms or comparisons within a sample, depends on the issue to be addressed. Given the importance of social comparison in this period (Hart, 1988), pubertal timing is generally regarded as a more crucial aspect of pubertal development than pubertal status in and of itself (e.g., Simmons, Blyth & McKinney, 1983). However, whereas social comparisons typically occur within the peer group (class, leisure time group, etc.), timing has, with the exception of two studies (Alsaker, 1992b; Silbereisen et al., 1989), been calculated on the basis of age or grade criteria.

The wide variety of methods and criteria makes a comparison of results very difficult. Furthermore, chronological age, pubertal development, and pubertal timing are intrinsically related to each other. Most studies, however, use one measure at a time and age is only rarely held constant.

Pubertal maturation and psychosocial adjustment: Conceptual considerations

One may consider the effects of pubertal changes on psychosocial adjustment from a biological perspective (e.g., effects of endocrinological changes), from an individual point of view (e.g., in terms of coping with developmental tasks), from a social one (in terms of roles), or from an interactional point of view. The latter perspective posits an interaction between the biological development, the social context and/or individual characteristics, and is by far in most widespread use in today's research on puberty. Direct effect models are hardly conceivable, because they implicitly assume a high degree of uniformity of behavior. The most plausible direct effects one may conceive of could be hormonal, or generally speaking biological, effects on moods and behavior.

Hormones and behavior

Hormonal effects on behavior have been repeatedly found in animal studies (Susman et al., 1985). Furthermore, there is evidence of a link to emotions and behavior in adults; dramatic psychiatric episodes (periodic psychosis) related to hormonal variations during the menstrual cycle in young adolescents have been reported (Berlin, Bergey & Money, 1985). The mechanisms that link hormones to behavior are still for the most part unknown. One can assume, however, that the considerable increases in hormones that occur during puberty might have activating effects (excitability, arousability; see Brooks-Gunn & Warren, 1989), or induce in the adolescent physiology a state of disequilibrium that could have emotional and behavioral effects.

Some clinical disorders seem to increase in early adolescence and hormonal factors have been postulated to account for at least some of the rise in incidence (Brooks-Gunn & Warren, 1989). Even within a biological frame of reference, however, most hypotheses include mediational variables. The influence of hormonal changes may also depend on earlier exposure to hormones, with permanent organizational effects on the central nervous system. Early exposure to gonadal steroids may sensitize individuals and lead to individual differences in responses to the same hormones during puberty (Susman et al., 1987). In addition, hormones are posited to affect behavior through their primary influence on variables such as emotionality or arousal (Inoff-Germain et al., 1988). It should also be noted that some domains of behavior, regulated by social norms or law, may be more dependent on the social context than others.

Pubertal maturation and cognition: Is there a link?

A certain level of cognitive development might be necessary to integrate the rapid biological changes (and others' reactions to these changes) in one's self-definition and to warrant the redefinitions involved in the transition from childhood to adolescence. Since pubertal maturation is characterized more by variation than uniformity in terms of age of onset and since pubertal and mental development are both controlled by the brain (Kohen-Raz, 1974), one may speculate whether cognitive and pubertal development may be linked in some way. The issue has already stimulated some research and several authors have provided overviews (Newcombe, Dubas, & Baenninger, 1989; Petersen, 1983). Some relation between physical and mental precocity has been reported (see Kohen-Raz, 1974) and there is some evidence for a small IQ advantage for early maturers (see Tanner, 1972). The results are relatively inconsistent, however, and cognitive maturation has also been found to follow chronological age rather than pubertal maturation (Petersen & Crockett, 1986).

On the basis of these rather inconclusive results, therefore, one should not expect young adolescents to be uniformly prepared for the task of self-redefinition, or to be all likely disrupted (Petersen & Crockett, 1986), from a cognitive point of view. Consequently, large individual differences should be expected in cognitive as well as other characteristics that may be central to psychosocial adjustment during pubertal development.

Psychosocial models and hypotheses

Psychosocial models are generally interactional models, proposing that effects of puberty are not a direct consequence of biological changes, but that individual factors, the social context, and cultural values play a central role in the process.

Individual factors. Among other things, individuals will differ in (1) the extent to which they perceive their pubertal development, (2) how they interpret the changes, (3) what kinds of expectations and attitudes they have, and (4) how they usually handle developmental tasks and transitions.

Individual differences in perception and interpretation of changes depend on cognitive abilities, on the individual's cognitive and personality style, including attribution style and defensiveness, on how much knowledge the young adolescent has about eventual body changes, and on the extent to which he or she is oriented toward her or his body (body-consciousness). The extent to which an individual perceives such changes is crucial to the way he or she will react.

Furthermore, the individual's own perception of timeliness, in pubertal development, may be essential in this context (Blyth, Simmons & Zakin, 1985; Brooks-Gunn, 1987). This perception is typically influenced by the reactions of others, the particular peer group which serves as a reference group, and the centrality of specific norms about pubertal status and conformity. Two young people who are equally mature may perceive themselves as on-time or off-time depending on the level of maturation of the adolescents with whom they associate. Only a moderate relation has been found between actual timing and perceived timing (e.g., Alsaker, 1992b; Stattin & Magnusson, 1990), and the importance of perception of timing has been shown in several studies, in which it has yielded much clearer results than timing in itself (e.g., Alsaker, 1992b; Rierdan & Koff, 1985; Sonis et al., 1987).

Individuals also differ in personality characteristics (e.g., self-concept, self-esteem, gender identity) and social competence. These differences are likely to play an important role in the way they solve tasks involving transition and adjustment. One may easily think of young adolescents who act as trendsetters, no matter how different they are from others (early or late maturers), whereas others would feel deviant in the same situation and possibly also be labelled as such by peers.

The social context: Others' reactions. As noticed by Clausen (1975), one's appearance acts as a signal to others. Therefore, the young developing adolescent, physically becoming more of an adult, will trigger reactions from others (see Brooks-Gunn and Warren, 1989, for a short review of reactions from parents and peers). Signals, like words, have denotative and connotative meanings. The denotative meaning of the physical changes at puberty is relatively clear: The child matures sexually and enters the transitional period heralding adulthood. The connotative meaning depends on the other's own experiences and value system, including attitudes toward her or his body, ideals of attractiveness, and adult sex roles. Petersen and Taylor (1980) noted, for example, that reactions from others may be more important than the actual physical changes.

Richards and Petersen (1987) noted that "once a young person looks like an adult, adult behavior and motivation are typically expected" (p. 37). Given the unclear position of young adolescents and the changing sex roles in today's Western societies, expectations of developing adolescents may vary to a large extent depending on context and culture and they are not necessarily similar to expectations of adults. It should also be recalled that pubertal maturity occurs at a younger age than some generations ago (Fig. 2.1). Although the secular acceleration has flattened, there is also a clear trend toward staying at school and remaining financially dependent on parents for a longer time. Therefore, the discrepancy between adult appearance and adult role has become larger than it was. Reactions biologically matured adolescents may encounter today are more likely to be insecurity and in some cases heightened control from their parents. In other words, reactions from adults may be relatively mixed. One may therefore raise the question as to whether this discrepancy between biological and social maturity (in terms of expected adult roles) can have contributed to a general worsening of adolescents' psychological well-being. Although the question is of great importance for preventive work, it is difficult to answer without comparing equivalent groups of adolescents on equivalent dimensions at different times over the last century. Furthermore, we should bear in mind that a majority of young people experienced an inverse asynchrony of maturation about a century ago. They were enrolled in adult workplaces long before they were biologically mature. According to the data presented in Figure 2.1, people born in the twenties in Europe probably experienced biological maturation at the time when they left school and started working. These adolescents, however, matured around the time preceding World War II and it may be difficult to compare them to today's adolescents. Nevertheless, given some results on the damaging effect of simultaneous changes (Simmons & Blyth, 1987), some asynchrony of maturation in different domains appears more positive than stressful. Today's asynchrony allows the adolescent to assimilate biological changes in his or her identity before meeting a new task. Entering the working world with an adult appearance places the (late) adolescent in a more comfortable position than the one adolescents, looking like children among adults, encountered two or three generations ago. Finally, an issue that needs to be addressed in this context is whether young adolescents who are biologically mature really look like adults.

Given the general tendency toward conformity in adolescence, perhaps the issue of what is normative at a certain time may be more important than the issue just discussed. Peers' reactions, for example, should be

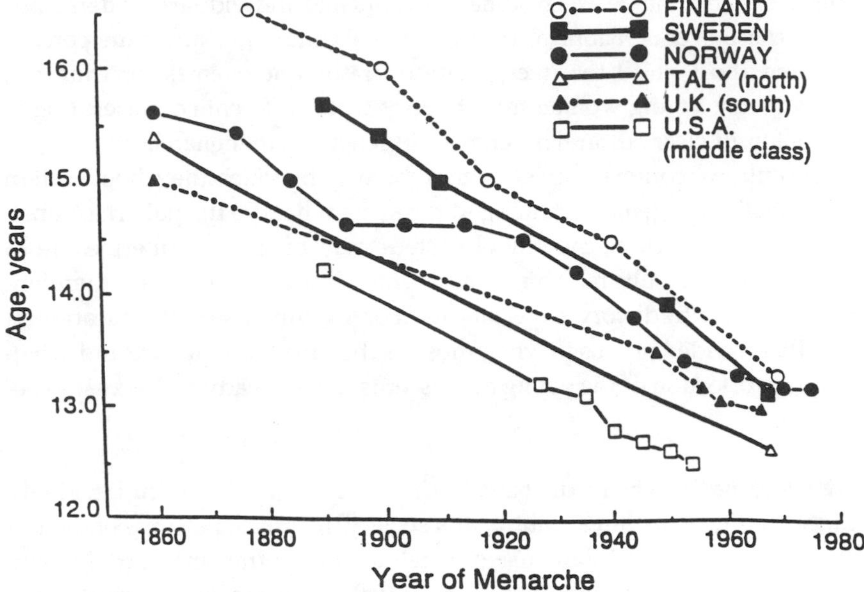

Figure 2.1 Secular trends in age of menarche, 1860–1970. (Tanner, 1989; reprinted with permission of Castlemead Publications.)

expected to be of greatest importance. Girls have declared that they do not want to be different from other girls (Tobin-Richards, Boxer, & Petersen, 1983). Depending on the peer group the young adolescent belongs to, expectations may also involve pressure toward certain types of activities.

In sum, the adolescent's developmental task during pubertal maturation is not merely one of adaptation to new characteristics due primarily to physiological changes, but also one of adaptation to a changing social environment (Petersen & Taylor, 1980) and of integration of discrepant reactions and expectations.

Cultural context. General attitudes toward maturation may be rather uniform in a culture, but they may also differ according to subcultural values. Such subcultures can include social class, educational level, ethnicity, religion, rural and urban areas, and even communities (see Richards & Petersen, 1987, for an example of the latter).

Another phenomenon that has been found to vary to a large extent across cultures (or subcultures) should be considered more seriously, and may differentially influence individuals' reactions to pubertal changes.

This is the relation between somatic events and individuals' understanding of these events (Fabrega, 1972). Cultural differences affect the perception and most of all the interpretation of somatic events. For example, interviewing young women from twenty-three different countries, Logan (1980) found clear cultural differences in reactions to menarche.

The cultural context also influences the way in which the school system and socializing agents pertaining to the system handle the pubertal transition. Systems such as the school system may be rather impermeable to rapid shifts in cultural values and young adolescents may therefore encounter contradictory expectations. For example, sexual education is usually provided at an age when most of the pupils are mature and when a large proportion of the young adolescents have already had sexual experiences.

The role of media. The media have traditionally passed on attitudes, ideals, and values held within a culture, or a society. Technical progress of the last decades, and especially the use of satellites in the transmission of television programs have, however, opened up a new era for the role of the media. The values conveyed do not necessarily conform to the values currently held at the receiver's site. Furthermore, due to economical and technical gaps between the different parts of the world, and the large entertainment industry in the United States, the cross-cultural influence through international media is largely unidirectional. This is true not only of film and television. Through the growing internationalization of advertising, local magazines often diffuse ideals of attractiveness fairly remote from their readers' appearance. This raises the question of where the ideals presented in the media come from and what role they play in defining bodily ideals.

Specific hypotheses. Most hypotheses primarily address the issue of the timing of changes. The specific models usually discussed in the literature on puberty are (1) the stage termination model, (2) the deviance model, and (3) the goodness of fit model.

The stage termination hypothesis suggests that the particular tasks pertaining to the different developmental stages require a certain amount of time to be resolved adequately. On the basis of this model, early maturation is claimed to interrupt the task of ego development prior to the pubertal stage (see Petersen & Taylor, 1980, for a detailed presentation of the hypothesis).

The deviance hypothesis states that negative effects of early or late maturation are linked to the fact that off-time maturation places young adolescents in a socially deviant category (Petersen & Taylor, 1980). On the basis of this hypothesis, an interaction effect between timing, grade, and gender should be expected. Effects should be stronger in lower grades for girls, when early maturing girls would be the first to show changes. For boys, effects of timing should be stronger in higher grades, when late maturing boys would be the very last to enter puberty. Note that the deviance hypothesis suggests a curvilinear relation between timing and other variables.

The goodness of fit hypothesis is closely related to the deviance hypothesis. It is based on the assumption that persons and contexts are distinct entities, displaying individual characteristics (Lerner, 1985). Consequently, a good fit between characteristics of the adolescent and the requirements made by the context is considered a prerequisite for psychological well-being. On-time maturers, for example, may be generally satisfied with the rate and timing of their pubertal changes, but they may be at risk in a context emphasizing the values of a prepubertal body build. The value of the hypothesis has been demonstrated regarding on-time girls among dancers (Brooks-Gunn & Warren, 1985).

In addition a simultaneous change hypothesis (Simmons & Blyth, 1987) and an ideal of thinness hypothesis (Blyth, Simmons, & Zakin, 1985) have been proposed. The first hypothesis states that pubertal development, one of many sources of change during early adolescence, interacts with other changes, and that negative effects partly depend on the number of changes occurring simultaneously with pubertal maturation. The second hypothesis posits that, given the widespread acceptance of the ideal of thinness in Western cultures, pubertal maturation will have a general negative effect on girls' body image.

Contrary to most of these hypotheses, based on the commonly held assumption that stressful life transitions may lead to change in behavior, Caspi and Moffitt (1991) have argued that "preexisting differences between people will be magnified and accentuated during times of life course discontinuities" (p. 158). Stressful pubertal changes are therefore expected to accentuate preexisting problems, leading to more difficulties for adolescents with a history of problems than for others.

In sum, the developing young adolescent may be considered a stimulus to the reactions of others but she or he is also an active processor of information and thus an actor in her or his own psychosocial development

(Lerner, 1985). Reactions to pubertal changes may well be influenced by hormonal factors, earlier personality and social development, and the social context, but they are not determined by these factors. Therefore, given equivalent contexts of development, adolescents will still be expected to show a high diversity of reactions.

Considering the assumed importance of the reactions of others for the psychological adjustment of the pubertal adolescent, the link between pubertal maturation and interpersonal relationships will be examined first, followed by a review of studies that have addressed a wide array of indicators of psychosocial adjustment. It should be noted that studies addressing reactions in the proximal social context (the microsystems, in Bronfenbrenner's terms, 1989) or values in the more distal cultural context (macrosystems) are sparse.

Interpersonal relationships and pubertal changes

The time around puberty is generally a period when interpersonal relationships are in transition. Young adolescents usually acquire more independence from their parents. The asymmetric relationship characteristic of childhood is expected to change into a more cooperative one (Youniss & Smollar, 1985) and peers become more important as a reference group (Hunter & Youniss, 1982). Therefore, the question has been posed, whether pubertal development in itself may, directly or indirectly, play some role in the observed changes during puberty.

Parent-adolescent relationships

In their thorough review of the literature on parent-child relationships at puberty, Paikoff and Brooks-Gunn (1991) have proposed three models of association between pubertal change and parent-child relationships. The first model implies a direct effect and/or an indirect effect (through emotional and behavioral changes) of hormonal changes on the parent-adolescent interaction. Only one of the reviewed studies had addressed the possible influence of pubertal hormones on behavior in the family. Inoff-Germain and colleagues (Inoff-Germain et al., 1988), who focused primarily on aggressive behavior, observed adolescents in interaction with their parents. Some association was shown between one testosterone index and an adrenal androgen and moderate signs of anger. The results were very inconsistent, however. In girls, estradiol and androstenedione levels were related to defiance, dominance, and anger toward parents.

The second model suggests primarily that changes in secondary sex characteristics, as well as rate and timing of change, through their stimulus (signal) value, would bring about changes in the parents' and adolescents' expectations of one another and thus in their mutual relationship. This model has, implicitly, received the most attention in the literature and, especially during the last decade, several studies have corroborated that behavior generally recognized as typical for young adolescents may be related to pubertal changes.

In agreement with earlier studies on menarche, indicating general changes in the mother-daughter relationship with the onset of menarche (Greif & Ulman, 1982), Hill and colleagues (Hill et al., 1985a, 1985b) have shown that some perturbation seems to occur immediately following menarche in girls, and at about the apex of pubertal development in boys. By that time, mothers are perceived as less accepting by their daughters, and sons are reported to be more confrontational and less involved in family activities.

Research conducted by Papini and colleagues has also contributed to an understanding of the period of most salient changes (called transpubertal) as a time of strain in terms of mutual dissatisfaction (Papini & Sebby, 1987), less affective and more assertive interactions (Papini, Datan, & McCluskey-Fawcett, 1988), and more conflicts with respect to personal habits (Papini & Clark, 1989). These studies have generally used observations of clothed adolescents to assess pubertal status. Studies based on more accurate and standard measures of pubertal maturation have demonstrated that higher pubertal status was related to increased conflict and diminished closeness in the parent-adolescent relationship in girls (Crockett & Petersen, 1987), but not in boys (Bulcroft, 1991; Crockett & Petersen, 1987). Note that these results, showing a linear association of pubertal development and relationship to parents in girls, do not replicate the former findings of transpubertal strain.

Studies focusing on pubertal timing have often come to dissimilar conclusions ranging from less conflict (Paikoff, Brooks-Gunn, & Carlton-Ford, 1991), through no effect (Simmons & Blyth, 1987; Stone & Barker, 1939, cited in Savin-Williams & Small, 1986) to more conflict or dissatisfaction with the parental relationship (Hill et al., 1985a; Petersen, 1985; Savin-Williams & Small, 1986; Stattin & Magnusson, 1990) in early maturing girls. Studies generally lead to the conclusion that in boys early maturing is accompanied by positive interactions (Simmons & Blyth, 1987; Savin-Williams & Small, 1986) whereas late maturing may show the opposite effect (Clausen, 1975; Jones & Mussen, 1958).

A note of caution is in order with respect to the results presented above. Most studies have failed to differentiate clearly between the roles of age, pubertal maturation, and timing. In a very careful study Steinberg (1987) has shown the value of controlling these three variables. Effects that could have been attributed to pubertal maturation on the basis of univariate analyses proved to be artifacts of age. In many cases pubertal development and age covaried in predicting the parent-adolescent relationship. Taken together, they predicted the relational variables significantly, but both yielded diminished, and even nonsignificant, coefficients when controlled for another.

On the basis of such cautious analyses (Steinberg, 1987) the general conclusion could be drawn that pubertal maturation seems to increase emotional distance between developing adolescents and their parents, independent of age. Pubertal maturation, in both girls and boys, is related to greater emotional autonomy and less closeness to parents. Conflicts between mothers and daughters increase in intensity with pubertal development. These results were replicated in a longitudinal analysis (Steinberg, 1988), using pubertal status at the first time of measurement to predict residual changes in the parent-adolescent variables. On the other hand, pubertal timing only rarely contributed to the prediction of parent-adolescent relationships and the results were equivocal.

Most studies mentioned above have been based on samples of intact families. Examining different types of families, Anderson, Hetherington, and Clingempeel (1989) reported findings generally in accordance with previous studies of nondivorced families. In divorced and remarried families the results were not significant or at best inconsistent. The only parenting variable that seemed to show a consistent pattern of relation with pubertal development was monitoring. As could be expected, monitoring declined with development in all families, independent of the gender of the child. Although this study, as do many others, suffers from a lack of correction for chronological age, it clearly points to the danger of considering only middle-class, white, and intact families in research on parent-adolescent relationships.

It may be hazardous to compare results from studies that have used different methods of assessment for pubertal status and relationships as well as different age ranges and statistical strategies, but some patterns seem to emerge. In sum, most studies addressing the issue of family relationships have shown some association between pubertal maturation and more independence, sometimes leading to less closeness and more conflict.

These effects, however, seem to be relatively small (Paikoff & Brooks-Gunn, 1991) and in many cases it is unclear whether they may be spurious and due more to maturation in other domains than to biological changes. The third model proposed by Paikoff & Brooks-Gunn (1991), assuming a joint influence of the various developmental processes, seems most appropriate to the study of relational changes in adolescence. This approach, however, goes far beyond the scope of this chapter and will not be discussed here.

It is also worth noting that most studies have focused on, and possibly overemphasized, conflicts, lack of warmth, and the like, and have labeled gains in autonomy and independence rather negatively. In addition, what is named "conflict" in many of the studies is far less dramatic than the connotation associated with the label. As noted by Greene and Grimsley (1990) research focusing mainly on increases in negative relationships, "stands in sharp contrast to the repeated observation that parent-adolescent relationships typically remain positive and of mutual importance during the adolescent transition" (p. 397). Stattin and Magnusson (1990) pointed out that although early maturing girls seemed to have somewhat less positive relationships to their mothers, they still had good relationships.

With respect to pubertal timing, findings have proved rather inconsistent, possibly indicating (aside from methodological reasons) that timing may not be a central dimension in the regulation of family relationships. We should recall that timing is primarily seen as crucial in contexts where conformity in appearance is highly valued, which is the case in the peer group but not in the family. Timing may play some role in the family, however, when it occurs off-time (especially too early) with respect to parents' expectations, producing a gap between the adolescents' physical maturity and parents' sensitivity to their needs, and when off-time maturing has an impact on the adolescents themselves (e.g., in terms of impaired or enhanced self-perception or/and peer relationships), leading to interaction changes in the family. Studies that reveal such effects are still needed.

Peer relationships

Considering the central role that peers are assumed to play in early adolescence, the number of studies on the influence of maturational timing on peer relationships is surprisingly low.

Girls. The only study reporting findings related to hormonal levels (Susman et al., 1985) concluded with null results in terms of number of friends. Findings based on different measures of pubertal development and thus also timing, have generally come to the same conclusion. That is, pubertal variables do not seem to be related to number of friends (Stattin & Magnusson, 1990; Susman et al., 1985), perceived popularity (Simmons & Blyth, 1987; Zakin, Blyth & Simmons, 1984), rejection (Silbereisen et al., 1989), or perceived acceptance (Crockett & Petersen, 1987). Brooks-Gunn & Warren (1988) have reported a positive effect of breast development which is often quoted and which should, therefore, be discussed here. This specific result may be related to the multidimensional character of pubertal development and thus indicate that changes in different characteristics may have different effects. Because breast development is more apparent than other pubertal changes, it may be an especially central event, more likely related to other variables (i.e., positively, as well as negatively). As the only evidence of a relation of pubertal development to peer acceptance, however, this finding clearly needs replication before elaborated explanations can be made.

One may question the adequacy and relevance of some of the measures of peer relationships in the context of biological maturation. Null results on general dimensions of peer acceptance do not imply that pubertal development has no effect on peer interactions. It seems, for example, that the onset of breast development in girls may trigger teasing from peers (essentially nonfriends; Brooks-Gunn, 1984). Furthermore, Stattin and Magnusson (1990) have shown that early maturing girls' peer relationships may differ from others in a crucial way, in terms of age and occupational status of close friends. Early maturers, who had experienced menarche prior to their eleventh birthday, had older friends and twice as many working friends as other girls their age. This turned out to be of decisive importance for the early start of these girls in drinking alcohol (see below).

Boys. Except for one study showing that boys' perception of rate of change was related to leadership experiences and to experiences of teasing by other boys (Bulcroft, 1991), studies have generally yielded null results as to the variables presented above (Bulcroft, 1991; Crockett & Petersen, 1987; Simmons & Blyth, 1987; Susman et al., 1985). It should be noted that one study found that social class interacted with pubertal maturation. Late maturers were less liked by peers in the working class, whereas there were no effects in middle class (Clausen, 1975).

In sum, studies have generally shown no effects, or inconsistent and isolated effects, of pubertal development on peer acceptance, but clear effects on the choice of friends. As noted by Stattin and Magnusson (1990) there are few specific hypotheses as to how pubertal development may affect peer relationships. Future research is needed to provide more specific hypotheses as to what kind of association one may expect between these two developmental areas. Two of the general hypotheses presented earlier may be of help in formulating at least general expectations. These are the deviance hypothesis, based on the idea that differential timing leads to differences in status among peers, and the goodness of fit model, stating that the effect of timing depends on the particular context in which biological maturation occurs. Following these models, one should expect early maturing to have a positive effect on peer relationships in contexts where maturing is highly valued, and vice versa.

Furthermore, due to the importance of social comparison in this period (Hart, 1988), pubertal timing should generally be expected to be a more crucial aspect of pubertal development than pubertal status in the context of peer relationships. The results showing that early maturing girls had older friends and that late maturers tended to have younger friends (Stattin & Magnusson, 1990) may indicate that off-time maturers often try to find matching friends, and thus redefine their peer network. Research is needed to examine possible changes of reference group and the consequences they may have for other domains of development or behavior. For example, finding matching friends may be positive for early maturers' body image, but it may also lead to more risk behavior. Remaining an off-time (early) maturer within one's peer group may be associated with greater internalizing problems and possibly a feeling of lesser acceptance by peers.

Pubertal changes and psychosocial adjustment: Empirical evidence

There is a high degree of consensus that pubertal maturation and timing often have an effect on psychological adjustment (Petersen & Crockett, 1985) and that the effect may be different for girls and boys. Early studies on pubertal maturation have often focused on its relation to what we may call normal psychosocial development, including personality as well as social dimensions (e.g., attitudes, interests, self-concept), whereas recent studies seem to be more oriented toward problem behavior.

Most early studies report positive effects of early maturing in boys. Among other things, they have been seen as more relaxed, attractive, self-confident, and conforming, and less dependent (see Petersen & Taylor, 1980). Results have usually yielded an inconsistent pattern in girls. For example, early maturing girls have been reported as submissive and listless and late maturers as having some of the qualities of early maturing boys. On the other hand, early maturing girls have also been found to be more reliable, to be less shy and less aggressive (Douglas, 1964, cited in Gross & Duke, 1980), to perceive themselves as generally more mature (not linked to pubertal changes; Stattin & Magnusson, 1990) and more independent (Simmons & Blyth, 1987). In this context of inconsistency, note that Clausen (1975) has pointed to the role social class may play. He has shown, for example, that early maturing middle-class girls could be characterized as self-confident, whereas early maturing had negative consequences in the working class.

Menarche, considered a special event in the pubertal development of girls, has received much attention. Although menarche has repeatedly been shown to be accompanied by negative feelings, some studies have shown it may have positive effects, essentially in terms of self-definition (Garwood & Allen, 1979; Greif & Ulman, 1982) and sexual differentiation (Koff, Rierdan & Silverstone, 1978; Rierdan & Koff, 1980).

The most robust findings, for both boys and girls, are usually linked to variables related to appearance, such as body image or feelings of attractiveness (Petersen, 1988). Body image represents a borderline area between personality development (integrating physical changes in one's self-representation) and pathology (highly devaluative attitudes toward one's body). The issue of dissatisfaction with one's body has been addressed in a large range of studies, and results from these studies will be presented first, followed by results from studies focusing on internalizing and externalizing problems. Finally, studies on heterosocial and heterosexual behavior will be examined.

Body image

Height, weight, and pubertal changes. Dissatisfaction with body has often been reported as strongly related to specific components of appearance: height (being too short) in boys (Duke-Duncan et al., 1985; Simmons & Blyth, 1987), and weight (being too heavy) in girls (Blyth et al., 1981; Dorn, Crockett, & Petersen, 1988; Hendry & Gillies, 1978; Mendelson & White, 1985). Early maturing boys have usually been found to be most satisfied with their height (Simmons & Blyth, 1987), whereas early maturing girls have generally been found to complain about their weight (Duke-Duncan et al., 1985; Stattin & Magnusson, 1990).

As noted earlier, pubertal changes in girls are accompanied by increases in body fat and weight (Garn & Clark, 1976). Given the emphasis most Western cultures place on leanness as a criterion for attractiveness (Cohn et al., 1987; Dornbusch, 1989; Zakin, Blyth, & Simmons, 1984), especially in females, and the fact that in early adolescence one usually starts to pay more attention to one's appearance and to attractiveness, we may expect pubertal weight increases to be rather upsetting and to lead to some negative effects of pubertal development on girls' body image. Reviewing the literature on pubertal development in girls, Stattin and Magnusson (1990) noted that the negative attitude toward their appearance found among early developing girls seemed to be "partly a function of their greater gain in body fat relative to other later-developed girls" (p. 115).

General satisfaction with body. In girls, pubertal development in itself, generally measured in terms of menarcheal status, has usually not been found to correlate with body satisfaction (Gargiulo et al., 1987; McGrory, 1990; Zakin, Blyth, & Simmons, 1984). Timing has proved to be a more powerful predictor of body satisfaction. Early maturing has been shown to have a negative effect (Brooks-Gunn & Warren, 1985; Çok, 1990). The effect of timing, however, may depend to a large extent on the social context. Late maturing dancers, for example, have been found to be more satisfied with their bodies than their on-time peers (in contrast to other late maturing girls, for whom no effects were demonstrated; Brooks-Gunn et al., 1989).

Such effects may also depend on the cultural context. Whereas Norwegian girls who perceived themselves as being on time or late did not differ in body satisfaction, American girls who perceived themselves as being on-time maturers were most satisfied with their bodies (Gargiulo et al., 1987; Tobin-Richards, Boxer, & Petersen, 1983). Furthermore, whereas some authors have shown a possibly greater dissatisfaction in North American early maturers with increasing grade (Petersen & Crockett, 1985; Simmons & Blyth, 1987), similar effects of early timing have been found to be strongest in younger girls in a large Norwegian sample (Alsaker, 1992b). This was still true when overweight was controlled for in the analyses.

Unfortunately, weight related variables have not always been included in studies on body image. Given that pubertal maturation is usually associated with weight gains early maturing girls differ from same-age girls not only in more advanced secondary sexual characteristics, but also in weight (Silbereisen & Kracke, 1994) and leanness. Therefore, some of the results reported in the literature may have been primarily due to differences in weight between early maturers and others, whereas other results may indicate a negative effect of changes in secondary sexual characteristics. This may explain some of the dissimilarity of results.

Results in boys have generally been highly consistent. Early maturing boys have been shown to feel more attractive (Tobin-Richards, Boxer, & Petersen, 1983), to be more satisfied with their bodies (Çok, 1990), their looks (Simmons & Blyth, 1987), and their muscle development (Blyth et al., 1981). Correspondingly, late developers have been found to be more dissatisfied with their bodies (Alsaker, 1992b).

In sum, early pubertal development is generally found to be related to higher satisfaction with one's appearance in boys but to more dissatisfaction in girls and the gender difference seems to be reversed in late maturers. Furthermore, dissatisfaction with one's body seems to be linked to the ideal of thinness that prevails in Western culture. It is worth noting that Cohn et al. (1987) found that 40 percent of early adolescent girls and 70 percent of college girls judge their bodies to be heavier than their ideal. This ideal weight was lower than what the same girls considered attractive to boys. Richards and colleagues (Richards et al., 1990) have found that early adolescent girls who categorized themselves as underweight were more satisfied with their bodies than others. The biological maturation does not necessarily in itself cause dissatisfaction in girls, but its side effects, in terms of weight (see Alsaker, 1992b), may.

Internalizing problems

On the basis of the finding that pubertal development seems to affect the body image of young adolescents, the next question might be formulated as follows: Does pubertal maturation, especially its timing, play some role in the onset or intensification of problems often reported to increase (in general or differentially for girls and boys) during adolescence?

The general concern with appearance in the adolescent period seems to make body image an important factor with respect to global self-esteem (e.g., Alsaker, 1992b; Secord & Jourard, 1953; Tobin-Richards, Boxer, & Petersen, 1983) and depressive cognitions. Moreover, some studies have indicated that pubertal maturation may, especially in girls, be associated with a proneness to depression (see Rutter, 1986) and results relating hormones (in mature women; see Brooks-Gunn and Warren, 1989) or particular menstrual phases (Parry, 1989) to depressive moods in women are also suggestive of possible negative effects of pubertal changes on internalizing problems.

Although there is no evidence for increased self-esteem problems during early adolescence on a group level (Alsaker & Olweus, 1993; Dusek & Flaherty, 1981; Simmons & Blyth, 1987), individuals have been shown to vary significantly in their rate of intraindividual change in self-esteem in early adolescence (Alsaker, 1992a). Changes in self-esteem do occur at puberty. Such changes are not the rule, however (stability over time is generally fairly high; see Alsaker & Olweus, 1992), and they occur in both positive and negative directions. Therefore, it is not reasonable to conceive of a general negative or positive effect of pubertal development (status) on self-esteem. The findings just reported may fit with a general interactional hypothesis, suggesting that pubertal development interacts with social or personality factors in affecting self-esteem.

Due to its generally high correlation with internalizing problems, self-esteem will be discussed in the present section. Given the somewhat different expectations that may be formulated for the two dimensions, however, results will be presented separately. Results pertaining to the area of self-esteem (or its opposite, negative self-evaluation or self-derogation) will be presented first, followed by results on general emotional difficulties. The latter category will include variables such as depression, anxiety, and psychosomatic problems. Results on moods will also be included, insofar as they indicate some proneness to depressive feelings.

Self-esteem. Most studies have reported pubertal status and pubertal timing to be unrelated to self-esteem in girls (Brack, Orr, & Ingersoll, 1988; Brooks-Gunn & Ruble, 1983; Garwood & Allen, 1979; McGrory, 1990; Simmons & Blyth, 1987; Zakin, Blyth, & Simmons, 1984). A positive effect of pubertal status has been reported, however, in one North American study (Jaquish & Savin-Williams, 1981),[2] and German girls who perceived themselves as early maturers have also been found to have less negative self-evaluations (Silbereisen et al., 1989). On the other hand, a Norwegian study based on very similar instruments (Alsaker, 1992b) has demonstrated an opposite effect.

2. It should be noted here that the study by Garwood and Allen (1979) is generally erroneously cited as demonstrating a positive relation between menarcheal status and self-esteem. The results presented in the paper were not significant ($p < 0.10$), and the author's conclusion of a positive effect (included in the abstract) was based on the interpretation of small and inconsistent differences between means in different postmenarcheal subgroups.

Girls who saw themselves as early maturers have been found to score higher on perceived instability of self (Alsaker, 1992b) and to show more variability of self-esteem (measured three times a week over a period of four weeks; Buchanan, 1991). These somewhat dissimilar results may underscore the possible influence of social and cultural contexts. Simmons and colleagues have shown that pubertal status may interact with the social context in terms of school transition. They found that whereas menstrual status was unrelated to self-evaluation before school transition, the girls with lowest self-esteem were those who experienced menarche and school transition at the same time (Blyth, Simmons, & Zakin, 1985).

Most studies reviewed here have yielded null results as to a possible effect of pubertal development and timing on self-esteem in boys (Blyth et al., 1981; Brack, Orr, & Ingersoll, 1988; Simmons & Blyth, 1987). When a relation has been reported (Alsaker, 1992b), it was in the disfavor of late maturers.

Emotional problems. In girls, timing in terms of high-for-age levels of follicle-stimulating hormone (FSH) has been found to correlate with Offer's Emotional Tone and Psychopathology subscales. The former scale taps essentially sadness, whereas the latter includes items ranging from anxiety to psychotic thinking (Susman et al., 1985). Levels of cortisol (C) and testosterone (T) have also been shown to predict interindividual differences in sadness (C & T), depressive symptoms (C), and anxiety (C) in concurrent analyses (Susman et al., 1991). The results were inconsistent across waves of data collection, however, and the association of symptoms with cortisol did not generally hold when corrected for age and pubertal status. There were no interactions of hormonal levels with symptoms in the prediction of later symptoms, and prior symptoms were the best predictors of the same symptoms one year later. Consequently, hormone levels could not be characterized as vulnerability factors. The relation of testosterone to sadness (a proxie of depressive feelings) could not be replicated in another study that also included a wide range of hormonal measures (Brooks-Gunn & Warren, 1989). Whereas most studies have been relatively inconclusive as to the role of hormones, pubertal status has been found to correlate with the intensity of negative moods (Buchanan, 1991). Early maturing girls have been reported as having more psychosomatic symptoms (Aro & Taipale, 1987; Stattin & Magnusson, 1990), to score higher on eating concerns (Brooks-Gunn et al., 1989), to score higher on Offer's psychopathology scale (Brooks-Gunn & Warren, 1985; Petersen & Crockett, 1985), on depressive feelings (Alsaker, 1992b; Stattin & Magnusson, 1990), and on sadness (Brooks-Gunn & Warren, 1985). In line with the already well documented inconsistency of results, it should be noted that null results have also been reported related to sadness (Petersen & Crockett, 1985).

Results concerning hormonal influences in boys have been somewhat inconsistent as to the hormones involved (Susman et al., 1985) and could generally not be replicated over several measurement times (see Susman, Dorn & Chrousos, 1991).

Results on emotional problems and pubertal status or timing in boys are not so clear as results on body image and self-esteem. Whereas early maturing has been shown in some studies to be associated with less sadness (Crockett & Petersen, 1987; Susman et al., 1985), it has also been found to be unrelated to the same dimension (Petersen & Crockett, 1985) and to be associated with more psychopathology (Petersen & Crockett, 1985), and depressive tendencies in younger boys (sixth graders, i.e. seventh graders in Norway; Alsaker, 1992b). The latter results corroborate results from the Berkeley Guidance Study (Peskin, 1967, cited in Petersen & Taylor, 1980) showing that early maturers were more somber and anxious than others. Pubertal status has also been reported to correlate positively with depressive symptoms and anxiety (Susman, Dorn, & Chrousos, 1991).

In sum, although the literature usually reports pubertal development, and especially early maturing as consistently favorable for boys (e.g., Zakin, Blyth, & Simmons, 1984), this general conclusion requires some revision.

Internalizing problems: Some conclusions. A note of caution is in order before the results are discussed. As in the area of parental relationships, measures of pubertal development and timing, as well as dimensions of psychological adjustment, vary to a great extent between studies. Given the diversity of measures and findings, the task is to locate some "Gestalt" in the results presented. As could be expected, pubertal status in itself was found to be generally unrelated to self-esteem. On the other hand, early timing may have a negative effect on girls' global self-evaluations and late timing may be related to more negative self-evaluations in boys. The effect in girls, however, may be dependent on age and/or culture, and studies including samples from different age groups and cultures are needed to explore this issue.

There may be indications of a negative effect of pubertal status, as well as early timing, on internalizing problems. As long as maturation in areas other than the physical one is not included in studies, however, it is hard to say if the negative effects attributed to pubertal status are due to pubertal maturation or just co-occur with it. Furthermore, problems seeming to arise with pubertal development may have been present, possibly in a somewhat different form, earlier (see Rutter, 1980). Therefore, longitudinal studies are needed that can control for the occurrence of psychopathology before the onset of puberty.

Turning now to timing, it seems that the general assumption with respect to the positive effects of early maturation in boys needs to be modified. Whereas early maturing boys, in general, seem to be more satisfied with their bodies than other boys, they have also scored repeatedly higher on indexes of psychopathology, and especially on depressive feelings. It should be noted that this differential finding, with respect to body image, self-esteem, and depression in boys, was also found when all variables were included in one and the same study (Alsaker, 1992b). It does not seem to be an artifact of differences in methods or samples.

Externalizing problems

Externalizing problems have received little attention, with respect to pubertal maturation, as compared to the dimensions presented so far. Possible associations of pubertal hormones with behavior problems and aggression have, however, attracted much research interest. Androgens, known to rise at puberty, are usually found to be related to aggressive behavior in animals (Inoff-Germain et al., 1988). Therefore the question has been raised, if some observed increases in antisocial, oppositional, or aggressive behavior observed in adolescence could be related to the endocrinological changes occurring during this period, either directly, or indirectly through changes in physical characteristics.

In boys, testosterone has been shown to be related to self-reported physical and verbal aggression, in responses to provocation and threat, to lack of frustration tolerance (Olweus et al., 1980, 1988), and to personality characteristics such as dominance, cynicism, and originality (Udry & Talbert, 1988). Studies have generally failed, however, to report a direct effect of testosterone on unprovoked aggressive and delinquent behavior (Susman et al., 1987). No effects have been found in girls (Brooks-Gunn & Warren, 1989; Susman et al., 1987).

In sum, the general pattern is one of associations between individual differences in pubertal hormones and aggression. The studies vary to a great extent, however, in statistical approaches and range of hormones used. Furthermore, the outcome variables have been operationalized in such different ways that it is hardly sensible to draw specific conclusions. Most studies have only addressed the issue in terms of interindividual differences in hormones and behavior. They have, therefore, failed to examine the core question associated with endocrinological changes at puberty: Do the hormonal changes that occur in the individual have any effect on behavior, and if so, under what circumstances?

The studies already mentioned have generally reported no effects of pubertal status or timing on aggression and delinquency. Although Simmons and Blyth (1987) reported no overall effect of timing (age at peak height velocity) on school-related behavior problems (girls and boys), they found younger postmenarcheal girls (sixth grade, i.e., early maturers) to score higher on these problems. This latter result agrees with findings reported by Stattin and Magnusson (1990) concerning early maturing girls, and findings indicating that girls with precocious puberty showed more behavior problems during IQ-testing situations and were reported by parents to have more behavior problems (Ehrhardt et al., 1984).

Magnusson and colleagues (Magnusson, Stattin, & Allen, 1986; Stattin & Magnusson, 1989, 1990) have reported clear effects of early maturing on what they have called "norm-violative activity." Turning first to drinking habits, they found a strong effect at age fourteen years and five months (14:5) with 63 percent of early maturing girls reporting to have been drunk at least once. Among late maturers only 29 percent had had this experience. The difference was even more marked in frequency of drunkenness (35 percent versus 6 percent). The effect was still present at age 14:10, but not at age 15:10. No systematic pattern was found when the girls' drinking habits were reassessed ten years later. Aro and Taipale (1987) reported a similar effect of early maturing on girls' alcohol consumption around age fifteen and found it to vanish around age sixteen. Furthermore, they found grade effects to be more important than pubertal timing in predicting drinking behavior.

In regard to other types of norm breaking, early maturing girls were found to be clearly more active than others (Magnusson, Stattin, & Allen, 1986). Their norm-breaking activities ranged from use of hashish and hard drugs, to provocations, stealing, and the like. The same early maturing girls were, however, only slightly more often represented in criminal records at age twenty-six, and the authors concluded that the results failed to provide evidence for an association of timing with persistent antisocial behavior.

Using self-reports and parents' reports, Caspi and Moffitt (1991) demonstrated that early maturing girls had engaged in more delinquent activities than their peers by the age of thirteen. It is important to note that early maturing girls who had a history of behavioral problems showed significantly more difficulties than early maturers without such a history and than other girls in general. When preexisting problems were held constant, early maturers were shown to experience more difficulties than their on-time peers.

Another important qualifying finding in this context is that reported by Magnusson, Stattin, and Allen (1986) who have shown that norm-violative activities were primarily related to the peer network of early maturing girls. As mentioned previously, early maturing girls were found to have older friends than on-time and late maturers. These older peers were also more often perceived as more tolerant toward norm-breaking behavior (Stattin & Magnusson, 1990). Silbereisen and colleagues (1989) have also reported that early maturing girls have more contact with "deviant" peers. This was only true, however, for eighth and ninth graders.

The issue of externalizing problems has been addressed in slightly different terms in studies focusing primarily on the physical characteristics of pubertal development than in studies focusing on hormones. Nevertheless, the inconsistency of results related to hormones and the converging findings on early timing in girls lead to the conclusion that early maturing girls are at risk for developing norm-breaking behavior habits and that the effect is mediated by social variables.

Results for boys are scarce and have generally shown no association between pubertal maturation and externalizing behavior. Off-time (early and late) maturing has, however, been shown to be related to drinking behavior (Anderson & Magnusson, 1990; Silbereisen & Kracke, 1994). Late maturers seemed to be at risk for later alcohol related problems (Anderson & Magnusson, 1990).

Heterosocial and heterosexual behavior

As stated by Susman and colleagues (1985), the influence of hormones on sexual behavior has often been demonstrated in animal studies, and female sexual motivation has also been shown to vary across the different phases of the menstrual cycle. Therefore, as with externalizing problems, there has been some interest in the possible direct and indirect effects of pubertal hormones on sexual motivation and behavior. Studies have usually also addressed behavior that may be characterized as preliminary to heterosexual behavior and may be labeled heterosocial. An example is dating. To the author's knowledge, the issue of homosexual motivation has been neglected in this context.

Girls. Hormonal levels were found to be mostly unrelated to dating behavior (Susman et al., 1985) and intercourse experience (Udry, Talbert, & Morris, 1986). However, the latter authors reported an association between testosterone (more precisely, the ratio of testosterone on testosterone binding globulin, also called Free Testosterone Index, FTI) and masturbation. It should be noted that pubertal development in itself seemed to be as important as FTI in the prediction of masturbation. Other androgens were also reported to be related to sexual motivation, and these effects seemed to be direct.

Heterosocial behavior has repeatedly been shown to occur more frequently in early maturing girls (Aro & Taipale, 1987; Crockett & Petersen, 1987; Simmons & Blyth, 1987; Stattin & Magnusson, 1990). Furthermore, early maturers have had intercourse at an earlier age than other girls (Robertson, Burchinal, & Martin, 1992) and are more likely to undergo at least one abortion before Grade 9 (Stattin & Magnusson, 1990). This finding fits well with results showing that precociously maturing girls were earlier than their pair-matched controls in onset of kissing behavior, intercourse (one to two years earlier), and masturbation (five and a half years earlier) (Meyer-Bahlburg et al., 1985).

Examining predictors of onset of intercourse, Udry and Billy (1987) found several social factors (e.g., best friends' sexual status) to be significant, in addition to effects of age in white girls. This finding may indicate that sexual behavior was highly controlled by social factors in these girls. In black girls, transition to intercourse was primarily predicted by pubertal development in itself.

Aro and Taipale (1987) have reported a strong relation between dating behavior and drinking. Fifty percent of girls with dating experience were found to drink at least once a month, whereas only 10 percent of nondating girls reported such drinking habits. As demonstrated earlier, pubertal development may affect young adolescents' peer group membership, which in turn may be crucial in determining the timing of other behaviors. The notion of timeliness is intrinsically linked to the concept of normative events and behavior at certain ages. To enter a group of older peers and be accepted as a member in this new group, an early maturing girl will generally have to learn what is normative for older peers and to behave like them. She is expected to behave "on-time" in the new context, and will, therefore, behave even more "off-time" (i.e., early) compared to classmates and girls her age. In addition, some types of behavior may facilitate, or trigger, the onset of other behavior. This again suggests that many of the dimensions examined as possible correlates of pubertal development ought to be studied simultaneously. Otherwise, many reported univariate results may be spurious.

Boys. Udry and colleagues (Udry et al., 1985) found testosterone, in terms of FTI, to be a strong predictor of sexual motivation and behavior in boys and the effect appeared to be direct. Pubertal status, in terms of physical characteristics, has failed to predict onset of coital experience over a two-year period (Udry & Billy, 1987). Whereas some studies have shown that pubertal status (Crockett & Petersen, 1987) and early timing (Simmons & Blyth, 1987) were positively related to heterosocial behavior, others have failed to demonstrate such effects (Susman et al., 1985; Udry & Billy, 1987).

With the exception of a few findings, the results just presented may be interpreted as showing a direct effect of hormones on sexual motivation and behavior, whereas heterosocial behavior may be more contingent on social context. Preliminary results presented recently by Halpern et al. (1992) seem to indicate, however, that whereas FTI failed to predict noncoital experience and transition to coital behavior (longitudinal analyses), pubertal development might be a better predictor. Thus, the conclusion was drawn that the social aspects of pubertal development may still play an important role in sexual behavior.

Discussion

Gender differences

Interactions of gender with pubertal change and timing have been repeatedly demonstrated. Effects are primarily evidenced in satisfaction with one's appearance in maturing boys and a corresponding dissatisfaction in girls. This difference in satisfaction is mainly linked to the weight gain in girls and the increased muscularity and height in boys, characteristics differentially attached to ideals of attractiveness in our culture. [3]

For further explanations of the gender differences, two issues should be mentioned. First, given the high percentage of young women reporting

3. In the same vein, it should be noted that, whereas boys experience gains in strength, girls experience mainly increases in size (Tanner, 1972). The combinination of increase in size (especially weight) and lack of increase in strength may have clear negative effects in athletic girls. This is especially true for swimmers who, despite continued training, often experience a drop in performance around mid-puberty (Finn Gnatt, national coach for female swimmers in Norway, personal communication, 1992).

dysmenorrhea and impairment of daily activities in relation to menstruation (Coupey & Ahlstrom, 1989), it is clear that some components of pubertal development represent real aversive somatic changes and concerns. The aversive character of these events may be exaggerated, however, in informally transmitted information, and young girls' expectations have been found to be negatively biased (Brooks-Gunn and Ruble, 1983; McGrory, 1990). As noted earlier, such expectations are assumed to affect the young adolescents' attitudes and experiences. Such clear negative experiences and expectations have not been reported in boys. Second, a question may be posed as to the centrality of adult sex roles in this context. Pubertal maturation heralds adulthood, signifying becoming a man or a woman in a certain society. Some of the differential effects associated with maturation could be due to the attitudes of adolescents toward adult sex roles.

Returning to the issue of timing, the general pattern of results clearly indicates that early maturing is a risk factor for psychosocial maladjustment in girls. It should be underscored that it is not always clear in boys whether early maturers are more satisfied than others, or whether the relation may be due to the greater dissatisfaction of late maturers (the latter was demonstrated in Alsaker, 1992b). Furthermore, although boys seem to value the changes much more than girls, early maturing has been shown to involve some negative emotions in boys as well as in girls. Therefore, on the basis of the often noted consensus on the positive effect of pubertal maturation in boys, the question ought to be raised: Have boys received fair treatment in research on pubertal changes? Issues that may be of concern in boys are almost never addressed, for instance, (1) the development of breasts that may occur at mid-puberty (see above), (2) the first ejaculation, also called "spermarche" (to my knowledge, this issue has been addressed in only one study, Gaddis & Brooks-Gunn, 1985), and (3) the size and shape of genitals (see Benson & Tomera, 1985). The exclusion of possible issues of concern in boys and the paucity of studies including boys, as compared to the number of studies that have focused on girls, may have led to some biases in conclusions. Many of the issues found to be important in girls have not been examined in boys.

Cultural differences

The differential findings as to the effect of hormones and pubertal development in black girls and white boys versus white girls (Udry et al., 1985; Udry & Billy, 1987) show the power of cultural regulations of sexual behavior. Masturbation, which is a private behavior, was less affected by social factors than by hormonal changes.

Studies conducted in different countries have yielded some slightly different results with respect to effects of timing. Given the general inconsistency of results, even within cultures, these differences should be replicated in studies including different cultures. Most important, the same methods should be used for all subjects. Furthermore, Clausen's (1975) differential findings with respect to timing in different social classes indicates the importance of taking subcultures into account.

General inconsistency of results

Regrettably, one of the rare areas of consensus in the pubertal literature is the lack of consistency across studies. Findings from the same study may prove to be inconsistent, depending on the use of subsamples (Simmons & Blyth, 1987) or of data from different waves of measurement. Because age, time, pubertal development, and timing of development are confounded, inconsistencies of findings may sometimes be difficult to disentangle from substantive effects or interactions. Dissimilarity of results may, to a great extent, be explained by the unreliability of measurement instruments and the wide variation in use (and sometimes also inadequate use) of methods (design, instruments, and statistics). Finally, due to the multiple sources of change during puberty, it may not be feasible to expect single factors to have large or consistent effects.

The role of hormones. Studies including hormonal assays have shown that hormones known to increase during pubertal maturation are only inconsistently associated with behavior and moods (see also the recent review by Buchanan, Eccles, & Becker, 1992). Hormonal effects on behavior have generally been found to be stronger, more frequent, and more consistent in boys than in girls (Susman et al., 1987). This may be due to the much larger and consistent increases in hormones that occur in boys as compared to girls. Furthermore, girls hormonal levels vary to a large extent during the menstrual cycle which may attenuate relations between hormonal levels and behavioral measures (Inoff-Germain et al., 1988). This has generally not been taken into account, except in one study (Udry et al., 1986). The aromatization of testosterone into estrogens in the fat tissue in girls also makes it difficult to interpret correlations of single hormones with behavior (Susman et al., 1985).

More generally, the recent results reported by Halpern and Udry (1992) on the variation in hormonal assays across laboratories, and even within laboratories as to saliva and serum samples, call for great caution. These authors demonstrated that the statistical relation between testosterone and pubertal or behavioral measures could be several times greater using values from some laboratories than from others. For example, correlations between plasma testosterone and pubertal development varied from a highly negative value of –0.62 to a positive value of 0.41. Furthermore, the variation in hormonal-behavioral results was not consistent across laboratories. In sum, there is no way to tell whether the negative or the positive coefficients, the significant or the nonsignificant results are the valid ones. Therefore, until results show clear consistency, no conclusion should be drawn concerning endocrinological changes and behavior. Even then, on the basis of our knowledge about behavioral effects on the activation of the hypothalamic-pituitary-adrenal axis (Susman et al., 1985), some prudence is recommended in interpreting hormonal-behavioral relations.

Finally, when the role of hormones in pubertal maturation is examined, the question should be raised whether the effects are peculiar to this transitional period. The issue of whether intraindividual changes in hormonal secretion can be shown to be related to changes in emotionality and behavior should be addressed. Finally, individual differences in hormonal changes and in the relation between hormonal changes and behavior should be examined.

Measurement issues. The extensive variety of measures of pubertal status was discussed earlier in this chapter. The variety in itself would not be a problem if the measures were reliable and valid. This, however, is not the case. Furthermore, results vary according to the components of maturation chosen to measure pubertal development (Brooks-Gunn & Warren, 1988). These results may indicate (1) that certain components of pubertal maturation develop relatively independently and cannot be considered equivalent events and (2) that some of these components are more relevant than others to particular domains of behavior. Unique values and attitudes may be attached to different events. Literature on possible differential effects of thelarche, adrenarche, and menarche, however, is still scarce and the fact that they occur at different ages may complicate the task.

One of the general problems in comparing results on pubertal timing is that the cutpoints for the standard trichotomization into early, on-time, and late maturation have varied to a substantial extent across studies, and even to some extent within studies (e.g., Paikoff, Brooks-Gunn, & Carlton-Ford, 1991). As an example, when menarcheal age has been used as a basis for timing classifications, different age limits have been used. In one study, cutpoints have been used that produce higher percentages of early and late maturers than on-time maturers (Simmons & Blyth, 1987). Such an operationalization of timing considerably attenuates the probability of finding effects of "off-time" maturation and cannot be used to test hypotheses based on the concept of deviance in status.

Moreover, the usual trichotomization, based on concurrent measures of pubertal maturation, fail to take into account the actual onset of puberty. That is, the early maturing group may include adolescents, especially girls, who have developed extremely early. The latter group may be qualitatively different from "normal early maturing" and a lack of control for actual age of pubertal onset might lead to inconsistent results across studies as to the effects of early maturing.

Finally, the outcome measures (behavior, emotional problems, etc.) not only vary across studies, but they are often poorly described and it is sometimes difficult to say if null or inconsistent results may be due to different and/or unreliable measures.

Methodological and statistical considerations. Unfortunately, studies on puberty are characterized by an extensive use of single item analyses. This may lead to attenuated results but it may also lead to results that are significant by chance. This is especially true when items or large numbers of indexes are entered in numerous univariate analyses, without any correction of the alpha level. Some authors have addressed this problem (e.g., Crockett & Petersen, 1987); they are, however, more the exception than the rule. Therefore, differences across studies, in reliability of measures and statistical analyses may explain some of the inconsistency of results. Furthermore, in many studies the only relationships examined have been linear. Given the possible qualitative differences between different pubertal stages and timing groups, curvilinear analyses should be routinely used in research on puberty.

Another methodological problem is linked to the age of subjects. In many studies, subjects are too old to yield valid information about the effects of the onset of puberty. This may not be the only central issue, but sampling differences, in terms of age, may also lead to different conclusions.

Multifaceted influences. As noted previously, early adolescence is a period of co-occurrence of changes and pubertal maturation is only one of the possible influences on behavior and emotions. It is therefore reasonable to expect only relatively small effects of pubertal changes. Reactions to pubertal changes have also been assumed to be affected by many factors. Both individual and contextual variables may be crucial in this context. The difficulty of controlling all possible sources of effect in the same study makes results extremely sensitive to normal sample fluctuations. The combination of expected small effects and sensitiveness to sample fluctuation may lead to lower consistency of findings in terms of statistical significance.

Consequently, it seems important not to rely exclusively on significance testing when results are reported in studies on pubertal timing, but to take the whole pattern of results into consideration (see Rosenthal, 1991). Furthermore, as proposed by Rierdan, Koff, and Stubbs (1987), some measures of effect size could be used that would make comparisons easier.

Moreover, attempts should be made to disentangle the effects of the different changes occurring around puberty. As shown by several authors (Brooks-Gunn & Warren, 1989; Petersen & Crockett, 1985) social factors may account for more variance in behavior and emotions than biological changes.

Persistence of effects

The question has been raised on several occasions as to the long lasting effects of early pubertal timing. Results concerning this issue come primarily from the longitudinal study conducted by Magnusson and colleagues and may indicate both long lasting and transient effects. The transitory effects pertain to the area of norm-breaking behavior. On the other hand, in showing that early maturing girls have often dated, had intercourse, married, and left school at an earlier age than others (Stattin & Magnusson, 1990) the Stockholm study clearly indicates that early maturing may have a great impact on a girl's entire life.

Although these girls did not drink more than others when they grew up, they did drink more and were more likely to act deviantly in early adolescence. Since some types of behavior may facilitate, or trigger, the onset of other behavior, it is sensible to assume that these girls are generally at risk for more severe problems. Note also that the Stockholm study was launched in the late sixties. Changes in the availability of hard drugs in most Western societies in the last decades may have aggravated the risks of long lasting negative effects of early maturing.

Another possible long lasting effect is one of transgenerational risks. Cognitive maturation has been found to be more age-graded than a function of pubertal maturation (Petersen & Crockett, 1986). Young post-menarcheal girls cannot be expected to be better able to take care of children than their young age indicates. They are, however, likely to get pregnant, and to marry at an earlier age than others. Their children are, on genetic grounds, expected to be early maturers themselves and since marriages at a young age (at least in Western societies) seem to be vulnerable, these children are more likely than others to grow up in a divorced family which may have additional negative effects. Instead of fading over time, negative effects may thus accumulate over generations.

The issue of possible long lasting effects of dissatisfaction with one's body has not received much attention. The increasing focus on dieting and on leanness in our culture, combined with some findings indicating that early maturing girls are at risk in terms of both body dissatisfaction and eating concerns (Brooks-Gunn et al., 1989) should incite researchers to look into possible long lasting effects of early maturation in this context.

Future research

Longitudinal studies

Longitudinal studies are needed to address questions of possible associations of intraindividual changes in different areas of development (see Alsaker, 1992a) and thus to try to disentangle the effects of pubertal maturation and other sources of change. Given the possibility to control for earlier problems, longitudinal studies would help answer questions about the role of pubertal development in the onset of psychopathology. Such studies ought to be conducted in different cultural contexts and should include a sufficient number of prepubertal subjects to capture the period of pubertal onset. This is especially important with respect to early maturing girls.

Heterogeneity of effects

The inconsistency of results has mainly been discussed in terms of possible methodological flaws but it may also reflect a genuine great heterogeneity of effects. Early maturing girls as a group have been found to show more internalizing problems and to some extent more externalizing problems. This does not mean, however, that all early maturing girls experience problems, or that they experience both types of problems. Depending on factors such as individual characteristics, the goodness of fit of the social context, or the availability of a good fitting context, some early maturing girls may experience their pubertal changes as positive. Some girls may feel bad about their bodies, become very concerned about their physical "deviance" and their weight, possibly start evaluating themselves rather negatively, and even develop more or less severe emotional problems (including dieting and eating problems). Still depending on the social context and personality characteristics, some girls may become very attractive to older boys. They may find the situation highly rewarding and enter adult life earlier than others (as demonstrated by Magnusson and colleagues, e.g., Stattin & Magnusson, 1990).

An important task for future research would be to look into this heterogeneity, rather than to look for small averaged effects, and to try to find the groups clearly at risk for concurrent and long lasting problems. Such an approach requires a focus on persons, or groups of persons, not only on variables over time (see Bergman & Magnusson, 1991).

Mechanisms rather than associations

A task related to the issue just addressed would be to focus more on mechanisms than merely on the presence of effects. This is especially important if we want to go beyond the descriptive level and plan intervention programs. Concepts such as cognitive strategies and social processes might become central in this context. As mentioned previously, recent research on puberty has mainly focused on problems. In the search for mechanisms that may explain the relationships between pubertal maturation and behavior, a focus on "normal" development in the presence of difficult situations is likely important. One may ask whether off-time maturers who differ in their reactions employ different strategies in the resolution of the developmental tasks involved in the pubertal process, and what characterizes the strategies employed by off-time maturers who feel good about their situation.

The somewhat different results obtained for the measures of actual timing and perceived timing in some studies and the general bias toward perceiving oneself as average (Alsaker, 1992b; Stattin & Magnusson, 1990), indicate that the perceptual process may be central. Moreover, differential findings as to actual and perceived early timing may indicate that the process of biased perception may have been effective in protecting at least some off-time maturers. The question thus arises as to what factors may affect the perception of maturation. The factors leading to biased perception toward average maturation as well as toward deviant maturation should be examined, and the issue of possible functionality or disfunctionality of biased perceptions should be addressed explicitly.

The strong desire of young adolescents for conformity in pubertal development should be taken into account. The increasing age segregation that is found in some cultures may intensify the negative effects of cross-aged peer relations in younger adolescents. Research is needed to illuminate the circumstances around, and the mechanisms active in, peer group transitions at puberty.

Prevention of negative effects

Given the possible heterogeneity of reactions to pubertal changes, prevention programs have to be differentiated. On the basis of the general risk factor for psychosocial maladjustment found in early maturing girls, however, any prevention should focus primarily on this group and hence start with rather young girls. The findings indicating that early maturing girls associate with older peers and possibly also with deviant peers (Magnusson et al., 1986) also underscore the necessity to work on the peer group level and to be attentive to such clustering changes.

Furthermore, considering the highly consistent findings as to the dissatisfaction of early maturing girls with their weight, and the fact that girls will continue to experience fat gains around puberty, despite cultural ideals of attractiveness, a clear preventive issue seems to emerge. At least one important move would be to provide prepubertal girls, parents, and teachers with appropriate information on the increase in body fat and weight that usually occurs during puberty and the problems this may entail. Aside from the overwhelming information about more or less serious dieting procedures in the media, the only information provided to young adolescents about weight comes from the growing number of campaigns for healthier life-styles, including the need to avoid overweight. Pediatricians have noted the possible danger of strict adherence to the low-fat, low-cholesterol diets typical of health campaigns for adult populations, during the adolescent growth spurt (Mansfield & Emans, 1989). An antidote to dissatisfaction with weight and body appearance may be found in athletic activities (Richards et al., 1990). The problem here is that early maturing girls may be less competent, athletically speaking, than other girls their age.

When it comes to boys, we still need more information about the long-term significance of late maturing and the possible negative impact of early maturing. Since, however, early maturing seems to be accompanied by some emotional distress in both girls and boys, and although it might be considered more an accentuating than a causal event (Caspi & Moffitt, 1991), people who work with adolescents should be cautioned as to the need to be more attentive to the problems of early developing young adolescents.

Finally, on the basis of findings on the early onset of drinking behavior and heterosexual activities in early maturing girls, and the possibly direct link between pubertal development and sexual behavior in boys, sex education ought to be provided at an early age, long before an early maturing girl might have undergone her first abortion.

References

Adams, J. F. (1981). Earlier menarche, greater height and weight: A stimulation-stress factor hypothesis. *Genetic Psychology Monographs*, 104, 3–22.

Alsaker, F. D. (1992a). Modelling quantitative developmental change. In *Framing Stability and Change: An Investigation into Methodological Reasoning*, ed. J.B. Asendorpf & J. Valsiner, pp. 88–109. Newbury Park, Ca.: Sage.

(1992b). Pubertal timing, overweight, and psychological adjustment. *Journal of Early Adolescence*, 12, 396–419.

Alsaker, F. D., & Olweus, D. (1992). Stability of self-evaluations in early adolescence. A cohort longitudinal study. *Journal of Research on Adolescence*, 2, 123–45.

Alsaker, F. D., & Olweus, D. (1993). Global self-evaluations and perceived instability of self in early adolescence: A cohort longitudinal study. *Scandinavian Journal of Psychology*, 34, 47–63.

Anderson, E. R., Hetherington, E. M., & Clingempeel, W. G. (1989). Transformations in family relations at puberty: Effects of family context. *Journal of Early Adolescence*, 9, 310–34.

Anderson, T., & Magnusson, D. (1990). Biological maturation and the development of drinking habits and alcohol abuse among young males: A prospective longitudinal study. *Journal of Youth and Adolescence*, 19, 33–41.

Aro, H., & Taipale, V. (1987). The impact of timing of puberty on psychosomatic symptoms among fourteen- to sixteen-year-old Finnish girls. *Child Development*, 58, 261–8.

Behrman, R. E., Kliegman, R. M., Nelson, W. E., & Vaughan III, V. C. (1992). *Nelson textbook of pediatrics*. Philadelphia: W. B. Saunders.

Belsky, J., Steinberg, L., & Draper, P. (1991). Childhood experience, interpersonal development, and reproductive strategy: An evolutionary theory of socialization. *Child Development*, 62, 647–70.

Benson, R. C., & Tomera, K. M. (1985). Significance of testicular size. *Medical Aspects of Human Sexuality*, 19, 157–73.

Bergman, L. R., & Magnusson, D. (1991). Stability and change in patterns of extrinsic adjustment problems. In *Problems and Methods in Longitudinal Research: Stability and Change*, ed. D. Magnusson, L. R. Bergman, G. Rudinger, & B. Torestad, pp. 323–46. Cambridge: Cambridge University Press.

Berlin, F. S., Bergey, G. K., & Money, K. (1985). Periodic psychosis at puberty. *Medical Aspects of Human Sexuality*, 19, 194.

Bierich, J. R. (1975). Physiologische und pathologische Aspekte der Adoleszenz [Psychological and pathological aspects of adolescence]. *Zeitschrift für Kinder und Jugendpsychiatrie*, 3, 300–11.

Blyth, D. A., Simmons, R. G., Bulcroft, R., Felt, D., Van Cleave, E. F., & Bush, D. M. (1981). The effects of physical development on self-image and satisfaction with body-image for early adolescent males. *Research in Community and Mental Health*, 2, 43–73.

Blyth, D. A., Simmons, R. G., & Zakin, D. F. (1985). Satisfaction with body image for early adolescent females: The impact of pubertal timing within different school environments. *Journal of Youth and Adolescence*, 14, 207–25.

Brack, C. J., Orr, D. P., & Ingersoll, G. (1988). Pubertal maturation and adolescent self-esteem. *Journal of Adolescent Health Care*, 9, 280–5.

Bronfenbrenner, U. (1989). Ecological systems theory. *Annals of Child Development*, 6, 187–249.

Brooks-Gunn, J. (1984). The psychological significance of different pubertal events to young girls. *Journal of Early Adolescence*, 4, 315–27.

(1987). Pubertal Processes: Their relevance for developmental research. In *Handbook of Adolescent Psychology*, ed. V. B. Van Hasselt & M. Hersen, pp. 111–30. New York: Pergamon Press.

(1988). Antecedents and consequences of variations in girls' maturational timing. *Journal of Adolescent Health Care*, 9, 365–73.

Brooks-Gunn, J., Attie, H., Burrow, C., Rosso, J. T., & Warren, M. P. (1989). The impact of puberty on body and eating concerns in athletic and nonathletic contexts. *Journal of Early Adolescence*, 9, 269–90.

Brooks-Gunn, J. & Petersen, A. C. (1984). Problems in studying and defining pubertal events. *Journal of Youth and Adolescence*, 13, 181–95.

Brooks-Gunn, J., Petersen, A. C., & Eichorn, D. (1985). The study of maturational timing effects in adolescence. *Journal of Youth and Adolescence*, 14, 149–61.

Brooks-Gunn, J., & Ruble, D. N. (1983). The experience of menarche from a developmental perspective. In *Girls at Puberty. Biological and Psychosocial Perspectives*, ed. J. Brooks-Gunn & A. C. Petersen, pp. 155–77. New York: Plenum Press.

Brooks-Gunn, J., & Warren, M. P. (1985). The effects of delayed menarche in different contexts: Dance and nondance students. *Journal of Youth and Adolescence*, 14, 285–300.

Brooks-Gunn, J., & Warren, M. P. (1988). The psychological significance of secondary sexual characteristics in eleven-year-old girls. *Child Development*, 59, 1061–9.

Brooks-Gunn, J., & Warren, M. P. (1989). Biological and social contributions to negative affect in young adolescent girls. *Child Development*, 60, 40–55.

Buchanan, C. M. (1991). Pubertal development, assessment of. In *Encyclopedia of Adolescence*, ed. R. M. Lerner, A. C. Petersen, & J. Brooks-Gunn, pp. 875–83. New York: Garland Publishing.

Buchanan, C. M., Eccles, J., & Becker, J. B. (1992). Are adolescents victims of their raging hormones: Evidence for activational effects of hormones on moods and behavior at adolescence. *Psychological Bulletin*, 111, 62–107.

Bulcroft, R. A. (1991). The value of physical change in adolescence: Consequences for the parent-adolescent exchange relationship. *Journal of Youth and Adolescence*, 20, 89–105.

Cairns, R. B., & Cairns, D. D. (1988). The sociogenesis of self-concepts. In *Persons in Context. Developmental Processes*, ed. N. Bolger, A. Caspi, G. Downey, & M. Moorehouse, pp. 181–202. Cambridge: Cambridge University Press.

Campbell, B. C., & Udry, J. R. (1992). *Mother's Age at Menarche, Not Stress, Accounts for Daughter's Age at Menarche*. Paper presented at the Biennial Meeting of the Society for Research on Adolescence, Washington, DC.

Caspi, A., & Moffit, T. E. (1991). Individual differences are accentuated during periods of social change: The sample case of girls at puberty. *Journal of Personality and Social Psychology*, 61, 157–68.

Clausen, J. A. (1975). The social meaning of differential physical and sexual maturation. In *Adolescence in the Life Cycle: Psychological Change and Social Context*, ed. S. E. Dragastin & G. H. Elder, pp. 25–47. Washington D.C.: Hemisphere.

Cohn, L. D., Adler, N. E., Irwin Jr., C. E., Millstein, S. G., Kegeles, S. M., & Stone, G. (1987). Body-figure preferences in male and female adolescents. *Journal of Abnormal Psychology*, 96, 276–9.

Çok, F. (1990). Body image satisfaction in Turkish adolescents. *Adolescence*, 25, 409–13.

Coupey, S. M., & Ahlstrom, P. (1989). Common menstrual disorders. *Pediatric Clinics of North America*, 36, 551–71.

Crockett, L. J., & Petersen, A. C. (1987). Pubertal status and psychosocial development: Findings from the early adolescence study. In *Biological Psychosocial Interactions in Early Adolescence*, ed. R. M. Lerner & T. T. Foch, pp. 173–88. Hillsdale, NJ: Erlbaum.

Dorn, L. D., Crockett, L. J., & Petersen, A. C. (1988). The relations of pubertal status to intrapersonal changes in young adolescents. *Journal of Early Adolescence*, 8, 405–19.

Dornbusch, S. M. (1989). The sociology of adolescence. *Annual Review of Sociology*, 15, 233–59.

Duke-Duncan, P., Ritter, P. L., Dornbusch, S. M., Gross, R. T., & Carlsmith, J. M. (1985). The effects of pubertal timing on body image, school behavior, and deviance. *Journal of Youth and Adolescence*, 14, 227–35.

Dusek, J. B., & Flaherty, J. F. (1981). The development of the self-concept during the adolescent years. [4, Serial No. 191]. *Monographs of the Society for Research in Child Development*, 46.

Ehrhardt, A. A., Meyer-Bahlburg, H. F., L, Bell, J. J., Susan, S. F., Healey, J. M., Stiel, R., Feldman, J. F., Morishima, A., & New, M. I. (1984). Idiopathic precocious puberty in girls: Psychiatric follow-up in adolescence. *Journal of the American Academy of Child Psychiatry*, 23, 23–33.

Eichorn, D. H. (1975). Asynchronizations in adolescent development. In *Adolescence in the Life Cycle: Psychological Change and Social Context*, ed. S. E. Dragastin & G. H. Elder Jr., pp. 81–96. Washington, DC: Hemisphere.

Fabrega, H. (1972). The study of disease in relation to culture. *Behavioral Science*, 17, 183–203.

Finkelstein, J. W. (1980). The endocrinology of adolescence. *Pediatric Clinics of North America*, 27, 53–69.

Gaddis, A., & Brooks-Gunn, J. (1985). The male experience of pubertal change. *Journal of Youth and Adolescence*, 14, 61–9.

Gargiulo, J., Attie, I., Brooks-Gunn, J., & Warren, M. P. (1987). Girls' dating behavior as a function of social context and maturation. *Developmental Psychology*, 23, 730–7.

Garn, S. M., & Clark, D. C. (1976). Trends in fatness and the origins of obesity. *Pediatrics*, 57, 443–56.

Garwood, S. G., & Allen, L. (1979). Self-concept and identified problem differences between pre- and postmenarcheal adolescents. *Journal of Clinical Psychology*, 35, 528–37.

Greene, A. L., & Grimsley, M. D. (1990). Age and gender differences in adolescents' preferences for parental advice: Mum's the Word. *Journal of Adolescent Research*, 5, 396–413.

Greif, E. B., & Ulman, K. J. (1982). The psychological impact of menarche on early adolescent females: A review of the literature. *Child Development*, 53, 1413–30.

Gross, R. T., & Duke, P. M. (1980). The effect of early versus late physical maturation on adolescent behavior. *Pediatric Clinics of North America*, 27, 71–7.

Hagenfeldt, K. (1985). Hormonelle forstyrrelser hos kvinder ved fysisk aktivitet. Rapport fra seminar i idraettens hus 27.-28.9.85. *At traene piger/kvinder*. Dansk Idraetsforbund, Brondby, Denmark.

Halpern, C. T., & Udry, J. R. (1992). Variations in adolescent hormones measures and implications for behavioral research. *Journal of Research on Adolescence*, 2, 103–22.

Halpern, C. T., Udry, J. R., Campbell, B., & Suchindran, C. (1992). *Hormonal influences on adolescent male sexual activity*. Paper presented at the Biennial Meeting of the Society for Research on Adolescence, Washington, DC.

Hart, D. (1988). The adolescent self-concept in social context. In *Self, Ego, and Identity*, ed. D. K. Lapsley & F. C. Power, pp. 71–90. New York: Springer-Verlag.

Hendry, L. B., & Gillies, P. (1978). Body type, body-esteem, school, and leisure: A study of overweight, average, and underweight adolescents. *Journal of Youth and Adolescence*, 7, 181–95.

Hill, J. P., Holmbeck, G. N., Marlow, L., Green, T. M., & Lynch, M. E. (1985a). Menarcheal status and parent-child relations in families of seventh-grade girls. *Journal of Youth and Adolescence*, 14, 301–16.

Hill, J. P., Holmbeck, G. N., Marlow, L., Green, T. M., & Lynch, M. E. (1985b). Pubertal status and parent-child relations in families of seventh-grade boys. *Journal of Early Adolescence*, 5, 31–44.

Hunter, F. T., & Youniss, J. (1982). Changes in functions of three relations during adolescence. *Developmental Psychology*, 18, 806–11.

Inoff-Germain, G., Arnold, G. S., Nottelmann, E. D., Susman, E. J., Cutler Jr, G. B., & Chrousos, G. P. (1988). Relations between hormonal levels and observational measures of aggressive behavior of young adolescents in family interactions. *Developmental Psychology*, 24, 129–39.

Jaquish, G. A., & Savin-Williams, R. C. (1981). Biological and ecological factors in the expression of adolescent self-esteem. *Journal of Youth and Adolescence*, 10, 473–86.

Jones, M. C., & Mussen, P. H. (1958). Self-conceptions, motivations, and interpersonal attitudes of early- and late-maturing girls. *Child Development*, 29, 491–501.

Koff, E., Rierdan, J., & Silverstone, E. (1978). Changes in representations of body image as a function of menarcheal status. *Developmental Psychology*, 14, 635–42.

Kohen-Raz, R. (1974). Physiological maturation and mental growth at pre-adolescence and puberty. *Journal of Child Psychology and Psychiatry and Allied Disciplines*, 15, 199–213.

Lerner, R. M. (1985). Adolescent maturational changes and psychosocial development; A dynamic interactional perspective. *Journal of Youth and Adolescence*, 14, 355–72.

Logan, D. D. (1980). The menarche experience in twenty-three foreign countries. *Adolescence*, 15, 247–56.

Magnusson, D., Stattin, H., & Allen, V. L. (1986). Differential maturation among girls and its relevance to social adjustment: A longitudinal perspective. In *Life-*

span Development and Behavior, vol. 7, ed. D. L. Featherman & R. M. Lerner, pp. 135–72. New York: Academic Press.

Mansfield, M. J., & Emans, S. J. (1989). Anorexia nervosa, athletics, and amenorrhea. *Pediatric Clinics of North America*, 36, 533–49.

McGrory, A. (1990). Menarche: Responses of early adolescent females. *Adolescence*, 25, 265–70.

Mendelson, B. D., & White, D. R. (1985). Development of self-body-esteem in overweight youngsters. *Developmental Psychology*, 21, 90–6.

Meyer, J. M., Eaves, L. J., Heath, A. C., & Martin, N. G. (1991). Estimating genetic influences on the age-at-menarche: A survival analysis approach. *American Journal of Medical Genetics*, 39, 148–54.

Meyer-Bahlburg, H. F. L., Ehrhardt, A. A., Bell, J. J., Cohen, S. F., Healey, J. M., Feldman, J. F., Morishima, A., Baker, S. W., & New, M. I. (1985). Idiopathic precocious puberty in girls: Psychosexual development. *Journal of Youth and Adolescence*, 14, 339–53.

Money, J., & Wolff, G. (1974). Late puberty, retarded growth and reversible hyposomatotropinism (psychological dwarfism). *Adolescence*, 9, 121–34.

Nadler, R. D., Wallis, J., Roth-Meyer, C., Cooper, R. W., & Baulieu, E. E. (1987). Hormones and behavior of prepubertal and peripubertal chimpanzees. *Hormones and Behavior*, 21, 118–31.

Newcombe, N., Dubas, J. S., & Baenninger, M. (1989). Associations of timing of puberty, spatial ability, and lateralization in adult women. *Child Development*, 60, 246–54.

Nottelmann, E. D., Susman, E. J., Dorn, L. D., Inoff-Germain, G., Loriaux, D. L., Cutler, G. B., & Chrousos, G. P. (1987). Developmental processes in early adolescence. *Journal of Adolescent Health Care*, 8, 246–60.

Olweus, D., Mattson, A., Schalling, D., & Low, H. (1980). Testosterone, aggression, physical, and personality dimensions in normal adolescent males. *Psychosomatic Medicine*, 42, 253–69.

Olweus, D., Mattson, A., Schalling, D., & Low, H. (1988). Circulating testosterone levels and aggression in adolescent males: A causal analysis. *Psychosomatic Medicine*, 50, 261–72.

Paikoff, R. L., & Brooks-Gunn, J. (1991). Do parent-child relationships change during puberty? *Psychological Bulletin*, 110, 47–66.

Paikoff, R. L., Brooks-Gunn, J., & Carlton-Ford, S. (1991). Effect of reproductive status changes on family functioning and well-being of mothers and daughters. *Journal of Early Adolescence*, 11, 201–20.

Papini, D. R., & Clark, S. (1989). Grade, pubertal status, and gender-related variations in conflictual issues among adolescents. *Adolescence*, 24, 977–87.

Papini, D. R., Datan, N., & McCluskey-Fawcett, K. A. (1988). An observational study of affective and assertive family interactions during adolescence. *Journal of Youth and Adolescence*, 17, 477–92.

Papini, D. R., & Sebby, R. A. (1987). Adolescent pubertal status and affective family relationships: A multivariate assessment. *Journal of Youth and Adolescence*, 16, 1–16.

Parry, B. L. (1989). Reproductive factors affecting the course of affective illness in women. *Psychiatric Clinics of North America*, 12, 207–20.

Petersen, A. C. (1983). Pubertal change and cognition. In *Girls at Puberty*, ed. J. Brooks-Gunn & A. C. Petersen, pp. 179–98. New York: Plenum Press.

(1985). Pubertal development as a cause of disturbance: Myths, realities, and unanswered questions. *Genetic, Social, and General Psychology Monographs*, 111, 205–32.

(1988). Adolescent development. *Annual Review of Psychology*, 39, 583–607.
Petersen, A. C., & Crockett, L. (1985). Pubertal timing and grade effects on adjustment. *Journal of Youth and Adolescence*, 14, 191–206.
Petersen, A. C., & Crockett, L. (1986). Pubertal development and its relation to cognitive and psychosocial development in adolescent girls: Implications for parenting. In *School-Age Pregnancy and Parenthood. Biosocial Dimensions*, ed. J. B. Lancaster & B. A. Hamburg, pp. 147–75. New York: Aldine De Gruyter.
Petersen, A. C., Crockett, L., Richards, M. H., & Boxer, A. M. (1988). A self-report measure of pubertal status: Reliability, validity, and initial norms. *Journal of Youth and Adolescence*, 17, 117–133.
Petersen, A. C., & Taylor, B. (1980). The biological approach to adolescence: Biological change and psychological adaptation. In *Handbook of Adolescent Psychology*, ed. J. Adelson, pp. 117–55. New York: John Wiley & Sons.
Richards, M. H., Boxer, A. M., Petersen, A. C., & Albrecht, R. (1990). Relation of weight to body image in pubertal girls and boys from two communities. *Developmental Psychology*, 26, 313–21.
Richards, M., & Petersen, A. C. (1987). Biological theoretical models of adolescent development. In *Handbook of Adolescent Psychology*, ed. V. B. Van Hasselt & M. Hersen, pp. 34–52. New York: Pergamon Press.
Rierdan, J., & Koff, E. (1980). The psychological impact of menarche: Integrative versus disruptive changes. *Journal of Youth and Adolescence*, 9, 49–58.
Rierdan, J., & Koff, E. (1985). Timing of menarche and initial menstrual experience. *Journal of Youth and Adolescence*, 14, 237–44.
Rierdan, J., Koff, E., & Stubbs, M. L. (1987). Depressive Symptomatology and Body Image in Adolescent Girls. *Journal of Early Adolescence*, 7, 205–16.
Robertson, E. B., Burchinal, M., & Martin, S. L. (1992). *Reproductive and social status consequences of early menarcheal timing*. Presented at the Biennial Meetings of the Society for Research on Adolescence, Washington, DC.
Rosenthal, R. (1991). Cumulating psychology: An appreciation of Donald T. Campbell. *Psychological Science*, 2, 213–21.
Rutter, M. (1980). *Scientific Foundations of Developmental Psychiatry*. London: Heinemann Medical.
(1986). The developmental psychopathology of depression: Issues and perspectives. In *Depression in Young People*, ed. C. E. Izard, P. B. Read & M. Rutter, pp. 3–30. New York: The Guilford Press.
Saucier, J.-F., & Marquette, C. (1985). Cycles de l'adolescence, processus sociaux et santé mentale. *Sociologie et societes*, 17, 27–32.
Savin-Williams, R. C., & Small, S. A. (1986). The timing of puberty and its relationship to adolescent and parent perceptions of family interactions. *Developmental Psychology*, 22, 342–7.
Secord, P. F., & Jourard, S. M. (1953). The appraisal of body-cathexis: Body-cathexis and the self. *Journal of Counsulting Psychology*, 17, 343–7.
Silbereisen, R. K., & Kracke, B. (1994). Variation in maturational timing and adjustment in adolescence. In *The Social Worlds of Adolescence*, ed. S. Jackson & H. Rodriguez-Tomé. East Sussex: Erlbaum.
Silbereisen, R. K., Petersen, A. C., Albrecht, H. T., & Kracke, B. (1989). Maturational timing and the development of problem behavior: Longitudinal studies in adolescence. *Journal of Early Adolescence*, 9, 247–68.
Simmons, R. G., & Blyth, D. A. (1987). *Moving into Adolescence. The Impact of Pubertal Change and School Context*. New York: Aldine de Gruyter.

Simmons, R. G., Blyth, D. A., & McKinney, K. L. (1983). The social and psychological effects of puberty on white females. In *Girls at Puberty: Biological and Psychosocial Perspectives*, ed. J. Brooks-Gunn & A. C. Petersen, pp. 229–72. New York: Plenum Press.

Slap, G. B. (1986). Normal physiological and psychological growth in the adolescent. *Journal of Adolescent Health Care*, 7 (Suppl), 13–23.

Sonis, W. A., Comite, F., Pescovita, O. H., Hench, K., Rahn, C. W., Cutler Jr., G. B., Loriaux, D. L., & Klein, R. P. (1987). Biobehavioral aspects of precocious puberty. *Annual Progress in Child Psychiatry and Child Development*, 140–51.

Stattin, H., & Magnusson, D. (1989). Social transition in adolescence: A biosocial perspective. In *Transition Mechanisms in Child Development: The Longitudinal Perspective*, ed. A. De Ribaupierre, pp. 147–90. Cambridge: Cambridge University Press.

Stattin, H., & Magnusson, D. (1990). *Pubertal maturation in female development*. Hillsdale, NJ: Erlbaum

Steinberg, L. (1987). Impact of puberty on family relations: Effects of pubertal status and pubertal timing. *Developmental Psychology*, 23, 451–60.

(1988). Reciprocal relation between parent-child distance and pubertal maturation. *Developmental Psychology*, 24, 122–8.

Susman, E. J., Dorn, L. D., & Chrousos, G. P. (1991). Negative affect and hormone levels in young adolescents: Concurrent and predictive perspectives. *Journal of Youth and Adolescence*, 20, 167–90.

Susman, E. J., Inoff-Germain, G., Nottelmann, E. D., Loriaux, D. L., Cutler Jr., G. B., & Chrousos, G. P. (1987). Hormones, emotional dispositions, and aggressive attributes in young adolescents. *Child Development*, 58, 1114–34.

Susman, E. J., Nottelmann, E. D., Inoff-Germain, G. E., Dorn, L. D., Cutler Jr., G. B., Loriaux, D. L., & Chrousos, G. P. (1985). The relation of relative hormonal levels and physical development and social-emotional behavior in young adolescents. *Journal of Youth and Adolescence*, 14, 245–64.

Tanner, J. M. (1972). Sequence, tempo, and individual variation in growth and development of boys and girls aged twelve to sixteen. In *Twelve to Sixteen: Early Adolescence*, ed. J. Kagan & R. Coles, pp. 1–24. New York: Norton.

(1989). *Foetus into Man: Physical Growth from Conception to Maturity*, 2d ed. Wale: Castlemead Publications.

Tobin-Richards, M. H., Boxer, A. M., & Petersen, A. C. (1983). The psychological significance of pubertal change. Sex differences in perceptions of self during early adolescence. In *Girls at Puberty: Biological and Psychological Perspectives*, ed. J. Brooks-Grunn & A. C. Petersen, pp. 127–54. New York: Plenum Press.

Udry, J. R., & Billy, J. O. (1987). Initiation of coitus in early adolescence. *American Sociological Review*, 52, 841–55.

Udry, J. R., Billy, J. O. G., Morris, N. M., Groff, T. R., & Raj, M. H. (1985). Serum androgenic hormones motivate sexual behavior in adolescent boys. *Fertility and Sterility*, 43, 90–4.

Udry, J. R., & Talbert, L. M. (1988). Sex hormone effects on personality at puberty. *Journal of Personality and Social Psychology*, 54, 291–5.

Udry, J. R., Talbert, L. M., & Morris, N. M. (1986). Biosocial foundations for adolescent female sexuality. *Demography*, 23, 217–30.

Warren, M. P. (1983). Physical and biological aspects of puberty. In *Girls at Puberty. Biological and Psychosocial Perspectives*, ed. J. Brooks-Gunn & A. C. Petersen, pp. 3–28. New York: Plenum Press.

Younnis, J., & Smollar, J. (1985). *Adolescent Relations with Mothers, Fathers, and Friends*. Chicago: The University of Chicago Press.

Zakin, D. F., Blyth, D. A., & Simmons, R. G. (1984). Physical attractiveness as a mediator of the impact of early pubertal changes for girls. *Journal of Youth and Adolescence*, 13, 439–50.

3. The challenge of teenage antisocial behavior

DAVID P. FARRINGTON

Teenage antisocial behavior

Aims and scope

This chapter aims to review what is known about teenage antisocial behavior. Generally, antisocial behavior does not appear in the teenage years without warning; it is commonly preceded by childhood antisocial behavior and followed by adult antisocial behavior. There seems to be continuity over time, since the antisocial child tends to become the antisocial teenager and then the antisocial adult, and the antisocial adult then tends to produce another antisocial child.

There appears to be significant consistency in the relative ordering of any cohort of people on some underlying dimension which might be termed "antisocial personality" (see Farrington, 1991a). The behavioral manifestations of this underlying personality change over time, however, and it is important to document and explain them. For example, the antisocial child may be troublesome and disruptive in school, the antisocial teenager may steal cars and burgle houses, and the antisocial adult male may beat up his wife and neglect his children. These changing manifestations reflect changes both within the individual (e.g., maturation) and in the environment (e.g., opportunities).

This chapter has a developmental focus in studying why people begin to display different types of antisocial behavior, why they continue or escalate, and why they eventually stop or change to other types. It is important to investigate developmental sequences over time where one behavior acts as a kind of stepping stone to another. Important risk factors for antisocial behavior are reviewed, especially individual difference factors such as high impulsivity and low intelligence, family influences such as poor child rearing and antisocial parents, peer influences, socioeconomic factors and situational influences. Biological, school, and community influences are not reviewed here, because they are reviewed in other chapters in this book. In light of the chapter's developmental focus, unchanging variables such as sex and race are not reviewed.

Fortunately or unfortunately, there is no shortage of factors that are significantly correlated with offending and antisocial behavior; literally thousands of variables differentiate significantly between official offenders and nonoffenders and correlate significantly with reports of antisocial behavior by teenagers, peers, parents, and teachers. In this chapter, I focus on some of the most influential risk factors.

The chapter also discusses protective factors and implications for preventive interventions. More is known about factors that facilitate antisocial behavior than about factors that inhibit it or that protect people against the influence of facilitating factors. The emphasis is on antisocial behavior by males, based on research carried out in the United Kingdom, the United States and similar Western democracies. Most research quoted here is on offending rather than other types of antisocial behavior.

Within the scope of a single chapter, it is obviously impossible to review everything that is known about antisocial behavior. (For more detailed reviews, see Rutter & Giller, 1983; Wilson & Herrnstein, 1985.) The chapter will focus on some of the more important and replicable findings obtained in some of the more methodologically adequate studies, especially longitudinal studies of large community samples. I shall refer especially to knowledge gained in the Cambridge Study in Delinquent Development, which is a prospective longitudinal survey of over four hundred London males from age eight to age thirty-two (Farrington & West, 1990). Similar results have been obtained in similar studies elsewhere in England (e.g., Kolvin et al., 1988b, 1990), in the United States (e.g., McCord, 1979; Robins, 1979), in the Scandinavian countries (e.g., Farrington & Wikstrom, 1994; Pulkkinen, 1988), and in New Zealand (e.g., Moffitt & Silva, 1988a).

Definitions and measurement

Teenage antisocial behavior covers a multitude of sins. It includes acts defined as delinquency and acts prohibited by the criminal law, such as theft, burglary, robbery, violence, vandalism, fraud, and drug use, and other clearly deviant behavior such as bullying, reckless driving, heavy drinking, and sexual promiscuity, and more marginally deviant acts such as heavy smoking, heavy gambling, employment instability, and conflict with parents. All these acts tend to be interrelated, in the sense that people who commit any one of them have a considerably increased risk of committing the others (West & Farrington, 1977).

Certain types of antisocial behavior are used as diagnostic criteria for the psychiatric category of conduct disorder in ICD-10 and DSM-IIIR (e.g. Robins, 1991). The major types are stealing, running away from home, lying, arson, truancy, burglary, vandalism, forced sex, fighting, robbery, and cruelty to people and animals. Conduct disorder is currently diagnosed when the disturbed behavior persists for at least six months and includes at least two (ICD-10) or three (DSM-IIIR) of the specified behaviors. Although this is usually termed childhood conduct disorder, the diagnosis can be made up to age seventeen, and hence often reflects teenage antisocial behavior. Whether this syndrome should be classified as a disorder, illness, or disease is arguable, since physical or biological causes of the syndrome have not been established conclusively.

Offending is commonly measured using either official records of arrests or convictions or self-reports of offending. The advantages and disadvantages of official records and self-reports are to some extent complementary. In general, official records include the worst offenders and the worst offenses, whereas self-reports include more of the normal range of delinquent activity. Self-reports have the advantage of including undetected offenses, but the disadvantages of concealment and forgetting. The key issue is whether the same results are obtained with both methods. For example, if official records and self-reports both show a link between parental supervision and delinquency, it is likely that the supervision is related to delinquent behavior (and that the finding is not due to any biases in measurement). This chapter focuses on such replicable results.

Teenage antisocial behavior is usually measured by conducting interviews with or obtaining ratings from parents, peers, teachers, or the teenagers themselves. Psychiatric diagnoses such as conduct disorder are usually made on the basis of clinical interviews. Conduct disorder can also be measured, however, by having parents, teachers, or adolescents complete checklists of specific symptoms (e.g., Achenbach & Edelbrock, 1984). Structured psychiatric interviews which can be administered by nonclinicians, such as the Diagnostic Interview Schedule for Children (DISC), and ratings based on systematic observation are also used. There is usually quite high concordance between different methods (e.g., Edelbrock & Costello, 1988).

Prevalence

The prevalence of offenders varies according to the definition of offending and the method of measurement (official records or self-reports, usually). For example, in the Cambridge Study, 96 percent of a sample of inner-city London males admitted committing at least one of ten common offenses (including theft, burglary, violence, vandalism, and drug abuse) at some time between the ages of ten and thirty-two, whereas only 33 percent had been convicted of at least one of these offenses during this age range (Farrington, 1989c). In order to compare offenders and nonoffenders, it is important to set a sufficiently high criterion for "offending" (e.g., in terms of frequency, seriousness, or duration, or in terms of arrests or convictions) so that the vast majority of the male population are not classified as offenders.

When the high rate of admission of minor offenses first became widely known in the 1960s, this led some sociologists to argue that there were no differences between offenders and nonoffenders (since "everybody does it"), and hence that the marked differences (especially in social class) seen in the official statistics reflected selection biases by the police or courts. More recent reviews (e.g., Hindelang, Hirschi, & Weis, 1981) show, however, that, with comparable criteria of seriousness of offending, official statistics and self-reports yield quite concordant results, and both demonstrate numerous significant differences between offenders and nonoffenders. This chapter focuses on these differences.

Generally, the worst offenders according to self-reports (taking account of frequency and seriousness) tend also to be the worst offenders according to official records (e.g., Farrington, 1973; Huizinga & Elliott, 1986). For example, in the Cambridge Study between ages fifteen and eighteen, 11 percent of the males admitted to burglary, and 62 percent of these males were convicted of burglary (West & Farrington, 1977). The correlates of official and self-reported burglary were very similar (Farrington, 1992b).

The prevalence of other types of antisocial behavior also varies with definitions and methods of measurement. According to the DSM-IIIR manual (American Psychiatric Association, 1987), about 9 percent of males and 2 percent of females under age eighteen meet the diagnostic criteria for conduct disorder. The most extensive information about the prevalence of psychiatric disorders in children and adolescents was collected in the large-scale Ontario Child Health Study in Canada (Offord, Boyle, & Racine, 1989). This was a survey of about 3,300 children. About 7 percent of males and 3 percent of females aged twelve to sixteen were conduct-disordered in the previous six months, according to reports by teachers and by the adolescents themselves.

Detailed figures for the prevalence of individual symptoms were provided by Offord, Alder, and Boyle (1986). For example, among twelve- to sixteen-year-olds, 10 percent of males and 9 percent of females admitted cruelty to animals; 14 percent of males and 8 percent of females admitted destroying other people's property. In the same survey, Boyle and Offord (1986) provided detailed figures for the prevalence of smoking, drinking and drug use. Extensive information about the prevalence of different antisocial symptoms at different ages between four or five and fifteen or sixteen can be found in Shepherd, Oppenheim, and Mitchell (1971) for English children, and Achenbach and Edelbrock (1983) and Loeber and colleagues (1989) for American children.

The antisocial syndrome

Although the acts included under the heading of delinquency are heterogeneous, it nevertheless makes sense to investigate the characteristics of delinquents. Juvenile delinquents are predominantly versatile rather than specialized (e.g., Klein, 1984; Farrington et al., 1988c). Those who commit one type of offense have a significant tendency to commit other types. For example, 86 percent of convicted violent offenders in the Cambridge Study also had convictions for nonviolent offenses (Farrington, 1991b).

Just as offenders tend to be versatile in their types of offending, they also tend to be versatile in their antisocial behavior. In the Cambridge Study, delinquents tended to be troublesome and dishonest in their primary schools, to be aggressive and frequent liars at the ages of twelve to fourteen, and to be bullies at age fourteen. By age eighteen, delinquents tended to be antisocial in a wide variety of respects, including heavy drinking, heavy smoking, using prohibited drugs, and heavy gambling. In addition, they tended to be sexually promiscuous, often beginning sexual intercourse under age fifteen, having several sexual partners by age eighteen, and usually having unprotected intercourse (Farrington, 1992c).

West and Farrington (1977) argued that delinquency (which is dominated by crimes of dishonesty) is only one element of a larger syndrome of antisocial behavior arising in childhood and usually persisting into adulthood. They developed a scale of "antisocial tendency" at age eighteen, based on factors such as an unstable job record, heavy gambling, heavy smoking, drug use, drunk driving, sexual promiscuity, spending time hanging about on the street, antisocial group activity, violence, and antiestablishment attitudes. Their aim was to devise a scale not based on the types of acts (thefts and burglaries) that usually lead to convictions. They showed that the convicted males were usually antisocial in several other respects. For example, two-thirds (67 percent) of the males convicted up to age eighteen had four or more of these antisocial features, compared with only 15 percent of the unconvicted males.

Farrington (1991a) developed comprehensive scales of "antisocial personality" at ages ten, fourteen, eighteen, and thirty-two, based on offending and on other types of antisocial behavior. For example, the scale at age fourteen included convictions, high self-reported delinquency, stealing outside home, regular smoking, had sexual intercourse, bullying, frequent lying, frequent disobedience, hostility to police, frequent truancy, daring, and poor concentration/restlessness. All these measures tended to be interrelated. The last two measures, however, riskiness and restlessness, are arguably causes of antisocial behavior rather than indicators of it. They were included for consistency with psychiatric criteria of antisocial personality disorder, but the general concept of impulsivity will be reviewed as a possible cause of antisocial behavior later in this chapter. It is often difficult to distinguish between causes and indicators.

These results are consistent with findings obtained in numerous other studies. For example, in a St. Louis survey of black males, Robins and Ratcliff (1980) reported that juvenile delinquency tended to be associated with truancy, precocious sex, drinking, and drug use. In two American studies separated by thirteen years, Donovan, Jessor, and Costa (1988) concluded that a single common factor accounted for the positive correlations among a number of adolescent antisocial behaviors, including problem drinking, marijuana use, precocious sexual intercourse, and delinquent behavior. Hence, as Jessor and Jessor (1977) argued, there is a syndrome of problem behavior in adolescence.

In the literature on childhood psychopathology, it is also customary to find a single syndrome including stealing, lying, cheating, vandalism, substance use, running away from home, and truancy (Achenbach et al., 1987). The key issue is how far aggressive acts are part of this syndrome. Conduct disorder is sometimes divided into an aggressive or overt type and a nonaggressive or covert type (Loeber & Schmaling, 1985). Since aggressive individuals tend to be serious and versatile in their antisocial behavior, it seems likely that the difference between overt and covert individuals is a difference in degree rather than kind. The difference may also reflect stages of development. Children who are nonaggressive at an early age may escalate to aggression later.

Antisocial behavior tends to be concentrated in certain people and certain families. In the Cambridge Study, although about one-third of the males were convicted of criminal offenses, it was also true that only 6 percent of the sample – the chronic offenders – accounted for about half of all the convictions (Farrington & West, 1993). Chronic offenders were disproportionately likely to commit other types of antisocial behavior. In numerous other projects such as the Philadelphia cohort study of Wolfgang, Thornberry, and Figlio (1987) and the Finland research of Pulkkinen (1988), there was a similar concentration of offending in a small proportion of the sample.

Magnusson and Bergman (1988) argued for a person-oriented rather than variable-oriented approach to the development of antisocial behavior. In their Swedish longitudinal survey, they noted the clustering of risk factors such as aggressiveness, restlessness, poor concentration, and underachievement among boys at age thirteen, and of outcomes such as crime, alcohol abuse, and psychiatric illness up to age twenty-three. Single risk factors such as aggressiveness significantly predicted single outcomes such as crime and alcohol abuse. When they excluded the 13 percent of boys with multiple risk factors from their analyses, however, these significant relationships disappeared. This suggests that many of the results obtained in variable-oriented research might be produced by a small minority of chronically antisocial people.

Childhood behavioral precursors

Robins (e.g., 1986) has consistently shown how a constellation of indicators of childhood antisocial behavior predicts a constellation of indicators of adult antisocial behavior. In several longitudinal studies, the number of different childhood symptoms predicted the number of different adult symptoms, rather than showing a linkage between specific childhood and adult symptoms (Robins & Wish, 1977; Robins & Ratcliff, 1978, 1980). Numerous other studies also show that childhood conduct problems predict later offending and antisocial behavior (e.g., Loeber & LeBlanc, 1990). For example, Spivack, Marcus, and Swift (1986) in Philadelphia discovered that troublesome behavior in kindergarten (ages three to four) predicted later police contacts; and Ensminger, Kellam, and Rubin (1983) in Chicago and Tremblay, LeBlanc, and Schwartzman (1988) in Montreal showed that ratings of aggressiveness by teachers and peers in the first grade (ages six to seven) predicted self-reported offending at ages fourteen to fifteen.

In the Cambridge Study there was similar evidence of continuity in antisocial behavior from childhood to the teenage years. The antisocial personality scale at age eight or ten correlated 0.50 with the corresponding scale at age fourteen and 0.38 with the scale at age eighteen (Farrington, 1991a). The second best predictor of the antisocial tendency scale at age eighteen was childhood troublesomeness at age eight to ten, rated by peers and teachers (Farrington, 1993a; the best predictor was having a convicted parent by age ten). In regard to specific types of antisocial behavior, troublesomeness was the only variable measured at age eight to ten that significantly predicted bullying at both ages fourteen and eighteen (Farrington, 1993c). Again, troublesomeness at age eight to ten was the best predictor of both truancy and aggression at age twelve to fourteen in the secondary schools (Farrington, 1980, 1989a).

There is also continuity in antisocial behavior at younger ages. For example, Rose, Rose, and Feldman (1989) in New York City found that externalizing scores on the Achenbach Child Behaviour Checklist (reflecting a broad-band antisocial syndrome; see Achenbach & Edelbrock, 1983), completed by parents, were significantly correlated (r = 0.57) between ages two and five. Furthermore, a mother's ratings of her boy's difficult temperament at age six months significantly predicted (r = 0.31) his externalizing scores at age eight in the Bloomington longitudinal survey (Bates et al., 1991). It might be argued that these kinds of relationships reflect the stability of the parent's personality rather than of the child's behavior, but similar results are obtained even with different data sources (parents at the earlier age and teachers later). In Outer London, Richman, Stevenson, and Graham (1985) reported that behavior problems tended to persist between ages three and eight, and in New Zealand White and colleagues (1990) showed that externalizing scores and being difficult to manage at age three predicted antisocial behavior at age eleven.

Adult behavioral sequelae

There is considerable continuity between juvenile and adult offending. In the Cambridge Study, nearly three-quarters of those convicted as juveniles (age ten to sixteen) were reconvicted between ages seventeen and twenty-four, and nearly half of the juvenile offenders were reconvicted between ages twenty-five and thirty-two (Farrington, 1992a). Furthermore, this continuity over time did not merely reflect continuity in police reaction to crime. Farrington (1989c) showed that, for ten specified offenses, the significant continuity between offending in one age range and offending in a later age range held for both self-reports and official convictions.

There is also continuity in other types of antisocial behavior from the teenage to the adult years, as the research of Robins (1979) has shown. The adult male with "antisocial personality disorder" generally fails to maintain close personal relationships with anyone else, performs poorly in his jobs, is involved in crime, fails to support himself and his dependents without outside aid, and tends to change his plans impulsively and to lose his temper in response to minor frustrations. As an adolescent, he tended to be restless, impulsive, and lacking in guilt, performed badly in school, truanted, ran away from home, was cruel to animals or people, and committed delinquent acts.

According to the DSM-IIIR manual (American Psychiatric Association, 1987), adult antisocial personality disorder can only be diagnosed if the antisocial adult had shown conduct disorder before age fifteen. This requirement was included because Robins's research (e.g., 1986) showed that, whereas no more than half of conduct-disordered children became antisocial adults, virtually all antisocial adults had previously shown symptoms of conduct disorder. For antisocial adults, the average age of the first childhood symptom was eight (Robins, Tipp, & Przybeck, 1991).

The Cambridge Study developed a measure of adult social dysfunctioning at age thirty-two, based on (in the previous five years) convictions, self-reported offending, poor home conditions, poor cohabitation history, child problems, poor employment history, substance abuse, violence, and poor mental health (a high score on the General Health Questionnaire; see Farrington et al., 1988b, and Farrington, 1989b). This measure of adult social dysfunctioning at age thirty-two was significantly predicted by the antisocial tendency measure at age eighteen (Farrington, 1993a). A measure of antisocial personality at age thirty-two, comparable to the earlier antisocial personality measures, was also developed. Antisocial personality at age eighteen correlated 0.55 with antisocial personality at age thirty-two (Farrington, 1991a).

Expressing this another way, 60 percent of the most antisocial quarter of males at age eighteen were still in the most antisocial quarter fourteen years later at age thirty-two. Bearing in mind the very great environmental changes between eighteen and thirty-two, as the males left their parental homes and eventually settled down in marital homes after a period of residential instability, this consistency over time seems likely to reflect consistency within the individual rather than consistency in the environment. It is often found that about half of any sample of antisocial children persist to become antisocial teenagers, and that about half of any sample of antisocial teenagers persist to become antisocial adults. It is important to investigate why some people persist and others improve or desist over time. Establishing the causes of desistance might help in devising effective methods of prevention and treatment.

Zoccolillo and colleagues (1992), in a follow-up of children who had been in care and control children, also demonstrated the continuity between childhood conduct disorder (at age nine to twelve) and adult social dysfunctioning (at age twenty-six) in areas of work and in social and sexual relationships. For example, 81 percent of those with three or more symptoms of conduct disorder in childhood showed adult dysfunctioning in two or more areas, compared with only 21 percent of those with zero to two symptoms of conduct disorder. Almost half (40 percent) of the males with three or more symptoms of conduct disorder showed persistent antisocial behavior after age eighteen and fulfilled the psychiatric criteria for adult antisocial personality disorder.

There is specific as well as general continuity in antisocial behavior from the teenage to the adult years. In the Cambridge Study, Farrington (1990a) developed measures of absolute change and relative consistency between ages eighteen and thirty-two. For example, the prevalence of marijuana use declined significantly, from 29 percent at age eighteen to 19 percent at age thirty-two. There was a significant tendency, however, for the users at age eighteen also to be users at age thirty-two (44 percent of users at age eighteen were users at age thirty-two, whereas only 8 percent of nonusers at age eighteen were users at age thirty-two). Other researchers (e.g., Ghodsian & Power, 1987) have also reported significant consistency in substance use between adolescence and adulthood.

In contrast, binge drinking and drunk driving increased significantly between ages eighteen and thirty-two, and there was again significant consistency over time. Heavy smoking did not change significantly between ages eighteen and thirty-two, and there was again significant consistency over time. Relative consistency thus coexisted with absolute increases, decreases, or constancy in the Cambridge Study. In the Netherlands, Verhulst, Koot, and Berden (1990) reported similar results for childhood antisocial behavior.

There is usually specific as well as general continuity in aggression and violence from the teenage to the adult years. In the Cambridge Study, aggression at age sixteen to eighteen was the best predictor of fighting at age thirty-two (Farrington, 1989a). Spouse assault at age thirty-two was significantly predicted by teacher-rated aggression at age twelve to fourteen, and by the antisocial personality measures at ages fourteen and eighteen, but not (surprisingly) by aggression at age eighteen (Farrington,

1994). Bullying at age thirty-two was specifically predicted by bullying at ages fourteen and eighteen independently of the continuity between aggression at ages fourteen and eighteen and aggression at age thirty-two (Farrington, 1993c). Furthermore, male bullying at ages fourteen and eighteen predicted bullying by his child when the male was thirty-two, showing intergenerational continuity in bullying. In their New York study, Eron and Huesmann (1990) also found that a boy's aggression at age eight predicted not only aggression and spouse assault at age thirty but the aggression of his child as well.

Antisocial careers

The prevalence of offending increases to a peak in the teenage years and then decreases in the twenties. This pattern is seen both cross-sectionally and longitudinally (Farrington, 1986a). The peak age of official offending for English males was fifteen until 1987, but it increased to eighteen in 1988 because of a decrease in detected juvenile shoplifting offenders (Barclay, 1990; Farrington & Burrows, 1993). The peak age for females was fourteen until 1985 when it increased to fifteen. In the Cambridge Study, the rate of convictions increased to a peak at age seventeen and then declined (Farrington, 1990a). The median age of conviction for most types of offenses (burglary, robbery, theft of and from vehicles, shoplifting) was seventeen; it was twenty for violence and twenty-one for fraud. In the Philadelphia cohort study of Wolfgang, Thornberry, and Figlio (1987), the arrest rate increased to a peak at age sixteen and then declined.

Self-report studies also show that the most common types of offending decline from the teens to the twenties. In the Cambridge Study, burglary, shoplifting, theft of and from vehicles, theft from slot machines, and vandalism all decreased from the teens to the twenties, but the same decreases were not seen for theft from work, assault, drug abuse, and fraud (Farrington, 1989c). For example, burglary (since the last interview) was admitted by 13 percent at age fourteen, 11 percent at age eighteen, 5 percent at age twenty-one, and 2 percent at the ages of twenty-five and thirty-two. In their American National Youth Survey, Elliott, Huizinga, and Menard (1989) found that self-reports of offending increased from eleven to thirteen to a peak at fifteen to seventeen and then decreased by the ages of nineteen to twenty-one.

Many theories have been proposed to explain why offending peaks in the teenage years (see Farrington, 1986a). Offending has been linked to testosterone levels in males, which increase during adolescence and early adulthood and decrease thereafter, and to changes in physical abilities or opportunities for crime. The most popular explanation focuses on social influence. From birth, children are under the influence of their parents, who generally discourage offending. During their teenage years, however, juveniles gradually break away from the control of their parents and become influenced by their peers, who may encourage offending. After age twenty, offending declines as peer influence gives way to a new set of family influences hostile to offending, originating in spouses and cohabitees.

The criminal career approach (e.g., Blumstein & Cohen, 1987; Blumstein et al., 1986) emphasizes the need to investigate such questions as why people start offending (onset), why they continue offending (persistence), why offending becomes more frequent or more serious (escalation), and why people stop offending (desistance). The factors influencing onset may differ from those influencing persistence, escalation, or desistance, if only because the different processes occur at different ages. Farrington and Hawkins (1991) found that there was no relationship between factors influencing prevalence (official offenders versus nonoffenders), those influencing early versus later onset, and those influencing desistance after age twenty-one; Loeber and colleagues (1991) in the Pittsburgh Youth Study reported no relationship between factors influencing onset and those influencing escalation.

To understand the causes of offending, it is important to study developmental processes such as onset, persistence, escalation, and desistance. It is also important not to restrict this study narrowly to offending, however, but also to study the onset, persistence, escalation, and desistance of other types of antisocial behavior. Loeber and LeBlanc (1990) used many other concepts to describe developmental processes in antisocial careers, including acceleration and deceleration, diversification, switching, stabilization, escalation, and deescalation. For example, retention (escalating to serious acts while still committing trivial acts) seems more common than innovation (escalating and giving up trivial acts).

In the Cambridge Study, the average age at the first conviction was seventeen and a half, and the average age at the last conviction (up to age thirty-two) was twenty-three years and four months, giving an average criminal career length of five years, ten months (Farrington, 1992a). The average number of offenses leading to convictions was 4.5. The males first convicted at the earliest ages (ten to thirteen) tended to become the most persistent offenders, committing an average of 8.1 offenses leading to convictions in an average criminal career lasting nine years, eleven months.

Over a quarter of all the convicted males had criminal careers lasting longer than ten years. It is generally true that an early onset of antisocial behavior predicts a long and serious antisocial career (Loeber & LeBlanc, 1990). Reitsma-Street, Offord, and Finch (1985) in Ontario found that on average antisocial teenagers had initiated smoking, drinking, drug use, and sexual behavior over two years before their nonantisocial siblings.

It is important to investigate developmental sequences in antisocial and criminal careers. In a study of Montreal delinquents, LeBlanc and Frechette (1989) discovered that shoplifting and vandalism tended to occur before adolescence (average age of onset, eleven), burglary and motor vehicle theft in adolescence (average onset, fourteen to fifteen), and sex offenses and drug trafficking in the later teenage years (average onset, seventeen to nineteen). In regard to other types of antisocial behavior, Loeber and colleagues (1992), on the basis of retrospective reports of parents of clinic-referred boys, found that rule breaking at home tended to begin at a median age of four and a half years, then cruelty to animals (five years), bullying (five and a half), lying, stealing, fighting (six), vandalism (six and a half) and eventually burglary (ten). It is desirable to investigate these kinds of sequences within individuals.

Loeber (1988) proposed that there were three different developmental pathways for antisocial behavior, which he labeled aggressive versatile, nonaggressive, and exclusive substance use. The aggressive versatile pathway included conduct disorder and had the earliest age of onset. The frequency of occurrence of any particular behavior predicted the likelihood of transition to the next most serious behavior. As noted earlier, these pathways may reflect differences in degree rather than in kind.

Three types of behavioral sequences can be distinguished (see Farrington et al., 1990a). First of all, different acts following each other may be different behavioral manifestations of the same underlying construct (e.g., antisocial personality) at different ages. Second, different acts may be different behavioral manifestations of the same or similar underlying constructs at different ages and also part of a developmental sequence, where one act is a stepping stone to or facilitates another (e.g., where smoking cigarettes leads to marijuana use). Third, different acts may be indicators of different constructs and part of a causal sequence, where changes in an indicator of one construct cause changes in an indicator of a different construct (e.g., where low attainment leads to truancy).

The recognition that there are changing manifestations of theoretical constructs at different ages implies that different operational definitions are needed to measure them. Some measures are only applicable at certain ages; for example, truancy from school could not be measured at age thirty, just as absenteeism from work could not be measured at age ten. There is also the complication that behavioral manifestations of antisocial tendency may be different at different time periods, for example, as fashionable drugs come and go (see, e.g., Farrington, 1990a).

A further problem is that the same indicator may reflect different underlying constructs at different ages (see also Rutter, 1989a). For example, having sexual intercourse at age thirteen is statistically deviant, but having sexual intercourse at age twenty-three is statistically normal. Only the developmental course or precocity of the behavior may be deviant or antisocial, not the behavior itself. When behavior is statistically normal, it tends not to be associated with other indicators of antisocial behavior. For example, Farrington (1991a) found that conflict with parents was related to other antisocial indicators at age thirty-two but not at age eighteen, when it was common; drunk driving was related to other antisocial indicators at age eighteen but not at age thirty-two (when the majority of drivers, in the previous five years, had driven after consuming at least ten units of alcohol).

Risk and protective factors

Establishing risk factors

Risk factors are prior factors that increase the risk of occurrence of a negative outcome such as antisocial behavior. Longitudinal data are required to establish the ordering of risk factors and outcomes. The focus in this chapter is on risk factors for the onset or prevalence of offending and antisocial behavior. Few studies have examined risk factors for continuation or desistance. In the Cambridge Study, however, Farrington and Hawkins (1991) investigated factors that predicted whether offenders convicted before age twenty-one would persist or desist between ages twenty-one and thirty-two. The best independent predictors of persistence included rarely spending leisure time with the father at age eleven or twelve, low intelligence at age eight or ten, employment instability at age sixteen, and heavy drinking at age eighteen. Nearly 90 percent of the convicted males who were frequently unemployed and heavy drinkers as teenagers went on to be reconvicted after age twenty-one.

It is also difficult to decide whether a given risk factor is an indicator (symptom) or a possible cause of antisocial tendency. For example, do heavy drinking, truancy, unemployment, and divorce measure antisocial tendency, or do they cause (an increase in) it? It is important not to include a measure of the dependent variable as an independent variable in causal analyses, because this will lead to false conclusions and an overestimation of explanatory or predictive power (see, e.g., Amdur, 1989).

It is not unreasonable to argue that the above examples may be both indicative and causal. For example, long-term variations *between* individuals in antisocial tendency may be mirrored by variations in alcohol consumption, just as short-term variations *within* individuals in alcohol consumption may cause more antisocial behavior during the heavier drinking periods. The interpretation of other factors may be more clear-cut. For example, being exposed as a child to poor parental child rearing techniques might cause antisocial tendency but would not be an indicator of it; and burgling a house might be an indicator of antisocial tendency but would be unlikely to cause it (although it might be argued that when an antisocial act is successful in leading to positive reinforcement, this reinforcement causes an increase in the underlying antisocial tendency).

Cross-sectional studies make it impossible to distinguish between indicators and causes, since they can merely demonstrate correlations between high levels of one factor (e.g., unemployment) and high levels of another (e.g., offending). Longitudinal studies can show, however, that offending is greater (within individuals) during some periods (e.g., of unemployment) than during other periods (e.g., of employment). Because within-individual studies have greater control over extraneous influences than between-individual studies, longitudinal studies can demonstrate with high internal validity in quasi-experimental analyses, that changes in unemployment within individuals cause offending (Farrington, 1988b; Farrington et al., 1986b). Longitudinal studies can also establish whether factors such as unemployment have the same or different effects on offending when they vary within or between individuals. Implications for prevention and treatment, which require changes within individuals, cannot necessarily be drawn from effects demonstrated only in between-individual research.

One of the greatest problems in interpreting results is that causal factors tend to be interrelated. For example, people living in criminal areas tend to be socioeconomically deprived, tend to use erratic methods of child rearing and to have poor supervision, tend to have children who are impulsive and who have low school attainment, and so on. The explanation, prevention, and treatment of delinquency requires some disentangling of the mass of intercorrelations, but this is very difficult to achieve convincingly.

It is important to establish which factors predict delinquency independently of other factors. In the Cambridge Study, it was generally true that each of six categories of variables (impulsivity, low intelligence, parenting, antisocial family, socioeconomic deprivation, child antisocial behavior) predicted offending independently of the other categories (Farrington, 1990b). A theory was proposed to explain the development of male property offending in general and the major results of the Cambridge Study in particular (Farrington, 1986b, 1992b, 1993b).

The major risk factors for antisocial behavior that are reviewed in this chapter are the individual difference factors of impulsivity and low intelligence, and family, peer, socioeconomic, and situational factors. These factors often have additive, interactive, or sequential effects (Rutter, 1979), but in the interests of simplicity I will consider them one by one.

Impulsivity

In the Cambridge Study, the boys nominated by teachers as restless or lacking in concentration, those nominated by parents, peers, or teachers as the most daring, and those who were the most impulsive on psychomotor tests all tended to be juvenile but not adult offenders (Farrington, 1992b). Later self-report questionnaire measures of impulsivity (including such items as "I generally do and say things quickly without stopping to think") were related to both juvenile and adult offending. Daring, poor concentration, and restlessness were all related to both official and self-reported delinquency (Farrington, 1992c). Daring at age eight to ten was an important independent predictor of antisocial tendency at age eighteen (Farrington, 1993a) and of violence and spouse assault at age thirty-two (Farrington, 1989a, 1994). Poor concentration or restlessness at age eight to ten was an important independent predictor of adult social dysfunctioning at age thirty-two (Farrington, 1993a).

Many other investigators have reported a link between the constellation of personality factors variously termed "hyperactivity-impulsivity-attention deficit" or HIA (Loeber 1987) and offending. For example, in Los Angeles, Satterfield (1987) tracked HIA and matched control boys between the ages of nine and seventeen, and showed that six times as many of the HIA boys were arrested for serious offenses. Similar results were reported by Gittelman and colleagues (1985) in New York. Other studies have shown that childhood hyperactivity predicts adolescent and adult antisocial behavior and substance use (e.g., Barkley et al., 1990; Mannuzza et al., 1991).

The major problem of interpretation in these projects centers on the marked overlap between hyperactivity and conduct disorder (e.g. Taylor, 1986). Many of the boys in these and other longitudinal studies of hyperactivity (e.g., Huessy & Howell, 1985; Nylander, 1979; Weiss & Hechtman, 1986) probably displayed not only HIA but also conduct disorder as well, making it difficult to know how far the results might have reflected the continuity between childhood antisocial behavior and later offending and adult antisocial behavior.

Farrington, Loeber, and Van Kammen (1990b) developed a combined measure of hyperactivity-impulsivity-attention deficit at age eight to ten and showed that it significantly predicted juvenile convictions independently of conduct problems at age eight to ten. Hence, it might be concluded that HIA is not merely another measure of antisocial personality, but is a possible cause, or an earlier stage in a developmental sequence. For example, Richman and colleagues (1985) found that restlessness at age three predicted conduct disorder at age eight. Other studies have also concluded that hyperactivity and conduct disorder are different constructs (e.g., Blouin et al., 1989; McGee, Williams, & Silva, 1985). Constructs similar to HIA, such as sensation seeking, are also related to delinquency (e.g., White, Labouvie, & Bates, 1985); low self-control is the central construct of Gottfredson and Hirschi's (1990) theory.

It has been suggested that HIA might be a behavioral consequence of a low level of physiological arousal. Offenders have a low level of arousal according to their low alpha (brain) waves on the EEG, or according to autonomic nervous system indicators such as heart rate, blood pressure, or skin conductance, or they show low autonomic reactivity (e.g., Venables & Raine, 1987). In his Swedish longitudinal survey, Magnusson (1988) demonstrated that low adrenaline levels at age thirteen, reflecting low autonomic reactivity, were related to aggressiveness and restlessness at that age and to later offending as an adult. Olweus (1987) also found that aggressive juveniles in Sweden tended to have low adrenaline levels. The causal links between low autonomic arousal, consequent sensation seeking, and offending are brought out explicitly in Mawson's (1987) theory of transient criminality.

Heart rate at age eighteen was measured in the Cambridge Study. Although a low heart rate correlated significantly with convictions for violence (Farrington, 1987), it did not significantly relate to delinquency in general. In addition, being tattooed was highly related to self-reported and official offending in the Cambridge Study (Farrington, 1992c). The meaning of this result is not entirely clear, but tattooing may reflect risk taking, daring, and excitement seeking.

Intelligence and attainment

Loeber and Dishion (1983) and Loeber and Stouthamer-Loeber (1987) extensively reviewed the predictors of male delinquency. They concluded that poor parental child management techniques, offending by parents and siblings, low intelligence and educational attainment, and separation from parents were all important predictors. Longitudinal (and cross-sectional) surveys have consistently demonstrated that children with low intelligence are disproportionately likely to become delinquents. Low intelligence and attainment are also related to childhood antisocial behavior (e.g., Rutter, Tizard, & Whitmore, 1970).

In the Cambridge Study, one-third of the boys scoring ninety or less on a nonverbal intelligence test (Raven's Progressive Matrices) at ages eight to ten were convicted as juveniles, twice as many as among the remainder (Farrington, 1992c). Low nonverbal intelligence was highly correlated with low verbal intelligence (vocabulary, word comprehension, verbal reasoning) and with low school attainment at age eleven; all these measures predicted juvenile convictions to much the same extent. In addition to their poor school performance, delinquents tended to be frequent truants, to leave school at the earliest possible age (which was then fifteen) and to take no school examinations.

Low nonverbal intelligence was especially characteristic of the juvenile recidivists (who had an average IQ of eighty-nine) and of those first convicted at the earliest ages (ten to thirteen). Furthermore, low intelligence and attainment predicted self-reported delinquency almost as well as convictions (Farrington, 1992c), suggesting that the link between low intelligence and delinquency was not caused by the less intelligent boys having a greater probability of being caught. Similar results have been obtained in other projects (e.g., Moffitt & Silva, 1988a; Wilson & Herrnstein, 1985). Low intelligence and attainment also predicted both juvenile and adult convictions (Farrington, 1992b). Low intelligence at age eight to ten was an important independent predictor of antisocial tendency at age eighteen (Farrington, 1993a) and of spouse assault at age thirty-two (Farrington, 1994). Low intelligence and attainment predicted aggression and bullying at age fourteen, and poor reading ability at age eighteen was the best predictor of having a child bully at age thirty-two (Farrington, 1989a, 1993c).

Low intelligence may lead to delinquency through the intervening factor of school failure. A plausible explanatory factor underlying the link between intelligence and delinquency, however, is the ability to manipulate abstract concepts. People who are poor at this tend to do badly in intelligence tests such as the Matrices and in school attainment, and they also tend to commit offenses, probably because of their poor ability to foresee the consequences of their offending and to appreciate the feelings of victims (i.e., their low empathy). Certain family backgrounds are less conducive than others to the development of abstract reasoning. For example, lower class, poorer parents tend to live for the present with little thought for the future, and tend to talk in terms of the concrete rather than the abstract. A lack of concern for future consequences, which is a central feature of Wilson and Herrnstein's (1985) theory, is also linked to the concept of impulsivity.

Modern research is studying not just intelligence but also detailed patterns of cognitive and neuropsychological deficit. For example, in a New Zealand longitudinal study of over 1,000 children from birth to age fifteen, Moffitt and Silva (1988b) found that self-reported delinquency was related to verbal, memory, and visual-motor integration deficits, independently of low social class and family adversity. Neuropsychological research might lead to important advances in knowledge about the link between brain functioning and delinquency. For example, the "executive functions" of the brain, located in the frontal lobes, include sustaining attention and concentration, abstract reasoning and concept formation, anticipation and planning, self-monitoring of behavior, and inhibition of inappropriate or impulsive behavior (Moffitt, 1990). Deficits in these executive functions are conducive to low measured intelligence and to delinquency. Moffitt and Henry (1989) found deficits in these executive functions especially among delinquents who were both antisocial and hyperactive.

Family factors

Loeber and Stouthamer-Loeber (1986) completed an exhaustive review of family factors as correlates and predictors of juvenile conduct problems and delinquency. They found that poor parental supervision or monitoring, erratic or harsh parental discipline, marital disharmony, parental rejection of the child, and low parental involvement with the child (as well as antisocial parents and large family size) were all important predictors.

In the Cambridge-Somerville study in Boston, McCord (1979) reported that poor parental supervision was the best predictor of both violent and property crimes. Parental aggressiveness (which included harsh discipline, shading into child abuse at the extreme) and parental conflict were significant precursors of violent but not property crimes, whereas the mother's attitude (passive or rejecting) was a significant precursor of property but not violent crimes. Robins (1979), in her long-term follow-up studies in St Louis, also found that poor supervision and discipline were consistently related to later offending, and Shedler and Block (1990) in San Francisco reported that hostile and rejecting mothers when children were aged five predicted frequent drug use at age eighteen.

Other studies also show the link between family factors and delinquency. In a Birmingham survey, Wilson (1980) concluded that the most important correlate of convictions, cautions, and self-reported delinquency was lax parental supervision. In their English national survey of juveniles aged fourteen to fifteen and their mothers, Riley and Shaw (1985) found that poor parental supervision was the most important correlate of self-reported delinquency for girls, and the second most important for boys (after delinquent friends). Family dysfunctioning is also related to conduct disorder (e.g., Offord, Boyle, & Racine, 1989).

In the Cambridge Study, West and Farrington (1973) found that harsh or erratic parental discipline, cruel, passive or neglecting parental attitude, poor supervision, and parental conflict, all measured at age eight, all predicted later juvenile convictions. Farrington (1992c) reported that poor parental child rearing behavior (a combination of discipline, attitude, and conflict), poor parental supervision, and low parental interest in education all predicted both convictions and self-reported delinquency. Poor parental child rearing behavior was related to early rather than later offending (Farrington, 1986b), and was not characteristic of those first convicted as adults (West & Farrington, 1977). Poor parental supervision, however, was related to both juvenile and adult convictions (Farrington, 1992b).

Offenders tend to have difficulties in their personal relationships. The Study males who were in conflict with their parents at age eighteen tended to be juvenile but not adult offenders. Conflict with parents at age thirty-two was not related to offending, however. Both juvenile and adult offenders tended to have a poor relationship with their wife or cohabitee at age thirty-two, or had assaulted her, and they also tended to be divorced and/or separated from their children (Farrington, 1992b).

In agreement with the hypothesis that being physically abused as a child foreshadows later violent offending (Widom, 1989), harsh parental discipline and attitude at age eight significantly predicted later violent, as opposed to nonviolent, offenders in the Cambridge Study (Farrington, 1978). However, more recent research has shown that it was equally predictive of violent and frequent offenders (Farrington, 1991b).

Broken homes and early separations also predict offending. In the Newcastle Thousand Family Study, Kolvin and colleagues (1990) reported that parental divorce or separation up to age five predicted later convictions up to age thirty-three. McCord (1982) carried out an interesting study of the relationship between homes broken by loss of the natural father and later serious offending. She found that the prevalence of offending was high for boys reared in broken homes without affectionate mothers (62 percent) and for those reared in united homes characterized by parental conflict (52 percent), irrespective of whether they had affectionate mothers. The prevalence of offending was low for those reared in united homes without conflict (26 percent) or in broken homes with affectionate mothers (22 percent).

These results suggest that it is not so much the broken home (or a single-parent female-headed household) which is criminogenic as the parental conflict which causes it. Teenage childbearing, however, combined with a single-parent, female-headed household is conducive to offending (Morash & Rucker, 1989). Single-parent families tended to have conduct-disordered and substance-abusing children in the Ontario Child Health Study, although such families were difficult to disentangle from low income families (Blum, Boyle, & Offord, 1988; Boyle & Offord, 1986).

The importance of the cause of the broken home is also shown in the English national longitudinal survey of over five thousand children born in one week of 1946 (Wadsworth, 1979). Boys from homes broken by divorce or separation had an increased likelihood of being convicted or officially cautioned up to age twenty-one in comparison with those from homes broken by death or from unbroken homes. Remarriage of a parent (which happened more often after divorce or separation than after death) was also associated with an increased risk of offending.

In the Cambridge Study, both permanent and temporary (more than one month) separations before age ten predicted convictions and self-reported delinquency, providing the separations were not caused by death or hospitalization (Farrington, 1992c). Homes broken at an early age (under age five), however, were not unusually criminogenic (West & Farrington, 1973). Separation before age ten predicted both juvenile and adult convictions (Farrington, 1992b), and was an important independent predictor of adult social dysfunctioning and spouse assault at age thirty-two (Farrington, 1993a, 1994).

Criminal, antisocial, and alcoholic parents also tend to have delinquent sons, as Robins (1979) found. For example, in her follow-up of over two hundred black males in St. Louis (Robins, West, & Herjanic, 1975), arrested parents (her subjects) tended to have arrested children, and the juvenile records of the parents and children showed similar rates and types of offenses. McCord (1977), in her thirty-year follow-up of about 250 treated boys in the Cambridge-Somerville study, also reported that convicted sons (her subjects) tended to have convicted fathers. Whether there is a specific relationship in her study between types of convictions of parents and children is not clear. McCord found that 29 percent of fathers convicted for violence had sons convicted for violence, in comparison with 12 percent of other fathers, but this may reflect the general tendency for convicted fathers to have convicted sons rather than any specific tendency for violent fathers to have violent sons.

Craig and Glick (1968) in New York City also showed that the majority of boys who became serious or persistent delinquents (84 percent) had criminal parents or siblings, in comparison with 24 percent of the remainder. Criminal parents tended to have conduct-disordered children in the Ontario Child Health Study (Offord, Boyle, & Racine, 1989), and substance use by parents predicted substance use by children in the Rutgers Health and Human Development project (e.g., Johnson & Pandina, 1991).

In the Cambridge Study, the concentration of offending in a small number of families was remarkable. West and Farrington (1977) discovered that less than 5 percent of the families were responsible for about half of the criminal convictions of all family members (fathers, mothers, sons, and daughters). West and Farrington (1973) showed that having convicted mothers, fathers, and brothers by a boy's tenth birthday significantly predicted his own later conviction. Furthermore, convicted parents and delinquent siblings predicted self-reported as well as official delinquency (Farrington, 1992c). Unlike most early precursors, a convicted parent was related less to offending of early onset (age ten to thirteen) than to later offending (Farrington, 1986b). A convicted parent also predicted which juvenile offenders went on to become adult criminals and which recidivists at age nineteen continued offending (West & Farrington, 1977). A convicted parent was the best predictor of antisocial tendency at age eighteen and of spouse assault at age thirty-two, and it was also an important independent predictor of bullying at age fourteen and adult social dysfunctioning at age thirty-two (Farrington, 1993a, 1993c, 1994).

These results are concordant with the psychological theory (e.g., Trasler, 1962) that antisocial behavior develops when the normal social learning process, based on rewards and punishments from parents, is disrupted by erratic discipline, poor supervision, parental disharmony, and unsuitable (antisocial or criminal) parental models. Some part of the link between antisocial parents and antisocial children may, however, reflect genetic influences.

Just as early family factors predict the early onset or prevalence of offending, later family factors predict later desistance. For example, it is often believed that male offending decreases after marriage, and there is some evidence in favor of this (e.g., Bachman, O'Malley, & Johnston, 1978). In the Cambridge Study, there was a clear tendency for convicted males who got married at age twenty-two or earlier to be reconvicted less often in the next two years than comparable convicted males who did not get married (West, 1982). However, in the case of both the males and their fathers, convicted males tended to marry convicted females, and convicted males who married convicted females continued to offend at the same rate after marriage as matched unmarried males. Offenders who married convicted females incurred more convictions after marriage than those who married unconvicted females, independently of their conviction records before marriage. Hence, it was concluded that the reformative effect of marriage was lessened by the tendency of male offenders to marry females who were also offenders. Rutter (1989b) has drawn attention to the importance of studying turning points in people's lives, such as marriage.

Peer factors

The reviews by Zimring (1981) and Reiss (1988) show that delinquent acts tend to be committed in small groups (of two or three people, usually) rather than alone. In the Cambridge Study, most officially recorded juvenile offenses were committed with others, but the incidence of co-offending declined steadily with age, from ten on. Burglary, robbery, and theft from vehicles were particularly likely to involve co-offenders, who tended to be similar in age and sex to the Study males and lived close to their homes and to the locations of the offenses. The Study males were most likely to offend with brothers when they had brothers who were similar in age to them (Reiss & Farrington, 1991). In Ontario, Jones, Offord, and Abrams (1980) discovered that male delinquents tended to have a preponderance of brothers, and proposed that there was male potentiation of antisocial behavior.

The major problem of interpretation is whether young people are more likely to commit offenses in groups than alone, or whether the high prevalence of co-offending merely reflects the fact that whenever young people go out they tend to go out in groups. Do peers tend to encourage and facilitate offending, or is it just that most kinds of activities out of the home (both delinquent and nondelinquent) tend to be committed in groups? Another possibility is that the commission of offenses encourages association with other delinquents, perhaps because "birds of a feather flock together" or because of the stigmatizing and isolating effects of court appearances and institutionalization. It is surprisingly difficult to decide among these various possibilities, although most researchers argue that peer influence is an important factor. For example, the key construct in Sutherland and Cressey's (1974) theory is the number of persons in a child's social environment with norms and attitudes favoring delinquency.

There is clearly a close relationship between the delinquent activities of a young person and those of his friends. In the United States (Hirschi, 1969) and England (West & Farrington, 1973), it has been found that a boy's reports of his own offending are significantly correlated with his reports of his friends' delinquency. In the American National Youth Survey of Elliott, Huizinga, and Ageton (1985), having delinquent peers was the best independent predictor of self-reported offending in a multivariate analysis. In the same study, Agnew (1991) showed that this relationship was greatest for teenagers who were most strongly attached to their peers and felt most peer pressure.

The major problem of interpretation is that, if delinquency is a group activity, delinquents will almost inevitably have delinquent friends, and this does not necessarily show that delinquent friends cause delinquency. Delinquent friends could be an indicator rather than a cause. In the National Youth Survey Elliott and Menard (1988) concluded that having delinquent peers increased a person's own offending and that a person's own offending also increased his likelihood of having delinquent peers. Hence, both effects seemed to be operating.

In the Cambridge Study, association with delinquent friends was not measured until age fourteen, and was therefore not investigated as a precursor of offending (which began at age ten). It was, however, a significant independent predictor of convictions at the young adult ages (Farrington, 1986b) and of teenage violence at age sixteen to eighteen (Farrington, 1989a). The recidivists at age nineteen who ceased offending differed from those who persisted, in that the desisters were more likely to have stopped going around in a group of male friends. Furthermore, spontaneous comments by the youths indicated that withdrawal from the delinquent peer group was seen as an important influence on ceasing to offend (West &

Farrington, 1977). Therefore, continuing to associate with delinquent friends may be an important factor in determining whether juvenile delinquents persist in offending as young adults or desist.

Delinquent peers are likely to be most influential where they have high status within the peer group and are popular. Studies in both the United States (Roff & Wirt, 1984) and England (West & Farrington, 1973) show, however, that delinquents are usually unpopular with their peers. It seems paradoxical for offending to be a group phenomenon facilitated by peer influence, and yet for offenders to be largely rejected by other adolescents (Parker & Asher, 1987). It may be, however, that offenders are popular in antisocial groups and unpopular in prosocial groups, or that rejected children band together to form adolescent delinquent groups (Hartup, 1983).

Socioeconomic factors

Most delinquency theories assume that delinquents disproportionately come from lower-class social backgrounds, and aim to explain why this is so. For example, Cohen (1955) proposed that lower-class boys found it hard to succeed according to the middle-class standards of school, partly because lower-class parents tended not to teach their children to delay immediate gratification in favor of long-term goals. Consequently, lower-class boys joined delinquent subcultures by whose standards they could succeed. Cloward and Ohlin (1960) argued that lower-class children could not achieve universal goals of status and material wealth by legitimate means and consequently resorted to illegitimate means.

The social class or socioeconomic status (SES) of a family has been measured by sociologists primarily according to rankings of the occupational prestige of the family breadwinner. Persons with professional or managerial jobs are ranked in the highest class, whereas those with unskilled manual jobs are ranked in the lowest. These occupational prestige scales may not, however, correlate very highly with real differences between families in socioeconomic circumstances. In general, the scales date from many years ago, when it was more common for the father to be the family breadwinner and for the mother to be a housewife. It may therefore be difficult to derive a realistic measure of socioeconomic status for a family with a single parent or with two working parents (Mueller & Parcel, 1981).

Over the years, many other measures of social class have become popular, including family income, educational levels of parents, type of housing, overcrowding in the house, possessions, dependence on welfare benefits, and family size. These may all reflect more meaningful differences between families than occupational prestige. For example, in his California self-report survey of over four thousand children, Hirschi (1969) concluded that offending was related to the family being on welfare and the father being unemployed, but not to the occupational or educational status of the father. Family size is highly correlated with other indices of socioeconomic deprivation, although its relationship with delinquency may reflect child-rearing factors (e.g., less attention to each child) rather than socioeconomic influences.

Beginning with the pioneering self-report research of Short and Nye (1957), it was common in the United States to argue that low social class was related to official offending but not to self-reported offending, and hence that the official processing of offenders was biased against lower-class youth. Unfortunately, as Thornberry and Farnworth (1982) pointed out, the voluminous literature on the relationship between SES and offending is characterized by inconsistencies and contradictions, and some reviewers (e.g., Hindelang, Hirschi, & Weis, 1981) have concluded there is no relationship between SES and either self-reported or official delinquency.

English studies have reported more consistent links between low social class and delinquency. In the English national survey, Douglas and colleagues (1966) showed that the prevalence of official juvenile delinquency in males varied considerably according to the occupational prestige and educational background of their parents, from 3 percent in the highest category to 19 percent in the lowest. In addition, Wadsworth (1979) reported that offending increased significantly with increasing family size. A similar link between family size and antisocial behavior was reported by Kolvin and colleagues (1988b) in their follow-up of Newcastle children from birth to age thirty-three, by Rutter, Tizard, and Whitmore (1970) in the Isle of Wight survey, and by Ouston (1984) in the Inner London survey.

Numerous indicators of SES were measured in the Cambridge Study, both for the male's family of origin and for the male himself as an adult, including occupational prestige, family income, housing, employment instability, and family size. Most of the measures of occupational prestige (based on the Registrar General's scale) were not significantly related to delinquency. In a reversal of the American results, however, low SES of the family when the boy was aged eight to ten significantly predicted his later self-reported but not official delinquency. More consistently, low family income, poor housing, and large family size predicted official and self-reported, juvenile and adult, offending (Farrington, 1992b, 1992c). Large family size at age ten was an important independent predictor of antisocial tendency at age eighteen and teenage violence; low family income at age eight was the best independent predictor of adult social dysfunctioning (Farrington, 1989a, 1993a). The Ontario Child Health Study (Offord, Boyle, & Racine, 1989) also showed that low income families tended to have conduct-disordered children.

Socioeconomic deprivation of parents is usually compared with offending by sons. When the sons grow up, however, their own socioeconomic deprivation can be related to their own offending. In the Cambridge Study, official and self-reported delinquents tended to have unskilled manual jobs and an unstable job record at age eighteen. Just as an erratic work record of the father predicted later offending by the Study male, an unstable job record of the male at age eighteen was one of the best independent predictors of his convictions between ages twenty-one and twenty-five (Farrington, 1986b). An unskilled manual job at age eighteen was also an important independent predictor of adult social dysfunctioning at age thirty-two (Farrington, 1993a). Between ages fifteen and eighteen, the Study males were convicted at a higher rate when they were unemployed than when they were employed (Farrington et al., 1986b), suggesting that unemployment in some way causes crime, and conversely that employment may lead to desistance from offending. Since crimes involving material gain (e.g., theft, burglary, robbery) especially increased during periods of unemployment, it seems likely that financial need is an important link in the causal chain between unemployment and crime.

Situational factors

It is plausible to suggest that criminal and antisocial behavior results from the interaction between a person (with a certain degree of underlying antisocial tendency) and the environment (which provides criminal opportunities). Given the same environment, some people will be more likely to commit offenses than others, and conversely the same person will be more likely to commit offenses in some environments than in others. Criminological research typically concentrates on either the development of criminal persons or the occurrence of criminal events, but rarely on both.

Most delinquency researchers have aimed to explain the development of offending people, but some have tried to explain the occurrence of offending events. As already mentioned, delinquents are predominantly versatile rather than specialized. Hence, in studying delinquents, it seems unnecessary to develop a different theory for each different type of offender. In contrast, if one is trying to explain why offenses occur, the situations are so diverse and specific to particular crimes that it probably is necessary to have different explanations for different types of offenses.

The most popular theory of offending events suggests that they occur in response to specific opportunities, when their expected benefits (e.g., stolen property, peer approval) outweigh their expected costs (e.g., legal punishment, parental disapproval). For example, Clarke and Cornish (1985) outlined a theory of residential burglary which included such influencing factors as whether a house was occupied, whether it looked affluent, whether there were bushes to hide behind, whether there were nosy neighbors, whether the house had a burglar alarm, and whether it contained a dog. Several other researchers have also proposed that offending involves a rational decision in which expected benefits are weighed against expected costs (e.g., Wilson & Herrnstein, 1985).

In the Cambridge Study, the most common reasons given for offending were rational ones, suggesting that most property crimes were committed because the offenders wanted the items stolen (West & Farrington, 1977). In Montreal, LeBlanc and Frechette (1989) also reported that most offenses were motivated by the utilitarian need for material goods. In addition, a number of cross-sectional surveys have shown that low estimates of the risk of being caught were correlated with high rates of self-reported offending (e.g., Erickson, Gibbs, & Jensen, 1977). Unfortunately, the direction of causal influence is not clear in cross-sectional research, since committing delinquent acts may lead to lower estimates of the probability of detection as well as the reverse. Farrington and Knight (1980) carried out a number of studies, using experimental, survey, and observational methods, that suggested that stealing involved risky decision-making. Hence, it is plausible to suggest that opportunities for delinquency, the immediate costs and benefits of delinquency, and the probabilities of these outcomes, all influence whether people offend in any situation.

Protective factors

There are several different definitions of protective factors. One is that protective factors are merely the opposite end of the scale from risk factors. For example, just as low intelligence is a risk factor, high intelligence may be a protective factor. Rae-Grant and colleagues (1989) used this definition in the Ontario Child Health Study and reported that the major protective factors for conduct disorder were getting along well with others, good academic performance, and participation in organized activities.

On other definitions, protective factors are not just the opposite of risk factors. For example, a variable with a nonlinear relationship to antisocial behavior might be regarded as a protective factor but not a risk factor. This would be true if the risk of antisocial behavior declined from medium to high levels of the factor but did not increase from medium to low levels. If high intelligence were linked to a low risk of antisocial behavior, whereas medium and low intelligence were linked to a fairly constant average risk, intelligence could be regarded as a protective factor but not a risk factor. The reverse finding is more common, however (Farrington & Hawkins, 1991). For example, in the Cambridge Study, the risk of conviction was high for males from large-sized families (with five or more children), but fairly constant over lower levels of family size. This is one reason for a discontinuous focus on the types of persons who are the extreme cases, rather than a continuous focus on the whole range of variation.

Another possible definition of a protective factor is a variable that interacts with a risk factor to minimize the risk factor's effects (Rutter, 1985). If low intelligence is related to offending only for males from low income families, and not for males from higher income families, then higher income might be regarded as a protective factor against the effects of the risk factor of low intelligence. Different types of people may vary considerably in their resilience in the face of stressors. It is usual to investigate protective factors by identifying a subsample at risk (with some combination of risk factors) and then searching for factors that predict successful members of this subsample (those who do not have the antisocial outcome). For example, high intelligence may be an important means of escape from a socioeconomically deprived background.

In Hawaii, Werner and Smith (1982) studied seventy-two children who possessed four or more risk factors for delinquency before age two but who nevertheless did not develop behavioral difficulties during childhood or adolescence. They found that the major protective factors included being first-born, being an active and affectionate infant, small family size, and receiving a large amount of attention from caretakers. Kandel and colleagues (1988) studied the sons of imprisoned fathers in a Danish birth cohort of nearly two thousand males born in Copenhagen, and found that those sons who avoided imprisonment had significantly higher intelligence than those imprisoned. Hence, they considered that high intelligence was a protective factor. In the Newcastle Thousand Family Study, Kolvin and colleagues (1988a) studied high-risk boys (from deprived backgrounds) who nevertheless did not become offenders. The major protective factors under age five seemed to be good mothering, good maternal health, an employed head of household, and being an oldest child. At ages eleven and fifteen, the most important protective factors were high intelligence, high school attainment, good concentration, good parental supervision, and membership in youth clubs.

In the Cambridge Study, Farrington and colleagues (1988a, 1988b) investigated vulnerable boys from typically criminogenic backgrounds (including at least three of these factors: low family income, large family size, a convicted parent, poor parental child rearing behavior, and low intelligence) who were not convicted up to age thirty-two. The most characteristic feature of these boys was that they had few or no friends at age eight. Although genuinely well-behaved at age thirty-two, they were often leading relatively unsuccessful lives, for example, living in dirty home conditions, alone, in rented quarters, never married, large debts, with low status, poorly paid jobs.

Therefore, for boys from vulnerable backgrounds, social isolation may act as a protective factor against offending but not against other kinds of social dysfunctioning. For adult social dysfunctioning in general, the most important protective factors for the vulnerable boys were the mother having a high opinion of the boy and the father not joining in the boy's leisure activities. If low intelligence had not been included in the definition of vulnerable backgrounds, it is likely that high intelligence would have emerged from these analyses as an important protective factor.

Implications for prevention

Causal factors

Methods of preventing or treating antisocial behavior should be based on empirically validated theories about causes. In this section, implications about prevention and treatment are drawn from some of the likely causes of antisocial behavior listed above. The major focus is on the prevention and treatment of offending. (For more extensive reviews of this topic, see Gordon & Arbuthnot, 1987; Kazdin, 1985; McCord & Tremblay, 1992.) The implications reviewed here are those for which there is some empirical justification, especially in randomized experiments. The effect of any intervention on delinquency can be demonstrated most convincingly in such experiments (Farrington, 1983; Farrington, Ohlin, & Wilson, 1986a).

It is difficult to know how and when it is best to intervene, because of the lack of knowledge about developmental sequences, ages at which causal factors are most salient, and influences on onset, continuation, and desistance. For example, if truancy leads to delinquency in a developmental sequence, intervening successfully to decrease truancy should lead to a decrease in delinquency. On the other hand, if truancy and delinquency are merely different behavioral manifestations of the same underlying construct, tackling one symptom would not necessarily change the underlying construct. Experiments are useful in distinguishing between developmental sequences and different manifestations, and Berg, Hullin, and McGuire (1979) found experimentally that decreases in truancy were followed by decreases in delinquency.

Causal factors may be more salient at some ages than others. For example, parental child rearing factors are likely to be most influential before the teenage years, so that the same intervention technique targeted on parents may be more effective for children aged eight than for those aged sixteen. Similarly, causal factors may have different effects on different stages of the criminal career. As an example, if delinquent peers affected continuation but not onset, an intervention technique targeted on peers should be applied after the criminal career has begun (as treatment) rather than before (as prevention).

It should be stated at the outset that many of the preventive effects are rather small in magnitude and have been demonstrated with small samples, and there is rarely evidence that they are sustained over several years. The intervention methods reviewed here often provide glimmers of hope rather than solid evidence of substantial reductive effects. This may be because, as Kazdin (1987) argued, chronic antisocial behavior tends to be persistent and long-lasting. He suggested that serious antisocial behavior might be viewed as a chronic disease that requires continuous monitoring and intervention over the life course. It might be desirable to distinguish chronic and less serious antisocial teenagers, and to apply different types of interventions to the two categories (LeBlanc & Frechette, 1989). If the chronics are the worst 5 percent, interventions applied to the next 10 percent may be more successful. Success may depend, however, on the extent to which risk factors specific to the next 10 percent can be identified.

Impulsivity

Impulsivity and other personality characteristics of offenders might be altered using the set of techniques variously termed cognitive-behavioral interpersonal skills training, which has proved to be quite successful (e.g., Michelson, 1987). For example, the methods used by Ross to treat juvenile delinquents (see Ross, Fabiano, & Ewles, 1988; Ross & Ross, 1988) are solidly based on some of the known individual characteristics of delinquents: impulsivity, concrete rather than abstract thinking, low empathy, and egocentricity.

Ross believes that delinquents can be taught the cognitive skills in which they are deficient, and that this can lead to a decrease in their offending. His reviews of delinquency rehabilitation programs (Gendreau & Ross, 1979, 1987) show that those which have been successful in reducing offending have generally tried to change the offender's thinking. Ross carried out his own "Reasoning and Rehabilitation" program in Canada, and found (in a randomized experiment) that it led to a significant decrease in reoffending for a small sample in a nine-month follow-up period. His training was carried out by probation officers, but he believes that it could be carried out by parents or teachers.

Ross's program aims to modify the impulsive, egocentric thinking of delinquents, to teach them to stop and think before acting, to consider the consequences of their behavior, to conceptualize alternative ways of solving interpersonal problems, and to consider the impact of their behavior on other people, especially their victims. It includes social skills training, lateral thinking (to teach creative problem solving), critical thinking (to teach logical reasoning), value education (to teach values and concern for others), assertiveness training (to teach nonaggressive, socially appropriate ways to obtain desired outcomes), negotiation skills training, interpersonal cognitive problem-solving (to teach thinking skills for solving interpersonal problems), social perspective training (to teach how to recognize and understand other people's feelings), role-playing and modeling (demonstration and practice of effective and acceptable interpersonal behavior).

Intelligence and attainment

If low intelligence and school failure are causes of offending, any program that leads to an increase in school success should lead to a decrease in offending. One of the most successful delinquency prevention programs was the Perry preschool project carried out in Michigan by Schweinhart and Weikart (1980). This was essentially a Head Start program targeted on disadvantaged black children, who were allocated (approximately at random) to experimental and control groups. The experimental children attended a daily preschool program, backed up by weekly home visits, usually lasting two years (covering ages three to four). The aim of the program was to provide intellectual stimulation, to increase cognitive abilities, and to improve later school achievement.

More than 120 children in the two groups were followed up to age fifteen, using teacher ratings, parent and youth interviews, and school records. As demonstrated in several other Head Start projects, the experimental group showed gains in intelligence that were rather short-lived. They were significantly better in elementary school motivation, however, school achievement at fourteen, teacher ratings of classroom behavior at six to nine, self-reports of classroom behavior at fifteen, and self-reports of offending at fifteen. Furthermore, a later follow-up of this sample by Berrueta-Clement and colleagues (1984) showed that, at age nineteen, the experimental group was more likely to be employed, more likely to have graduated from high school, more likely to have received college or vocational training, and less likely to have been arrested. The beneficial effects also persisted up to age twenty-seven (Schweinhart, Barnes, & Weikart, 1993). Hence, this preschool intellectual enrichment program led to decreases in school failure and to decreases in delinquency.

The Perry project is admittedly only one study based on relatively small numbers. Its results become more compelling, however, when viewed in the context of ten other similar American Head Start projects followed up by the Consortium for Longitudinal Studies (1983). With quite impressive consistency, all eleven studies showed that preschool intellectual enrichment programs had long-term beneficial effects on school success, especially in increasing the rate of high school graduation and deceasing the rate of special education placements. The Perry project was the only one to study offending, but the consistency of the school success results in all eleven projects suggests that the effects on offending might be replicable.

Family factors

If poor parental supervision and erratic child rearing behavior are causes of delinquency, it seems likely that parent training might succeed in reducing offending. Many different types of family therapy have been used (see e.g., Kazdin, 1987), but the behavioral parent training developed by Patterson (1982) in Oregon is one of the most hopeful approaches. His careful observations of parent-child interaction showed that parents of antisocial children were deficient in their methods of child rearing. These parents failed to tell their children how they were expected to behave, failed to monitor the behavior to ensure that it was desirable, and failed to enforce rules promptly and unambiguously with appropriate rewards and penalties. The parents of antisocial children used more punishment (such as scolding, shouting, or threatening), but failed to make it contingent on the child's behavior.

Patterson attempted to train these parents in effective child rearing methods, namely, noticing what a child is doing, monitoring behavior over long periods, clearly stating house rules, making rewards and punishments contingent on behavior, and negotiating disagreements so that conflicts and crises did not escalate. His treatment was shown to be effective in reducing child stealing and antisocial behavior over short periods in small-scale studies (Dishion, Patterson, & Kavanagh, 1992; Patterson, Chamberlain, & Reid, 1982; Patterson, Reid, & Dishion, 1992).

It is often useful to combine parent training with other types of interventions, as Kazdin and colleagues (1987) argued. In Montreal, Tremblay and colleagues (1991, 1992) identified about 250 disruptive boys at age six for a prevention experiment. Between the ages of seven and nine, the experimental group received training to foster social skills and self-control, while their parents were trained using Patterson's techniques. By age twelve, the experimental boys committed less burglary and theft, and were less likely to get drunk, than the controls. It is interesting that the differences in antisocial behavior between experimental and control boys increased as the follow-up progressed.

In Seattle, Hawkins, Von Cleve, and Catalano (1991; Hawkins et al., 1992b) combined parent training, teacher training, and skills training for children. About five hundred first grade children in twenty-one classes in eight schools were randomly assigned to experimental or control classes. The parents and teachers of the experimental children were trained to reinforce socially desirable behavior. The experimental boys proved to be significantly less aggressive in a follow-up than the control boys, and the experimental girls were significantly less self-destructive, anxious, and depressed than the control girls. By the fifth grade, the experimental children were less likely to have initiated delinquency and alcohol use. It might be expected that a combination of interventions might in general be more effective than a single technique, although combining interventions makes it harder to identify the active ingredient.

Peer influence

If having delinquent friends causes offending, then any program which reduces their influence or increases the influence of prosocial friends could have a reductive effect on offending. Several studies show that schoolchildren can be taught to resist peer influences that encourage smoking, drinking and marijuana use. (For detailed reviews of these programs, see Botvin, 1990; Hawkins, Catalano, & Miller, 1992a.) For example, Telch and colleagues (1982) in California employed older high school students, using modeling and guided practice, to teach younger ones to develop counterarguing skills to resist peer pressure to smoke. This approach was successful in decreasing smoking by the younger students, and similar results were reported by Botvin and Eng (1982) in New York City. Murray and colleagues (1984) in Minnesota used same-age peer leaders to teach students how to resist peer pressures to begin smoking, and Evans and colleagues (1981) in Houston used films.

Using high status peer leaders, alcohol and marijuana use can be reduced as well as smoking (e.g., Klepp, Halper, & Perry, 1986; McAlister et al., 1980). Botvin and colleagues (1984) in New York compared the application of a substance use prevention program by teachers and peer leaders. The program aimed to foster social skills and teach students ways of resisting peer pressure to use these substances. They found that peer leaders were effective in decreasing smoking, drunkenness, and marijuana use, but teachers were not. A large-scale meta-analysis of 143 substance use prevention programs by Tobler (1986) concluded that programs using peer leaders were the most effective in reducing smoking, drinking, and drug use. These techniques, designed to counter antisocial peer pressures, could also help to decrease offending.

Socioeconomic deprivation

If socioeconomic deprivation causes offending, then providing increased economic resources for the more deprived families should lead to a decrease in offending by their children. The major problem is to identify the active ingredient to be targeted. Low income, poor housing, and large family size are all interrelated, but the causal chain linking these factors with offending is unclear. Experiments are needed which target each of these factors separately. It seems likely that relative rather than absolute income, housing quality, and family size are important, since there have been great changes in recent years in the absolute values of these variables.

The most relevant studies are probably the income maintenance experiments carried out in the United States, which provided extra income for poor families. The only evaluation of the effect of income maintainance on children's behavior (Groeneveld, Short, & Thoits, 1979) did not, however, yield positive results. There were no significant differences between the experimental and control groups in the later official offending records of children who were aged nine to twelve at the time of the treatment. Nevertheless, there is some evidence that extra welfare benefits given to ex-prisoners can in some instances lead to a decrease in their offending (Rossi, Berk, & Lenihan, 1980). In light of the clear link between socioeconomic deprivation and antisocial behavior, it is surprising that more prevention experiments targeting this factor have not been conducted.

Situational factors

A number of crime prevention methods have been based on situational influences on crime. These methods are typically aimed at specific types of offenses and are designed to change the environment to decrease criminal opportunities (e.g., Clarke, 1983). They include increasing surveillance (e.g., by installing closed-circuit television cameras in subway stations), hardening targets (e.g., by replacing aluminum coin boxes by steel ones in public telephone kiosks), and managing the environment (e.g., by paying wages by check rather than by cash). These techniques proved effective in reducing crime in experimental and time series studies (Clarke, 1992).

The major difficulty with this approach is displacement. If some people have criminal tendencies, and if one outlet for these is blocked, they will seek other outlets, other types of crimes, other methods of committing crimes, other targets, and so on. Situational prevention is not likely to be effective with chronic offenders, and hence should be targeted on more opportunistic and less committed offenders. As Clarke (1983) pointed out, situational approaches also provoke fears of "big brother" forms of state control and of a fortress society in which frightened citizens scuttle from their fortified houses, in their fortified cars, to their fortified workplaces, avoiding contact with other citizens. Nevertheless, situational crime prevention is clearly an important approach which holds out the promise of decreasing offending.

As mentioned earlier, situational approaches are often linked to a rational decision-making theory of crime (e.g., Cornish & Clarke, 1986). If offending involves a rational decision in which the costs are weighed against the benefits, it might be deterred by increasing the costs of offending or by increasing the probability of costs (e.g., the risk of detection). Experimental and quasi-experimental research on drunken driving (e.g., Ross, Campbell, & Glass, 1970), driving with worn tires (e.g., Buikhuisen, 1974), and domestic violence (e.g., Sherman & Berk, 1984) suggests that adults can be deterred in this way. The attempt to deter juveniles in the "Scared Straight" program, however, by having adult prisoners tell them about the horrors of imprisonment, was not successful (e.g., Finckenauer,

1982; Lewis, 1983). Given the "macho" orientation of many young offenders, it may be that these warnings made offending seem riskier and hence more attractive.

Conclusions

A great deal has been learned in the last twenty years, particularly from longitudinal surveys, about the causes of offending and other types of antisocial behavior. Offenders differ significantly from nonoffenders in many respects, including impulsivity, intelligence, family background, peer influence, and socioeconomic deprivation. These differences are often present before, during, and after criminal careers. The precise causal chains that link these factors with antisocial behavior, and the ways in which these factors have independent or interactive effects, are not known, but it is clear that children at risk can be identified with reasonable accuracy. Researchers should focus especially on the small minority of individuals who are the most chronically antisocial and who account for a significant proportion of all types of antisocial acts.

It is plausible to suggest that there is an antisocial personality that arises in childhood and persists into adulthood, with numerous different behavioral manifestations, including offending. The Cambridge Study shows that the typical delinquent – a male property offender – tends to be born in a low income, large-size family and to have criminal parents. When he is young, his parents supervise him rather poorly, use harsh or erratic child rearing techniques, and are likely to be in conflict and to separate. He tends to have low intelligence and poor attainment at school, is troublesome, hyperactive and impulsive, and often truants. He tends to associate with delinquents.

After leaving school, the delinquent tends to have a record of low status jobs punctuated by periods of unemployment. His antisocial behavior tends to be versatile rather than specialized. He not only commits property offenses such as theft and burglary but also engages in violence, vandalism, drug use, excessive drinking, reckless driving, and sexual promiscuity. His likelihood of offending reaches a peak during his teenage years and then declines in his twenties, when he is likely to get married or cohabit with a woman.

There is continuity over time in antisocial behavior, but changes are also occurring. It has often been found that about half of a sample of antisocial children go on to become antisocial teenagers, and about half of antisocial teenagers go on to become antisocial adults. More research is needed on factors that vary within individuals and that predict these changes over time. Research is especially needed on changing behavioral manifestations and developmental sequences at different ages. More effort should be made to identify factors that protect vulnerable children from developing into antisocial teenagers.

Research is needed on methods of preventing and treating the antisocial personality syndrome. Some hopeful techniques were reviewed in the previous section, but the most that can be said about them is that they warrant large-scale testing. More systematic research is needed to establish with what samples and in what circumstances different techniques are optimally effective. Rather than targeting the most chronically antisocial individuals, it may be more effective to target the next most serious group. In order to advance knowledge about the causes, prevention, and treatment of delinquency, a new generation of longitudinal studies on offending and antisocial behavior is needed, including testing of the effects of experimental interventions on the natural history of delinquency and crime (see Farrington, 1988a; Farrington et al., 1986a; Tonry, Ohlin, & Farrington, 1991).

Because of the link between delinquency and numerous other social problems, any measure that succeeds in reducing delinquency will have benefits that go far beyond this. Any measure that reduces delinquency will probably also reduce alcohol abuse, drunk driving, drug abuse, sexual promiscuity, family violence, truancy, school failure, unemployment, marital disharmony, and divorce. It is clear that problem children tend to grow up into problem adults, and that problem adults tend to produce more problem children. Major efforts to reduce antisocial tendency and delinquency are urgently needed.

References

Achenbach, T. M., & Edelbrock, C. S. (1983). *Manual of the Child Behavior Checklist and Revised Child Behavior Profile*. Burlington, Vermont: University of Vermont Department of Psychiatry.

Achenbach, T. M., & Edelbrock, C. S. (1984). Psychopathology of childhood. *Annual Review of Psychology*, 35, 227–56.

Achenbach, T. M., Verhulst, F. C., Baron, G. D., & Althaus, M. (1987). A comparison of syndromes derived from the child behavior checklist for American and Dutch boys aged 6–11 and 12–16. *Journal of Child Psychology and Psychiatry*, 28, 437–53.

Agnew, R. (1991). The interactive effects of peer variables on delinquency. *Criminology*, 29, 47–72.

Amdur, R. L. (1989). Testing causal models of delinquency: A methodological critique. *Criminal Justice and Behavior*, 16, 35–62.

American Psychiatric Association (1987). *Diagnostic and Statistical Manual of Mental Disorders*, 3d ed., revised. Washington, DC: American Psychiatric Association.

Bachman, J. G., O'Malley, P. M., & Johnston, J. (1978). *Youth in Transition*, Vol. 6. Ann Arbor, Mich.: University of Michigan Institute for Social Research.

Barclay, G. C. (1990). The peak age of known offending by males. *Home Office Research Bulletin*, 28, 20–3.

Barkley, R. A., Fischer, M., Edelbrock, C. S., & Smallish, L. (1990).The adolescent outcome of hyperactive children diagnosed by research criteria. I. An 8-year prospective follow-up study. *Journal of the American Academy of Child and Adolescent Psychiatry*, 29, 546–57.

Bates, J. E., Bayles, K., Bennett, D. S., Ridge, B., & Brown, M. M. (1991). Origins of externalizing behavior problems at 8 years of age. In *The Development and Treatment of Childhood Aggression*, ed. D. J. Pepler & K. H. Rubin, pp. 93–120. Hillsdale, N.J.: Erlbaum.

Berg, I., Hullin, R., & McGuire, R. (1979). A randomly controlled trial of two court procedures in truancy. In *Psychology, Law and Legal Processes*, ed. D. P. Farrington, K. Hawkins & S. Lloyd-Bostock, pp.143–51. London: Macmillan.

Berrueta-Clement, J. R., Schweinhart, L. J., Barnett, W. S., Epstein, A. S., & Weikart, D.P. (1984). *Changed Lives*. Ypsilanti, Mich.: High/Scope.

Blouin, A. G., Conners, C. K., Seidel, W. T., & Blouin, J. (1989). The independence of hyperactivity from conduct disorder: Methodological considerations. *Canadian Journal of Psychiatry*, 34, 279–82.

Blum, H. M., Boyle, M. H., & Offord, D. R. (1988). Single-parent families: Child psychiatric disorder and school performance. *Journal of the American Academy of Child and Adolescent Psychiatry*, 27, 214–9.

Blumstein, A., & Cohen, J. (1987). Characterizing criminal careers. *Science*, 237, 985–91.

Blumstein, A., Cohen, J., Roth, J. A., & Visher, C. A. (eds.) (1986). *Criminal Careers and "Career Criminals."* Washington, DC: National Academy Press.

Botvin, G.J. (1990). Substance abuse prevention: Theory, practice and effectiveness. In *Drugs and Crime*, ed. M. Tonry & J.Q. Wilson, pp. 461–519. Chicago: University of Chicago Press.

Botvin, G.J., Baker, E., Renick, N.L., Filazzola, A.D. & Botvin, E.M. (1984). A cognitive-behavioral approach to substance abuse prevention. *Addictive Behaviors*, 9, 137–47.

Botvin, G. J., & Eng. A. (1982). The efficacy of a multicomponent approach to the prevention of cigarette smoking. *Preventive Medicine*, 11, 199–211.

Boyle, M. H., & Offord, D. R. (1986). Smoking, drinking and use of illicit drugs among adolescents in Ontario: Prevalence, patterns of use and socio-demographic correlates. *Canadian Medical Association Journal*, 135, 1113–21.

Buikhuisen, W. (1974). General deterrence: Research and theory. *Abstracts in Criminology and Penology*, 14, 285–98.

Clarke, R. V. (ed.) (1992). *Situational Crime Prevention*. New York: Harrow and Heston.

(1983). Situational crime prevention: Its theoretical basis and practical scope. In *Crime and Justice*, Vol. 4, ed. M. Tonry & N. Morris, pp. 225–56. Chicago: University of Chicago Press.

Clarke, R. V., & Cornish, D. B. (1985). Modeling offenders' decisions: A framework for research and policy. In *Crime and Justice*, Vol. 6, ed. M. Tonry & N. Morris, pp.147–85. Chicago: University of Chicago Press.

Cloward, R. A., & Ohlin, L. E. (1960). *Delinquency and Opportunity*. New York: Free Press.

Cohen, A. K. (1955). *Delinquent Boys*, Glencoe, Ill.: Free Press.

Consortium for Longitudinal Studies (1983). *As the Twig is Bent...Lasting Effects of Pre-School Programs*. Hillsdale, N.J.: Erlbaum.

Cornish, D. B., & Clarke, R. V. (eds.) (1986). *The Reasoning Criminal*. New York: Springer-Verlag.

Craig, M. M., & Glick, S. J. (1968). School behavior related to later delinquency and non-delinquency. *Criminologica*, 5, 17–27.

Dishion, T. J., Patterson, G. R., & Kavanagh, K. A. (1992). An experimental test of the coercion model: Linking theory, measurement and intervention. In *Preventing Antisocial Behavior*, ed. J. McCord & R. Tremblay, pp. 253–82. New York: Guilford.

Donovan, J. E., Jessor, R., & Costa, F. M. (1988). Syndrome of problem behavior in adolescence: A replication. *Journal of Consulting and Clinical Psychology*, 56, 762–5.

Douglas, J. W. B., Ross, J. M., Hammond, W. A., & Mulligan, D. G. (1966). Delinquency and social class. *British Journal of Criminology*, 6, 294–302.

Edelbrock, C., & Costello, A. J. (1988). Convergence between statistically derived behavior problem syndromes and child psychiatric diagnoses. *Journal of Abnormal Child Psychology*, 16, 219–31.

Elliott, D. S., Huizinga, D., & Ageton, S. S. (1985). *Explaining Delinquency and Drug Use*. Beverly Hills, Calif.: Sage.

Elliott, D. S., Huizinga, D., & Menard, S. (1989). *Multiple Problem Youth*. New York: Springer-Verlag.

Elliott, D. S., & Menard, S. (1988). *Delinquent Behavior and Delinquent Peers: Temporal and Developmental Patterns*. Unpublished manuscript.

Ensminger, M. E., Kellam, S. G., & Rubin, B. R. (1983). School and family origins of delinquency. In *Prospective Studies of Crime and Delinquency*, ed. K.T. Van Dusen & S.A. Mednick, pp. 73–97. Boston: Kluwer-Nijhoff.

Erickson, M., Gibbs, J. P., & Jensen, G. F. (1977). The deterrence doctrine and the perceived certainty of legal punishment. *American Sociological Review*, 42, 305–17.

Eron, L. D., & Huesmann, L. R. (1990). The stability of aggressive behavior – even unto the third generation. In *Handbook of Developmental Psychopathology*, ed. M. Lewis & S.M. Miller, pp. 147–156. New York: Plenum.

Evans, R. I., Rozelle, R. M., Maxwell, S. E., Raines, B. E., Dill, C. A., Guthrie, T. J., Henderson, A. H., & Hill, P. C. (1981). Social modeling films to deter smoking in adolescents: Results of a three-year field investigation. *Journal of Applied Psychology*, 66, 399–414.

Farrington, D. P. (1973). Self-reports of deviant behavior: Predictive and stable? *Journal of Criminal Law and Criminology*, 64, 99–110.

(1978). The family backgrounds of aggressive youths. In *Aggression and Antisocial Behaviour in Childhood and Adolescence*, ed. L. Hersov, M. Berger, & D. Shaffer, pp. 73–93. Oxford: Pergamon.

(1980). Truancy, delinquency, the home and the school. In *Out of School: Modern Perspectives in Truancy and School Refusal*, ed. L. Hersov & I. Berg, pp. 49–63. Chichester: Wiley.

(1983). Randomized experiments on crime and justice. In *Crime and Justice*, Vol. 4, ed. M. Tonry & N. Morris, pp. 257–308. Chicago: University of Chicago Press.

(1986a). Age and crime. In *Crime and Justice*, Vol. 7, ed. M. Tonry & N. Morris, pp.189–250. Chicago: University of Chicago Press.

(1986b). Stepping stones to adult criminal careers. In *Development of Antisocial and Prosocial Behavior*, ed. D. Olweus, J. Block, & M. R. Yarrow, pp. 359–84. New York: Academic Press.

(1987). Implications of biological findings for criminological research. In *The Causes of Crime: New Biological Approaches*, ed. S. A. Mednick, T. E. Moffitt, & S. A. Stack, pp. 42–64. Cambridge: Cambridge University Press.

(1988a). Advancing knowledge about delinquency and crime: The need for a coordinated program of longitudinal research. *Behavioral Sciences and the Law*, 6, 307–31.

(1988b). Studying changes within individuals: The causes of offending. In *Studies of Psychosocial Risk*, ed. M. Rutter, pp. 158–83. Cambridge: Cambridge University Press.

(1989a). Early predictors of adolescent aggression and adult violence. *Violence and Victims*, 4, 79–100.

(1989b). Later adult life outcomes of offenders and non-offenders. In *Children at Risk: Assessment, Longitudinal Research, and Intervention*, ed. M. Brambring, F. Losel, & H. Skowronek, pp. 220–44. Berlin: De Gruyter.

(1989c). Self-reported and official offending from adolescence to adulthood. In *Cross-National Research in Self-Reported Crime and Delinquency*, ed. M. W. Klein, pp. 399–423. Dordrecht, Netherlands: Kluwer.

(1990a). Age, period, cohort, and offending. In *Policy and Theory in Criminal Justice: Contributions in Honour of Leslie T. Wilkins*, ed. D. M. Gottfredson & R. V. Clarke, pp. 51–75. Aldershot: Avebury.

(1990b). Implications of criminal career research for the prevention of offending. *Journal of Adolescence*, 13, 93–113.

(1991a). Antisocial personality from childhood to adulthood. *The Psychologist*, 4, 389–94.

(1991b). Childhood aggression and adult violence: Early precursors and later life outcomes. In *The Development and Treatment of Childhood Aggression*, ed. D. J. Pepler & K. H. Rubin, pp. 5–29. Hillsdale, N.J.: Erlbaum.

(1992a). Criminal career research in the United Kingdom. *British Journal of Criminology*, 32, 521–36.

(1992b). Explaining the beginning, progress and ending of antisocial behavior from birth to adulthood. In *Facts, Frameworks and Forecasts: Advances in Criminological Theory*, Vol. 3, ed. J. McCord, pp. 253–86. New Brunswick, N.J.: Transaction.

(1992c). Juvenile delinquency. In *The School Years*, 2d ed., ed. J. C. Coleman, pp. 123–63. London: Routledge.

(1993a). Childhood origins of teenage antisocial behaviour and adult social dysfunction. *Journal of the Royal Society of Medicine*, 86, 13–7.

(1993b). Motivations for conduct disorder and delinquency. *Development and Psychopathology*, 5, 225–41.

(1993c). Understanding and preventing bullying. In *Crime and Justice*, Vol. 17, ed. M. Tonry, pp. 381–458. Chicago: University of Chicago Press.

(1994). Childhood, adolescent and adult features of violent males. In *Aggressive Behavior: Current Perspectives*, ed. L. R. Huesmann, pp. 215-40. New York: Plenum.

Farrington, D. P., and Burrows, J. N. (1993). Did shoplifting really decrease? *British Journal of Criminology*, 33, 57–69.

Farrington, D. P., Gallagher, B., Morley, L., St Ledger, R. J., & West, D. J. (1986b). Unemployment, school leaving, and crime. *British Journal of Criminology*, 26, 335–56.

Farrington, D. P., Gallagher, B., Morley, L., St Ledger, R. J., & West, D. J. (1988a). A 24-year follow-up of men from vulnerable backgrounds. In *The Abandonment of*

Delinquent Behavior, ed. R. L. Jenkins & W. K. Brown, pp.155–73. New York: Praeger.
Farrington, D. P., Gallagher, B., Morley, L., St Ledger, R. J., & West, D. J. (1988b). Are there any successful men from criminogenic backgrounds? *Psychiatry*, 51, 116–30.
Farrington, D. P., & Hawkins, J. D. (1991). Predicting participation, early onset, and later persistence in officially recorded offending. *Criminal Behaviour and Mental Health*, 1, 1–33.
Farrington, D. P., & Knight, B. J. (1980). Four studies of stealing as a risky decision. In *New Directions in Psycholegal Research*, ed. P.D. Lipsitt & B.D. Sales, pp. 26–50. New York: Van Nostrand Reinhold.
Farrington, D. P., Loeber, R., Elliott, D. S., Hawkins, J. D., Kandel, D. B., Klein, M. W., McCord, J., Rowe, D. C., & Tremblay, R. E. (1990a). Advancing knowledge about the onset of delinquency and crime. In *Advances in Clinical Child Psychology*, Vol. 13, ed. B.B. Lahey & A.E. Kazdin, pp. 283–342. New York: Plenum.
Farrington, D. P., Loeber, R., & Van Kammen, W. B. (1990b). Long-term criminal outcomes of hyperactivity-impulsivity-attention deficit and conduct problems in childhood. In *Straight and Devious Pathways From Childhood to Adulthood*, ed. L.N. Robins & M. Rutter, pp. 62–81. Cambridge: Cambridge University Press.
Farrington, D. P., Ohlin, L. E., & Wilson, J. Q. (1986a). *Understanding and Controlling Crime*. New York: Springer-Verlag.
Farrington, D. P., Snyder, H. N., & Finnegan, T. A. (1988c). Specialization in juvenile court careers. *Criminology*, 26, 461–87.
Farrington, D. P., & West, D. J. (1990). The Cambridge study in delinquent development: A long-term follow-up of 411 London males. In *Criminality: Personality, Behaviour, Life History*, ed. H-J. Kerner & G. Kaiser, pp. 115–38. Berlin: Springer-Verlag.
Farrington, D. P., & West, D. J. (1993). Criminal, penal and life histories of chronic offenders: Risk and protective factors and early identification. *Criminal Behaviour and Mental Health*, 3, 492–523.
Farrington, D. P., & Wikstrom, P-O. H. (1994). Criminal careers in London and Stockholm: A cross-national comparative study. In *Cross-National Longitudinal Research on Human Development and Criminal Behavior*, ed. E. G. M. Weitekamp & H-J. Kerner, pp. 65–89. Dordrecht, Netherlands: Kluwer.
Finckenauer, J. O. (1982). *Scared Straight*. Englewood Cliffs, N.J.: Prentice-Hall.
Gendreau, P., & Ross, R. R. (1979). Effective correctional treatment: Bibliotherapy for cynics. *Crime and Delinquency*, 25, 463–89.
Gendreau, P., & Ross, R. R. (1987). Revivification of rehabilitation: Evidence from the 1980s. *Justice Quarterly*, 4, 349–407.
Ghodsian, M., & Power, C. (1987). Alcohol consumption between the ages of 16 and 23 in Britain: A longitudinal study. *British Journal of Addiction*, 82, 175–80.
Gittelman, R., Mannuzza, S., Shenker, R., & Bonagura, N. (1985). Hyperactive boys almost grown up. *Archives of General Psychiatry*, 42, 937–47.
Gordon, D. A., & Arbuthnot, J. (1987). Individual, group and family interventions. In *Handbook of Juvenile Delinquency*, ed. H. C. Quay, pp. 290–324. New York: Wiley.
Gottfredson, M., & Hirschi, T. (1990). *A General Theory of Crime*. Stanford, Calif.: Stanford University Press.
Groeneveld, L. P., Short, J. F., & Thoits, P. (1979). *Design of a Study to Assess the Impact of Income Maintenance on Delinquency*. Final Report to the National Institute of Juvenile Justice and Delinquency Prevention, Washington, DC.

Hartup, W. W. (1983). Peer relations. In *Handbook of Child Psychology*, Vol. 4, ed. P. H. Mussen, pp. 103–96. Toronto: Wiley.

Hawkins, J. D., Catalano, R. F., & Miller, J. Y. (1992a). Risk and protective factors for alcohol and other drug problems in adolescence and early adulthood: Implications for substance use prevention. *Psychological Bulletin*, 112, 64–105.

Hawkins, J. D., Catalano, R. F., Morrison, D. M., O'Donnell, J., Abbott, R. D., & Day, L. E. (1992b). The Seattle social development project: Effects of the first four years on protective factors and problem behaviors. In *Preventing Antisocial Behavior*, ed. J. McCord & R. Tremblay, pp. 139–61. New York: Guilford.

Hawkins, J.D., Von Cleve, E. & Catalano, R.F. (1991). Reducing early childhood aggression: Results of a primary prevention program. *Journal of the American Academy of Child and Adolescent Psychiatry*, 30, 208–17.

Hindelang, M. J., Hirschi, T., & Weis, J.G. (1981). *Measuring Delinquency*. Beverly Hills, California: Sage.

Hirschi, T. (1969). *Causes of Delinquency*. Berkeley, California: University of California Press.

Huessy, H. R., & Howell, D. C. (1985). Relationships between adult and childhood behaviour disorders. *Psychiatric Journal of the University of Ottawa*, 10, 114–9.

Huizinga, D., & Elliott, D. S. (1986). Reassessing the reliability and validity of self-report measures. *Journal of Quantitative Criminology*, 2, 293–327.

Jessor, R., & Jessor, S. L. (1977). *Problem Behavior and Psychosocial Development*. New York: Academic Press.

Johnson, V., & Pandina, R. J. (1991). Effects of the family environment on adolescent substance use, delinquency and coping styles. *American Journal of Drug and Alcohol Abuse*, 17, 71–88.

Jones, M.B., Offord, D.R. & Abrams, N. (1980). Brothers, sisters and antisocial behaviour. *British Journal of Psychiatry*, 136, 139–45.

Kandel, E., Mednick, S. A., Kirkegaard-Sorenson, L., Hutchings, B., Knop, J., Rosenberg, R., & Schulsinger, F. (1988). IQ as a protective factor for subjects at high risk for antisocial behavior. *Journal of Consulting and Clinical Psychology*, 56, 224–26.

Kazdin, A. E. (1985). *Treatment of Antisocial Behavior in Children and Adolescents*. Homewood, Ill.: Dorsey Press.

(1987). Treatment of antisocial behavior in children: Current status and future directions. *Psychological Bulletin*, 102, 187–203.

Kazdin, A. E., Esveldt-Dawson, K., French, N. H., & Unis, A. S. (1987). Effects of parent management training and problem-solving skills training combined in the treatment of antisocial child behavior. *Journal of the American Academy of Child and Adolescent Psychiatry*, 26, 416–24.

Klein, M. W. (1984). Offence specialization and versatility among juveniles. *British Journal of Criminology*, 24, 185–94.

Klepp, K-I., Halper, A., & Perry, C. L. (1986). The efficacy of peer leaders in drug abuse prevention. *Journal of School Health*, 56, 407–11.

Kolvin, I., Miller, F. J. W., Fleeting, M., & Kolvin, P. A. (1988a). Risk/protective factors for offending with particular reference to deprivation. In *Studies of Psychosocial Risk*, ed. M. Rutter, pp. 77–95. Cambridge: Cambridge University Press.

Kolvin, I., Miller, F. J. W., Fleeting, M., & Kolvin, P. A. (1988b). Social and parenting factors affecting criminal-offence rates: Findings from the Newcastle Thousand Family Study (1947–1980). *British Journal of Psychiatry*, 152, 80–90.

Kolvin, I., Miller, F. J. W., Scott, D. M., Gatzanis, S. R. M., & Fleeting, M. (1990). *Continuities of Deprivation*? Aldershot: Avebury.

LeBlanc, M., & Frechette, M. (1989). *Male Criminal Activity From Childhood Through Youth*. New York: Springer-Verlag.

Lewis, R. V. (1983). Scared straight – California style. *Criminal Justice and Behavior*, 10, 209–26.

Loeber, R. (1987). Behavioral precursors and accelerators of delinquency. In *Explaining Criminal Behavior*, ed. W. Buikhuisen & S. A. Mednick, pp. 51–67. Leiden, Netherlands: Brill.

(1988). Natural histories of conduct problems, delinquency and associated substance use: Evidence for developmental progressions. In *Advances in Clinical Child Psychology*, Vol. 11, ed. B. B. Lahey & A. E. Kazdin, pp. 73–124. New York: Plenum.

Loeber, R., & Dishion, T. (1983). Early predictors of male delinquency: A review. *Psychological Bulletin*, 94, 68–99.

Loeber, R., Green, S. M., Lahey, B. B., Christ, M. A. G., & Frick, P. J.(1992). Developmental sequences in the age of onset of disruptive child behaviors. *Journal of Child and Family Studies*, 1, 21–41.

Loeber, R., & LeBlanc, M. (1990). Toward a developmental criminology. In *Crime and Justice*, Vol. 12, ed. M. Tonry & N. Morris, pp. 375–473. Chicago: University of Chicago Press.

Loeber, R., & Schmaling, K. B. (1985). Empirical evidence for overt and covert patterns of antisocial conduct problems. *Journal of Abnormal Child Psychology*, 13, 337–52.

Loeber, R., & Stouthamer-Loeber, M. (1986). Family factors as correlates and predictors of juvenile conduct problems and delinquency. In *Crime and Justice*, Vol. 7, ed. M. Tonry & N. Morris, pp. 29–149. Chicago: University of Chicago Press.

Loeber, R., & Stouthamer-Loeber, M. (1987). Prediction. In *Handbook of Juvenile Delinquency*, ed. H. C. Quay, pp. 325–82. New York: Wiley.

Loeber, R., Stouthamer-Loeber, M., Van Kammen, W. B., & Farrington, D. P. (1989). Development of a new measure of self-reported antisocial behavior for young children: Prevalence and reliability. In *Cross-National Research in Self-Reported Crime and Delinquency*, ed. M.W. Klein, pp. 203–25. Dordrecht, Netherlands: Kluwer.

Loeber, R., Stouthamer-Loeber, M., Van Kammen, W. B., & Farrington, D. P. (1991). Initiation, escalation and desistance in juvenile offending and their correlates. *Journal of Criminal Law and Criminology*, 82, 36–82.

Magnusson, D. (1988). *Individual Development From an Interactional Perspective*. Hillsdale, N.J.: Erlbaum.

Magnusson, D., & Bergman, L. R. (1988). Individual and variable-based approaches to longitudinal research on early risk factors. In *Studies of Psychosocial Risk*, ed. M. Rutter, pp. 45–61. Cambridge: Cambridge University Press.

Mannuzza, S., Klein, R. G., Bonagura, N., Malloy, P., Giampino, T. L., & Addalli, K. A. (1991). Hyperactive boys almost grown up. V. Replication of psychiatric status. *Archives of General Psychiatry*, 48, 77–83.

Mawson, A. R. (1987). *Transient Criminality*. New York: Praeger.

McAlister, A., Perry, C., Killen, J., Slinkard, L. A., & Maccoby, N. (1980). Pilot study of smoking, alcohol and drug abuse prevention. *American Journal of Public Health*, 70, 719–21.

McCord, J. (1977). A comparative study of two generations of native Americans. In *Theory in Criminology*, ed. R. F. Meier, pp. 83–92. Beverly Hills, Calif.: Sage.

(1979). Some child-rearing antecedents of criminal behavior in adult men. *Journal of Personality and Social Psychology*, 37, 1477–86.

(1982). A longitudinal view of the relationship between paternal absence and crime. In *Abnormal Offenders, Delinquency, and the Criminal Justice System*, ed. J. Gunn & D. P. Farrington, pp. 113–28. Chichester: Wiley.

McCord, J., & Tremblay, R. E. (eds.) (1992). *Preventing Antisocial Behavior*. New York: Guilford.

McGee, R., Williams, S., & Silva, P. A. (1985). Factor structure and correlates of ratings of inattention, hyperactivity and antisocial behavior in a large sample of 9-year-old children from the general population. *Journal of Consulting and Clinical Psychology*, 53, 480–90.

Michelson, L. (1987). Cognitive-behavioral strategies in the prevention and treatment of antisocial disorders in children and adolescents. In *Prevention of Delinquent Behavior*, ed. J. D. Burchard & S. N. Burchard, pp. 275–310. Beverly Hills, Calif.: Sage.

Moffitt, T. E. (1990). The neuropsychology of juvenile delinquency: A critical review. In *Crime and Justice*, Vol. 12, ed. M. Tonry & N. Morris, pp. 99–169. Chicago: University of Chicago Press.

Moffitt, T. E., & Henry, B. (1989). Neuropsychological assessment of executive functions in self-reported delinquents. *Development and Psychopathology*, 1, 105–18.

Moffitt, T. E., & Silva, P. A. (1988a). IQ and delinquency: A direct test of the differential detection hypothesis. *Journal of Abnormal Psychology*, 97, 330–3.

Moffitt, T. E., & Silva, P. A. (1988b). Neuropsychological deficit and self-reported delinquency in an unselected birth cohort. *Journal of the American Academy of Child and Adolescent Psychiatry*, 27, 233–40.

Morash, M., & Rucker, L. (1989). An exploratory study of the connection of mother's age at childbearing to her children's delinquency in four data sets. *Crime and Delinquency*, 35, 45–93.

Mueller, C. W., & Parcel, T. L. (1981). Measures of socio-economic status: Alternatives and recommendations. *Child Development*, 52, 13–30.

Murray, D. M., Luepker, R. V., Johnson, C. A., & Mittelmark, M. B. (1984). The prevention of cigarette smoking in children: A comparison of four strategies. *Journal of Applied Social Psychology*, 14, 274–88.

Nylander, I. (1979). A 20-year prospective follow-up study of 2,164 cases at the child guidance clinics in Stockholm. *Acta Paediatrica Scandinavica*, supplement 276.

Offord, D. R., Alder, R. J., & Boyle, M. H. (1986). Prevalence and sociodemographic correlates of conduct disorder. *American Journal of Social Psychiatry*, 6, 272–8.

Offord, D. R., Boyle, M. H., & Racine, Y. (1989). Ontario Child Health Study: Correlates of disorder. *Journal of the American Academy of Child and Adolescent Psychiatry*, 28, 856–60.

Olweus, D. (1987). Testosterone and adrenaline: Aggressive antisocial behavior in normal adolescent males. In *The Causes of Crime: New Biological Approaches*, ed. S.A. Mednick, T.E. Moffitt, & S.A. Stack, pp. 263–82. Cambridge: Cambridge University Press.

Ouston, J. (1984). Delinquency, family background, and educational attainment. *British Journal of Criminology*, 24, 2–26.

Parker, J. G., & Asher, S. R. (1987). Peer relations and later personal adjustment: Are low accepted children at risk? *Psychological Bulletin*, 102, 357–89.

Patterson, G. R. (1982). *Coercive Family Process*. Eugene, Ore.: Castalia.

Patterson, G. R., Chamberlain, P., & Reid, J. B. (1982). A comparative evaluation of a parent training program. *Behavior Therapy*, 13, 638–50.

Patterson, G. R., Reid, J. B., & Dishion, T. J. (1992). *Antisocial Boys*. Eugene, Ore.: Castalia.

Pulkkinen, L. (1988). Delinquent development: Theoretical and empirical considerations. In *Studies of Psychosocial Risk*, ed. M. Rutter, pp. 184–99. Cambridge: Cambridge University Press.

Rae-Grant, N., Thomas, B. H., Offord, D. R., & Boyle, M. H. (1989). Risk, protective factors, and the prevalence of behavioral and emotional disorders in children and adolescents. *Journal of the American Academy of Child and Adolescent Psychiatry*, 28, 262–8.

Reiss, A. J. (1988). Co-offending and criminal careers. In *Crime and Justice*, Vol. 10, ed. M. Tonry & N. Morris, pp. 117–70. Chicago: University of Chicago Press.

Reiss, A. J., and Farrington, D. P. (1991). Advancing knowledge about co-offending: Results from a prospective longitudinal survey of London males. *Journal of Criminal Law and Criminology*, 82, 360–95.

Reitsma-Street, M., Offord, D. R., & Finch, T. (1985). Pairs of same-sexed siblings discordant for antisocial behaviour. *British Journal of Psychiatry*, 146, 415–23.

Richman, N., Stevenson, J., & Graham, P. (1985). Sex differences in the outcome of pre-school behaviour problems. In *Longitudinal Studies in Child Psychology and Psychiatry*, ed. A.R. Nicol, pp. 75–89. Chichester: Wiley.

Riley, D., & Shaw, M. (1985). *Parental Supervision and Juvenile Delinquency*. London: Her Majesty's Stationery Office.

Robins, L. N. (1979). Sturdy childhood predictors of adult outcomes: Replications from longitudinal studies. In *Stress and Mental Disorder*, ed. J. E. Barrett, R. M. Rose & G. L. Klerman, pp. 219–35. New York: Raven Press.

(1986). Changes in conduct disorder over time. In *Risk in Intellectual and Social Development*, ed. D.C. Farran & J.D. McKinney, pp. 227–59. New York: Academic Press.

(1991). Conduct disorder. *Journal of Child Psychology and Psychiatry*, 32, 193–212.

Robins, L. N., & Ratcliff, K. S. (1978). Risk factors in the continuation of childhood antisocial behavior into adulthood. *International Journal of Mental Health*, 7, 96–116.

Robins, L. N., & Ratcliff, K. S. (1980). Childhood conduct disorders and later arrest. In *The Social Consequences of Psychiatric Illness*, ed. L. N. Robins, P. J. Clayton & J. K. Wing, pp. 248–63. New York: Brunner/Mazel.

Robins, L. N., Tipp, J., & Przybeck, T. (1991). Antisocial personality. In *Psychiatric Disorders in America*, ed. L. N. Robins & D. Regier, pp. 259–90. New York: Macmillan/Free Press.

Robins, L. N., West, P. J., & Herjanic B. L. (1975). Arrests and delinquency in two generations: A study of black urban families and their children. *Journal of Child Psychology and Psychiatry*, 16, 125–40.

Robins, L. N., & Wish, E. (1977). Childhood deviance as a developmental process: A study of 223 urban black men from birth to 18. *Social Forces*, 56, 448–73.

Roff, J. D., & Wirt, R. D. (1984). Childhood aggression and social adjustment as antecedents of delinquency. *Journal of Abnormal Child Psychology*, 12, 111–26.

Rose, S. L., Rose, S. A., & Feldman, J. F. (1989). Stability of behavior problems in very young children. *Development and Psychopathology*, 1, 5–19.

Ross, H. L., Campbell, D. T., & Glass, G. V. (1970). Determining the social effects of a legal reform: The British breathalyzer crackdown of 1967. *American Behavioral Scientist*, 13, 493–509.

Ross, R. R., Fabiano, E. A., & Ewles, C. D. (1988). Reasoning and rehabilitation. *International Journal of Offender Therapy and Comparative Criminology*, 32, 29–35.

Ross, R. R., & Ross, B. D. (1988). Delinquency prevention through cognitive training. *New Education*, 10, 70–5.

Rossi, P. H., Berk, R. A., & Lenihan, K. J. (1980). *Money, Work and Crime*. New York: Academic Press.

Rutter, M. (1979). *Changing Youth in a Changing Society*. London: Nuffield Provincial Hospitals Trust.

(1985). Resilience in the face of adversity: Protective factors and resistance to psychiatric disorder. *British Journal of Psychiatry*, 147, 598–611.

(1989a). Age as an ambiguous variable in developmental research: Some epidemiological considerations from developmental psychopathology. *International Journal of Behavioral Development*, 12, 1–34.

(1989b). Psychosocial risk trajectories and beneficial turning points. In *Early Influences Shaping the Individual*, ed. S. Doxiadis, pp. 229–39. New York: Plenum.

Rutter, M., & Giller, H. (1983). *Juvenile Delinquency: Trends and Perspectives*. Harmondsworth: Penguin.

Rutter, M., Tizard, J., & Whitmore, K. (1970). *Education, Health and Behaviour*. London: Longman.

Satterfield, J. H. (1987). Childhood diagnostic and neurophysiological predictors of teenage arrest rates: An 8-year prospective study. In *The Causes of Crime: New Biological Approaches*, ed. S. A. Mednick, T. E. Moffitt & S. A. Stack, pp.146–67. Cambridge: Cambridge University Press.

Schweinhart, L. J., Barnes, H. V., & Weikart, D. P. (1993). *Significant Benefits*. Ypsilanti, Mich.: High/Scope.

Schweinhart, L. J., & Weikart, D. P. (1980). *Young Children Grow Up*. Ypsilanti, Mich.: High/Scope.

Shedler, J., & Block, J. (1990). Adolescent drug use and psychological health. *American Psychologist*, 45, 612–30.

Shepherd, M., Oppenheim, B., & Mitchell, S. (1971). *Childhood Behaviour and Mental Health*. London: University of London Press.

Sherman, L. W., & Berk, R. A. (1984). The specific deterrent effects of arrest for domestic assault. *American Sociological Review*, 49, 261–72.

Short, J. F., & Nye, F. I. (1957). Reported behavior as a criterion of deviant behavior. *Social Problems*, 5, 207–13.

Spivack, G., Marcus, J., & Swift, M. (1986). Early classroom behaviors and later misconduct. *Developmental Psychology*, 22, 124–31.

Sutherland, E. H., & Cressey D. R. (1974). *Criminology*, 9th ed. Philadelphia: Lippincott.

Taylor, E. A. (1986). Childhood hyperactivity. *British Journal of Psychiatry*, 149, 562–73.

Telch, M. J., Killen, J. D., McAlister, A. L., Perry, C. L., & Maccoby, N. (1982). Long-term follow-up of a pilot project on smoking prevention with adolescents. *Journal of Behavioral Medicine*, 5, 1–8.

Thornberry, T. P., & Farnworth, M. (1982). Social correlates of criminal involvement: Further evidence on the relationship between social status and criminal behavior. *American Sociological Review*, 47, 505–18.

Tobler, N. S. (1986). Meta-analysis of 143 drug treatment programs: Quantitative outcome results of program participants compared to a control or comparison group. *Journal of Drug Issues*, 16, 537–67.

Tonry, M., Ohlin, L. E., & Farrington, D. P. (1991). *Human Development and Criminal Behavior*. New York: Springer-Verlag.

Trasler, G. B. (1962). *The Explanation of Criminality*. London: Routledge and Kegan Paul.

Tremblay, R. E., LeBlanc, M., & Schwartzman, A. E. (1988). The predictive power of first-grade peer and teacher ratings of behavior: Sex differences in antisocial behavior and personality at adolescence. *Journal of Abnormal Child Psychology*, 16, 571–83.

Tremblay, R. E., McCord, J., Boileau, H., Charlebois, P., Gagnon, C., LeBlanc, M., & Larivee, S. (1991). Can disruptive boys be helped to become competent? *Psychiatry*, 54, 148–61.

Tremblay, R. E., Vitaro, F., Bertrand, L., LeBlanc, M., Beauchesne, H., Boileau, H., & David, L. (1992). Parent and child training to prevent early onset of delinquency: The Montreal longitudinal-experimental study. In *Preventing Antisocial Behavior*, ed. J. McCord & R. Tremblay, pp. 117–38. New York: Guilford.

Venables, P. H., & Raine, A. (1987). Biological theory. In *Applying Psychology to Imprisonment*, ed. B.J. McGurk, D.M. Thornton & M. Williams, pp. 3–27. London: Her Majesty's Stationery Office.

Verhulst, F. C., Koot, H. M., & Berden, G. F. M. G. (1990). Four-year follow-up of an epidemiological sample. *Journal of the American Academy of Child and Adolescent Psychiatry*, 29, 440–8.

Wadsworth, M. (1979). *Roots of Delinquency*. London: Martin Robertson.

Weiss, G., & Hechtman, L. T. (1986). *Hyperactive Children Grown Up*. New York: Guilford Press.

Werner, E. E., & Smith, R. S. (1982). *Vulnerable but Invincible*. New York: McGraw-Hill.

West, D. J. (1982). *Delinquency: Its Roots, Careers and Prospects*. London: Heinemann.

West, D. J., & Farrington, D. P. (1973). *Who Becomes Delinquent?* London: Heinemann.

West, D. J., & Farrington, D. P. (1977). *The Delinquent Way of Life*. London: Heinemann.

White, H. R., Labouvie, E. W., & Bates, M. E. (1985). The relationship between sensation seeking and delinquency: A longitudinal analysis. *Journal of Research in Crime and Delinquency*, 22, 197–211.

White, J. L., Moffitt, T. E., Earls, F., Robins, L. N., & Silva, P. A. (1990). How early can we tell? Predictors of child conduct disorder and adolescent delinquency. *Criminology*, 28, 507–33.

Widom, C. S. (1989). The cycle of violence. *Science*, 244, 160–6.

Wilson, H. (1980). Parental supervision: A neglected aspect of delinquency. *British Journal of Criminology*, 20, 203–35.

Wilson, J. Q., & Herrnstein, R. J. (1985). *Crime and Human Nature*. New York: Simon and Schuster.

Wolfgang, M. E., Thornberry, T. P., & Figlio, R. M. (1987). *From Boy to Man, From Delinquency to Crime*. Chicago: University of Chicago Press.

Zimring, F. E. (1981). Kids, groups and crime: Some implications of a well-known secret. *Journal of Criminal Law and Criminology*, 72, 867–85.

Zoccolillo, M., Pickles, A., Quinton, D., & Rutter, M. (1992). The outcome of childhood conduct disorder: Implications for defining adult personality disorder and conduct disorder. *Psychological Medicine*, 22, 971–986.

4. The challenge of depressive disorders in adolescence

KATHLEEN RIES MERIKANGAS & JULES ANGST

Introduction

Melancholia in children is characteristically spontaneous, unprecipitated, psychic pain, with corresponding changes in emotions, thinking, and motivation. (Emmingshaus, 1887)

Despite the assertion in clinical reviews that depression in childhood and adolescence was not considered as a diagnostic entity prior to 1960, descriptions of melancholia in children date back to the middle of the eighteenth century. In 1863, Berkhan presented a review of the literature on childhood melancholia, and Emmingshaus' 1887 book on psychiatric syndromes in childhood included chapters on melancholia and mania.

During the last two decades, there has been a burgeoning of research in affective disorders emerging in childhood and adolescence. With the rediscovery that depression does indeed occur even among children (Rutter, Tizard, & Whitmore, 1970; Posnanski , Krahenguhl, & Zrull, 1976; Carlson, 1990), hundreds of papers have reported studies of the phenomenology, assessment, magnitude, risk factors, and consequences of depression first experienced in childhood and adolescence. Knowledge of the now well-established biases of clinical samples of children with depression has led to a substantial body of research which has been devoted to gaining understanding of the magnitude and risk factors for depression in children selected from nonclinical samples.

Because of the comprehensiveness of several scholarly reviews of the phenomenology, assessment, and magnitude of adolescent depression (see Angold, 1988; Fleming & Offord, 1990; Rutter, Izard, & Read, 1986),

This Research was supported in part by Research Scientist Development Awards K02-MH00499–02, R01-AA07080–06, and R01-DA05648–05 from the National Institutes of Health to Dr. Merikangas; the John D. and Catherine T. MacArthur Foundation, Mental Health Network I on the Psychobiology of Depression and Other Affective Disorders; and Grants 3.804.76 and 3.948.0.85 from the Swiss National Science Foundation to Professor Angst.

this chapter will provide only a broad overview of the current issues in measurement, diagnosis, epidemiology, risk factors, and longitudinal studies of depression commencing in childhood. We will focus on two key areas of relevance to adolescent depression: comorbidity of depression and other syndromes, and familial and genetic studies that have assessed depression in children and adolescents. The importance of integration of adult and child psychiatric research in these domains will be emphasized. The present review will be restricted to studies that employed standardized criteria for affective disorders.

Methodological issues

Definition and description

The measurement of depression has been extensively studied in both adult and child psychiatry. Because depression is a normal human emotion that exists on a continuum from normal response to an adverse event to an extreme expression of sadness characterized by incapacity, profound hopelessness, and suicidal ideation, the major issue with respect to measurement involves the identification of the threshold at which depression becomes a disorder (Angold, 1988).

Although childhood depression differs from that in adulthood in terms of demographic features, the phenomenology of depression in adolescence is generally believed to be similar to adult manifestations (Angst, 1988). The artificial distinction between cognitive and emotional disorders is nowhere more apparent than in the expression of depression, in which an individual's view of the world is not commensurate with the reality observed by others. The "black cloud" of depression completely obscures positive characteristics of the individual and his or her surroundings. In adolescence, the salience of family input to emerging cognition of self-image is gradually replaced by extrafamilial input, particularly with respect to interpersonal relationships. The interpretation of both internal and external events is thus strongly influenced by the stage of cognitive development of the individual, coupled with previous experience of the event (Beck et al., 1979). For example, the development of the self-concept may be an important factor in models in the interpretation of the interaction between the expression of inner emotional states and external events.

Assessment

There is an extensive literature on the measurement of depression in children and adolescents. Standardized assessments of adolescents range from self-report symptom checklists to highly structured diagnostic instruments. The advantages and disadvantages of each of these approaches have been summarized by Orvaschel (1985). In brief, the symptom checklists are dimensional, thereby avoiding arbitrary discrimination between affected and unaffected respondents; have well-established psychometric properties; and often have extensive normative data available. Disadvantages of such checklists include a lack of specificity of high scores, partially attributable to lack of data on the context, and frequency and severity of symptom expression; restricted time period of assessment, generally limited to the current date or past week; the generation of insufficient information with which to assess diagnostic criteria; and weak evidence on the criterion validity of such measures (Brunshaw & Szatmari, 1988).

In contrast, structured diagnostic interviews provide uniformity of data collection in the clinical interview setting, generate criteria to yield standardized diagnoses, assess the context, frequency, duration, and impairment of symptom constellations, and generally provide the best approximation to the clinical interview. Weaknesses often include a lack of flexibility in the use of clarification and symptom probes by the interviewer; the use of a flowchart format based on diagnostic thresholds, which precludes the collection of subthreshold data on symptoms, duration, frequency, or impairment; and the lack of clinical judgment on the part of the interviewer in interpreting the interview responses.

The use of structured diagnostic interviews in child psychiatry has evoked abundant research on the reliability of diagnoses in children and adolescents. Although the wide discrepancy between child and parent reports has alarmed investigators in child psychiatry, the differences are often greater in family studies of adults. Most studies of adolescents employ the children themselves as the major source of information, with ancillary information from parents being of secondary importance in rendering diagnostic information (Orvaschel, Sholomskas, & Weissman, 1980).

Epidemiology of depression in adolescents

Prevalence rates

Reviews of the epidemiology of adolescent depression are convergent in identifying the methodological inconsistencies that preclude aggregation of current studies (Angold, 1988; Fleming & Offord, 1990). The most prominent differences were the sampling sources, which ranged from junior high schools to female colleges, the age of the samples, the response

Table 4.1 *Community surveys of depressive symptoms in adolescents*

Authors (Year)	Number	Source	Age	DX Interview	Assessment Period	Percent Exceeding Depressive Cut-Off Score
Rutter (1979)	2303	Community	14–15	Clinical Interview	Current	40
Kandel & Davies (1982)	8206	Senior high school	13–19	SCL-90[1]	1 year	25
Schoenbach et al (1982)	384	Junior high school	12–16	CES-D[2]	1 week	50
Teri (1982)	568	Senior high school	14–17	BDI[3]	2 weeks	34
Kaplan et al (1984)	385	Junior/senior high school	11–17	BDI[3]	2 weeks	23
Offord et al (1987)	1230	Community	12–16	CBCL[4]	6 months	46
Garrison et al (1989)	677	Junior high school	11–17	CES-D[2]	1 week	5
Reinherz et al (1989)	378	Ninth grade	13–16	CDI[5]	Lifetime	21

[1] Symptom Checklist-90 (Derogatis, 1977).
[2] Center for Epidemiologic Studies Depression Scale (Radloff, 1977).
[3] Beck Depressive Inventory (Beck, Ward, & Mendelson, 1961).
[4] Achenbach Child Behavior Checklist (Achenbach & Edelbrock, 1983).
[5] Children's Depression Inventory (Kovacs & Beck, 1977).

rates, and the diagnostic procedures including instrumentation, criteria, and informants.

Numerous studies have assessed the frequency of depressive symptoms in samples from the general population. In the studies listed in Table 4.1, adolescents between ages twelve and seventeen were recruited from junior and senior high schools in the community. The range in the period of prevalence of depressive symptoms ranged from one week to one year. The average frequency of subjects who had experienced depressive symptoms of sufficient severity to surpass the cut-off score was 34 percent, with a range of 22.7 percent to 50 percent across the eight studies. The assessment period was not systematically associated with the proportion of subjects who exceeded the threshold for depression.

Prevalence rates of depression defined according to standardized diagnostic criteria are shown in Table 4.2. The most substantial amount of data on adolescent depression has been collected on the point prevalence of major depression. Of the seven studies listed in Table 4.2, the average prevalence of a current episode of major depression is 3.4 percent, with a range of 0.4 percent to 5.7 percent. The average six-month prevalence rate across three studies was 5.1 percent. Lifetime rates of major depression in older adolescents reported by Deykin, Levy, and Wells (1987) and Lewinsohn and colleagues (1991) were 8.3 and 25.3 percent, respectively. Although both studies sampled from school settings, the former study was based on a college setting, whereas the latter was conducted in a representative sample of high schools. Rates of dysthymic disorder were widely divergent in the three studies, with a range of 0.5 to 8.0 percent, again reflecting methodological variation. Finally, in a study by Lewinsohn and colleagues (1986), the five-year incidence rate of depression over the age interval twelve to seventeen was 17/1000.

Longitudinal studies

Longitudinal studies are critical in the assessment of the persistence, stability, and consequences of depression in adolescence. Several investigators have conducted follow-ups of children and adolescents with depression identified in clinical (Kovacs et al., 1984; Harrington et al., 1990) or epidemiologic samples (Kandel & Davies, 1986; McGee et al., 1992; Rutter et al., 1976b; McGee & Williams, 1988; Keller et al., 1992). The majority of these studies were uncontrolled and the investigators were rarely blind to the original diagnosis of the index case. Moreover, the study of Harrington and colleagues (1990) was the only follow-up study of a clinical sam-

Table 4.2 *Community surveys of depressive disorders in adolescents*

Authors (Year)	Number	Source	Age	DX Interview	DX Criteria	Major Depression (percent)	Dysthymia
Rutter et al. (1970)	2303	Community	14–15	Clinical Interview	—	1.5	—
Deykin et al. (1987)	424	Colleges	16–19	DIS[1]	DSM-III	6.8 LT	—
Kashani et al. (1987b)	150	Community	14–16	DICA[2]	DSM-III	4.7 point	8.0* point
McGee & Williams (1988)	943	Community	15	DISC[3]	DSM-III	1.2 point 1.9 LT	1.1 point
Velez et al. (1989)	456	Community	13–18	DISC[3]	DSM-III-R	3.7 point	—
Fleming et al. (1989)	1230	Community	12–16	SDI[4]	DSM-III	9.8 6-mnths	—
Whitaker et al. (1990)	356	High school	14–17	Clinical Interview	DSM-III	4.0 LT	4.9 LT
Lewinsohn et al. (1991)	1710	High school	14–18	K-SADS-E[5]	DSM-III-R	18.4 LT 2.9 point	3.2 LT

* 8.0% was also the rate for Dysthymia & MDD.
[1] Diagnostic Interview Schedule (Robins, Helzer, & Croughan, 1981).
[2] Diagnostic Interview for Children and Adolescents (Reich et al., 1982).
[3] Diagnostic Interview Schedule for Children (Costello et al., 1984).
[4] Survey Diagnostic Instrument (Boyle, Offord, & Hofmann, 1987).
[5] Schedule for Affective Disorders & Schizophrenia for School Aged Children: Epidemiologic Version (Chambers et al., 1985).

ple to include a control group. The usual length of follow-up in prospective studies was five years (apart from Harrington et al. [1990], in which the follow-up was some fifteen years).

The results of the longitudinal studies of clinical samples of depressed adolescents suggest that adolescents in treatment for depression exhibit marked recurrence of affective symptoms and syndromes over time. Follow-up of afflicted adolescents into adulthood also reveals that depressive disorder is characterized by considerable diagnostic specificity. In epidemiologic studies adolescents with depressive symptoms or syndromes continue to report depression as long as eight years after the initial assessment. In general, stability of depression is greatest among those with early onset of depression, a comorbid disorder, and recurrence of depressive episodes. The poor social functioning of adults with a history of adolescent depression may be associated with the impact of depression exerting a major influence on the pathways of development of educational, social, and occupational skills.

Consequences of adolescent depression

The most alarming consequence of depression in adolescents is suicide. Rates of suicide in this age group have increased over the past decades. However, depression is rarely the sole disorder in suicidal adolescents (Hoberman & Bergmann, 1992). Depression is often comorbid with substance abuse and anxiety disorders among suicidal adolescents. Moreover, personality disorders, when coupled with major depression, are particularly associated with repeated suicide attempts (Hoberman & Bergmann, 1992).

In a prospective longitudinal study of an epidemiologic sample of a cohort from Zurich, Switzerland, in their late teens, Angst, Degonda, and Ernst (1992) found that the major risk factors for suicide attempts were similar to those in adulthood. The patterns of comorbidity among suicide attempters were also similar to those reported in adults: affective disorders, antisocial personality, and drug abuse. One finding that was particularly relevant to the design of suicide prevention programs was the association between suicide attempts and Recurrent Brief Depression, which was more strongly associated with suicide attempts than any of the other affective disorders (Merikangas, Wick, & Angst, 1994).

The other major consequence of depression in youth is the interruption of the completion of developmental tasks in the educational, social, and psychological spheres. Impairment in relationships with family and friends is a frequent sequela of depression. The subsequent lack of social support may generate a negative feedback loop in which the consequences of depression may actually serve to maintain the depressive episode.

The long-term sequelae of the interruption in social and psychological development and educational achievement have not been well established. However, depending on the chronicity, recurrence, severity, and comorbid conditions, depression in adolescence would be expected to lead to consequences in social relationships and restricted occupational choice in adulthood as well.

Risk factors for affective disorders

Individual characteristics that appear to potentiate the risk of depression in adolescents include increasing age, female gender, low socioeconomic status, precipitating environmental factors including bereavement, parental separation and divorce, and other life events interpreted as stressful by the child. Specific temperaments or personality traits may also be associated with an increased risk of depression. Alternatively, such traits may constitute an early form of expression of depression or they may be residual to depressive episodes. In a prospective longitudinal study of 1,144 women, Rodgers showed that childhood neurosis was associated with adulthood psychopathology only in the presence of provocative events in adulthood (Rodgers, 1990). There is a consistent association between neuroticism, interpersonal sensitivity, and depression. The nature of this relationship awaits further clarification in longitudinal studies (Angst, 1988; Boyce et al., 1991).

Gender

The results of longitudinal studies of depression have revealed that whereas males report greater rates of depression prior to age twelve, there is a dramatic reversal in the sex ratio thereafter. For example, in a longitudinal follow-up of a large community sample, McGee and colleagues (1992) reported a male to female sex ratio of 4.3:1 at age eleven and 0.4:1 at age fifteen, attributable to the increase in the incidence of depression among females after age twelve. Although the symptoms of depression are similar among male and female adolescents, Allgood-Merton, Lewinsohn, and Hops (1990) found that poor self-esteem and negative body image were more common among female adolescents. Moreover, these characteristics constituted the major antecedents of depressive episodes in young females.

Age of onset

There is great variability in the estimates of the age of initial onset of depression. Prior to the recent generation of studies which have investigated depressive syndromes and diagnoses in children and adolescents, estimates of the age of onset of depression were derived from retrospective studies of adults with depression. There are, however, numerous references to depression in childhood and adolescence in clinical literature of the early part of this century (Angst, 1988). Of particular interest is the frequency with which case reports of adolescent onset depression described concomitant disorders including eating disorders, hyperactivity, and schizophrenia.

Although the age of onset of bipolar disorder derived from retrospective studies is unreliable, first admission rates of bipolar depression reveal that there is a dramatic increase in first admissions of both males and females after age fifteen. In a study of first admissions for manic-depressive psychosis in the United Kingdom, there were no females and 0.6/1000 males between the ages of ten and fourteen; the rates per thousand of first admissions in the age interval of fifteen to nineteen increased to 24.6 and 25.6 (Sibisi, 1990). Several investigators have reported that the initial onset of bipolar disorder may present with minor depression, mild mood swings or cyclothymia, hypomania, or atypical depression (Carlson, Davenport, & Jamison, 1977; Akiskal et al., 1977; Kovacs et al., 1984; Angst, 1988). Therefore, it is likely that the initial symptoms of bipolar disorder may begin in the early teen years, followed by inception of the full-blown manifestation of the disorder in the late teens.

Evidence from prospective epidemiologic studies reveals a dramatic change in the prevalence of major depressive episodes after age eleven. Prior to that age, depression is very rare; whereas by age fifteen, the estimates of the prevalence of depression are quite high (McGee et al., 1992). The incidence of depression continues to increase throughout early adulthood, peaking between forty-five and fifty-five years of age (Lewinsohn et al., 1986).

The parallel course of the risk of affective symptoms and syndromes with the reproductive cycle in women has been extensively noted, yet little scientific evidence is available to distinguish the neurochemical basis from the life changes which accompany the reproductive milestones.

Although the increased risk of depression among girls in the early teens has been widely described, there is little empirical evidence regarding a direct relationship between the onset of depression and levels of reproductive hormones. There are also profound social changes with adolescence which may be strongly linked to the development of self-esteem.

Biologic factors

Although several biologic parameters have been investigated among depressed adolescents, the studies have generally been quite small and inadequately controlled. The most consistently studied parameters are cortisol secretion, growth hormone, sleep EEG, and response to thyroid stimulating hormone. As in adult affective disorder, none has been confirmed as a trait marker for childhood depression (Kutcher & Marton, 1989).

Protective factors

Results of longitudinal studies have revealed that there are also several unique individual characteristics that appear to be protective against the risk of psychopathology. The most consistent factors are academic achievement, involvement in extracurricular activities, social competence and positive relationships with adults outside the family (Rutter, 1979; Merikangas, 1984). Individual factors that protected against depression in the study by Reinherz et al. (1989) were self-perception of attractiveness, intellectual competence, and popularity, as well as adequate social supports.

Family history

Because a family history of depression has been the strongest and most potent non-demographic risk factor for the affective disorders, it is critical to include familial factors in systematic investigations of the etiology of depression. Despite the abundance of well-controlled family and genetic studies that have employed sophisticated methodology to investigate the transmission of affective disorders among adults, there are only a limited number of controlled family studies that have focused on the manifestation of affective disorders among adolescents. Reviews of early family studies of parents with affective illness have been presented by Beardslee and colleagues (1983), and there are more recent studies by LaRoche and colleagues. (1987) and Downey and Coyne (1990). Methodological limitations of these studies, including a lack of adequate comparison and control groups, absence of blindness to parental diagnostic status, biased samples of proband parents, and nonstandardized assessments of disorders in children, have been well recognized and have been rectified in recent studies. Nevertheless, integration of the findings across studies is still precluded by wide variation in the demographic and clinical features of the samples. Tables 4.3 and 4.4 present a summary of controlled studies of offspring of parents with bipolar and nonbipolar depression, respectively. The studies reviewed herein are limited to those in which offspring in the age range of adolescence were assessed.

The five controlled studies of offspring of parents with bipolar disorder exhibit wide variation in the frequency of affective disorders among offspring of affected parents (a range of 26 percent to 67 percent – see Table 4.3). Similar variation among the controls suggests major methodological differences in the selection and assessment across studies. The relative risk among children of the cases compared to control parents was elevated in four of the five studies. The most remarkable finding in these studies was the high rates of all psychiatric disorders, which exceeded 50 percent in most studies. The finding that the majority of disorders in these offspring were comprised of affective syndromes demonstrates some specificity of transmission of the affective disorders. The absence of cases of bipolar disorder or mania in these children is, however, most likely attributable to the youthful age of the offspring, which averaged fourteen in these studies. Longitudinal data are necessary to determine the proportion of offspring in whom the expression of affective disorders and symptoms represents an early manifestation of the same affective subtype for which their parents had sought treatment.

Table 4.4 summarizes the studies of offspring of parents with unipolar (or nonbipolar) affective disorder. There was an approximately four-fold increased risk of affective disorders , and a two-fold increase in the rates of psychiatric syndromes in general among the offspring of depressed parents when compared to those of controls. In contrast to the offspring of bipolar parents, the children of unipolar parents exhibited an increased risk of diverse psychiatric disorders including substance abuse, conduct disorder, and anxiety disorders. In many studies, the rates and/or relative risks of the anxiety disorders exceeded those of the affective disorders. Thus, despite the elevated relative risk of affective disorders in these offspring, the high rates of nonaffective disorders suggest that there is less specificity of transmission of affective disorders among the unipolar than among bipolar probands. Similar findings have emerged from family

Table 4.3 *Controlled studies of the offspring of parents with bipolar depression*

	Proband		Controls	
Authors (Year)	Number	Source	Number	Source
Decina et al. (1983)	18	Outpatient	14	Psych outpatient
Klein & Depue (1985)	26	Inpatient	22	Psych outpatient
Gershon et al. (1985)	16	Inpatient/ Outpatient	19	Normal
Hammen et al (1987)	9	Female outpatient	14 22	a) Medical ill b) Normal
Nurnberger et al. (1988)	32	Inpatient	39	Volunteer
Grigoroiu-Serbanescu et al. (1989)	47	Inpatient	61	Normal

Table 4.4 *Controlled studies of offspring of parents with unipolar/major depression*

	Proband		Controls		Offspring	
Authors (Year)	Number	Source	Number	Source	Number of Cases	Number of Controls
Welner et al. (1977)	29	Inpatient	41	School	75	152
Cytryn et al. (1982)	13	Inpatient	15	Normals	19	21
Keller et al. (1986) Beardslee et al. (1983)	57	Inpatient Outpatient		Neighborhood acquaintance	108	64
Weissman et al. (1987)	56	Inpatient / Outpatient	35	Community	125	95
Hammen et al. (1987)	13	Female outpatient	14 22	(a)Medical ill (b) Community	19	(a) 18 (b) 35
Turner et al. (1987)	11	Outpatient dysthymic	10	Advertisement	14	13
Orvaschel et al. (1988)	34	Recurrent outpatient	29	Community	61	16
Sylvester et al. (1988)	45	Outpatient	26	Normals	11	47
Klein & Depue (1985)	47	Inpatient	38 33	(a) Psych ill (b) Medical ill	47	38

Table 4.3 *Continued*

				Disorders In Offspring (Rates/100)			
Offspring				Affective		Any DX	
Number of Cases	Number of Controls	Age	DX Interview	Cases	Controls	Cases	Controls
31	18	7–14	MHAF[1]	26	0	52	5
41	22	15–21	SADS-L[2]	38	5	43	18
29	37	6–17	K-SADS	41	38	72	51
12	a) 18 b) 35	8–16	K-SADS	67	17	92	29
53	39	15–25	SADS-L[2]	43	10	72	31
72	72	10–17	K-SADS	10	1	61	25

[1] Mental Health Assessment Form (Kestenbaum & Bird, 1978).
[2] Schedule for Affective Disorders & Schizophrenia (Endicott & Spitzer, 1978).

Table 4.4 *Continued*

		Lifetime Disorders In Offspring (Rates/100)					
Offspring		Affective		Anxiety		Any DX	
Age	DX Interview	Cases	Controls	Cases	Controls	Cases	Controls
6–16	DICA	7	0	—	—	—	—
5–15	None	70	23	—	—	—	—
11–19	DICA	38	23	16	—	65	—
6–23	K-SADS	28	13	40	18	76	57
8–16	K-SADS	74	(a) 44 (b) 17	32	(a) 17 (b) 11	74	(a) 50 (b) 29
7–12	CAS[1]	0	0	21	9	22	8
6–17	K-SADS	21	4	20	9	41	15
7–17	DICA	29	5	34	6	—	—
14–22	SADS-L	32	0	—	—	51	24

[1] Child Assessment Schedule (Hodges et al., 1982).

studies of adults which reveal greater specificity and familial aggregation of bipolar disorder than unipolar disorder (McGuffin & Katz, 1989).

Although these studies provide evidence for the involvement of familial factors in the etiology of affective disorders, the observation of an increased risk of disorders in children sheds little light on possible mechanisms through which such factors may operate to produce depression and other psychopathology in children. Familial aggregation of depression may result from shared genes, common environmental factors, or a combination thereof.

Genetic factors

The bulk of evidence regarding the role of genetic factors in the etiology of the affective disorders has been derived from studies of manic- or bipolar depression. The results of family, twin, and adoption studies have yielded strong evidence for the involvement of genetic factors in the etiology of bipolar depression (McGuffin & Katz, 1989). The adoption studies of Cadoret and colleagues (1985), and twin studies of Kendler, Heath, and Martin (1986), Torgersen (1990), McGuffin, Katz, and Rutherford (1991), and Clifford, Hopper, and Fulker (1984) have revealed that although genetic factors are involved in the etiology of nonbipolar depression, the heritability (i.e., degree of variance attributable to genetic factors) is substantially lower than that of bipolar affective disorder. The rate-limiting step in the genetic studies to date, however, is the lack of valid definitions of nonbipolar depression. This may be attributable in part to its heterogeneity. There is substantial evidence that the affective disorders are comprised of a heterogeneous set of conditions (Weissman et al., 1986), some of which are primary and others of which are secondary manifestations of personality disorders, other disorders such as alcoholism or anxiety disorders, or neurologic conditions including migraine, or developmental disorders.

Transmissible familial factors

Parental psychopathology comprises the most powerful predictor of the subsequent development of depression in their offspring. The specific mechanism through which parental illness exerts an influence is not clear. Although some parental disorders exhibit specificity of transmission to offspring, as reviewed above, depression in parents is more strongly associated with anxiety disorders than with depression in children. The early expression of anxiety could constitute expression of an underlying vulnerability to emotional disorders through transmissible biologic factors, or the deficits in the home environment of children exposed to parental depression and its sequelae. Moreover, the results of some of the adoption studies of offspring of alcoholic parents have shown that depression is associated both with a biologic background of alcoholism and with depression in the adoptive home. These findings demonstrate the importance of environmental contributors to depression (Goodwin, Schulsinger, & Knop, 1977).

Several of the family studies of adolescents and children of depressed parents have incorporated measures of potential mechanisms for the familial transmission of affective disorders. In general, the findings converge in demonstrating that unipolar subtype, chronicity and severity of depression, and affective illness in the mother were associated with increased risk of disorders among the offspring. Most surprising was the lack of specificity of transmission of nonbipolar depression, as revealed by elevation of nonaffective disorders in the children. Most of these family studies did not provide systematic information on comorbid disorders in the parents, however, thereby limiting conclusions regarding the specificity of transmission of affective and nonaffective conditions.

Chronicity and severity of parental disorder have consistently been shown to be associated with an elevated risk of depression among offspring. The mechanism for this observation is not clear, however. Increased severity could indicate greater underlying genetic risk or could be associated with greater disruption in the child's environment, or both. The features of the home environment that may potentiate or protect against the expression of depression in offspring have been reviewed by Rutter (1989), Angold (1988), and Downey and Coyne (1990). The family environment of depressed adults, particularly mothers, has been shown to be characterized by family and parental discord, divorce, inattention, rejection, and abuse. Holmes and Robins (1988) reported that depressed women were more likely than alcoholic mothers to severely punish their children and to apply an inconsistent pattern of interaction with their children. Similarly, prospective longitudinal studies of Cohen and colleagues (1990) showed that the combination of power assertive punishment and lack of consistency in parenting was more strongly related to the persistence of depression than was a family structure in which the child was reared by only one parent. Familial risk factors for depression in childhood were also investigated in the Zurich Cohort Study (Angst et al., 1990a) in which the major predictors of depression were psychiatric illness in first degree relatives, and lack of care and interpersonal conflict in parents.

Parker, Tupling, and Brown (1979) have examined the relationship between the two major dimensions of parental behavior and attitudes and psychopathology in their offspring. They found that a parental discipline pattern of affectionless control was strongly associated with depressive disorders in adolescents. Moreover, this association has been found to be specifically associated with "neurotic depression" or a combination of anxiety and depression, since studies of bipolar depressives reveal normal parental levels of these dimensions (Parker, 1979). A recent study confirmed the association between psychopathology and a perceived parental bonding style of high over-control and low care in an epidemiologic sample of adolescents. In contrast to previous studies of adults, however, the impact of paternal behavior on child psychopathology was of equal importance to that of the mother (Klimidis et al., 1992).

An extensive review of the association between parenting behavior of depressed parents and child maladjustment revealed that the unidirectional model of intergenerational transmission of depression is insufficient to explain the lack of specificity of the parenting difficulties among depressed mothers. Indeed, chronic distress was found to have a more powerful influence on parenting behavior than did clinical depression. Moreover, the impact of children's behavior on the maintenance of depression in parents has rarely been considered. There appears to be a reciprocal relationship between parental depression and child maladjustment (Downey & Coyne, 1990).

There are several alternative models that link the effects of marital turmoil on parental depression and depression among exposed children. Downey and Coyne (1990) provided a detailed explication of possible alternatives, but evidence supporting the directionality and specific role of these factors in childhood depression is lacking. The effects of these phenomena on adolescents has received scant attention. Studies that have investigated the effects of familial and individual characteristics on adolescents have tended to focus on the risk of externalizing conditions, particularly drug abuse. Information is clearly needed to gain understanding of the complex relationship between familial factors and individual factors in the etiology of the affective disorders.

Although parental concordance for psychiatric disorders has been studied fairly extensively among adult offspring of parents with psychopathology, the above-cited studies were quite variable in the degree to which the effects of the sex of the affected parent and the illness in the co-parent were assessed routinely. The studies that did examine the effect of the sex of the parent yielded inconsistent findings; the study of Keller and colleagues (1986) revealed greater disturbance in the children of depressed mothers, compared with those of depressed fathers, whereas other studies reported no systematic differences in child psychopathology as a function of the sex of the affected parent (Weissman et al., 1987; Orvaschel, Walsh-Allis, & Ye, 1988). Most of these studies, however, did not simultaneously assess such factors as comorbidity and clinical severity, which may differ according to the sex of the affected parent.

The effect of dually affected parents in increasing the risk of psychopathology and difficulties in adjustment among their offspring appears to vary according to the specific disorders manifested by the parents. A recent study of parental concordance for drug abuse revealed a strong monotonic trend in the risk of drug abuse among children (Merikangas, Rounsaville, & Prusoff, 1991). In contrast, most studies reveal a lack of specificity of the effect of parental concordance for psychopathology. That is, the risk of disorders among offspring of couples who exhibit concordance for specific disorders has not been shown to differ from that of couples who manifest different disorders, such as alcoholism in one parent and depression in the other (Merikangas, Prusoff, & Weissman, 1988). This suggests that the mechanism for the increased risk of illness among children may be associated with detrimental environmental factors produced by impairment secondary to the specific disorders manifest in the parents. Although life events have generally been considered as an environmental contributor to depression, the findings of a recent family study revealed that both depression and adverse life events clustered in families. This suggests that the propensity to experience adversity and depression may represent an expression of the same underlying diathesis (McGuffin & Bebbington, 1988).

Environmental factors

Environmental risk factors unique to individual family members may be distinguished from transmissible environmental familial factors according to the degree of sharing of such factors within families. Although marital and family discord may be shared among all family members, the negative effects could interact with individual susceptibility to stress to produce dramatically different outcomes in same sex siblings who are close in age. Thus, the unique characteristics of each family member are critical in determining the effect of environmental phenomena on either elevating or diminishing the risk of manifestation of underlying liability factors for depression. It is these interactions that need to be the focus of future research on the etiology of affective syndromes, for it is clear that simplistic models of univariate external factors on the risk for depression are insufficient to explain the etiology of such a common and relatively nonspecific condition.

Life events not shared within families are an important source of unique environmental contributions to depression. The major events associated with depression in both retrospective and prospective studies are early separation from a parent by death or divorce, serious illnesses, particularly those which are chronic, and sexual and physical abuse (Reinherz et al., 1989; Roy, 1985). It is likely, however, that adverse life events may comprise nonspecific risk factors for depression. These events may exert their influence through the degree of disruption, chronicity, and severity of their impact on the individual's life. For example, Kendler and colleagues (1992) have recently shown that parental loss prior to age seventeen was significantly related to five of the six major psychiatric disorders investigated in their study of female twins.

Comorbidity of depression and other disorders

Evidence from clinical, epidemiologic, longitudinal, and family study data consistently demonstrates that affective disorders in adolescents are characterized by a substantial degree of comorbidity, particularly with anxiety disorders and conduct problems. A summary of epidemiologic data presented in Table 4.5 reveals that the majority of adolescents with depressive disorders exhibit concomitant disorders in either the emotional or behavioral spheres. Angst and colleagues (1990a) reported that both anxiety and conduct symptoms in childhood were associated with depression in early adulthood. Different patterns of comorbidity are evident for specific affective subtypes, however. That is, similar degrees of comorbidity with nonaffective disorders have been reported between dysthymia and major depression, which demonstrate a significant degree of overlap themselves, whereas bipolar disorder rarely co-occurs with other conditions among adolescents (Rohde, Lewinsohn, & Steeley, 1991).

Anxiety disorders are the most common concomitant to depression in both childhood and adolescence, with as many as three-quarters of depressed adolescents reporting manifestations of anxiety disorders as well. Studies of clinical samples of adolescents with depression and those with anxiety disorders including phobia, separation anxiety, and overanxious disorder, reveal a high degree of co-occurrence between symptoms and disorders in each of the two domains (Bernstein, 1991; Strauss et al.,

1988; Mitchell et al., 1988; Kovacs et al., 1989; Bernstein & Garfinkel, 1986). Epidemiologic studies of adolescents from which rates of comorbidity between depression and anxiety could be extracted are presented in Table 4.5. This compilation of data illustrates that the anxiety disorders are the conditions by far the most commonly associated with depression, ranging from approximately 20 percent to 75 percent of subjects with depression.

Conduct disorder is also frequently associated with affective disorders in community samples, with an average of one-third of adolescents with depression having a history of conduct disorders (Table 4.5). In a comprehensive review of comorbidity between conduct and affective disorders, Zoccolillo (1992) concluded that conduct disorders are far more frequently associated with depression than chance expectations in both clinical (Puig-Antich, 1982; Marriage et al., 1986; Kovacs et al., 1988; Woolston et al., 1989) and community samples (Anderson et al., 1987; Kashani et al., 1987a; McGee et al., 1990). In the vast majority of cases, the onset of conduct disorder precedes that of depression in both retrospective and prospective studies (Kovacs et al., 1988; Harrington et al., 1991). In contrast to the relationship between anxiety disorders and depression, however, empirical evidence supports the theory that conduct is the primary disorder in most cases with concomitant depression, and that the latter disorder represents a complication of either the conduct disorder or some associated risk factor. This confirms the observation of Rutter and colleagues (1976b) that conduct problems with depression are more similar to conduct without depression than to depression alone.

An association between affective disorders and other psychiatric and nonpsychiatric disorders has also been reported among adolescents identified in epidemiologic samples. For example, the prevalence of affective disorders has been shown to be significantly greater among adolescents with eating disorders, substance abuse (Rohde, Lewinsohn, & Seeley, 1991), and attention deficit disorder (McClellan et al., 1990). An association between depression and somatic illnesses, particularly those involving the central nervous system (Rutter et al., 1976b), such as migraine (Merikangas, Angst, & Isler, 1990), has also been reported.

Clinical characteristics of comorbid disorders

Substantial evidence reveals that comorbidity of affective and nonaffective disorders is associated with greater severity of depression. Adolescents with both syndromes have a greater number and severity of depressive symptoms (Mitchell et al., 1989; Kashani & Orvaschel, 1990), more

Table 4.5 *Comorbidity of affective disorders in epidemiologic studies of adolescents*

			Number with Depression (percent)	
Authors (Year)	Number	Age	Lifetime	Current
Rutter et al. (1976b)	2303	14–15	—	35 (1.5%)
Deykin et al. (1987)	424 female	16–19	35 (8.3%)	—
Kashani et al. (1987a)	150	14–16	—	7 (4.7% MDD, 8.0% Dysth)
Kashani et al. (1989)	140	12, 17	—	7 (4.7%)
McGee et al. (1990)	943	15	18 (1.9%)	11 (1.2%)
Rohde et al. (1991)	1710	14–18	347 (20.3%)	50 (2.9%)

severe anxiety symptoms (Strauss et al., 1988), a greater number of episodes of depression, and more suicide attempts (Rohde, Lewinsohn, & Seeley, 1991). In many studies, adolescents with depression only were more similar to the controls than they were to the persons with comorbid affective disorders (Strauss et al., 1988). Comorbidity for anxiety and depression could be attributed partially to a less crystallized manifestation of the disorders at early stages of development, particularly those in the emotional sphere. Rutter, Graham, and Chadwick (1976a) suggested that neurotic disorders of childhood and adolescence were less differentiated than neuroses in adults.

The presence of more than one diagnostic entity is far more common than that of single disorders among adolescents. Comorbidity may reflect true associations between syndromes, or may arise from several methodological artifacts including diagnostic imprecision, such as symptom overlap among conditions, sampling biases emerging from clinical samples or unbalanced representation of population strata, or a positive response set of the subjects. The consistency of findings across diverse study paradigms with respect to the magnitude, patterns, and longitudinal course of comorbid disorders associated with depression among adolescents sug-

Table 4.5 *Continued*

Percent of Depressed Adolescents with Comorbid Disorders								
Anxiety		Conduct			Alcohol/Drug Abuse		All	
Lifetime	Current	Lifetime	Current	Attention Deficit Disorder	Lifetime	Current	Lifetime	Current
—	74.0	—	—	—	—	—	—	—
—	—	—	—	—	23.0	—	—	—
—	87.8	—	30.7	8.0	—	25.0	—	100.0
—	75.0	—	33.3	8.0	—	25.0		100.0
—	30.8	—	33.3	—	—	—	—	64.1
21.0	18.0	12.1	8.0	—	19.9	14.0	42.9	42.0

gests that comorbidity is not an artifact of sampling bias. The co-occurrence of these conditions could, however, still arise from a lack of nosologic precision or from the lack of specificity of expression of the symptoms of these conditions during the early stages of their inception.

A review of possible mechanisms for comorbidity among children and adolescents is presented by Caron and Rutter (1991) as follows: The two disorders result from shared and overlapping risk factors; apparent co-occurring conditions comprise a single condition with multiple manifestations; or one of the disorders causes or lowers the threshold for the expression of the other. Evidence from longitudinal and family genetic studies constituted the most powerful methods with which to discriminate between possible explanations for associations between disorders, after methodological factors have been excluded. For example, evidence for cross-transmission of "pure" forms of anxiety and depression among the relatives of probands with these conditions suggests that depression and anxiety among adults result from shared underlying etiologic factors (Merikangas, 1990; Merikangas, Risch, & Weissman, 1994). Moreover, assessment of the specificity of concordance for depressive symptoms and disorder among adult monozygotic twins reveals that the cotwin is as likely to manifest anxiety alone as depression (Torgersen, 1990; Clifford, Hopper, & Fulker, 1984; Kendler, Heath, & Martin, 1986).

Comorbidity in family studies

Although comparable twin data have not been reported among adolescents, some of the family studies of adolescent offspring of parents with depression or anxiety disorders provide evidence regarding the co-transmission of these conditions. A review of the association between affective and anxiety disorders in family studies of parents with both affective and anxiety disorders was presented by Weissman (1990). She concluded that anxiety and depression co-occur in children and adolescents and in their families. This review did not, however, present a mutually exclusive categorization of anxiety and depression among the offspring.

In order to investigate the degree of co-transmission between the disorders, it is necessary to classify the diagnoses in the offspring into mutually exclusive categories. The results of controlled family studies of adolescents in which these data were available are presented in Table 4.6. These studies reveal a lack of specificity of transmission of depression because of the low rates of pure depression among the offspring. The prevalence of pure anxiety disorders was greater than that of pure depressive disorders among the offspring of depressed parents. When depression was manifest among the offspring of parents with anxiety disorders, it often co-occurred with depression.

Similarly, the studies that have investigated the prevalence of anxiety and depression among parents of depressed adolescents reveal a lack of specificity of expression of depression. Mitchell and colleagues (1989) reported that a maternal history of anxiety or substance abuse was associated with depression in the offspring. Major depression in either the father or mother was not associated with an increased risk of depression among the offspring relative to the controls.

This was confirmed in an extensive analysis of the transmission of depression and anxiety in a family study in which the joint effects of parental comorbidity and mating type for these conditions on comorbidity among the adolescent offspring were examined (Table 4.7) (Merikangas, Prusoff, & Weissman, 1988). Although the original design of the study focused on the risk of depression among offspring of parents in treatment for major depression, stronger transmissibility was found for anxiety disorders plus depression than for major depression alone. There was no

Table 4.6 *Comorbidity in offspring in controlled family studies of parents with depression or anxiety*

	Proband Groups		DX in Offspring (Rates/100)		
Authors (Year)	Number of Parents	Number of Children	Depression & Anxiety	Depression Only	Anxiety Only
Decina et al. (1983)	18 Bipolar	31	12.9	12.9	3.2
	14 Controls	16	—	—	—
Turner et al. (1987)	13 Anxiety	16	0	6.3	37.5
	11 Dysthymic	14	0	0	21.4
	10 Normal	13	0	0	9.0
Merikangas et al. (1988)	33 Both Dep & Anx or 1 Dep/1 Anx	77	63.6	18.1	32.5
	30 One Dep & Anx	71	16.9	16.9	19.7
	5 One Dep	9	22.2	11.1	22.2
	4 One Anx	10	10.0	0	10.0
	20 Both Normal	52	7.7	17.3	9.6
McClellan et al. (1990)	16 Depression	27	34.0	18.0	27.0
	29 Panic	50	27.0	12.0	23.0
	26 Normal	48	20.0	11.0	13.0

Table 4.7 *Effects of logistic regression analysis of parental diagnosis on disorders in offspring*

Main Effects		Disorders In Offspring: Adjusted Odds Ratio (+/- 95% Confidence Intervals)			
		Major Depression	Depression Only	Anxiety Only	Anxiety & Depression
Diagnosis In Mother	Depression	N.S.	N.S.	N.S.	N.S.
	Anxiety	N.S.	N.S.	N.S.	4.2 (1.7–10.6)
	Alcoholism	4.8 (1.5–15.8)**	N.S.	N.S.	N.S.
Diagnosis In Father	Depression	N.S.	N.S.	6.7 (2.3–19.8)**	N.S.
	Anxiety	N.S.	N.S.	0.4 (2.3–19.8)**	N.S.
	Alcoholism	N.S.	N.S.	N.S.	N.S.
Parent Proband		N.S.	N.S.	0.1 (0.03–0.4)**	N.S.
Age of Offspring (Continuous)		***	***	**	**
Sex of Offspring		2.2 (1.2–4.2)*	N.S.	N.S.	3.5 (1.3–7.0)*
Interactions	Depression Mother† Anxiety Mother	N.S.	N.S.	7.9 (2.6–23.8)**	N.S.
	Anxiety Mother† Anxiety Father	3.1 (1.5–6.5)**	N.S.	N.S.	N.S.

*P<0.05, **P<0.01, ***P<0.001.
(Merikangas, Prusoff, & Weissman, 1988).

association between parental depression and depression alone among offspring. The only parental diagnosis associated with an increased risk of depression in offspring was maternal alcoholism.

These findings confirm the overlap in the transmission of depression and anxiety shown in the studies summarized in Table 4.5, as well as those in family studies of adult relatives of probands with affective disorders. Moreover, retrospective data on the adolescent offspring in this study suggest that anxiety may constitute an early form of expression of affective disorders. The lack of transmission of "pure depression" suggests that depression among the adolescent offspring may result from nontransmissible factors either familial or unique to the individual child. The results of an earlier uncontrolled study of offspring of bipolar parents by Conners and colleagues (1979) also revealed that anxiety symptoms tended to precede those of depression, particularly among the female offspring of unipolar probands. The lack of an association among the offspring of bipolar probands was interpreted as a differential manifestation of genetic susceptibility underlying the expression of bipolar disorder and unipolar disorder. Whereas children of bipolar probands tend to manifest few symptoms and mainly within the affective domain, children of unipolar probands exhibit more diverse symptom patterns.

Longitudinal studies of comorbidity

In the assessment of the longitudinal course of anxiety and depression, anxiety disorders have consistently been shown to precede the onset of depression. Several prospective longitudinal studies reported that anxiety preceded the onset of depression in more than 60 percent of the persons with concomitant expression of the two syndromes (Reinherz et al., 1989; Rohde, Lewinsohn, & Seeley, 1991). Moreover, Angst and colleagues (1990b) demonstrated that when changes occurred over time in the expression of either "pure" depression or anxiety, the majority of cases exhibited anxiety first and developed depression over time. Conversely, pure depressives rarely developed pure anxiety at follow-up. Reinherz and colleagues (1989) also reported that anxiety in the third grade was a major predictor of depression at age fifteen.

Longitudinal studies of clinical samples also exhibit the same pattern of onset of the two disorders; the onset of anxiety preceded that of depression in the majority of the depressed adolescents with concomitant anxiety. The prospective studies of clinically depressed children and adolescents of Kovacs and colleagues (1989; 1988) revealed that the onset of comorbid disorders generally preceded that of depression, and often persisted beyond the cessation of depressive episodes. This suggests that anxiety may comprise an early vulnerability factor for depression, with the onset of the depression emerging in late adolescence or adulthood.

Summary and future studies

1. *Establishment of valid classification and assessment of adolescent depression*

Empirical evidence for the validity of the definition of depression, in both adolescents and adults, is quite sparse. Moreover, the point at which the threshold should be drawn to discriminate between normal expression of a depressed mood and depressive disorder is not known. The lack of availability of trait markers for depression, coupled with the lack of specificity of transmission of depression in families after accounting for comorbidity suggests that depression in adolescence is still heterogeneous and may not constitute a valid and discrete syndrome. Further studies are needed to complement the evidence for the stability of depression commencing in adolescence from longitudinal studies of nonclinical samples, particularly with respect to the role of comorbid disorders in the maintenance of the continuity between adolescent and adult depression.

2. *Epidemiology of depression in adolescence*

Epidemiologic studies of depression in adolescents reveal that symptoms of depression are quite common in this age group, with more than 50 percent exhibiting elevated levels of depressive symptomatology and its concomitants. The point prevalence of depressive disorders is quite low, however, with an average rate of 3.4 percent across studies. Despite the low rates, the consequences of depression in this age group can be quite severe, with suicide the most serious consequence and impairment in social, educational, and psychological development a frequent depressive concomitant.

3. *Comorbidity of depression among adolescents*

Comorbidity of depression with anxiety disorders and behavior disorders appears to be as common among adolescents as it is among adults. Other conditions comorbid to depression which have been investigated include eating disorders and substance abuse. There is a gap in knowledge regarding the association between physical illness and depression. Longitudinal and family studies of adolescents suggest that comorbidity expressed in adulthood is likely to be present during the early phases of depressive illness, and does not generally constitute a consequence of depression. Rather, anxiety and behavior disorders tend to precede the onset of depression, with depression representing a complication or secondary manifestation of the underlying disorder. Systematic family studies designed to address specifically the mechanisms for comorbid associations between depression and other disorders among offspring of parents with both conditions are notoriously lacking. Such studies could elucidate the nature of the association between depression and other disorders. Because aggregate evidence suggests that depression comorbid to other conditions is more severe in terms of chronicity and severity, prospective longitudinal studies within family study designs could provide evidence regarding the impact of comorbidity on the course and outcome of depression, and on its nosological implications. The lack of evidence regarding the efficacy of the standard treatments of depression in adults when applied to depressed adolescents may be attributable to the presence of comorbid disorders in these subjects.

4. *Risk factors*

Inconsistent methodology and constellations of risk factors preclude aggregation across studies of risk factors for depression in adolescence. The causal relationships between depression and putative risk factors have not been elucidated. The most consistent correlates of adolescent depression are demographic characteristics. Numerous studies have investigated patterns of family interaction without accounting for parental psychopathology; whereas family studies often limit assessments to diagnoses in the parents and children. Nevertheless, disturbances in parenting, non-intact and dysfunctional families, and low socioeconomic status have been consistently associated with depression in adolescents (Fleming & Offord, 1990). Future studies should discriminate between risk factors for depression and those for comorbid disorders. Biologic factors are notoriously absent from studies of premorbid risk factors for depression. Future research should also focus on the interactions between vulnerability and environmental factors in the etiology of depression.

5. *Longitudinal studies*

Although there are numerous prospective longitudinal epidemiologic studies of psychopathology as assessed by dimensional scales among children and adolescents, there are very few prospective longitudinal studies of epidemiologic samples of children in which diagnostic criteria have been systematically applied. These studies are critical in elucidating the patterns of age of onset, premorbid risk factors, the temporal order of onset of disorders comorbid to depression. Hypothesis-driven short-term prospective longitudinal studies that focus on specific periods of development are likely to be fruitful in identifying factors which potentiate or inhibit the expression of underlying vulnerability for depression.

References

Achenbach, T. M., & Edelbrock, C. (1983). *Manual for the Child Behavior Checklist and Revised Behavior Profile.* Burlington: University of Vermont Department of Psychiatry.

Akiskal, H. S., Djenderedjian, A. H., Rosenthal, R. H., & Khani, M. K. (1977). Cyclothymic disorder: Validating criteria for inclusion in the bipolar affective group. *American Journal of Psychiatry*, 134,1227–33.

Allgood-Merton, B., Lewinsohn, P. M., & Hops, H. (1990). Sex differences and adolescent depression. *Journal of Abnormal Psychology*, 99, 55–63.

Anderson, J. C., Williams, S., McGee, R., & Silva, P. A. (1987). DSM-III disorders in preadolescent children: prevalence in a large sample from the general population. *Archives of General Psychiatry*, 44, 69–76.

Angold, A. (1988). Childhood and adolescent depression: I. Epidemiological and aetiological aspects. *British Journal of Psychiatry*, 152, 601–17.

Angst, J. (1988). Clinical course of affective disorders. In *Depressive Illness: Prediction of Course and Outcome,* ed. T. Helgason & R.J. Daly, pp. 1–48. Berlin: Springer-Verlag.

Angst, J., Degonda, M., & Ernst, C. (1992). The Zurich Study XVI: Suicide attempts in a cohort from age 20 to 30. *European Archives of Psychiatry and Clinical Neuroscience*, 242, 135–141.

Angst, J., Merikangas, K. R., Scheidegger, P., & Wicki, W. (1990a). Recurrent brief depression: a new subtype of affective disorder. *Journal of Affective Disorders*, 19, 37–8.

Angst, J., Vollrath, M., Merikangas, K. R., & Ernst, C. (1990b). Comorbidity of anxiety and depression in the Zurich cohort study of young adults. In *Comorbidity of Mood and Anxiety Disorders,* ed. J.D. Maser & C.R. Cloninger, pp. 123–38. Washington, DC: American Psychiatric Press, Inc..

Beardslee, W. R., Bemporad, J., Keller, M. B., & Klerman, G. L. (1983). Children of parents with major affective disorder: A review. *American Journal of Psychiatry*, 140, 825–32.

Beck, A. T., Rush, A. J., Shaw, B. F., & Emery, G. (1979). *Cognitive Therapy of Depression.* New York: Guilford.

Beck, A. T., Ward, G. H., & Mendelson, M. (1961). An inventory for measuring depression. *Archives of General Psychiatry*, 4, 561–71.

Berkhan, D. (1863). Irreseinbeikindern. *Correspondenzbl Deutsch Gesellsch Psychiatr*, 10, 65–76.

Bernstein, G. A. (1991). Comorbidity and severity of anxiety and depressive disorders in a clinic sample. *Journal of the American Academy of Child and Adolescent Psychiatry*, 30, 43–50.

Bernstein, G. A., & Garfinkel, B. D. (1986). School phobia: The overlap of affective and anxiety disorders. *Journal of the American Academy of Child Psychiatry*, 25, 235–41.

Boyce, P., Parker, G., Barnett, B., Cooney, M., & Smith, F. (1991). Personality as a vulnerability factor to depression. *British Journal of Psychiatry*, 159, 106–14.

Boyle, M. H., Offord, D. R., & Hofmann, H. G. (1987). Ontario Child Health Study: I. Methodology. *Archives of General Psychiatry*, 44, 826–31.

Brunshaw, J. M., & Szatmari, P. (1988). The agreement between behaviour checklists and structured psychiatric interviews for children. *Canadian Journal of Psychiatry*, 33, 474–80.

Cadoret, R. J., O'Gorman, T. W., Heywood, E., & Troughton, E. (1985). Genetic and environmental factors in major depression. *Journal of Affective Disorders*, 9, 155–64.

Carlson, G. A. (1990). Bipolar disorders in children and adolescents. In *Psychiatric Disorders in Children and Adolescents*, ed. B. D. Garfinkel, G. A. Carlson & E. B. Weller, pp. 21–36. Philadelphia: W.B. Saunders Company.

Carlson, G. A., Davenport, Y. B., & Jamison, K. (1977). A comparison of outcome in adolescent and late onset bipolar manic depressive illness. *American Journal of Psychiatry*, 134, 919–22.

Caron, C., & Rutter, M. (1991). Comorbidity in child psychopathology: Concepts, issues and research strategies. *Journal of Child Psychology and Psychiatry*, 32: 1063–80.

Chambers, W. J., Puig-Antich, J., Hirsch, M., Paez, P., Ambrosini, P. J., Tabrizi, M. A., & Davies, M. (1985). The assessment of affective disorders in children and adolescents by semistructured interview: Test-retest reliability of the Schedule for Affective Disorders and Schizophrenia for School-Age Children, Present Episode Version. *Archives of General Psychiatry*, 42, 696–702.

Clifford, C. A., Hopper, J. L., & Fulker, D. W. (1984). A genetic and environmental analysis of a twin family study of alcohol use, anxiety, and depression. *Genetic Epidemiology*, 1, 63–79.

Cohen, P., Brook, J. S., Cohen, J., Velez, N., & Garcia, M. (1990). Common and uncommon pathways to adolescent psychopathology and problem behavior. In *Straight and Devious Pathways from Childhood to Adulthood*, ed. L. Robins & M. Rutter, pp. 242–58. London: Cambridge University Press.

Conners, C. K., Himmelhoch, H., Goyette, C. H., Ulrich, R. F., & Neil, J. F. (1979). Children of parents with affective illness. *Journal of the American Academy of Child and Adolescent Psychiatry*, 18, 600–7.

Costello, A. J., Edelbrock, C. S., Dulcan, M. K., & Kalas, R. (1984). *Testing of the NIMH Diagnostic Interview Schedule for Children (DISC) in a Clinical Population: Final Report*. Rockville, Maryland: Center for Epidemiological Studies, National Institute of Mental Health.

Cytryn, L., McKnew, D. H., Jr., Bartko, J. J., Lamour, M., & Hamovitt, J. H. (1982). Offspring of patients with affective disorders: II. *Journal of the American Academy of Child and Adolescent Psychiatry*, 21, 389–91.

Decina, P., Kestenbaum, C. J., Farber, S., Kron, L., Gargan, M., Sackeim, H. A., & Fieve, R. R. (1983). Clinical and psychological assessment of children of bipolar probands. *American Journal of Psychiatry*, 140: 548–53.

Derogatis, R. L. (1977). *Symptom Checklist 90, R-Version Manual I: Scoring, Administration and Procedures for the SCL-90*. Baltimore: Johns Hopkins University Press.

Deykin, E. Y., Levy, J. C., & Wells, V. (1987). Adolescent depression, alcohol and drug abuse. *American Journal of Public Health*, 77, 178–82.

Downey, G., & Coyne, J. C. (1990). Children of depressed parents: An integrative review. *Psychological Bulletin*, 108: 50–76.

Emmingshaus, H. (1887). *Die Psychischen Storungen des Kindersalters*. Tubingen: Verlag der H. Lauppschen buchhandlung.

Endicott, J., & Spitzer, R. L. (1978). A diagnostic interview: The Schedule for Affective Disorders and Schizophrenia – lifetime version. *Archives of General Psychiatry*, 35, 837–44.

Fleming, J. E., & Offord, D. R. (1990). Epidemiology of childhood depressive disorders: A critical review. *Journal of the American Academy of Child and Adolescent Psychiatry*, 29, 571–80.

Fleming, J. E., Offord, D. R., & Boyle, M. H. (1989). Prevalence of childhood and adolescent depression in the community – Ontario Child Health Study. *British Journal of Psychiatry*, 155, 647–54.

Garrison, C. Z., Schluchter, M. D., Schoenbach, V. J., & Kaplan, B. K. (1989). Epidemiology of depressive symptoms in young adolescents. *Journal of the American Academy of Child and Adolescent Psychiatry*, 28: 343–51.

Gershon, E. S., McKnew, D., Cytryn, L., Hamovit, J., Schreiber, J., Hibbs, E., & Pellegrini, D. (1985). Diagnoses in school-age children of bipolar affective disorder patients with normal controls. *Journal of Affective Disorders*, 8: 283–91.

Goodwin, D. W., Schulsinger, F., & Knop, J. (1977). Psychopathology in adopted and non-adopted daughters of alcoholics. *Archives of General Psychiatry*, 34: 1005–9.

Grigoroiu-Serbanescu, M., Christodorescu, D., Jipescu, I., Totoescu, A., Marinescu, E., & Ardelean, V. (1989). Psychopathology in children aged 10–17 of bipolar parents: Psychopathology rate and correlates of the severity of the psychopathology. *Journal of Affective Disorders*, 16: 167–79.

Hammen, C., Gordon, D., Burge, D., Adrian, C., Jaenicke, C., & Hiroto, D. (1987). Maternal affective disorders, illness and stress: Risk for children's psychopathology. *American Journal of Psychiatry*, 144, 6.

Harrington, R., Fudge, H., Rutter, M., Pickles, A., & Hill, J. (1990). Adult outcomes of childhood and adolescent depression: I. Psychiatric status. *Archives of General Psychiatry*, 47, 465–73.

Harrington, R., Fudge, H., Rutter, M., Pickles, A., & Hill, J. (1991). Adult outcomes of childhood and adolescent depression: II. Links with antisocial disorders. *Journal of the American Academy of Child and Adolescent Psychiatry*, 30, 434–9.

Hoberman, H. M., & Bergmann, P. E. (1992). Suicidal behavior in adolescence. *Current Opinion in Psychiatry*, 5, 508–17.

Hodges, K., McKnew, D., Cytryn, L., Stern, L., & Kline, J. (1982). The Child Assessment Schedule (CAS) diagnostic interview: A report on reliability and validity. *Journal of the American Academy of Child and Adolescent Psychiatry*, 21, 468–73.

Holmes, S. J., & Robins, L. N. (1988). The role of parental disciplinary practices in the development of depression and alcoholism. *Psychiatry*, 51, 24–36.

Kandel, D. B., & Davies, M. (1982). Epidemiology of depressive mood in adolescents. *Archives of General Psychiatry*, 39, 1205–12.

Kandel, D. B., & Davies, M. (1986). Adult sequelae of adolescent depressive symptoms. *Archives of General Psychiatry*, 43, 255–65.

Kaplan, S. L., Hong, G. K., & Weinhold, C. (1984). Epidemiology of depressive symptomatology in adolescents. *Journal of the American Academy of Child Psychiatry*, 23: 91–8.

Kashani, J. H., Beck, N. C., Hoeper, E. W., Corcoran, C. M., McAllister, J. A., Fallahi, C., Rosenberg, T. K., & Reid, J. C. (1987a). Psychiatric disorders in a community sample of adolescents. *American Journal of Psychiatry*, 144, 584–9.

Kashani, J. H., Carlson, G. A., Beck, N. C., Hoeper, E. W., Corcoran, C. M., McAllister, J. A., Fallahi, C., Rosenberg, T. K., & Reid, J. C. (1987b). Depression, depressive symptoms, and depressed mood among a community sample of adolescents. *American Journal of Psychiatry*, 144, 931–4.

Kashani, J. H., & Orvaschel, H. (1990). A community study of anxiety in children and adolescents. *American Journal of Psychiatry*, 147, 313–8.

Kashani, J. H., Orvaschel, H., Rosenberg, T. K., & Reid, J. C. (1989). Psychopathology in a community sample of children and adolescents: A developmental perspective. *Journal of the American Academy of Child and Adolescent Psychiatry*, 28, 701–6.

Keller, M. B., Beardslee, W. R., Dorer, D. J., Lavori, P. W., Samuelson, H., & Klerman, G. L. (1986). Impact of severity and chronicity of parental affective illness on adaptive functioning and psychopathology in children. *Archives of General Psychiatry*, 43, 930–7.

Keller, M. B., Lavori, P. W., Wunder, J., Beardslee, W. R., Schwartz, C. E., & Roth, J. (1992). Chronic course of anxiety disorders in children and adolescents. *Journal of the American Academy of Child and Adolescent Psychiatry*, 31, 595–9.

Kendler, K. S., Heath, A., & Martin, N. G. (1986). Symptoms of anxiety and depression in a volunteer twin population. *Archives of General Psychiatry*, 43, 213–21.

Kendler, K. S., Neale, M. C., Kessler, R. C., Heath, A. C., & Eaves, L. J. (1992). Childhood parental loss and adult psychopathology in women. *Archives of General Psychiatry*, 49, 109–16.

Kestenbaum, C. J., & Bird, H. R. (1978). A reliability study of the mental health assessment form for school age children. *Journal of the American Academy of Child Psychiatry*, 17, 338–47.

Klein, D. N., & Depue, R. A. (1985). Obsessional personality traits and risk for bipolar affective disorder: An offspring study. *Journal of Abnormal Psychology*, 94: 291–7.

Klimidis, S., Minas, I. H., Ata, A. W., & Stuart, G. W. (1992). Construct validation in adolescents of the brief current form of the parental bonding instrument. *Comprehensive Psychiatry*, 33, 378–83.

Kovacs, M., & Beck, A. T. (1977). An empirical-clinical approach toward a definition of childhood depression. In *Depression in Childhood: Diagnosis and Treatment and Conceptual Models*, ed. J.G. Schulterbrandt & A. Raskin. New York: Raven Press.

Kovacs, M., Feinberg, T. L., Crouse-Novak, M. A., Paulauskas, S. L., & Finkelstein, R. (1984). Depressive disorders in childhood: I. A longitudinal prospective study of characteristics and recovery. *Archives of General Psychiatry*, 41, 229–37.

Kovacs, M., Gatsonis, C., Paulauskas, S. L., & Richards, C. (1989). Depressive disorders in childhood: IV. A longitudinal study of comorbidity with and risk for anxiety disorders. *Archives of General Psychiatry*, 46, 776–82.

Kovacs, M., Paulauskas, S., Gatsonis, C., & Richards, C. (1988). Depressive disorders in childhood: III. A longitudinal study of comorbidity with and risk for conduct disorders. *Journal of Affective Disorders*, 15, 205–17.

Kutcher, S. P., & Marton, P. (1989). Parameters of adolescent depression: A review. *Psychiatric Clinics of North America*, 12, 895–918.

LaRoche, C., Sheiner, R., Lester, E., Benierakis, C., Marrache, M., Engelsmann, F., & Chiefetz, P. (1987). Children of parents with manic-depressive illness: A follow-up study. *Canadian Journal of Psychiatry*, 32, 563–9.

Lewinsohn, P. M., Duncan, E. M., Stanton, A. K., & Hautzinger, M. (1986). Age at first onset for nonbipolar depression. *Journal of Abnormal Psychology*, 95, 378–83.

Lewinsohn, P. M., Rohde, P., Seeley, J. R., & Hops, H. (1991). Comorbidity of unipolar depression: I. Major depression with dysthymia. *Journal of Abnormal Psychology*, 100, 205–13.

Marriage, K., Fine, S., Moretti, M., & Haley, G. (1986). Relationship between depression and conduct disorder in children and adolescents. *Journal of the American Academy of Child and Adolescent Psychiatry*, 25, 687–91.

McClellan, J. M., Rubert, M. P., Reichler, R. J., & Sylvester, C. E. (1990). Attention deficit disorder in children at risk for anxiety and depression. *Journal of the American Academy of Child and Adolescent Psychiatry*, 29, 534–9.

McGee, R., Feehan, M., Williams, S., & Anderson, J. (1992). DSM-III disorders from age 11 to age 15 years. *Journal of the American Academy of Child and Adolescent Psychiatry*, 31, 50–9.

McGee, R., Feehan, M., Williams, S., Partridge, F., Silva, P. A., & Kelly, J. (1990). DSM-III disorders in a large sample of adolescents. *Journal of the American Academy of Child and Adolescent Psychiatry*, 29, 611–9.

McGee, R., & Williams, S. (1988). A longitudinal study of depression in nine-year-old children. *Journal of the American Academy of Child and Adolescent Psychiatry*, 27, 342–8.

McGuffin, P., & Bebbington, P. (1988). The Camberwell Collaborative Depression Study. III. Depression and adversity in the relatives of depressed probands. *British Journal of Psychiatry*, 152, 775–82.

McGuffin, P., & Katz, R. (1989). The genetics of depression and manic-depressive disorder. *British Journal of Psychiatry*, 155, 294.

McGuffin, P., Katz, R., & Rutherford, J. (1991). Nature, nurture and depression: A twin study. *Psychological Medicine*, 21, 329.

Merikangas, K. R. (1984). Divorce and assortative mating among depressed patients. *American Journal of Psychiatry*, 141: 74–6.

(1990). Co-morbidity for anxiety and depression: Review of family and genetic studies. In *Comorbidity of Mood and Anxiety Disorders*, eds. J. D. Maser & C. R. Cloninger, pp. 331–48. Washington DC: American Psychiatric Press, Inc. .

Merikangas, K. R., Wick, W., & Angst, J. (1994). Heterogeneity of depression: Classification of depressive subtypes by longitudinal course. *British Journal of Psychiatry*, 164, 342–8.

Merikangas, K. R., Angst, J., & Isler, H. (1990). Migraine and psychopathology: Results of the Zurich cohort study of young adults. *Archives of General Psychiatry*, 47, 849–53.

Merikangas, K. R., Prusoff, B. A., & Weissman, M. M. (1988). Parental concordance for affective disorders: Psychopathology in offspring. *Journal of Affective Disorders*, 15, 279–90.

Merikangas, K. R., Risch, N. J., & Weissman, M. M. (1994). Comorbidity and cotransmission of alcoholism, anxiety and depression. *Psychological Medicine*, 24, 69–80.

Merikangas, K. R., Rounsaville, B. J., & Prusoff, B. A. (1991). Familial factors in vulnerability to substance abuse. In *Vulnerability to Drug Abuse*, ed. M. Glantz & R. Pickens, pp. 79–98. Washington, DC: American Psychological Association Press.

Mitchell, J., McCauley, E., Burke, P., Calderon, R., & Schloredt, K. (1989). Psychopathology in parents of depressed children and adolescents. *Journal of the American Academy of Child and Adolescent Psychiatry*, 28: 352–7.

Mitchell, J., McCauley, E., Burke, P. M., & Moss, S. J. (1988). Phenomenology of depression in children and adolescents. *Journal of the American Academy of Child and Adolescent Psychiatry*, 27, 12–20.

Nurnberger, J. I., Hamovit, J., Hibbs, E., Pellegrini, D., Guroff, J. J., Maxwell, M. E., Smith, A., & Gershon, E. S. (1988). A high-risk study of primary affective disorder: Selection of subjects, initial assessment, and 1- to 2-year follow-up. In *Relatives at Risk for Mental Disorder*, ed. D. L. Dunner, E. S. Gershon, & J. E. Barrett, pp. 161–77. New York: Raven Press.

Offord, D. R., Boyle, M. H., Szatmari, P., Rae-Grant, N., Links, P. S., Cadman, D. T., Byles, J. A., Crawford, J. W., Blum, H. M., Byrne, C., Thomas, H., & Woodward, C. A. (1987). Ontario Child Health Study: II. Six-month prevalence of disorder and rates of service utilization. *Archives of General Psychiatry*, 44, 832–6.

Orvaschel, H. (1985). Psychiatric interviews suitable for use in research with children and adolescents. *Psychopharmacology Bulletin*, 21, 737–45.

Orvaschel, H., Sholomskas, D., & Weissman, M. M. (1980). *The Assessment of Psychopathology and Behavioral Problems in Children: A Review of Scales Suitable for Epidemiological and Clinical Research (1967–1979)*. Rockville, Maryland: Alcohol, Drug Abuse and Mental Health Administration.

Orvaschel, H., Walsh-Allis, G., & Ye, W. (1988). Psychopathology in children of parents with recurrent depression. *Journal of Abnormal Child Psychology*, 16: 17–28.

Parker, G. (1979). Parental characteristics in relation to depressive disorders. *British Journal of Psychiatry*, 134, 138–47.

Parker, G., Tupling, H., & Brown, L.B. (1979). A parental bonding instrument. *British Journal of Medical Psychology*, 52, 1–10.

Posnanski, E. O., Krahenguhl, V., & Zrull, J. P. (1976). Childhood depression – a longitudinal perspective. *Journal of the American Academy of Child Psychiatry*, 15, 491–501.

Puig-Antich, J. (1982). Major depression and conduct disorder in prepuberty. *Journal of the American Academy of Child Psychiatry*, 21, 118–28.

Radloff, L. S. (1977). The CES-D scale: A self-report depression scale for research in the general population. *Applied Psychological Measurement*, 1, 385–401.

Reich, T., Herjanic, B., Welner, Z., & Gandhy, P. R. (1982). Development of a structured psychiatric interview for children: Agreement on diagnosis comparing child and parent interviews. *Journal of Abnormal Child Psychology*, 10, 325–36.

Reinherz, H. Z., Stewart-Berghauer, G., Pakiz, B., Frost, A. K., Moeykens, B. A., & Holmes, W. M. (1989). The relationship of early risk and current mediators to depressive symptomatology in adolescence. *Journal of the American Academy of Child and Adolescent Psychiatry*, 28, 942–7.

Robins, L. N., Helzer, J. E., & Croughan, J. L. (1981). The NIMH diagnostic interview schedule: Its history, characteristics, and validity. *Archives of General Psychiatry*, 39, 381–9.

Rodgers, B. (1990). Behaviour and personality in childhood as predictors of adult psychiatric disorder. *Journal of Child Psychology and Psychiatry*, 31, 393–414.

Rohde, P., Lewinsohn, P. M., & Seeley, J. R. (1991). Comorbidity of unipolar depression: II. Comorbidity with other mental disorders in adolescents and adults. *Journal of Abnormal Psychology*, 100, 214–22.

Roy, A. (1985). Early parental separation and adult depression. *Archives of General Psychiatry*, 42, 987–91.

Rutter, M. (1979). *Changing Youth in a Changing Society: Patterns of Adolescent Development*. London: Nuffield Provincial Hospital Trust.

(1989). Isle of Wight revisited: Twenty-five years of child psychiatric epidemiology. *Journal of the American Academy of Child and Adolescent Psychiatry*, 28, 633–53.

Rutter, M., Graham, P., & Chadwick, O. (1976a). Adolescent turmoil: Fact or fiction? *Journal of Child Psychology and Psychiatry*, 17, 35–6.

Rutter, M., Izard, C. E., & Read, P. B. (1986). *Depression in Young People*. New York: Guilford Press.

Rutter, M., Tizard, J., & Whitmore, K. (1970). *Education, Health, and Behaviour*. New York: Longman, Inc.

Rutter, M., Tizard, J., Yule, W., Graham, P., & Whitmore, K. (1976b). Research report: Isle of Wight studies, 1964–1974. *Psychological Medicine*, 6, 313–32.

Schoenbach, V. J., Kaplan, B. H., Grimson, R. C., & Wagner, E. H. (1982) Use of a symptom scale to study the prevalence of a depressive syndrome in young adolescents. *American Journal of Epidemiology*, 116: 791–800.

Sibisi, C. D. T. (1990). Sex difference in the age of onset of bipolar affective illness. *British Journal of Psychiatry*, 156, 842–5.

Strauss, C. C., Last, C. G., Hersen, M., & Kazdin, A. E. (1988). Association between anxiety and depression in children and adolescents with anxiety disorders. *Journal of Abnormal Child Psychology*, 16, 57–68.

Sylvester, C. E., Hyde, T. S., & Reichler, R. J. (1988). Clinical psychopathology among children of adults with panic disorder. In *Relatives at Risk for Mental Disorder*, ed. D. L. Dunner, E. S. Gershon, & J. E. Barrett, pp. 87–99. New York: Raven Press.

Teri, L. (1982). The use of the Beck Depression Inventory with adolescents. *Journal of Abnormal Child Psychology*, 10, 277–84.

Torgersen, S. (1990). A twin-study perspective of the comorbidity of anxiety and depression. In *Comorbidity of Mood and Anxiety Disorders*, ed. J. D. Maser & C. R. Cloninger, pp. 367–80. Washington, DC: American Psychiatric Press, Inc.

Turner, S. M., Beidel, D. C., & Costello, A. (1987). Psychopathology in the offspring of anxiety disorders patients. *Journal of Consulting and Clinical Psychology*, 55: 229–35.

Velez, C. N., Johnson, J., & Cohen, P. (1989). A longitudinal analysis of selected risk factors for childhood psychopathology. *Journal of the American Academy of Child and Adolescent Psychiatry*, 28, 861–4.

Weissman, M. M. (1990). Evidence for comorbidity of anxiety and depression: Family and genetic studies of children. In *Comorbidity of Mood and Anxiety Disorders*, ed. J. D. Maser & C. R. Cloninger, pp. 349–68. Washington DC: American Psychiatric Press, Inc.

Weissman, M. M., Gammon, G. D., John, K., Merikangas, K. R., Prusoff, B. A., & Scholomskas, D. (1987). Children of depressed parents: Increased psychopathology and early onset of major depression. *Archives of General Psychiatry*, 44, 847–53.

Weissman, M. M., Merikangas, K. R., Wickramaratne, P. J., Kidd, K. K., Prusoff, B. A., Leckman, J. F., & Pauls, D. L. (1986). Understanding the clinical heterogeneity of major depression using family data. *Archives of General Psychiatry*, 43, 430–4.

Welner, Z., Welner, A., McCrary, M. D. ,& Leonard, M. A. (1977). Psychopathology in children of inpatients with depression: A controlled study. *Journal of Nervous and Mental Disease*, 164, 408–13.

Whitaker, A., Johnson, J., Shaffer, D., Rapoport, J. L., Kalikow, K., Walsh, B. T., Davies, M., Braiman, S., & Dolinsky, A. (1990). Uncommon troubles in young people: Prevalence estimates of selected psychiatric disorders in a nonreferred population. *Archives of General Psychiatry*, 47, 487–96.

Woolston, J. L., Rosenthal, S. L., Riddle, M. A., Sparrow, S. S., Cicchetti, D., & Zimmerman, L. (1989). Childhood comorbidity of anxiety/affective disorders and behavior disorders. *Journal of the American Academy of Child and Adolescent Psychiatry*, 28, 707–13.

Zoccolillo, M. (1992). Co-occurrence of conduct disorder and its adult outcomes with depressive and anxiety disorders: A review. *Journal of the American Academy of Child and Adolescent Psychiatry*, 31, 547–56.

5. Towards explaining patterns and trends in youth crime

DAVID J. SMITH

Introduction

The largest body of research on crime and conduct disorders has been concerned to understand why some individuals are disposed toward criminal behavior or conduct disorder whereas others are not. This involves describing patterns of criminal behavior, showing the distribution of those disposed toward crime or conduct disorder among social and cultural groups, comparing the personal and psychological characteristics of offenders and nonoffenders, and studying the process of individual development that leads to criminal behavior. Although this body of research springs from a concern to understand how individual differences arise, and fits most easily with a theory that sees crime as the result of the dispositions of individuals, it has produced a rich body of data that can be used to test a wider range of theories. At the same time, a number of intellectual innovations and social pressures have broadened the field of inquiry well beyond individual differences and their origins in the developmental process. Various sociological theories, all loosely related to Marxist class analysis, have tried to show how crime can be the product of social structures and institutions. More important, perhaps, is the growing pressure on both theory and policy caused by the continuing rise in the aggregate level of crime. It seems unlikely that these increases can be explained wholly in terms of the predispositions of individuals. These broad societal trends are not what dispositional theories were formulated to deal with. This has led to various newer styles of research and analysis that focus on explaining trends in aggregate crime rates, or on explaining crime by reference to the opportunities available for it and not by reference to individual dispositions.

This chapter aims to bring together the main findings from these different and to some extent separate traditions of research and analysis. The

This chapter is based on a fuller presentation of the evidence in the Academia Europaea Study Group report (Rutter, M. & Smith, D. J. [eds.] *Psychosocial Disorders in Young People: Time Trends and Their Causes*, Chichester: Wiley, 1995), and I am grateful for permission to include portions of the report here.

central objective is to review explanations of the continuing rise in the aggregate crime rate in the light of the available evidence.

In all developed countries except Japan there have been very large increases in the level of recorded crime during the present century, and the increases since the Second World War have been substantial. A few crimes, such as murder and some white collar crimes, are mostly committed by mature adults. Crimes that make up the bulk of those officially recorded, that is, robbery, theft, burglary, assault, and damage to property, are mostly committed by teenagers and young adults in their twenties. The peak age, even for fraud and forgery, is nineteen. Studies based on people's own accounts of their behavior show the same strong relationship between age and crime. The first section of the chapter considers this relationship in greater detail, and shows that the enormous rise in crime in the present century is essentially an increase in misconduct among young people up to the age of twenty-nine. It also reviews the explanations that have been put forward to account for the age–crime curve.

The next three sections review the evidence on the continuity between crime and conduct disorders, on the individual characteristics of offenders, and on the social and cultural correlates of offending. This prepares the way for a discussion of secular trends in the aggregate crime rate and cross-national comparisons. The principal theories put forward to account for crime are then reviewed in the light of the available evidence, with a focus on their ability to explain the rising crime rate in most developed countries.

Age and crime

Probably the most important single fact about crime is that it is committed mainly by teenagers and young adults. The crime rate increases swiftly to a peak in the teenage years between fifteen and seventeen, then decreases more gradually with increasing age. The pattern is illustrated by the official statistics for England and Wales on males convicted by the courts or officially cautioned.[1] In 1988, the number of offenses per one hundred males was 0.8 for those aged ten, 2.5 for those aged twelve, 7.4 for those aged fifteen, and 7.6 for those aged eighteen. The rate declined steadily thereafter.

1. These statistics cover indictable offenses only (this excludes the least serious ones). If they admit the offense, in some cases offenders may be cautioned rather than prosecuted, and these cases are included. Since 1985, however, police forces have increasingly used unrecorded warnings rather than recorded cautions for apprehended juvenile offenders (aged under seventeen), and these are not covered by the quoted statistics.

Prospective longitudinal studies provide closely similar findings on the relationship between age and officially recorded offending. In England, the Cambridge Study in Delinquent Development has been a rich source of data on this topic (for a general description of the study, see Farrington & West, 1990). This is a prospective longitudinal study of 411 males living in a working-class area of London in 1961–62, when they were first contacted at the age of eight or nine. Information on offenses committed by this group was collected through repeated searches at the Criminal Record Office; minor crimes such as common assault (not causing marks or injury), traffic infractions, and drunkenness are not normally recorded there and were therefore excluded. There were 1.7 offenses leading to conviction per one hundred males at age ten, rising to a peak of 16.8 at age seventeen, and then falling to 3.0 at age thirty-one, the last age with reasonably complete conviction data. These findings count offenses rather than people (the same person may commit many offenses). To obtain a prevalence rate, it is necessary to count people rather than offenses. The cumulative prevalence rate is the proportion of people who have been convicted of one or more offenses up to a given age. In the Cambridge Study, the cumulative prevalence rate was 4.9 percent by the age of twelve, 13.1 percent by the age of fourteen, 20.7 percent by the age of sixteen, 27 percent by the age of eighteen, 31.2 percent by the age of twenty, and 36.1 percent by the age of thirty (Farrington, 1990).

Although the Cambridge Study is of boys from one particular part of London, and is based on a small sample size, national statistics are remarkably similar. The Home Office has calculated official offending rates of English males born in four randomly chosen weeks of 1953 (Home Office Statistical Bulletin, 1987, 1989). This provides information for the whole of England for males born in the same year as the Cambridge cohort (which is focused on a working-class area of London). The pattern of change in rates of offending by age is closely similar for the national and local cohorts. The national cohort also shows a cumulative rate of official offending of 32.6 percent by the age of thirty, only about 3 percent less than in the inner-city London sample of the Cambridge Study. These findings show that in England for a young male to have been convicted of breaking the law is hardly deviant in a statistical sense. Equally striking, however, is the decrease in law breaking after the peak at the age of seventeen. One-quarter of the cohort were convicted of an offense between the ages of thirteen and eighteen, compared with 12 percent between the ages of twenty-seven and thirty-two.

The findings quoted so far relate to officially recorded offending, but a closely similar relationship between age and crime is also shown in the large number of studies based on respondents' own accounts of offenses they have committed. The Cambridge Study, for example, collected information about offending from self-reports as well as official records. Comparisons between self-reports and court records show that the self-reports have a high level of validity; but the self-reports provide a wider measure of offending, one less dependent on the reactions of the police and the courts.[2] At the age of eighteen, respondents were asked about offending in the past three years; at the age of thirty-two they were asked about the past five years. Despite this difference in the time window, the proportion who said they had offended decreased very sharply between these two ages. The proportion admitting to one or more of six nonviolent offenses[3] declined from 45 percent at the age of eighteen to 11 percent at the age of thirty-two. The proportion who said they had been involved in fights declined from 63 percent to 37 percent between these two ages.

The constancy of the age–crime curve

So far, this account of the relationship between age and crime has concentrated on males in England, but the relationship remains much the same for different times, places, and social groups. Hirschi and Gottfredson have put forward the extreme view that the relationship is invariant (Hirschi & Gottfredson, 1983; Gottfredson & Hirschi, 1990). Although that is certainly an exaggeration, the level of constancy in the relationship is striking. Thus, Gottfredson and Hirschi (1990) are able to show that the age–crime curve in England and Wales was much the same in 1842–44, in 1903, and in 1965; that the curves are similar for males and females if the rate of offending is standardized to cancel out the large difference at all ages between the sexes; that the curves for the United States and for England and Wales are similar; that the curves are similar for different ethnic groups in the United States. Studies in many other countries also show a similar relationship: A recent example is the longitudinal study of official offending among a cohort in Stockholm (Wikström, 1990).

2. Self-reports may not be completely independent of the reactions of the criminal justice system, however. Whether respondents remember offenses, or think them worth reporting, may be influenced by whether the matter came to light, and by whether they were punished. In addition, although self-reports have been shown to have validity in general terms, the relationship between self-reported and official offending may perhaps vary in important ways between population groups, with important consequences, for example, for our understanding of the relationship between crime and ethnic group.
3. Burglary, theft of vehicles, theft from vehicles, shoplifting, theft from slot machines, vandalism.

In spite of these striking regularities, Farrington (1986) has shown that there are also some potentially significant variations. The crime rate for English males peaked at age thirteen in 1938, at age fourteen in 1961, and at age fifteen in 1983. This raises the possibility that some social change (such as the raising of the school leaving age) has caused offending to peak at progressively later ages over the present century. Unfortunately, however, the interpretation cannot be straightforward, since the pattern of change for females is different. These changes over time are in any case small. Much larger are the differences according to the type of offense. Clear differences of this kind have been shown from analysis of American official arrest statistics. For example, Cline (1980) divided offenses into three broad groups according to the median age of arrest (shown in parentheses below).

1. Vandalism (17); motor vehicle theft, arson, burglary, larceny-theft, liquor law violations (18).
2. Handling stolen property (20); narcotic law violations (21); violence, disorderly conduct, prostitution (24); sex offenses other than forcible rape and prostitution (26); white-collar offenses such as forgery and fraud (26); abuse and neglect of family and children (28).
3. Drunkenness and drunk driving (35); gambling (37).

Wilson and Herrnstein (1985), using FBI figures for 1985, showed a similar change in the pattern of offenses by age. Longitudinal studies of officially recorded offending confirm that "changes in offending patterns with age seen in national statistics . . . are at least partly due to crime switching by offenders" (Farrington, 1986: 209). The self-report data from the Cambridge Study "showed that most offenses peaked during the period fifteen to eighteen, although shoplifting and burglary peaked earlier" (idem: 210).

Explaining the age–crime curve

Although the age–crime curve is the most basic fact of criminology, social scientists are very far from understanding its significance, or explaining the developmental processes that give rise to it. As Rutter (1989: 2) has argued, "age as such cannot be used as an explanation for behavioral change; either physical maturation or experience may be operative." Either of these basic types of explanation requires a great deal of further elaboration.

The constancy of the age–crime relationship suggests that it springs from some very basic features of human development. Particularly indicative is the evidence collected by Gottfredson and Hirschi on misbehavior in prison, and motor vehicle accidents, which are related to age in much the same way as crime. Surprisingly, however, the evidence does not seem consistent with the idea that the age–crime curve reflects a changing disposition to offend as the individual moves through the life cycle. If that were so, then a gradual change would occur in the individual life course, so that incidence (the number of offenses committed by each offender) as well as prevalence (the proportion of people offending) would vary with age. In fact, it seems that the individual life course is characterized not by smooth change in the disposition to offend, but by fairly abrupt changes. This suggests that explaining the age–crime curve will eventually involve explaining why individuals at some point abandon crime.[4]

Gottfredson and Hirschi convincingly demonstrate the weaknesses of explanations of desistance so far put forward. Theories that emphasize social bonds cannot explain why these become more effective in adulthood than in childhood; sociological theories, which explain crime in terms of power relationships between social classes, or labeling by the criminal justice system, or associating with others who are criminally minded, have nothing to say about why crime should decline with age – in fact, they ought to predict a continuous increase. Gottfredson and Hirschi cite an explanation by Trasler (1979; 1980) of desistance from crime in terms of social bonds and social situations.

> The simplest . . . explanation . . . is one which concentrates upon the satisfactions of delinquent conduct . . . which maintain such behaviour during adolescence, but cease to do so when the individual becomes an adult. I suggested earlier that much teenage crime is fun . . . But as they grow older most young men gain access to other sources of achievement and social satisfaction – a job, a girlfriend, a wife, a home, and eventually children – and in doing so become gradually less dependent upon peer-group support. What is more to the point, these new life-patterns are inconsistent with delinquent activities. (Trasler, 1980: 11–12)

In spite of the plausibility of this kind of explanation, the evidence for the effect of these factors is surprisingly weak, especially in the light of the overwhelming strength of the age–crime relationship. Although those who have been delinquent from childhood are much more likely than nondelinquents to have frequent periods of unemployment (West &

4. This is, however, a simplification. The fall in the crime rate after the peak age arises partly because lifetime prevalence increases more slowly after that age (there are comparatively few "late entrants") as well as because of desistance.

Farrington, 1977), the evidence that getting a job is associated with desistance from crime is far from clear-cut. A longitudinal study by Bachman, O'Malley, and Johnston (1978) suggested that there may be some relationship of that kind, but it is not a powerful one. There is no evidence that having a girlfriend is associated with giving up crime. On the contrary, "dating can be equated with smoking and drinking in terms of its connection with delinquency" (Gottfredson & Hirschi, 1990: 139). In their review of the effects of marriage, Rutter and Giller (1983) indicate that the findings are contradictory and inconclusive. They conclude that "whether marriage increases or decreases delinquent tendencies may well be largely determined by what sort of change (if any) in social group and personal relationships it entails" (234). There is no evidence that having children is associated with a reduction in criminal activity, and looking at the matter the other way about, there is ample evidence that the children of offenders also tend to become offenders.

None of these processes has been studied in sufficient depth and detail. Further research may well be able to show that in some circumstances (depending, for example, on the type of job, the age of marriage, or the characteristics of the marriage partner) these factors are associated with desistance from crime. The weakness of the relationships so far discovered is, however, at least enough to show that factors such as these cannot possibly account for the greater part of the immensely strong relationship between age and crime.

Perhaps the underlying mechanisms will be better understood when different groups of offenders are separated out. As might be expected, a high proportion of crime is committed by persistent offenders. For example, Stattin and Magnusson (1991) used a longitudinal study to identify males who were officially recorded offenders at all three stages of their development (up to age fourteen, between ages fifteen and twenty, and between ages twenty-one and thirty). This group accounted for 5 percent of all subjects and for 14 percent of those with criminal records at any stage, but for 62 percent of recorded crime occasions. Those who had recorded offenses during adolescence only, or during early adulthood only, together accounted for 20 percent of subjects, but for only a small proportion of offending occasions. Clearly, the relationship between age and crime differs in an important way between these groups, although even the persistent offenders tend strongly to desist after the age of thirty.

It seems likely that the age–crime curve largely reflects processes of biological development and maturation, but if so the specific processes involved have not been identified, and why they should result in a pattern of fairly abrupt desistance is not understood.

Continuity between crime and conduct disorders

The foregoing account of the age–crime curve has emphasized the fall after the peak age of offending rather than the rise before that age. That is because the apparent rise before the age of fourteen or fifteen is probably misleading. Rutter and Giller explain the matter as follows.

> Of course official statistics show that delinquency reaches a peak during the middle or late teens, with many individuals not receiving their first conviction until well into adolescence or even early adult life. But this simply reflects the fact that, by law, young children cannot be convicted, that the police are less likely to prosecute young first offenders and that it may take some time for delinquent activities to be detected. Certainly, both self-report data and behavioral ratings from teachers and others make clear that most delinquent individuals already show some form of antisocial behavior during middle childhood or pre-adolescence. (Rutter and Giller, 1983: 51; their citations have been omitted.)

In most jurisdictions, young children cannot be convicted of a criminal offense, and special criminal justice procedures apply to teenagers (up to an age boundary between juveniles and adults which varies widely from one country to another). For that reason alone, there is a need for a wider and inevitably vaguer concept than crime, such as antisocial behavior, conduct disorder, or delinquency, when discussing the behavior of juveniles. Broader concepts of this kind can also be useful as a background to our understanding of adult criminal behavior.

Among the conduct disorders that have been included in studies of antisocial behavior and delinquency are disruptive aggression such as teasing, quarrelsomeness, lying, malicious mischief and fire-setting, stealing, truancy, staying out late at night, running away from home, and gang activities. There is some disagreement about the importance of distinguishing between different types of conduct disturbance in children. Robins and her colleagues (Robins, 1978; Robins & Ratcliff, 1979) have argued that there is a single syndrome of antisocial behaviors, citing the intercorrelations between different forms of childhood deviance, and between various forms of childhood deviance and total adult deviance.

Research on child development before the peak age of offending at fourteen or fifteen suggests that specific forms of antisocial behavior peak at different ages; the peak in offending in the teenage years may reflect a shift, associated with the passage into the adult world, toward types of antisocial behavior regarded as criminal, rather than an increase up to that age in the amount of antisocial behavior.

An impressive body of evidence from longitudinal studies demonstrates the continuity between antisocial behavior in childhood and in adulthood. Summarizing these findings, Robins (1978) claimed that although adult antisocial behavior is nearly always preceded by childhood antisocial behavior, most antisocial children do not become antisocial adults (because of the familiar decline in the prevalence of crime or antisocial behavior with age). This conclusion was strengthened recently by the results of a large prospective study from birth to age fifteen in Dunedin, New Zealand.

> Eighty-four per cent of children found to be 'uncontrolled' at age 11 met criteria for stable and pervasive antisocial disorder when reassessed at 13. Antisocial behavior at 13 was predicted by 'externalizing behavior' at age 3 and behavior problems at age 5, long before a diagnosis of conduct disorder could be made. Further, these early behaviors were stronger predictors than IQ, mothers' attitudes, language level, or any other variable tested. (Robins, 1991: 202)

Robins also pointed out that aggressive behavior in childhood is the most stable of all early detectable personality characteristics. A review of eighteen follow-up studies estimated a 0.63 correlation between earlier and later measurements. Magnusson (1987) found, however, from a longitudinal study in Stockholm, that the apparent link between aggressiveness in childhood and later criminality arises because there is a group of boys having a combination of characteristics including both aggressiveness and hyperactivity (which is shown to be related to a low level of responsiveness by the autonomic nervous system). Boys who were hyperactive and aggressive were likely to become persistent offenders, whereas those who were aggressive but not hyperactive had no more than an average chance of offending later.

In spite of the high level of continuity overall, West and Farrington (1977) showed that a minority of adult criminals were free of conduct disturbance during childhood, and that late onset was associated with low social status and criminality of the parents.

The Epidemiological Catchment Area (ECA) Study has measured antisocial personality within a large cross-sectional survey of Americans in both private households and institutions such as prisons and hospitals

(Robins & Regier, 1991). In the broadest terms, "antisocial personality is characterized by the violation of the rights of others and a general lack of conformity to social norms" (Robins, Tipp, & Przybeck, 1991). In more specific terms, the diagnosis requires three childhood problems out of a possible twelve before age fifteen, and four adult problems out of a possible ten, together with continuity of symptoms and occurrence. Among the childhood symptoms are five related to aggressiveness, including weapon use, cruelty to animals, cruelty to people, forcing sex on others, and stealing with confrontation. Other childhood symptoms are vandalism, truancy, other school problems, drug use, and early sexual activity. Among the adult symptoms are lack of remorse, work problems, marital problems, child neglect, violence, transiency, illegal behaviors, promiscuous sexual behavior, and lying.

All the items are highly intercorrelated. Nevertheless, the findings show that while criminality is one of the symptoms of antisocial personality, it is neither a necessary nor a sufficient condition. Lifetime prevalence of antisocial personality among this general population sample was 2.6 percent, which is far lower than the prevalence of arrests or criminal convictions. Of those with antisocial personality, 47 percent had been arrested more than once for a non-traffic offense; of those with two or more such arrests, 37 percent had antisocial personality.

For the adults covered by the survey, the relationship between age and antisocial personality was broadly similar to the age–crime curve. Among those who had ever had antisocial personality, the proportion who had not had it over the past year (the rate of remission) increased from 39 percent among those under thirty years of age, through 59 percent among those aged thirty to forty-four and 86 percent among those aged forty-five to sixty-four to 100 percent for those aged sixty-five or more. Although antisocial personality eventually remits, just as offenders desist from crime, it nevertheless has a long duration. Among those with no symptoms in the past year, the average duration from first to last symptom was nineteen years.

Most antisocial children recover without developing the diagnosis of antisocial personality in adulthood. Overall, only 26 percent of children who had met the childhood criteria for antisocial personality also met the adult criteria. The ECA, however, like earlier longitudinal studies, confirmed that childhood problems are a strong predictor of adult antisocial personality. The more symptoms a child has shown, the more likely the adult is to be diagnosed as having antisocial personality. In addition, early onset in childhood predicts adult antisocial personality, though not so strongly as the number of childhood symptoms.

Taken together, the findings outlined in this section show that there is a close connection between criminal behavior in adulthood and a wider range of conduct disorders in childhood. The work of Robins also shows that in adulthood a cluster of antisocial behaviors can be identified that vary by age in much the same way as criminal behavior.

Personal characteristics of offenders

IQ and scholastic attainment

There is a substantial body of research that shows a consistent association between lower IQ and an increased risk of delinquency (Hirschi & Hindelang, 1977). The association remains regardless of the way that delinquency is measured. There is also a similar relationship between delinquency and low educational attainment (which in turn is closely related to IQ).

These relationships probably reflect rather complex underlying processes. It is not the case that delinquency causes lower IQ or school failure, because in many studies the lower IQ has been measured before delinquency became manifest. Part of the explanation may lie, however, in a link at an early age between lower IQ and troublesome behavior, which is a predictor of later delinquency.

There is some support for the theory that educational failure through lowered self-esteem and antagonism to school causes delinquency. For example, the longitudinal study by Elliott and Voss (1974) showed that the delinquency of school dropouts (which was higher than for those who stayed on) markedly diminished at the time when they left school.

Personality

A considerable body of research has failed to show convincingly that personality is a consistent or significant explanation of crime. One of the major problems with this line of research, as Gottfredson and Hirschi (1990) argued, is that there are important overlaps between supposedly distinct personality dimensions, and between each of these dimensions and delinquency: That is, the personality scales incorporate items that refer to conduct disorder or offending. The results of studies relating Eysenck's neuroticism scale (N) and extraversion scale (E) to delinquency have produced inconsistent results; where relationships are shown, they tend to be quite small; and for cross-sectional studies there is the problem that high E could be a consequence of imprisonment rather than a cause of offending.

Other personal characteristics

Although a number of earlier studies found that mesomorphic (muscular) body build was associated with delinquency, this was probably because of the limitations of method of the studies concerned (inadequate control groups, use of institutionalized populations). Studies of general population samples have found either no relationship of this kind (West & Farrington, 1973), or a contrary relationship between delinquency and light build or late puberty (Wadsworth, 1979) which disappeared when social factors were taken into account.

In summarizing the research findings on a number of physiological and psychological characteristics as determinants of offending, Rutter and Giller (1983) concluded that those who persist in offending into adult life tend to show hyperactivity, attentional defects, low autonomic reactivity (for example, low pulse rate even when stressed), impaired avoidance learning in response to punishment (involving reduced anxiety and low response to pain), and a greater than normal need for stimulation. The longitudinal study in Stockholm directed by Magnusson and others provided support for the theory that low autonomic reactivity (as measured by adrenaline excretion) and hyperactivity (from teachers' ratings) are predictors of later criminality among boys (Magnusson, 1987, 1988; Magnusson & Bergman, 1990). Also, the level of adrenaline excretion at the age of ten or thirteen predicted the level of criminal activity *after* the age of twenty better than the level *before* the age of twenty (Magnusson, 1988). This may indicate that boys with low adrenaline excretion are likely to become persistent offenders.

Genetic factors

Rutter and Giller (1983) concluded that the weight of evidence from twin studies suggests that genetic factors probably play a significant role in antisocial personality disorders that continue into adult life. The data from studies of nonadopted children (e.g., Osborn & West, 1979) show that there is a strong association between repeat offending in the father and repeat offending persisting into adult life in the sons.

Sociocultural patterns

Sex

Official statistics,[5] studies of self-reported offending, and studies of self-reported conduct disorders or antisocial personality all show much higher rates of offending among males than among females. Wilson and Herrnstein (1985) showed female suspects as a percentage of total suspects for twenty-five countries in 1963–72. The proportion ranged from 2 percent in Brunei to 21 percent in the West Indies. The larger European countries lie around or above the midpoint of this range: Netherlands, 10 percent; England and Wales, 14 percent; France, 14 percent; West Germany, 17 percent.

Reviews of both self-report studies and official statistics have concluded that "Sex differences are larger in official data than in self-reports. They are greater for adults than for juveniles, for property offenses than for personal offenses, for more serious crimes than for less serious ones, and for whites than for nonwhites." (Wilson & Herrnstein, 1985: 114). The last statement refers to comparisons between white and black people in the United States. For certain ethnic minorities – for example, people in Britain originating from the Indian subcontinent – the difference in rates of offending between males and females is exceptionally large, because offending among females is so rare. The difference between official statistics and self-report studies noted by Wilson and Herrnstein and all other writers on this subject may not be genuine. Nearly all self-report studies cover children and young people only, and most cover noncriminal misconduct as well as criminal offenses. The lower sex differences in the self-report studies may therefore arise because the findings (compared with those of official statistics) are weighted toward less serious kinds of misconduct and the younger age groups for which sex differences are known to be less marked.

In many countries, the difference between the sexes in the rate of offending has narrowed over the past forty years, although the male preponderance remains very great. In England and Wales, the sex ratio[6] dropped from around eleven to one in 1957 to around five to one in 1977. Since 1977, however, the ratio has remained completely stable. The pattern of change in the United States was similar over the 1960s and 1970s. In both countries, the difference between the sexes has narrowed most mark-

5. Of arrests, where available, or of persons convicted or cautioned.

6. Persons cautioned or convicted for indictable offenses per 100,000 population. The source for these statistics is Home Office (1978; 1992).

edly for petty property crimes (Wilson & Herrnstein, 1985); in Britain at least, the difference between the sexes in the prevalence of violent offenses has narrowed as well.

In spite of these recent changes, the large difference in criminal behavior and conduct disorders between the sexes is on the whole strikingly stable across cultures and periods. Along with the age–crime curve, this is one of the two most basic facts of criminology. The difference in crime rates is clearly connected in some way with the substantial difference (on average) in overt aggression between males and females. Most personal as opposed to property offenses are manifestly aggressive acts, but it is important to consider whether aggressive antisocial behavior in the child is a predictor of aggressive criminal behavior in the adult. Many retrospective and prospective longitudinal studies suggest that it is (e.g., Farrington, 1978). Aggressiveness itself is a relatively stable characteristic over the life course (Olweus, 1979). Furthermore, there is a link between aggression and nonviolent crime, although this seems to be largely because there is a group of young boys who are both aggressive and steal.[7] Hence, there is evidence that a difference in aggressiveness between males and females leads to a difference in the prevalence of criminal and antisocial behavior.

Against this Magnusson (1987) has argued from analyses of the Stockholm longitudinal study that the apparent relationship between childhood aggression and adult criminality only arises because there is a group of hyperactive boys who are also aggressive and often become persistent offenders. More generally, Magnusson and Bergman (1990) argued for a person-oriented as opposed to a variable-oriented approach to understanding these relationships. On this view, the difference in criminality between males and females arises because the two groups vary in a complex cluster of characteristics, and follow widely divergent developmental paths in a variety of ways. Aggression on its own might be a relatively unimportant aspect of these differences.

There is a consistent body of evidence (reviewed by Maccoby & Jacklin, 1980a; 1980b) to show that males are more aggressive than females from an early age. Among the arguments for the view that the difference has a biological basis are that it starts from an early age, that it is reproduced

7. Farrington (1978) showed that boys who were aggressive at the age of eight or ten had an increased risk of nonviolent as well as violent crime, although the link with violent crime was stronger. The indications from other research (Moore et al., 1979), however, are that children who steal but do not show aggressive antisocial behavior have no increased risk of committing violent offenses later, although they do have an increased risk of committing property offenses.

across many cultures, and that alterations in male hormone levels have been shown through experiments to have an effect on aggressiveness.

Another line of explanation involves the male and female roles, and the stresses and criminal opportunities attaching to them. It seems plausible that changes in the roles and usual activities of men and women will largely explain the narrowing of the male-female crime ratio of the past forty years, but explanations of this kind are not yet supported by detailed analysis. It has not been demonstrated that the changes in the male-female crime ratio, which have occurred over a fairly limited period of fifteen years or so, have coincided with a period of exceptional change in female roles; closer specification of the important dimensions of female roles is needed before the matter can be fully analyzed. It is not clear, without detailed analysis, that the more traditional female roles offer fewer opportunities than the male ones for committing either property or personal offenses. It is striking, for example, that men are more likely than women to be violent within the family, although women spend much more time interacting with children and parents in the family setting than do men.

Ethnic group

There is a considerable body of writing attempting to explain the high crime rate among American blacks. By contrast, discussion of the European data is at a much earlier stage; it has been mainly concerned, up to now, with how far apparent differences in crime rates between ethnic groups are a consequence of law enforcement practices and the operation of the criminal justice system. It seems likely from the available evidence that in Britain and the Netherlands, at least, there is a substantially higher than average rate of offending for certain minority groups, but not for others: a higher than average rate for Afro-Caribbeans in England, and for Moroccans in the Netherlands; a lower than average rate for south Asians in England; and perhaps slightly above average rates for Surinamers and Turks in the Netherlands. This at least shows that the causes of high crime rates are specific to particular ethnic groups, and are not a consequence of the process of migration and adaptation over the recent postwar period which is largely shared by these groups.

The explanation for the high crime rate among Black Americans is highly controversial. A number of different factors and processes are probably involved, including inadequate socialization connected with stressed family circumstances, a breakdown of social controls in largely black inner-city areas, and perceptions of a lack of legitimate opportunities.

Social class

Many sociological theories have assumed that both youth and adult crime is much more common among the lower than among the higher social classes, but evidence to support the assumption has always been weak. This matter became the subject of academic controversy in the United States in the late 1970s and early 1980s. An enormous number of studies collected relevant results. Braithwaite (1981) listed thirty-one studies in the period 1958 to 1969, and forty studies from the 1970s. From a secondary analysis of thirty-five studies, Tittle, Villemez, and Smith (1978) concluded that there was a slight negative relationship between class and criminality. Self-report studies produced lower associations than official statistics studies. One possible reason for this is that many of the behaviors covered by self-report studies are noncriminal and even trivial. Another is that the association with social class in studies of official statistics arises from selective law enforcement practices. In addition, Tittle, Villemez, and Smith found a historic decline in the strength of the association; by the 1970s no association appears in either self-report or official statistics studies. Braithwaite (1981) challenged the conclusion of a decline. He also showed that studies of advanced societies tended to find little association between social class and criminality. This point was taken up by Axenroth (1983) who found, using both official statistics and self-report data, a strong association between class and criminality in Korea. He concluded that social class may be strongly associated with criminality in less developed or developing societies, but not in advanced industrial societies.

Rutter and Giller summarized the British evidence on this question as follows.

> The evidence suggests that there is a modest (but not strong) association between low social status and delinquency, but that this association applies mainly at the extremes of the social scale, that it is due in part to social class differentials in detection and prosecution, and that in so far as it applies to real differences in delinquent activities, the association is largely confined to the more serious delinquencies. Moreover, even that association is more strongly evident with measures of parental unemployment or reliance on welfare than with indices of parental occupation or education. (Rutter and Giller, 1983: 136–7)

They thought at least some of the data suggested that the social class–delinquency association may be slightly stronger in Britain than in the United States. They also concluded that measures of poverty, unemployment, and reliance on welfare showed stronger associations with delinquency than parental occupation or education.

There is some evidence that the effect of social class on delinquency may be mediated by other factors associated with low social status. Farrington (1979) found that the association disappeared when the effect of parental supervision was taken into account. West and Farrington (1973) also found that although parental criminality and family income were associated with each other and each was associated with delinquency, the effect of parental criminality was more basic, for it tended to remain after controlling for family income, whereas the reverse was not the case.

Family influences

Loeber and Stouthamer-Loeber (1986) have reported the results of a meta-analysis of a large number of American, British, and Scandinavian studies on the relation of family factors to juvenile conduct problems and delinquency. They included both longitudinal and concurrent studies, ones using self-reports and official data on delinquency, ones based on normal samples, and others comparing delinquents with nondelinquents, and aggressive with nonaggressive children. As a method of organizing the data, they distinguished four paradigms of family influences. First, there is the neglect paradigm, in which parents spend too little time interacting with their children and are often unaware of the mischief they are getting into. The pattern has two distinct aspects: a lack of supervision and a lack of involvement. Second, there is the conflict paradigm, a pattern of escalating conflict between child and parents. Aspects of the pattern are inadequate, inappropriate, or inconsistent disciplining, and rejection (of the child by the parents or of the parents by the child). The third paradigm concerns deviant behaviors and values. Parents may be delinquent themselves, or they may hold attitudes that condone lawbreaking. Fourth, there is the disruption paradigm. Neglect and conflict may arise because of marital discord, breakup of the marriage with the subsequent absence of one parent, and parental illness.

Variables belonging to all four paradigms were found to be consistently related to conduct problems or delinquency. These relationships tended to be strongest for the neglect paradigm, intermediate for the deviant behaviors and attitudes and the conflict paradigms, and lowest for the disruption paradigm. Broadly speaking, socialization variables (such as parents' involvement with children) were more strongly related than familial background variables (such as the absence of a parent).

The familial variables are related to the full range of child problems captured by self-reports of conduct and delinquency and by arrest or court records. The amount of supervision was related (inversely) to the seriousness or amount of delinquency, and the association was stronger for official than for self-reported delinquency. The same was true for several other familial variables.

Various findings suggest that different family handicaps interlock and jointly increase the chances that children will become delinquent. The risk of child problem behavior increases rapidly as the number of family handicaps increases. Child conduct problems can be divided into those that are overt and confrontational (arguing, fighting, etc.) and those that are covert (stealing, vandalism, truancy, drug use, etc.). There is some evidence that distinct patterns of familial handicaps may be associated with the two kinds of problem behavior.

Use of alcohol and illicit drugs

There is overwhelming evidence of a strong association between use of alcohol and aggression, including violent crime, and between use of various illicit drugs and a wide range of delinquent and criminal activities (Hore, 1990; Evans, 1990; Gordon, 1990; Fagan, 1990; Chaiken & Chaiken, 1990). As Fagan (1990) pointed out, however, there is little explanatory power to the intoxication-aggression association when the effects of culture and social interaction are removed. A satisfactory explanation must describe the interactions between use of psychoactive substances and the way people perceive the social setting and their own and others' behavior, the expectations they form, cultural beliefs about the effects of the substance, and the operation of social controls; it is only when these combine together in specific ways that they produce aggressive behaviors.

Although the link between alcohol and aggression is certainly not straightforward, there is good evidence from time series analyses of data for Scandinavian countries (Wiklund & Lidberg, 1990) and Australia (Smith, 1990) that changes in the total consumption of alcohol are associated with changes in the level of recorded violent crime.

According to Chaiken and Chaiken (1990) in a recent review of the results of American research on the relation between drugs and predatory crime, "there is strong evidence that predatory offenders who persistently and frequently use large amounts of multiple types of drugs commit crimes at significantly higher rates over longer periods than do less drug-involved offenders, and predatory offenders commit fewer crimes during periods in which they use no heroin." Although these multiple heavy users of multiple types of drugs probably account for a considerable proportion of predatory crime, they are a special group; the relation between drugs and crime for the majority of offenders and drug users is entirely different. Most adolescents and adults who use illicit drugs do not commit predatory crimes. About half of delinquent youngsters are delinquent before they start using drugs, whereas the remaining half start concurrently or after. This suggests that prevention of delinquency is likely to be a better approach than prevention of drug use among adolescents.

In broad terms, the evidence suggests that use of drugs is more an aspect than a cause of delinquency. Since, however, there is an important group of persistent and frequent offenders who are also persistent users of heroin and other drugs, it seems that use of drugs may be a cause of crime among a minority of offenders who account for a substantial proportion of all offenses.

Social geography

A long tradition of British and American research documents variations in crime rates between areas, and analyzes these differences in terms of social geography or ecology: that is, in terms of the social composition and physical layout of areas, rather than the characteristics of individuals. Large differences in crime rate can be demonstrated between different types of area. For example, an analysis of data from the British Crime Survey of 1984 (Hope & Hough, 1988) compared crime victimization rates within eleven types of areas. The areas used in the analysis are census enumeration districts which contain on average 150 households, grouped into the eleven types on the basis of a cluster of sociodemographic characteristics.[8] The proportion of households that were victims of burglary varied from 1 percent in "agricultural areas" through 4 percent in "poor quality older terraced housing" to 12 percent in "poorest quality council estates." The analysis showed that the risk of burglary was strongest for council tenants in areas consisting mostly or entirely of council housing. This demonstrates an ecological effect on top of the effect due to the tenure of the individual family.

8. The ACORN classification used for the analysis was derived from a principal components analysis of a range of enumeration-level census variables.

Explaining such area differences is a more difficult matter. A great deal of attention and research effort has been devoted in recent years to the "broken windows" hypothesis put forward by Wilson and Kelling (1982). They argued that minor disorder and incivility undermine the informal processes by which communities normally maintain order. In support of this idea, Hope and Hough (1988) have shown that types of areas with high levels of perceived incivilities tend also to have high levels of crime as measured by total or burglary victimization. The shape of the relationship also suggests an accelerating process of decline associated with the positive feedback process envisaged by Wilson and Kelling (for example, rising crime increases fear and further discourages residents from trying to exert informal social controls).

A different approach to explaining area differences is to consider the opportunities for crime afforded by different types of area. These would be shaped by physical layout and routine activities of residents as well as by informal social controls. According to this approach, the tradition that explains criminal behavior in terms of an assessment of perceived risks by a potential offender should be informed by the ecological tradition. The criminal's decision-making will be influenced by perceptions of risk associated with the perceived characteristics of areas (Gottfredson & Taylor, 1988). As yet, there is little systematic evidence supporting this idea.

Using data from the British Crime Survey of 1982, Sampson and Wooldredge (1987) have shown that as well as being associated with the characteristics of individuals or families, burglary risk was associated with characteristics of the local area: the proportion of single-person households, the rate of unemployment, and housing density. Personal theft was also related to area as well as individual characteristics.

Thus, studies integrating area-level and individual-level information about victimization are now beginning to show that both levels are important in shaping the individual's vulnerability to crime. Studies integrating area-level and individual-level information about offending are at an early stage (Gottfredson & Taylor, 1988). So far, they tend to show that individual characteristics overwhelm area characteristics as determinants of offending.

Trends in crime and cross-national comparisons

Conceptual and measurement issues

There are three basic elements in the idea of crime: moral wrong, transgression of a legal code, and a decision to use the resources of the criminal justice system to deal with the matter. Any method of measuring crime must be bound up with the changing content of legal codes, changing moral perceptions, and changing methods of dealing with offensive behavior. Different methods of measurement place varying degrees of emphasis on the three main elements. Recorded crime is a count of incidents referred to the authorities, and classified by them as breaking the legal code. Victim surveys report incidents people know about and remember, and which the surveyors regard as being against the law. These include many not referred to the authorities, although people are still influenced in deciding what to mention in the survey by their conception of what it might be worth reporting to the police. Studies of self-reported offending also cover a wider field than recorded crime. Both victim surveys and self-report studies of offending are subject to biases caused by forgetting and distortion, by mistaking when an event occurred, and by a reluctance to mention certain incidents.

The serious measurement problems involved in making cross-national comparisons have been carefully enumerated by Mayhew (1992). She divided the problems in making use of statistics of recorded crime into "cultural" differences and "system" differences. "The nuances of culture are reflected most intangibly in which forms of deviance are 'socially' defined as criminal by victims, and which – within wide ranges of discretion it seems – are 'officially' so defined by criminal justice agencies. Descriptions of particular systems have documented some official differences, but we have nothing approaching a systematic index." It has been shown that local rates of recorded crime may vary widely because of enforcement strategy or recording practice (Reynolds & Blyth, 1975; McCleary, Nienstadt, & Erven, 1982; Farrington & Dowds, 1985), and this suggests that similar differences between countries are likely. As Mayhew pointed out, "thresholds for offenses involving sexual behaviour or assault can be particularly problematic" but "even seemingly straightforward offenses such as burglary, vehicle theft or homicide can pose problems in comparisons." There is wide variation in the extent to which less serious offenses are counted in official statistics, which means that comparing the total of all recorded offenses between countries is particularly perilous. The proportion of offenses reported to the police may vary between countries: It has certainly been shown to change over time in the United States. Changes in recording practice can take place because of directives, shifting perceptions among staff, or organizational changes such as computerization which reduce the scope for discretion. An example of the effects of reporting and recording changes is the divergence in

England and Wales over a fifteen-year period in survey-measured trends in burglary, which rose by 17 percent, and that for recorded offenses, which rose by 127 percent (Mayhew, Elliott & Dowds, 1989).[9] These changes may be related to increasing house ownership and insurance.

The method followed in victim surveys is to ask respondents whether each of a number of specific things has happened to them over a reference period (often twelve months). The incidents are mostly described in simple language, sometimes without reference to the word describing the corresponding criminal offense. The respondent's description is not tested: For example, someone who says that her purse was stolen will not be asked more detailed questions to explore the possibility that she lost or mislaid it. Victim surveys count many incidents that are not counted in recorded crime. Many incidents that might sometimes be recorded as crimes are not mentioned in victim surveys, because the respondent did not notice or care about or recall them, or did not want to think of them as crime, or did not want to tell anyone about them. This is particularly true of sexual offenses, and of violence between people who know each other well.

Incidents counted in victim surveys but not in the statistics of recorded crime are offenses having identifiable victims which were either not reported or not recorded. Offenses counted in statistics of recorded crime but not in victim surveys are chiefly those without any victim or which are generated by law enforcement or regulation: possession of illicit drugs, prostitute soliciting, obstructing a police officer, and contravention of traffic regulations. Finally, some types of offense are seldom recorded by either method: corruption, tax fraud, white-collar crime, and contravention of public safety and health regulations.

The great bulk of crime revealed by victim surveys is theft, damage to property, and assault, and these are probably the kinds of crimes which cause greatest public concern. For England and Wales and for the United States it is now possible to make a close comparison between victim-survey results and counts of recorded crime for selected offenses of this kind (Mayhew, 1992). Except for motor vehicle theft, the victim-survey counts are higher than the counts of recorded crime by factors of two and a half or more. The near-universal insurance of motor vehicles accounts for the fact that nearly all thefts of motor vehicles are recorded.

9. This may overestimate the divergence, because the two different surveys used over the fifteen-year period were not entirely comparable. The British Crime Survey in 1981–87 shows a 59 percent increase in burglary versus 38 percent in comparable recorded offenses (Mayhew, Elliott, & Dowds, 1989).

In spite of this wide difference in coverage, the results of victim surveys over time show trends fairly similar to the statistics of recorded crime. The main difference, in both the United States and England and Wales, is that the curves shown by victim-survey statistics are flatter and smoother. Between 1981 and 1987, crime counted by the British Crime Survey rose by 30 percent, as against a 41 percent rise in recorded offenses (Mayhew, Elliott & Dowds, 1989). The size and direction of the divergence over time between police and survey statistics vary in a complex way between types of offense.

The results from asking people about offenses they have committed have been compared with their official convictions. All the relevant studies show that self-reported offenders are more likely to be official offenders than are self-reported nonoffenders, and conversely that official offenders are more likely to be self-reported offenders than are the official nonoffenders (Huizinga & Elliott, 1986). Although these results have been taken to demonstrate the validity of the self-report method, another possible interpretation is that those who are officially recorded become more willing to admit their delinquent acts. The most convincing demonstration of the validity of self-report, therefore, is to show, as Farrington (1973; 1989) has done, that self-reported offending predicts future convictions among those who are currently unconvicted. At the same time, self-reports yield far more incidents than are counted in official statistics of recorded crime. Many studies show that the probability of a self-reported offender becoming an officially recorded offender is quite low. Unlike victim surveys, self-report studies have not generally been used as a method of estimating the volume of crime. It has been sufficient for the purposes of these studies to show that there is a clear connection between self-reported and official offending.

From this discussion it should be clear that the concept of crime is elusive, and that it is captured by different measures in markedly different ways. Different measures are subject to different influences, and emphasize different elements of the idea of crime – perception of moral wrong, infraction of a legal code, or processing by the criminal justice system. There is a substantial overlap between them, but the interpretation of statistics of recorded crime and of victim survey results must be hedged around with qualifications.

Crime rates since the Second World War

The International Criminal Police Organisation (Interpol) has since 1950 reported statistics of recorded crime collected from a range of countries.

Although broad guidelines are given on counting and classification, countries derive the statistics entered on the form from the official statistics available, which are shaped by the national legal code. Hence the statistics provide no more than a rough and ready basis for comparison between countries. Comparison of trends over time between countries may be somewhat more reliable. The crime classification method used by Interpol was changed to a more detailed one in 1977. It is possible to make a continuous series from 1950 by aggregating certain of the categories used since 1977. Generally, the results show a smooth trend over this break in classification between 1976 and 1977 when the later categories are aggregated in this way.

Figures 5.1 to 5.4 illustrate the trends shown by the Interpol data for selected countries, always expressing recorded crime as a rate per 1000 population, or 100,000 in the case of homicide. Figure 5.1 shows a large rise in the total crime rate between 1951 and 1990 for all countries except Japan. As mentioned earlier, the total crime rate is more subject to measurement error than the rates for more specific offenses, since it is sensitive to the inclusion or exclusion of less serious offenses. It is nevertheless useful as an indicator of the huge expansion for nearly all countries in the amount of crime that impinges on the criminal justice system. The highest increases in total crime rate recorded for the selected countries are for Spain (by a factor of twenty-nine) and Canada (by a factor of twenty-seven). There were also exceptionally steep increases for Sweden (factor of fourteen) and Norway (factor of thirteen). For the remaining countries except Japan, the crime rate increased over this period by a factor of between two and six. Remarkably, in the context of the trends for other countries, the total crime rate in Japan declined slightly over the forty-year period. There are some differences between countries in the shape of the upward trend. Unfortunately, the Interpol figures recorded for the United States are incomplete, but the detailed statistics (available in the Uniform Crime Reports) show a decline in the total crime rate during the 1980s, following the earlier upward trend. Canada and Australia similarly registered a decline in the 1980s. In the remaining countries (always excepting Japan) the upward trend continued.[10]

The story of steeply rising crime rates is confirmed when more specific offenses are considered rather than total crime. Over the full time series, property crimes are encompassed by the broadly interpreted categories of aggravated theft and other theft. Although there are many detailed varia-

10. A more short-lived reversal of the upward trend is evident in some countries, for example England and Wales, if year by year statistics are studied.

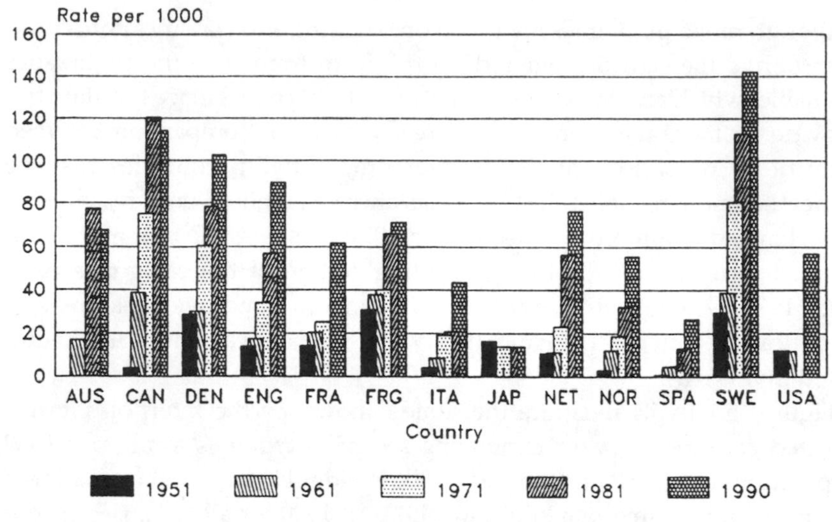

Figure 5.1. Total recorded offenses, 1951–1990. (Interpol data)

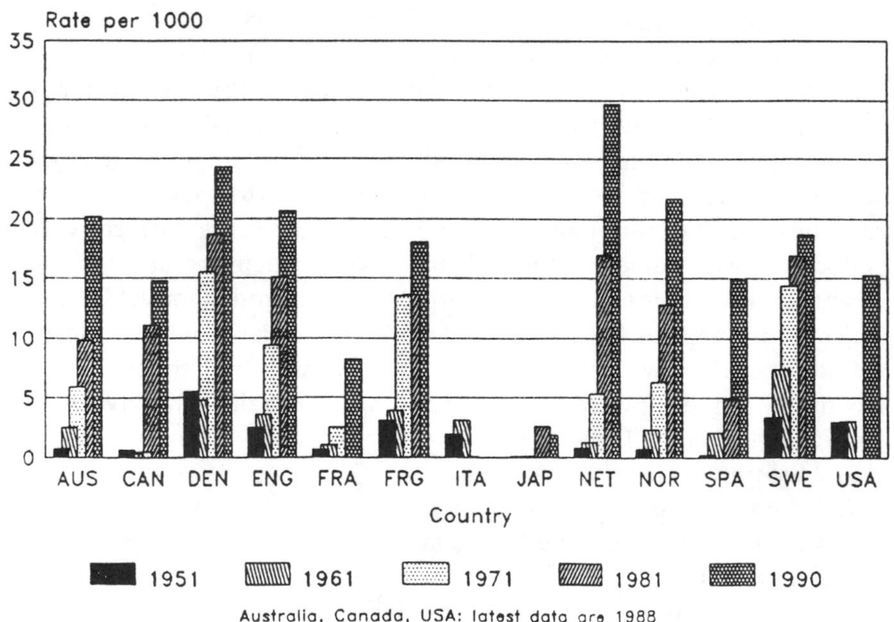

Figure 5.2. Aggravated theft, 1951–1990. (Interpol data)

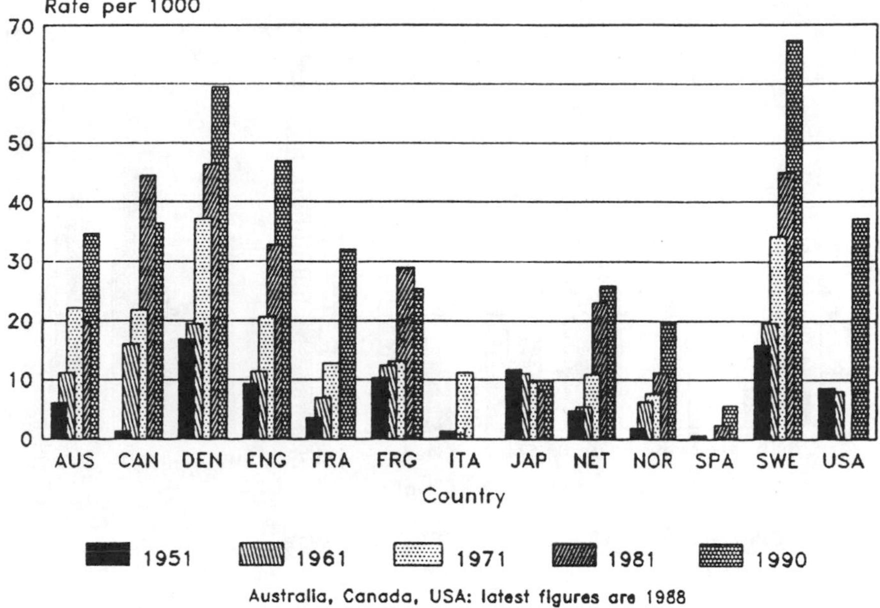

Figure 5.3. Theft (excluding aggravated), 1951–1990. (Interpol data)

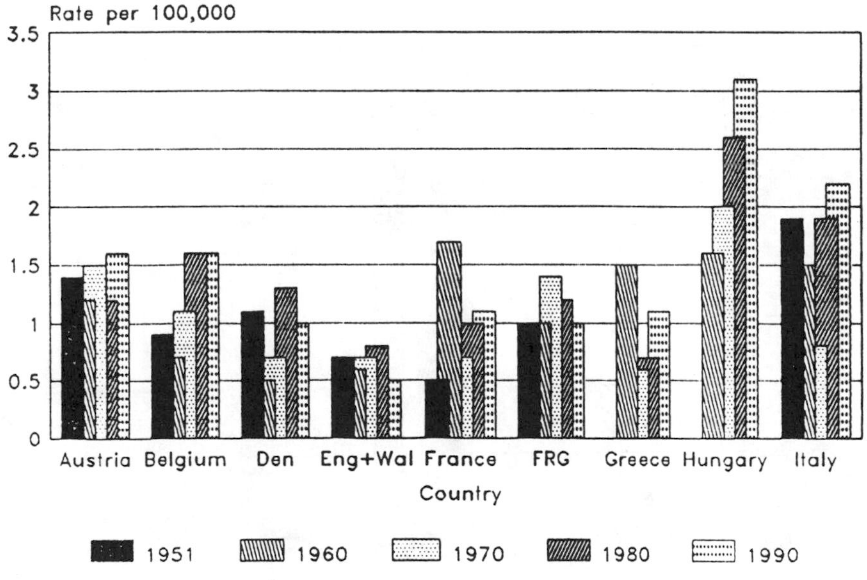

Figure 5.4a. Homicide, 1951–1990. (World Health Organization data)

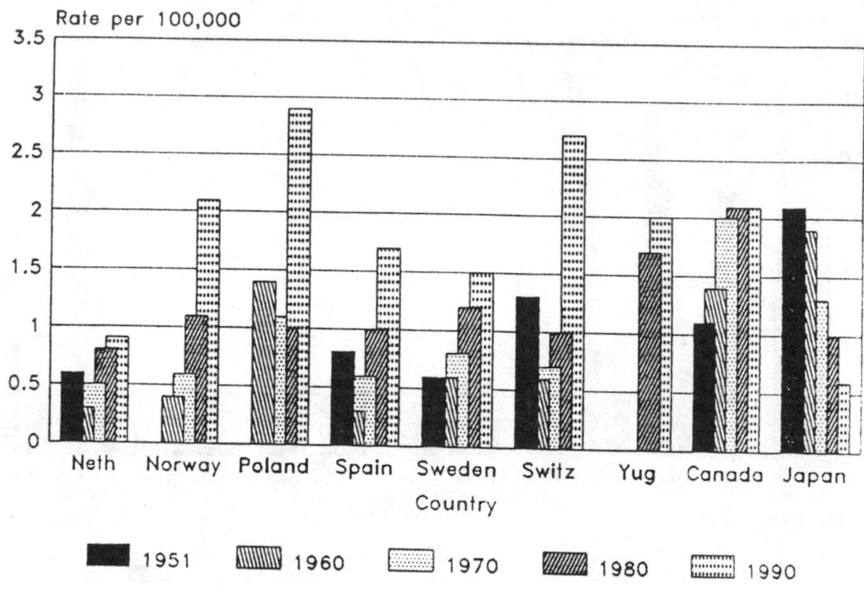

Figure 5.4b. Homicide, 1951–1990. (World Health Organization data)

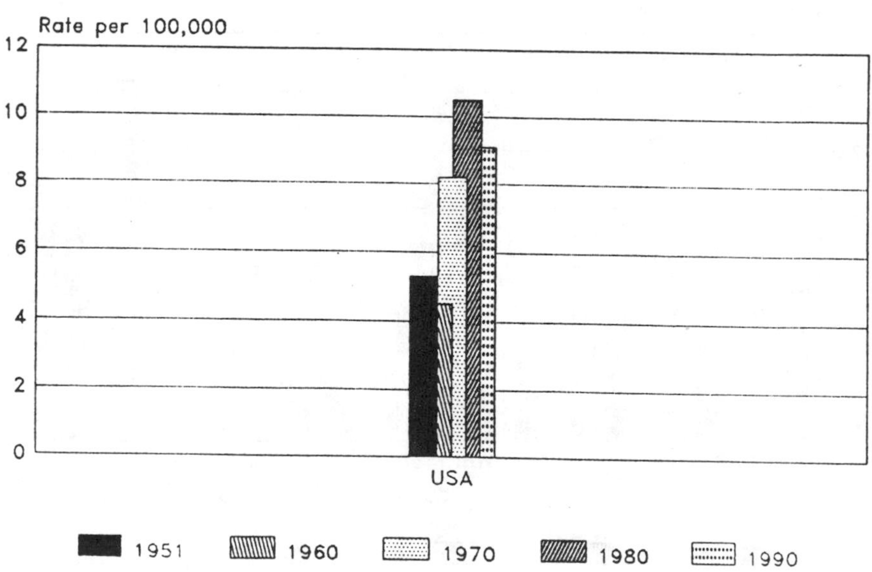

Figure 5.4c. Homicide, U.S.A., 1951–1990. (World Health Organization data – note change of scale)

tions between countries, the trends for aggravated theft and other theft are comparable to those for total crime rates. In England and Wales, for example, the total crime rate increased by a factor of five and a half, aggravated theft by a factor of seven and a half, and other theft by a factor of four and a half. The pattern of change for two more specific offenses – theft of motor vehicles and breaking and entering – can be traced for the more recent period starting in 1977. Substantial increases are again registered for many countries in the crime rates for these more specific offenses over a much shorter time period.

Crimes of violence other than homicide cannot be identified in the Interpol statistics until 1977. Since then, there have been substantial increases in the rates of serious assault in Australia, Denmark, England and Wales, and the United States.

For all the offenses so far considered, the great majority of offenders are teenagers and young adults in their twenties. The same is not true of homicide, but homicide rates are of special interest because most homicides are probably recorded in all the countries considered here. As homicide is much rarer than other crimes, the rates have been expressed per 100,000 population.[11] There has been a substantial increase in homicide rates in most of the selected countries since 1951, but these increases are considerably smaller, in most countries, than the increases in the rates of other crimes. In Japan the homicide rate has declined to 40 percent of the 1951 rate.

Trends in juvenile crime. In England and Wales the official figures on juvenile offending show the numbers of convictions and cautions of persons aged ten to sixteen for indictable[12] offenses per 1,000 population in this age group. On this definition, offending by males "increased to a peak from 1961 to the mid 1970s, then decreased somewhat in the late 1970s, then increased again to a greater peak in 1985, before decreasing again up to 1989." Offending by females "increased fairly steadily to a peak in 1985 before decreasing up to 1989. The changes are quite dramatic" (Farrington, 1992). Neither the earlier increases nor the recent decline in officially recorded juvenile offending is, however, a true reflection of changes in juvenile behavior. Rather, it reflects changes in policy for dealing with juvenile offenders (in the proportion of cases where the juvenile was formally charged with an offense). Similar patterns of change in offi-

11. The Interpol statistics on homicide include attempts up to 1976 but exclude them thereafter, except in the case of the Netherlands. For that reason, the figures for the Netherlands shown in the chart for 1981 and 1990 are out of line with those for other European countries.
12. Excludes the least serious offenses.

cially recorded juvenile delinquency have been observed in many European countries. Kyvsgaard (1991) drew attention to the widespread recent decline in official juvenile offending and quotes the relevant statistics for a range of countries. Although she assumed that these statistics indicate a decline in juvenile misbehavior, she quoted no convincing evidence in support of this view. Mayhew (1992) writes that "after a period of increasing numbers of juveniles before the courts, in most countries the proportion of juvenile offenders prosecuted has decreased over time, reflecting both demographic change and a general increase in formal or informal cautioning. In a sample of thirteen countries,[13] the number of juvenile offenders fell by 21% between 1980 and 1989, the sharpest drops being in Greece, Northern Ireland and West Germany."

Cross-national comparisons of rates of recorded crime

So far it has been established that most recorded crime is committed by teenagers and adults in their twenties, and that in most developed countries, with the signal exception of Japan, there have been enormous increases in the rates of recorded crime in the postwar era.[14] These changes are in part due to changing perceptions, laws, institutions, and ways of dealing with offensive behavior, but there has clearly been a substantial increase in crime, in criminal behavior, and in the prevalence of offending, on any appropriate definition. Although there have been declines during the 1980s in the prevalence of officially recorded juvenile offending in many countries, these probably reflect for the most part changes in response of the criminal justice system. Contrary to the trend in most countries, however, there was a marked decrease in crime in the United States during the 1980s; the contrasting trends in England and the United States are confirmed by close comparisons of official and victim-survey data.

The Interpol statistics also show wide differences in rates of recorded crime between countries at any one time. For the period 1986–88, for example, the rate of burglary per 100,000 population was 2,776 in the Netherlands, 1,965 in West Germany, 1,769 in England and Wales, 1,010 in Switzerland, 828 in Austria, 697 in France, 588 in Belgium, 257 in Greece, and 228 in Japan. The rate of recorded burglary in the Netherlands was therefore 2.7 times the rate in Switzerland, and 12.2 times the rate in Japan.

13. The countries were Austria, Canada, England and Wales, Finland, France, Greece, Japan, Luxembourg, Netherlands, Northern Ireland, Norway, Scotland, and West Germany.
14. Switzerland is probably a second exception, although it is not included in the figures because Interpol data are not available for earlier years.

No very clear pattern emerges from the various attempts to interpret these striking cross-national differences. One reason for this is the large amount of "noise" in the statistics compiled. Even allowing for these data problems, however, it is clear that the most popular theories either do not fit the facts, or else are so vaguely specified that they will fit any facts. They tend to deal in broad-brush accounts of societal structures, because writers lack the detailed information about individual countries that would allow them to describe mechanisms that might link broad structure with the control of crime. Mayhew (1992) has summed up most of these theories as relying on a broad notion of "modernization." The germ of the idea is that crime was low in earlier societies based mainly on agriculture and that rising crime is a product of the process of development to modern industrial or postindustrial society. Writers mention a number of features of the process of development or modernization as being important: for example, the move from agriculture to industry, the concentration of population in large towns, increasing social heterogeneity brought about by the mobility of the population, the destruction of small, tightly knit village communities, the growth of individualism, a weakening of community controls associated with all these developments, a decline in fatalistic acceptance of a low position in a preordained hierarchy, increasing affluence creating more goods to be stolen, increasing feelings of relative deprivation. The question not yet answered is which specific aspects of development, or what specific pattern of interactions between different factors, accounts for the striking differences in recorded crime rates between developed nations. Any appeal to a general process of development assumed to be similar in all countries is bound to fail, since the most highly developed country, Japan, not only has very low crime rates, but has always had very low crime rates (at any rate since the Second World War). For the moment, cross-national comparisons do not seem to have got very far; in order to move toward explaining rising crime, we will have to look to more detailed studies of crime and the conditions that give rise to it in specific societies.

Cross-national comparisons of survey data

One reason why cross-national studies of recorded crime rates have been inconclusive is that – for all the reasons already rehearsed – these crime rates mean different things in different countries. Comparisons based on the results of victim surveys have begun to suggest that cross-national differences on survey-based measures tend to be smaller. For example, rates of recorded crime are substantially higher in Scotland than in England and Wales for all offenses except violence against the person. In 1982, the first British Crime Survey was carried out on a closely comparable basis in England, Wales, and Scotland. The results showed few differences in survey-based crime rates between the two countries, and where there are differences, some of them run in the opposite direction (show higher rates in England and Wales than in Scotland). Mayhew and Smith (1985) concluded that for the most part the differences in rates of recorded crime between the two countries are due to differences in counting practices.

A number of comparisons have also been made between the results of crime surveys carried out independently in Canada, England and Wales, Australia, the Netherlands, and the United States. Although there are important differences between the methods used in these various surveys, the results do fit reasonably well with the statistics of recorded crime, although substantial differences in recorded crime between countries are in some cases not replicated in survey-based estimates, and may arise from differences in counting procedures. National victim surveys cannot yet, however, provide a basis for systematic comparison of crime rates between countries. The 1989 International Crime Survey for the first time makes possible a more systematic comparison of this kind (see van Dijk, Mayhew, & Killias, 1991). The survey has some fairly severe limitations. Sample sizes were fairly small (two thousand households in most countries) and for the most part the survey was carried out through computer-assisted telephone interviews. Where telephone interviewing was used, at least 70 percent of households had telephones, and in most countries the figure was 90 percent or higher. The response rates from the telephone interviews were variable, however, and generally low. They ranged from 30 percent to 71 percent, and the average was 41 percent. Response rates of this order leave substantial scope for biases that may be just as important as the reporting and recording problems underlying official statistics.

Despite these faults and limitations, there is a fairly high correlation between the ranking of countries on survey victimization measures and on recorded crime rates. These findings indicate that in time the survey method will produce data of great value for international comparative studies of crime. They show that national statistics of recorded crime do provide a useful measure of incidents that are reported to the police, but that, to a considerable extent, variations in rates of recorded crime between countries reflect variations in the propensity of the public to report incidents to the police.

The pattern that emerges from comparing the rates of victimization between countries, as shown by the International Crime Survey, is similar in many respects to the pattern shown for the rates of recorded crime in Figure 5.1: For example, Canada, Australia, and the United States have high rates on both measures, whereas Japan has a low rate on both. Spain is low on recorded crime but much higher on victimization rate, probably because the proportion of incidents reported to the police is low.

One clear finding that emerges from the survey is an association between the proportion of the national population living in large cities of 100,000 inhabitants or more and the national risk of victimization ($r = 0.64$). Major exceptions to the general pattern are Japan, where the rate of victimization is low in relation to the high proportion living in cities, and the United States and the Netherlands, where the rate of victimization is high in relation to the proportion living in cities. It has long been known that within countries the rate of crime (however measured) is much higher in large cities than elsewhere, but this finding suggests that national differences in crime rates arise, to a considerable extent, because of national differences in the urban/rural mix. A similar result was obtained by Pease and Harvey (1988) from analysis of United Nations surveys; they showed that at the national level population density is a strong predictor of overall crime rates. This at least shows that crime is related to one specific aspect of "modernization" or "development" – the gathering of the population into large cities. This may point the way toward an explanation of crime, as discussed in a later section.

Theories

Many ideas and theories have been put forward to explain the patterns and trends of crime and conduct disorders. The abundance of explanations is apt to become chaotic. They often originate from different disciplines, may be intended to explain different things, or apply to different levels of explanation, yet frequently overlap, are recombined, and emerge in a new shape. It may help to divide them into four broad types.

1. *Dispositional theories* seek to explain why some individuals are more disposed to crime than others. A dominant strain is the idea that a disposition to crime is the result of a process of socialization in the setting of the family or (less prominently) the school. A disposition to crime may also be related to fixed, or relatively fixed, personal characteristics such as sex, IQ, physiological and personality attributes.

2. *Social control theories* start from the need to explain why people don't normally commit crimes, rather than why they sometimes do. They say that criminal behavior is inhibited by the painful, uncomfortable, or embarrassing consequences caused by formal and informal sanctions. Social control is achieved through direct supervision and sanctions, at varying levels of formality, for example by the family, the school, peers, acquaintances in the neighborhood, or strangers. Some of these (particularly family and school) may also be important as agents of socialization: the process whereby rules and values are internalized becomes part of a person's outlook, and forms the nucleus of a system of self-regulation (Bandura, 1991).

3. *Opportunity or limited rationality theories* are closely allied to social control theories, but explain criminal behavior as the outcome of a decision-making process in which costs and benefits are weighed. They differ from social control theories in that they emphasize the calculation of benefits as well as risks. Limited rationality theories do not assume a perfect or idealized calculation of risks, costs, and benefits, but an actor making choices on the basis of a faulty and biased assessment of limited information. Relevant to this type of theory is research on social geography, the physical environment, situational prevention, the risk of conviction, and life-styles and routine activities as determinants of criminal opportunities. Broad social or economic changes, such as the increase in the number of goods that people own, may shape opportunities for crime.

4. *Sociological theories* explain crime as the consequence of social structures or institutions, especially social class divisions. For example, crime is caused by the gap between the cultural goals of the working class and the means available for achieving them; or crime is the normal and accepted behavior of deviant subcultures; or it results from the labeling of the relatively weak as criminals, or from the widening of the net of the criminal justice system. Theories that explain the growth of crime by reference to unemployment, poverty, or inequality belong under this head.

Most theorists have been interested in just a few of the many mechanisms that underlie crime and conduct disorders. Often an account of one mechanism among the many involved is presented as an explanation of the total pattern. An example is Sutherland's (1956) theory that people become criminal because of the company they keep. Clearly, a complete theory would have to bring together elements from a number of the types reviewed here. Before starting to build such a theory (which is well beyond the scope of this chapter) it is important to consider which elements of the various types of theories may be worth retaining.

Dispositional theories

The two most basic facts about crime and conduct disorders are the age–crime curve and the much greater level of offending among males than among females. The reasons for the age–crime curve, and in particular the reasons why most young men give up crime, are not well understood. Desistance probably cannot be explained by changing opportunities or by increased social control, so it probably does reflect a change in disposition, probably biologically determined in some way. The large difference between the sexes is connected in some way with a difference in aggressiveness, which is probably biologically determined. This may, however, be just one of a complex cluster of characteristics which vary systematically between males and females.

A large body of research shows that processes of socialization within the family have a strong influence on the likelihood that a child will become a persistent and serious offender. There is evidence that schools, too, vary in their effectiveness in preventing absenteeism and delinquency (Rutter et al. 1979).

The sex difference and the age–crime curve do not seem to offer an explanation for the rise in crime over the past forty years. Changes in the shape of the age–crime curve could, in principle, lead to a rise in crime, but in practice the curve seems to remain fairly constant. Although female crime has risen more quickly than male crime in recent years (from a very low base), most of the rise in aggregate crime can be attributed to males.

Changes in family functioning could be a powerful explanation of rising crime. Conflict associated with marriage break-ups is strongly associated with delinquency in children, so the rising number of divorces could help to explain the rise in crime. The evidence does not suggest that the absence of a parent is a particularly important factor in itself, so it is not clear that the rise in the number of single-parent families is an important cause of the rise in crime. The largest rise in crime probably happened before the largest rise in the number of single-parent households in most countries. Changes in family functioning (regardless of family structure) could have an important influence on the level of crime, but it is not known whether there have been negative changes of that kind.

Although school socialization has been shown to have some importance, there is no evidence that this has become less effective over time.

Social control and self-regulation

Within each country, crime rates are much higher in large cities than elsewhere, and as pointed out earlier, there is a fairly high correlation between the ranking of countries by crime rate and by proportion of the population in towns of 100,000 or more inhabitants. Just what are the characteristics of large towns that lead to higher crime rates is a matter that would repay further study; one possibility is lower social control and surveillance, arising from mobility and heterogeneity of the population, lack of consensus on social norms, and less interaction with neighbors. Increasing urbanization cannot account for rising crime in Britain during the postwar period, or in a number of other European countries such as the Netherlands and Belgium, since over this period the population was tending to spread out rather than concentrate further into cities.

Bandura's social cognitive theory (1991) attempts to give a completely general account of the causal relationships underlying all behavior, including crime. It does not therefore belong within any particular type of crime theory, but is mentioned here because it places considerable emphasis on self-reactive influences and self-regulatory mechanisms. Much popular thinking would ascribe the rise in crime to a decline in moral standards, or a loss of self-control. Against that, Bandura argues that there is no invariant superego, and that self-reactive influences do not operate unless they are activated. There are four mechanisms through which moral standards can be disengaged: by reconstruing conduct, so that it appears not to transgress the code; by displacing or diffusing responsibility from oneself; by disregarding or misrepresenting the consequences of an act; and by blaming or devaluing the victim. There is good experimental evidence to demonstrate that these mechanisms of moral disengagement do operate. If societal trends tend to strengthen some or all of these mechanisms, the increase in crime could be explained not by a decline in personal or moral standards, but by an increasing tendency to disengage these standards in a selective and self-serving manner. Bandura argues, in particular, that many features of modern life are conducive to impersonalization and dehumanization. This might be particularly true of life in large cities, and would then help to explain the difference in crime rates between urban and rural areas, and the association between urbanization and crime rates at the national level of analysis.

Rates of crime also vary widely between small areas, and there is evidence that at least one of the reasons for such differences is the effectiveness of informal social controls rather than self-regulatory mechanisms. It is possible that the postwar rise in crime was associated with a weakening of informal social controls in specific types of areas within the cities, although there seems to be no way of testing this hypothesis at present. All sorts of methods can be proposed, however, for improving the effectiveness of social controls in high crime areas in future. Many such programs have been started over the past ten years in France, the United States and Britain, but their effectiveness has rarely been scientifically evaluated.

The evidence on the effect of formal sanctions is not clear-cut. In high crime periods and countries the risk of conviction is generally low, because the resources of the police and courts are stretched in dealing with the high volume of crime. In low crime periods and countries, the converse tends to be true. The critical question, therefore, is whether a *change* in the conviction rate can bring about a *change* in the crime rate. In order to address this question, Farrington and Langan (1992) have carried out a careful analysis of the contrasting trends in England and the United States between 1981 and 1986/7 both in crime rates and in the chances of conviction. They do not, however, come to a firm conclusion on the central issue. "Changes in the risk of conviction or imprisonment emerged as one plausible explanation for our results, but we cannot be at all confident that this factor would have appeared plausible if we had studied more countries, more time points, or different periods."

Opportunity and limited rationality

The broad theory of opportunity or limited rationality is that offending arises from an interaction between the individual and a constellation of competing risks and rewards. A large number of factors may influence the risks and rewards and the way they are perceived by the offender. These include the physical environment, social geography, the amount and nature of goods available to be stolen, how business is organized (for example, whether payments are made by cash, by check, or by credit card), and the life-styles and routine activities of people in the neighborhood. The opportunity theory therefore opens up many detailed possibilities for crime prevention, which may be tested individually, and some have been shown to work (Heal & Laycock, 1986; Clarke, 1992).

The emphasis on opportunity since the late 1970s was driven by policy imperatives rather than theoretical considerations. According to the account of Clarke (1992) it developed out of the failure of the policy of rehabilitation of offenders, which was the counterpart of dispositional theories. If criminal behavior is seen as a consequence of relatively stable dispositions, it may seem that the best policy is to change those dispositions. This runs up against two problems. First, the dispositions are, *ex hypothesi*, relatively stable, and hence hard to change. Second, the available institutions, such as prisons, are more likely to strengthen dispositions to crime (for example, through association with other criminals) than the opposite. If we go back further, and consider the factors (such as poor family functioning) which cause young people to become disposed to crime, we are again faced with a problem in policy terms. It is easy to see that happy families do not produce criminals. It is very hard to see how public policy can decree that family relationships be constructive and positive.

It seems far more likely that public policy can reduce the opportunities for crime, and this perception led to the increased emphasis on opportunity. It follows that opportunity theories do not deny the importance of dispositional factors. Crime is seen as the product of a motivated offender and his assessment on the basis of limited information of the risks and opportunities. The reason for emphasizing the risks and opportunities, rather than the offender's motivation, is that they can more easily be manipulated.

Situational prevention is the term used by Clarke (1992) to describe techniques that aim to manipulate the opportunities to reduce the level of crime. "Situational prevention comprises opportunity-reducing measures that are (1) directed at highly specific forms of crime (2) that involve the management, design or manipulation of the immediate environment in as systematic and permanent way as possible (3) so as to increase the effort and risks of crime and reduce the rewards as perceived by a wide range of offenders" (Clarke, 1992: 4).

Although the need to find credible crime prevention policies was the spur to the development of situational crime prevention, this approach is increasingly grounded in a general theory connected with both economics and psychology. Economics provides the model of the reasoning criminal making choices on the basis of incomplete information. Interactionist psychology provides the model of the individual with a repertoire of different attitudes, perceptions, and predispositions that are selectively brought into play depending on the specific situation. Hence, the theory that behavior is determined to a large extent by situations rather than by fixed dispositions that operate equally in all situations is one that fits well with some recent developments in psychology.

Much of the early opposition to opportunity theory and to situational prevention in particular was based on the assumption that dispositions to crime are relatively fixed, so if one set of opportunities is closed, the offender will find another. There is now a considerable body of well designed studies showing that at least in some cases not all of the crime prevented by opportunity reduction is displaced to other targets. There is evidence of displacement in some cases, but there is also evidence of what Clarke calls diffusion in others: That is, crime prevention efforts focusing on one area or type of target also reduce crime in neighboring areas or against related targets.

Thus, research in the tradition of situational crime prevention has demonstrated that opportunity is an important factor in specific cases, including some where motivation is extremely strong. The researchers in this tradition have shown little interest, however, in the question whether the general growth of crime is a consequence of a change in the structure of opportunities. It is feasible, though difficult, to consider how to reduce the opportunities for specific crimes. It is much more difficult – and probably impossible – to assess whether the whole "constellation of risks and opportunities" has shifted in favor of the offender over the postwar period. That is because there are innumerable specific situations, and situational prevention insists on the need to analyze each one individually.

Research (e.g., Sampson & Wooldredge, 1987) has shown that some aspects of social geography are associated with local crime rates, as predicted by the life-style/routine activities model: For example, burglary was associated with a high proportion of single-person households and with properties often left empty. These findings suggest that the general reduction in the size of households and the increase in the proportion of single-person households may be a cause of rising crime, through a change in the pattern of opportunity.

Broad economic changes might be expected to have an effect on the pattern of opportunity. In an econometric study of crime trends in England and Wales since the Second World War, Field (1990) constructed a regression model including growth in consumption and unemployment as explanatory variables, along with a considerable number of others. The results showed no effect of unemployment on the growth of crime, and this remained true whether unemployment in the current year, or one or two years previously, was considered. Growth in property crime was found to have an inverse relation to consumption growth in the short run, but to have no relation in the long run. Growth in personal crime, including violence against the person and sexual offenses, was found to be positively associated with growth in consumption both in the short and long run. Field explained these findings in terms of an economic theory of crime, in which increased consumption has three kinds of effect: It increases the opportunities for theft, it gives people the expectation of higher lifetime income from legitimate activity and therefore reduces the motivation to steal, and it increases the amount of time spent outside the home, and hence the opportunities for crime. The findings of this study suggest that increasing consumption is not the explanation for the long-term rise in property crime, but may be part of the explanation for rising personal crime. As most crime is theft, this still leaves most of the increase in crime to be explained.

Easterlin (1968) advanced the hypothesis that persons in large age cohorts will face greater competition combined with fewer social controls, so crime rates in these cohorts will rise. This may possibly be interpreted as a theory turning on the assessment by young people of the risks and opportunities available to them. Because most crime is committed by young men, an increase in the number of young males can be expected to have a substantial effect on the crime rate. Some econometric research (e.g., Field, 1990) does show a relationship in the short term between growth in crime and growth in the number of young men in the population. Over the longer term (the last 100 years), however, there has been a substantial reduction in all developed countries in the proportion of the population accounted for by young people. Hence, Easterlin's hypothesis cannot possibly explain the long-term increase in crime.

Sociological influences

In general, the sociological theories of crime belong to a form of class analysis ultimately deriving from Marx. According to Merton's strain theory (1938; 1957), crime is caused by the strain or gap between cultural goals and the means available for achieving them. He thought that young people in the lower social strata experience frustration from the lack of opportunity to participate in the rewards of economic success. One reaction to this strain, to adopt illegitimate means to achieve the goals, was the main explanation of the origin of crime. Thus, crime could be seen as a strategy used by the dispossessed to deal with class oppression.

The subcultural approach suggests that delinquency is "normal" behavior for a particular (working class) subculture and hence is learned like any other behavior (Mays, 1954; Willmott, 1966; Downes, 1966). This too springs from a class analysis. By adopting this strategy, sections of the working class succeed in denying or bypassing the demands of the dominant class, expressed in the morality and ideology it seeks to impose on the whole society.

As set out in an earlier section, there is evidence that in the late 1960s in England and Wales the police began to arrest people they would previously have dealt with informally. Evidence of this kind gives rise to the more general theory that increases in crime are due to a "widening of the net" – an enlargement of the scope of matters dealt with by formal process. This idea can be linked with labeling theory, which states that criminal process is a method of marking people as deviant, so they can be controlled and dealt with in ways that would not be acceptable in the case of mainstream citizens. (Garfinkel even went so far as to describe trials as "degradation ceremonies.") Putting these two ideas together, it might be suggested that crime increases because the criminal justice system widens the scope of the behavior and people it stigmatizes. Once a larger number of people have been labeled as deviant, there is a larger target for further police action leading to an increase in the number of offenses. These ideas are less closely linked with class analysis than with strain theory and subcultural theory; nevertheless, there may be the suggestion that net widening and labeling are methods used by the ruling class to stigmatize and oppress increasingly large numbers of the working class.

The central problem for these three sociological theories is that the relationship between social class and delinquency is not strong. For some versions of the theories, it may also be a problem that it is implausible to see crime as an aspect of class conflict, if that means that crime is an attack by one class on another. Offenders and their victims tend to belong to the same social class, ethnic group, social networks, and geographical area.

Nevertheless, there is some association between social class (particularly parental unemployment and poverty) and crime, and each of these theories has some value and incorporates some important insights. The labeling theory can be taken as an example. Farrington (1977) set out evidence from the Cambridge cohort that boys convicted between the ages of fourteen and eighteen reported more delinquency at eighteen than those not so convicted. A difference remained after controlling for early factors predictive of delinquency (criminality of parents, family income, family size, IQ, global index of parental behavior). There was some evidence to show that the order of causation was from labeling to deviance and not the opposite. Repeated labeling increased deviance amplification. Cautions (as opposed to convictions) did not lead to deviance amplification. Farrington was further able to show that some but not all the deviance amplification effect was an increased tendency to admit offenses. A more recent analysis of the Stockholm longitudinal study also supports the view that boys who become official offenders at an early age are more likely to offend as adults (Magnusson & Bergman, 1990).

Although ethnographic research adopting the subcultural perspective in England and America has provided valuable insights into the life and world view of delinquent boys, quantitative research has always disconfirmed the idea that these boys have value systems fundamentally different from the dominant ones. On the other hand, there may well be settings, in southern Italy for example, where young boys are socialized into deviant life-styles associated with organized crime, because the crime organizations are the main power base and source of employment and security.

The general conclusion of these three sociological theories is that although they provide interesting insights, they cannot explain any of the main sources of variation in observed patterns of crime.

Other sociological theories connect crime with unemployment, poverty, or inequality. Some studies on the individual level have suggested that people are more likely to commit crimes when unemployed (Farrington et al, 1986) but evidence from studies on aggregate data is equivocal (Orsagh & Witte, 1981). As already mentioned, in an econometric study of crime trends in England and Wales since the Second World War, Field (1990) found no effect of unemployment on the growth of crime, and this remained true whether considering unemployment in the current year, or one or two years previously.

In broad terms, theories linking crime with poverty or inequality are implausible, because, first, crime tends to be much higher in the rich, developed countries than in the developing countries, and second, income tends to be more equally distributed in the developed than in the developing countries.

Conclusions

In spite of the extensive body of research on crime and conduct disorders, this review has shown that it is extraordinarily difficult to explain why crime, most of it committed by young people, has increased so much in most developed countries in the postwar period. The most important factors are probably changes in family functioning, decline in the effectiveness of informal social controls in local communities, and changes in the pattern of crime opportunities and the associated risks.

The central conclusion to be drawn for policy is that decisions should not be taken solely or primarily on the basis of an assessment of the likely effect on future levels of crime, because those effects cannot now be assessed with any certainty, and perhaps they never will be. That point is highlighted by a discussion of the effect in America of an increase in the proportion of offenders convicted and imprisoned. The findings are consistent with the theory that the declining crime rate in America in the 1980s was caused by an increase in the likelihood that an offender would be convicted and imprisoned. Yet they cannot now, and they probably never will, establish that conclusion with any degree of certainty. On the other hand, there is much clearer evidence that the conviction of adolescent boys increases their level of delinquency. The deterrent effect of an increased risk of conviction on those not convicted or imprisoned would therefore have to be weighed against the amplification of delinquency among those convicted "pour encourager les autres." Mathematically and morally, that would be an equation with no solution.

It follows that policy must concentrate on pursuing objectives indubitably good in themselves. That means trying to improve family functioning and school socialization, improving the effectiveness of informal social controls in local communities, and reducing the opportunities for crime.

References

Axenroth, J. B. (1983). Social class and delinquency in cross-cultural perspective. *Journal of Research in Crime and Delinquency*, July, 164–82.

Bachman, J. G., O'Malley, P. M., & Johnston, J. (1978). *Adolescence to Adulthood – Change and Stability in the Lives of Young Men. Youth in Transition*, Vol. 6, Institute for Social Research, University of Michigan.

Bandura, A. (1991). Social cognitive theory of moral thought and action. In *Handbook of Moral Behaviour and Development*, Vol. 1: Theory, ed. W. M. Kurtines & J. L. Gewirtz, pp. 45–103. Hillsdale, N.J.: Erlbaum.

Braithwaite, J. (1981) The myth of social class and criminality reconsidered. *American Sociological Review* 46, 36–57.

Chaiken, J. M. & Chaiken, M. R. (1990). Drugs and predatory crime. In *Drugs and Crime: Crime and Justice, A Review of Research*, Vol. 13, ed. M. Tonry & J. Q. Wilson, pp. 203–40. University of Chicago Press.

Clarke, R. V. (ed.) (1992). *Situational Crime Prevention: Successful Case Studies.* New York: Harrow and Heston.

Cline, H. F. (1980). Criminal behavior over the life span. In *Constancy and Change in Human Development*, ed. O. G. Brim & J. Kagan, 641–74. Cambridge, Mass.: Harvard University Press.

Downes, D. (1966) *The Delinquent Solution: A Study of Subcultural Theory*. London: Routledge & Kegan Paul.

Easterlin, R. A. (1968). *Population, Labor Force and Long Swings in Economic Growth: The American Experience.* New York: National Bureau of Economic Research.

Elliott, D. S., & Voss, H. L. (1974). *Delinquency and Dropout*. Lexington Books.

Evans, M. (1990). Unsocial and criminal activities and alcohol. *Handbook of Forensic Psychiatry*, ed. R. Bluglass & P. Bowden, pp. 881–95. Edinburgh: Churchill Livingstone.

Fagan, J. (1990). Intoxication and aggression. In *Drugs and Crime: Crime and Justice, A Review of Research*, Vol. 13, ed. M. Tonry & J. Q. Wilson, pp. 241–320. Chicago: University of Chicago Press.

Farrington, D. P. (1973). Self-reports of deviant behaviour: Predictive and stable? *Journal of Criminal Law and Criminology*, 64, 99–110.

(1977). The effects of public labelling. *British Journal of Criminology*, 17, 112–25.

(1978). The family backgrounds of aggressive youths. In *Aggression and Antisocial Behaviour in Childhood and Adolescence*, ed. L. A. Hersov, M. Berger, & D. Shaffer, pp. 73–93. Oxford: Pergamon.

(1979). Environmental stress, delinquent behavior, and convictions. In *Stress and Anxiety*, Vol. 6, ed. I. G. Sarason & C. D. Spielberger, pp. 93–107. Washington, DC: Hemisphere.

(1986). Age and crime. In *Crime and Justice: An Annual Review of Research*, Vol. 7, ed. M. Tonry & N. Morris, pp. 189–250. Chicago: University of Chicago Press.

(1989). Self-reported and official offending from adolescence to adulthood. In *Cross-National Research in Self-Reported Crime and Delinquency*, ed. M. W. Klein, 399–423. Dordrecht: Kluwer.

(1990). Age, period, cohort and offending. In *Policy and Theory in Criminal Justice: Contributions in Honour of Leslie T. Wilkins*, ed. D. M. Gottfredson & R. V. Clarke. Aldershot: Avebury.

(1992). Trends in English juvenile delinquency and their explanation. *International Journal of Comparative and Applied Criminal Justice*, 16.2, 151–3.

Farrington, D. P., & Dowds, E. A. (1985). Disentangling criminal behaviour and police reaction. In *Reactions to Crime: The Public, the Police, Courts and Prisons*, ed. D. P. Farrington & J. Gunn, pp. 41–72. Chichester: Wiley.

Farrington, D. P., Gallagher, B., Morley, L., St. Ledger, R. J., & West, D. J. (1986). Unemployment, school leaving and crime. *British Journal of Criminology*, 26.4, 335–56.

Farrington, D. P., & Langan, P. A. (1992). Changes in crime and punishment in England and America in the 1980s. *Justice Quarterly*, 9, 5–46.

Farrington, D. P., & West, D. J. (1990). The Cambridge Study in Delinquent Development: A long-term follow-up of 411 London males. In *Criminality: Personality, Behaviour and Life History*, ed. H. J. Kerner & G. Kaiser. Heidelberg, Germany: Springer-Verlag.

Field, S. (1990). *Trends in Crime and Their Interpretation: A Study of Recorded Crime in Post-war England and Wales*. Home Office Research Study 119, London: Her Majesty's Stationery Office.

Gordon, A. (1990). Drugs and criminal behaviour. In *Principles and Practice of Forensic Psychiatry*, ed. R. Bluglass & P. Bowden, pp. 897–901. Edinburgh: Churchill Livingstone.

Gottfredson, M. R., & Hirschi, T. (1990). *A General Theory of Crime*. Stanford: Stanford University Press.

Gottfredson, S. D., & Taylor, R. B. (1988). Community contexts and criminal offenders. In *Communities and Crime Reduction*, ed. T. Hope & M. Shaw, pp. 62–80. London: Her Majesty's Stationery Office.

Heal, K., & Laycock, G. (1986). *Situational Crime Prevention: From Theory into Practice*. London: Her Majesty's Stationery Office.

Hirschi, T., & Gottfredson, M. (1983). Age and the explanation of crime. *American Journal of Sociology*, 89, 552–84.

Hirschi, T., & Hindelang, M. J. (1977). Intelligence and delinquency: a revisionist view. *American Sociological Review*, 42, 571–87.

Home Office (1978). *Criminal Statistics England and Wales 1977*. London: Home Office.

(1992). *Criminal Statistics England and Wales 1990*. London: Home Office.

Home Office Statistical Bulletin (1987). *Criminal Careers of Those Born in 1953: Persistent Offenders and Desistance*. London: Home Office.

(1989). *Criminal and Custodial Careers of Those Born in 1953, 1958 and 1963*. London: Home Office.

Hope, T., & Hough, M. (1988). Area, crime and incivilities: a profile from the British Crime Survey. In *Communities and Crime Reduction*, ed. T. Hope & M. Shaw, pp. 30–47. London: Her Majesty's Stationery Office.

Hore, B. (1990). Alcohol and crime. In *Principles and Practice of Forensic Psychiatry*, ed. R. Bluglass & P. Bowden, pp. 873–80. Edinburgh: Churchill Livingstone.

Huizinga, D., & Elliott, D. S. (1986). Reassessing the reliability and validity of self-report delinquency measures. *Journal of Quantitative Criminology*, 2, 293–327.

Kyvsgaard, B. (1991). The decline in child and youth criminality: possible explanations of an international trend. In *Youth, Crime and Justice: Scandinavian Studies in Crime*, Vol. 12, ed. A. Snare. Norwegian University Press.

Loeber, R., & Stouthamer-Loeber, M. (1986). Family factors as correlates and predictors of juvenile conduct problems and delinquency. In *Crime and Justice: An Annual Review of Research*, Vol. 7, ed. M. Tonry & N. Morris, pp. 29–149. Chicago: University of Chicago Press.

Maccoby, E. E., & Jacklin, C. N. (1980a). Psychological sex differences. In *Scientific Foundations of Developmental Psychiatry*, ed. M. Rutter, pp. 92–100. London: Heinemann Medical Books.

Maccoby, E. E., & Jacklin, C. N. (1980b). Sex differences in aggression: a rejoinder and reprise. *Child Development*, 51, 964–80.

Magnusson, D. (1987). Adult delinquency in the light of conduct and physiology at an early age: a longitudinal study. In *Psychopathology*, ed. D. Magnusson & A. Öhman, pp. 221–234. Orlando, Fla.: Academic Press.

(1988). Antisocial behaviour of boys and autonomic activity/reactivity. In *Biological Contributions to Crime Causation*, ed. T. E. Moffitt & S. A. Mednick, pp. 135–46. Dordrecht: Martinus Nijhoff.

Magnusson, D., & Bergman, L. R. (1990). A pattern approach to the study of pathways from childhood to adulthood. In *Straight and Devious Pathways from Childhood to Adulthood*, ed. L. N. Robins & M. Rutter, pp. 101–15. Cambridge: Cambridge University Press.

Mayhew, P. (1992). Cross-national comparisons of crime and victimisation. Unpublished paper. London: Home Office.

(1992). Law and justice systems. *The Economist Atlas of the New Europe*, London: Economist Books.

Mayhew, P., Elliott, D., & Dowds, L. (1989). *The 1988 British Crime Survey*, Home Office Research Study No. 111. London: Her Majesty's Stationery Office.

Mayhew, P., & Smith, L. J. F. (1985). Crime in England and Wales and Scotland: a British Crime Survey comparison. *British Journal of Criminology*, 25.6, 148–59.

Mays, J. B. (1954). *Growing up in the City*. Liverpool: University Press.

McCleary, R., Nienstadt, B. B., & Erven, J. M (1982). Interrupted time series analysis of Uniform Crime Reports: the case of organisational reforms. In *Quantitative Criminology*, ed. J. Hagan, pp. 13–37. Beverly Hills, Calif.: Sage.

Merton, R. K. (1938). Social structure and anomie. *American Sociological Review*, 3.6, 672–82.

(1957). *Social Theory and Social Structure*. New York: Free Press.
Moore, D. R., Chamberlain, P., & Mukai, L. H. (1979). Children at risk for delinquency: A follow-up comparison of aggressive children who steal. *Journal of Abnormal Child Psychology*, 7, 345–55.
Olweus, D. (1979). Stability of aggressive reaction patterns in males: A review. *Psychological Bulletin*, 86, 852–75.
Orsagh, T., & Witte, A. D. (1981). Economic status and crime: implications for offender rehabilitation. *Journal of Criminal Law and Criminology*, 72.3, 1055–71.
Osborn, S. G., & West, D. J (1979). Conviction records of fathers and sons compared. *British Journal of Criminology*, 19, 120–33.
Pease, K., & Harvey, L. (1988). Quantitative information from the second UN Crime Survey: An overview. University of Manchester, mimeograph.
Reynolds, D. A., & Blyth, P. D. (1975). Sources of variation affecting the relationship between police and survey-based estimates of crime rates. In *Victimology: A New Focus*, Vol. 3, ed. I. Drapkin & E. Viano, pp. 201–25. Lexington, Mass.: D. C. Heath.
Robins, L. (1978). Sturdy childhood predictors of adult antisocial behaviour: replications from longitudinal studies. *Psychological Medicine*, 8, 611–22.
(1991). Conduct disorder. *Journal of Child Psychology and Psychiatry*, 32.1: 193–212.
Robins, L. N., & Ratcliff, K. S. (1979). Risk factors in the continuation of childhood antisocial behaviours into adulthood. *International Journal of Mental Health*, 1, 96–116.
Robins, L. N., & Regier, D. A. (eds.) (1991), *Psychiatric Disorders in America: The Epidemiological Catchment Area Study*. New York: The Free Press.
Robins, L. N., Tipp, J., & Przybeck, T. (1991). Antisocial personality. In *Psychiatric Disorders in America: The Epidemiological Catchment Area Study*, ed. L. N. Robins & D. A. Regier, pp. 258–90. New York: The Free Press.
Rutter, M. (1989). Age as an ambiguous variable in developmental research: some epidemiological considerations from developmental psychopathology. *International Journal of Behavioural Development*, 12, 1–24.
Rutter, M., & Giller, H. (1983). *Juvenile Delinquency: Trends and Perspectives*. Harmondsworth: Penguin Books.
Rutter, M., Maughan, B., Mortimore, P., Ouston, J., with Smith, A. (1979). *15000 Hours: Secondary Schools and Their Effects on Children*. London: Open Books; Cambridge, Mass: Harvard University Press.
Sampson, R. J., & Wooldredge J. D. (1987). Linking the micro- and macro-level dimensions of lifestyle-routine activity and opportunity models of predatory victimisation. *Journal of Quantitative Criminology*, 3.4, 371–93.
Smith, I. (1990). Alcohol and crime: the problem in Australia. In *Principles and Practice of Forensic Psychiatry*, ed. R. Bluglass & P. Bowden, pp. 947–51. Edinburgh: Churchill Livingstone.
Stattin, H., & Magnusson, D. (1991). Stability and change in criminal behaviour up to age 30. *British Journal of Criminology*, 31.4, 327–46.
Sutherland, E. H. (1956). *The Sutherland Papers*, ed. A. K. Cohen, A. R. Lindesmith, & K. Schuessler. Bloomington: Indiana University Press.
Tittle, C. R., Villemez, W. J., & Smith, D. A. (1978). The myth of social class and criminality: an empirical assessment of the empirical evidence. *American Sociological Review*, 43, 643–56.
Trasler, G. B. (1979). Delinquency, recidivism, and desistance. *British Journal of Criminology*, 19, 314–22.

Trasler, G. B. (1980). Aspects of causality, culture and crime. Paper presented at the 4th International Seminar at the International Center of Sociological, Penal and Penitentiary Research and Studies, Messina, Italy.

van Dijk, J. J. M., Mayhew, P., & Killias, M. (1991). *Experiences of Crime across the World*, 2d ed. Deventer and Boston: Kluwer.

Wadsworth, M. (1979). *Roots of Delinquency: Infancy, Adolescence and Crime*. Oxford: Martin Robertson.

West, D. J., & Farrington, D. P. *Who Becomes Delinquent?* London: Heinemann.

West, D. J., & Farrington, D. P. (1977). *The Delinquent Way of Life*. London: Heinemann Educational Books.

Wiklund, N., & Lidberg, L. (1990). Alcohol as a causal criminogenic factor: The Scandinavian experience. In *Principles and Practice of Forensic Psychiatry*, ed. R. Bluglass & P. Bowden, pp. 941–45. Edinburgh: Churchill Livingstone.

Wikström, P.-O. H. (1990). Age and crime in a Stockholm cohort. *Journal of Quantitative Criminology*, 6.1, 61–83.

Willmott, P. (1966). *Adolescent Boys in East London*. London: Routledge & Kegan Paul.

Wilson, J. Q., & Herrnstein, R. (1985). *Crime and Human Nature*. New York: Simon & Schuster.

Wilson, J. Q., & Kelling, G. (1982). Broken windows. *The Atlantic Monthly*, March, 29–38.

6. Depression and suicidal behaviors in adolescence: Sociocultural and time trends

RENÉ F.W. DIEKSTRA

Introduction

Recent summaries of physical health status indicators have suggested an emerging trend of healthier adolescents in developed countries (Irwin & Vaughan, 1988). A more comprehensive picture of the current state of adolescent health, however, seems to point otherwise. If parameters of adolescent health include mental and psychosocial conditions and behaviors having more long-term implications for health such as school dropout, sexual activity, substance abuse, and inclination to violence, current data do not provide unequivocal support for the view of improving health and social well-being for the adolescent population.

This chapter discusses the available evidence for a secular increase in depressive disorders and suicidal behaviors.

The literature on adolescent depression and suicide that is available for answering these questions can be divided into six approaches or research lines (Petersen, Compas, & Brooks-Gunn, 1993; Fombonne, in press; Diekstra, Kienhorst, & De Wilde, in press): (1) depressed mood; (2) depressive syndrome; (3) clinical depression or depressive disorder; (4) suicidal ideation; (5) parasuicide or attempted suicide; and (6) suicide. Each of these approaches not only encompasses an emphasis on different aspects of depressive and/or suicidal phenomena but also a different theoretical and/or empirical tradition. Suicidology or the separate study of suicidal behaviors, for example, has emerged from research showing that the correlation between suicidal reactions and depression in *sensu strictu* or mental illness in general is far from perfect. The separate study of parasuicide

This chapter is based on a fuller presentation of the evidence in the Academia Europaea Study Group report (Rutter, M. & Smith, D. J. [eds.] *Psychosocial Disorders in Young People: Time Trends and Their Causes*, Chichester: Wiley, 1995), and I am grateful for permission to include portions of the report here.

in adolescence suggests that parasuicidal behavior is different from suicide in terms of etiology, functionality, demography, and behavioral characteristics (Rutter, 1986).

We will first discuss the issues of definition and operationalization or measurement of these six concepts. Against that background we will review the available evidence on rising secular trends among adolescents. We will conclude with a discussion of possible causal mechanisms, priorities for future research, and for public health care.

Definitions

Depression

The words depression and depressed are used in everyday life to refer to both a feeling state and a disorder that involves associated symptoms such as social withdrawal, agitation or suicidal inclination. On the base of intensity, length, and disruptiveness of the depressed feeling and related symptoms more or less normal states are distinguished from pathological ones.

Depressed mood refers first of all to a loss of positive affect and emotional involvement with self, others, or situations. It is often also characterized, however, by the so-called cognitive triad (Beck, 1976) of thoughts of unworthiness and self-blame, feelings of helplessness to change the situation, and hopelessness about the future (Rutter, 1986). Depressed mood tends to be accompanied by inefficient coping with normal life demands and stressful events. In this, it is different from normal feelings of sadness, grief, or disappointment. It has been shown to be one of the main characteristics differentiating adolescents referred for clinical help from those not referred (Achenbach, 1991).

The term *depressive syndrome* tends to be used when, in addition to depressed mood, there are anxiety, loneliness, death wishes, guilt feelings, sleep problems, and the like (Achenbach, 1991). Such syndromes include dysthymia, meaning milder, less incapacitating but chronic forms of depressive disturbance. The large majority of adolescents with dysthymia never come to the attention of health care professionals; when they do, it is usually because of some more acute problems.

A *major depressive disorder* is marked by a depressed mood and/or a loss of interest or pleasure in almost all activities, as well as at least three of the following symptoms: marked weight loss or gain when not dieting (or failure to make the necessary weight gains in adolescence), constant problems in sleeping, agitated or greatly slowed-down behavior, tiredness, reduced concentration and decision-making ability, feelings of worthlessness or abnormal guilt, and frequent thoughts about death and/or suicide, suicide plans, or suicidal acts.

There is evidence (Strober & Carlson, 1982) that up to a quarter of adolescents with major depression also have so-called manic or hypomanic episodes and therefore suffer from a bipolar mood disorder. There is some evidence that bipolar disorders are often not recognized as such among adolescents, possibly because of the difficulty of distinguishing between "normal" levels of activity in adolescence and hypomanic behavior. In one study of adults suffering from bipolar disorders it was found retrospectively that many of them had shown evidence of the disorder as adolescents (Roy-Byrne et al., 1985).

Several studies (Weinstein et al., 1990; Petersen, Compas, & Brooks-Gunn, 1993) suggest that a gradient of severity is implied from depressed mood via depressive syndrome to depressive disorder. With regard to affect and cognitive characteristics there is a great deal of similarity between the three, although only for depressive disorder do clear-cut length-of-time or chronicity criteria exist. In addition, a diagnosis of depressive disorder requires the existence of physical symptoms (such as psychomotor, sleep, or energy problems).

It is also assumed that there are developmental pathways that sequentially link one to another, but there is a paucity of evidence on the transition from depressed mood to depressive syndrome, and from depressive syndrome to depressive disorder.

Suicidal behavior

The words suicide and suicidal are used in everyday life to refer to self-chosen behavior intended to bring about one's own death on the short(est) term. Of all the behaviors and experiences to which these words are attached, however, many are not or might not be motivated by a wish to die or to do away with oneself for good. Often they are meant only to express or communicate feelings such as despair, hopelessness, and anger. Contemporary literature, therefore, usually divides suicidal behavior into three categories. *Suicidal ideation* refers to cognitions that can vary from fleeting thoughts that life is not worth living, via very concrete well-thought-out plans for killing oneself, to an intense delusional preoccupation with self-destruction (Goldney et al., 1989).

The term *parasuicide* covers behaviors that can vary from suicidal gestures and manipulative attempts to serious but unsuccessful attempts to kill oneself. It refers to any deliberate act with nonfatal outcome that might cause or actually causes self-harm, or that without intervention from others, would have done so, or that consists of ingesting a substance in excess of its generally recognized or prescribed therapeutic dose (Kreitman, 1977).

More and more authors on the subject prefer the term parasuicide to attempted suicide or suicide attempt since it makes no reference to intention. As Kreitman (1977) has pointed out, intention cannot be used as a criterion since the person's motive may be too uncertain or too complex to ascertain readily. When asked "Why did you do it?" most will deny (afterwards) that they wanted to kill themselves. Many will reply "I just don't know." Since parasuicide, particularly during adolescence and young adulthood, is usually carried out at the height of an interpersonal crisis by an individual feeling desperate and confused, such obscurity of intent is not at all surprising. Moreover, approximately two thirds of the men and nearly half of the women who present as parasuicides have taken alcohol within a few hours of the act (Kreitman, 1977).

This points to another important aspect of the definition of parasuicide: The act should be nonhabitual. A habitual user of excessive quantities of alcohol or a habitual user of dangerous quantities of (hard) drugs, if found unconscious as a result of an overdose (assuming that other information indicating suicidal intent such as a suicide note is not present), is not considered a parasuicide. Nor is habitual self-mutilation (cutting, piercing, head banging) implied under the term parasuicide.

The term *suicide* refers to any death that is the direct or indirect result of a positive or negative act accomplished by the victim, knowing or believing the act will produce this result (Maris, 1991). This definition implies, first, that the term suicide should be applied only in case of a death. Second, risk-taking that leads to death, if the indirect causal sequence can be specified and was intentional, is suicide. Indirect suicide is a common but neglected form of suicide. Some authors (Farberow, 1980) believe it is particularly common in adolescence and young adulthood and that a considerable number of road traffic fatalities in young males are in actual fact suicides. Third, self-neglecting behavior, sometimes referred to as suicidal "erosion," such as hunger strike or refusal to take life-preserving medication, if it results in death, is also considered suicide.

It is apparent from these definitions, as research has indeed shown, that there is considerable overlap between the three classes of suicidal behavior. There is also some evidence of developmental pathways that sequentially link suicidal ideation to parasuicide to suicide. Little is known, however, about the causes and patterns of recruitment from suicidal ideation to parasuicide and from parasuicide to suicide or about the factors that precipitate or protect against these transformations.

Measurements

An important obstacle to satisfactorily answering the question central to this chapter is the differences in quantity as well as in quality of the data available for each of the six categories of depressive and suicidal phenomena. There are no countries in the world that keep national statistics or registers for any of these categories with the sole exception of suicide. No health surveillance systems exist, not even at a regional or local level, that allow for monitoring the prevalence and incidence of depressive conditions or nonfatal suicidal phenomena among adolescents over significant periods of time (Fombonne, in press; Diekstra, Kienhorst, & De Wilde, in press). The only exceptions are a few research centers that over several decades have collected all cases of hospital-admitted parasuicides in a well-defined catchment area (Platt, 1988; Diekstra, Kienhorst, & De Wilde, in press). The lower age limit for case identification in these centers, however, has been fifteen years, so no data are available on early adolescence.

In the few countries where repeated national surveys of adolescent mental and behavioral health are carried out (such as the Monitoring the Future projects in the United States, see Bachman, Johnston, & O'Malley, 1986, and the Netherlands, see Diekstra et al., 1991), measures of depression and suicidal reactions are either not included (United States) or the studies are not long enough in place (the Netherlands) to allow for any solid conclusions with regard to secular trends. In addition, longitudinal studies of birth cohorts that could provide information on the life course proportional vulnerability in adolescence for depressive and nonfatal suicidal conditions are not yet available.

Depressive conditions

Depressive conditions are usually measured in one of two ways: (self-report) questionnaires and structured or semi-structured diagnostic interviews (Merikangas and Angst, this volume). Because these vary in the time frame covered (from "now" or "last week" to "last year"), comparisons across studies are difficult. There are also substantial differences in the severity cutoffs used, which add to the problem. In order to assess possible trends over time in rates of depressive disorder, there is the additional need to rely on retrospective reports (Fombonne, in press, for a discussion of the methodological issues involved).

Suicidal behaviors: Suicidal ideation and parasuicide

There are three major ways to measure suicidal behaviors: self-report, interview, and administrative procedures. For the assessment of suicidal ideation a number of psychometrically sound questionnaires do exist (Goldney et al., 1989), but they do not appear to have been widely used thus far. The same is the case with so-called suicide attitude scales measuring, among other things, affective, cognitive, and instrumental attitudes toward one's own suicide (Diekstra & Kerkhof, 1989). Most studies have tended to use their own individual questions or questions included in commonly used instruments for assessing (mental) health status such as the General Health Questionnaire (GHQ; Goldney et al., 1989). Consequently, is it difficult to compare results between studies. The more so, because the period of enquiry varies substantially between studies, from "over the past weeks" via "over the last year" to "ever."

With regard to parasuicide, most studies have used hospital admission data, which are essentially administrative data, for case identification. Since criteria for regarding a case as a parasuicide/suicide attempt are often obscure and vary considerably both in and between countries, comparison between studies of prevalence/incidence and characteristics of parasuicides is clearly limited. Furthermore, there is evidence of a relationship between method (not just medical seriousness) and probability of hospital referral of parasuicide cases. There are substantial differences between countries and regions in customs and procedures for referral to hospitals. Consequently, hospital based data may provide a much more valid estimate of the parasuicide incidence in one place than in another. Either way, hospital based rates significantly underestimate "true" rates as community surveys have shown (Diekstra, Kienhorst, & De Wilde, in press). This seems to be particularly the case amongst adolescents and young adults. The exact magnitude of the dark number remains obscure, however, because of differences in identification and measurement of parasuicide between surveys. Most surveys, with a few exceptions (Kienhorst et al., 1990a; Diekstra et al., 1991; Centers of Disease Control [CDC], 1991), do not cover the whole adolescent age spectrum (the lower age limit is usually fifteen years). The ways in which parasuicide is measured vary considerably. For example, in the National Institute of Mental Health Epidemiological Catchment Area studies in the United States

(Moscicki et al., 1989) respondents are asked the question "Have you ever attempted suicide?" Surveys in other countries (Diekstra, Kienhorst, & De Wilde, in press) have sometimes used a so-called Selfdestructive Behavior Questionnaire in which the terms "attempted suicide" and "suicide attempt" are deliberately avoided. Instead respondents are asked questions like "Have you ever because of social, emotional or other problems: – tried to hang yourself?; – taken an overdose of . . . ?" and eight other possible methods. Whenever respondents tick one or more of these (potentially) self-harming behaviors, they are asked to provide further details on each episode as well as circumstantial evidence. Only those episodes meeting certain informational criteria are scored as parasuicides.

A slightly adapted version of this method is being used in the Parasuicide Monitoring Project of the World Health Organization's Regional Office for Europe. This study is currently in progress in sixteen centers in eleven European countries. Most of these centers collect cases of parasuicide from a variety of sources: hospitals, general practitioners, outpatient clinics, mental health centers, social work agencies, and the like. A preliminary report of this study has been published so far (Platt, Bille-Brahe, & Kerkhof, 1992) and although it should soon provide the first internationally comparable data on period prevalence (twelve months) and lifetime prevalence (retrospectively) of parasuicide, such data are not yet available.

Suicidal behaviors: Suicide

The preliminary conclusion from the discussion on measurements so far is that, however strange it may be, our only hope for answering the question about secular trends lies with suicide. In many European countries as well as in the United States, Australia, and Japan suicide rates have been recorded for at least a century. These data might suggest answers to such questions as: What has been the trend in suicide among adolescents over the course of the twentieth century? Is suicide mortality among the young on the increase?

The validity of the answers to these questions is a direct function of the validity of the data used, in this case national suicide statistics. Therefore, any discussion of secular trends in suicide has first to address the issue of the validity and reliability of the available data. The salient question is whether methods and criteria in identifying suicides vary so much among different populations that they may account for the differences in rates. Several authors have argued that cultural attitudes toward suicide so affect certification that official suicide statistics are valueless (Douglas, 1967).

In 1968 The World Health Organization (WHO) established a working group on the comparability of suicide statistics that in its report stated: "The inescapable conclusion is that the present official suicide statistics are only of limited value. Constructing epidemiological and sociodemographic theories about suicide, therefore, will remain hazardous" (WHO Chronicle, 1975: 193). Only seven years later another WHO working group came to an almost opposite conclusion expressing "confidence in the use of official suicide statistics from European countries for trend-analysis" (WHO, 1982: 19). This conclusion was reached after a careful examination of the available empirical evidence.

Differences in ascertainment procedures clearly do not explain differences in suicide rates between populations. In a now classical study Sainsbury and Barraclough (1968) compared the rank order of the suicide rates of immigrants to the United States of eleven countries with the rates reported by their countries of origin. Cases of suicide in the various immigrant groups were all identified by United States procedures, whereas suicides in the home countries were identified by the particular method(s) of each country. The rank order of the two sets appeared to be nearly identical ($r = 0.90$).

A study of suicide mortality statistics of immigrants to Australia confirmed this finding (Whitlock, 1971; Lester, 1972) and also showed that it holds for both sexes. The correlation between the suicide rates of male immigrants from sixteen countries and their countries of birth was 0.79; for females it was 0.76. Considering the small number of suicides in some immigrant groups and hence the large standard error of their rates, the correlations are surprisingly high.

There is yet another aspect of the problem that needs to be mentioned. Suicide is underreported to a greater or lesser extent everywhere (e.g. McCarthy & Walsh, 1975, for Ireland; Jobes, Berman, & Josselson, 1986 for the United States). In any country the agent responsible for certifying deaths who has doubts about recording a suicide probably records either an undetermined death or an accidental death. The report of the 1968 WHO working group (WHO Chronicle, 1975) found wide variation in the extent to which agents resort to these alternatives. It is therefore of considerable interest to examine how the varying tendencies of nations to use these two categories rather than suicide alters their suicide rates relative to other nations. Barraclough (1973) was the first to look into this matter. He found that the rank order of officially reported suicide rates of twenty-two countries and the rank order of a rate derived by combining suicide and undetermined mortality rates were highly correlated (r = 0.89). Sainsbury, Jenkins, and Baert (1981) reported a study that showed that variations in the use of the categories "accidental" and "undetermined" causes of death contribute little toward explaining differences between the suicide rates of European countries.

If, as the studies mentioned show, differences in the rank order of suicide rates of countries or cultural groups are barely altered when the effects of varying methods of ascertainment are controlled, national suicide mortality statistics can be assumed to be a valuable source of data on which to base comparative epidemiological studies. This conclusion is supported by the fact that consistent differences in rates between national, demographic, and social groups have been recorded over very long periods, in several instances far more than one century, differences which persist despite political changes that in many countries have altered ascertainment procedures. To ignore the implications of such conspicuous regularities as the higher suicide rates of males, of those living alone or divorced, of the mentally ill, and of the strong increase in youth suicide over the last three decades, and so on, is surely a failure of vision. In summary, suicide is underreported for a number of reasons and the rates are subject to many errors of a kind encountered in reporting mortality figures in general. Nevertheless, the evidence from studies designed to settle this point clearly indicate that these errors are random, at least to an extent that allows the epidemiologist profitably to compare rates between countries, within them, and over time. A note of caution should be struck, however, with regard to extending this general conclusion to all age groups in the same way. Most work on the reliability and validity of suicide statistics has been limited to data from those fifteen years of age and over.

Prevalence or incidence of suicidal behaviors in adolescence

It is clear that our cartography of the territory of emotional disturbances in adolescence is still very incomplete, particularly if seen from an international perspective. In addition to the discrepancies and deficiencies in data sources and measurement methods, there are also discrepancies in methods of sampling, size and characteristics of samples, and methods of data analyses that make comparison of studies hazardous.

The following overall conclusions with regard to point prevalence as well as lifetime prevalence or lifetime risk of depressive conditions and suicidal behaviors in adolescence should therefore be considered very tentative. The findings on depression are summarized in the chapters by

Merikangas and Angst, and by Petersen and Leffert (this volume); those on suicidal behaviors are considered here.

Suicidal ideation

A review of community survey studies on adolescent populations (defined here as high school student populations) published after 1985 reveals that estimates of the prevalence of suicidal thoughts range from 3.5 percent (Kienhorst et al., 1990b), 14 percent (Canton et al., 1989), 15.4 percent (Pronovost, Cote, & Ross, 1990), 18.9 percent (Diekstra et al., 1991), 23.3 percent (Nagy & Adcock, 1990), 38 percent (Watanabe et al., 1988), 52.1 percent (Smith & Crawford, 1986), to 52.9 percent (Harkavy Friedman et al., 1987). To a large extent, the differences in rates reported can be explained by differences in definition of suicidal ideation and differences in period of reference. In some studies the subjects have been asked about "recent" suicidal thinking (Kienhorst et al., 1990a), in others about suicidal thoughts during the past year (Diekstra et al., 1991; Dubow et al., 1989; Nagy & Adcock, 1990), and in yet others for suicidal ideation "ever" or "at least once" (Pronovost, Cote, & Ross, 1990; Smith & Crawford, 1986; Harkavy Friedman et al., 1987). Not surprisingly, the longer the period of assessment (retrospectively) the higher the rate tends to be. If the reasonable assumption is made that measuring suicidal ideation "ever" or "at least once" can be equated with measuring lifetime prevalence rate, we find a range of about 15 to 53 percent, which proves it to be a phenomenon quite common indeed in adolescence. Most of the studies reviewed show a clear preponderance of suicidal girls. There is also some evidence of a positive correlation of prevalence of suicidal ideation and age, at least over the period of twelve through seventeen years of age, and more prominently in girls than in boys (Diekstra et al., 1991). No data are available on pre- and postpuberty differences with regard to the prevalence of suicidal ideation, but as we shall see later, it seems safe to assume that it increases during the teenage years.

Parasuicide

A review of ten community survey studies on samples of adolescents (high school students), published after 1986, showed estimates of year prevalence of parasuicidal acts to vary between 2.4 and 20 percent (Dubow et al., 1989; Pronovost, Cote, & Ross, 1990; Rubenstein et al., 1989; Nagy & Adcock, 1990; CDC, 1991) whereas lifetime prevalence rates range from 2.2 to 20 percent (Diekstra, Kienhorst, & De Wilde, in press;

Kienhorst et al., 1990b; Smith & Crawford, 1986; Rubenstein et al., 1989; Andrews & Lewinsohn, 1990; Harkavy Friedman et al., 1987). These differences in rates must be interpreted in the light of differences in case definition and measurement.

All studies report a clear preponderance of girls but the data they present on the relationship between parasuicide prevalence and incidence and age are less uniform. Some studies report a clear increase in parasuicide rate with each year in the teenage period (Kreitman, 1977), but others (Diekstra et al., 1991) report that rates peak in midadolescence (around sixteen to seventeen years of age) and thereafter level off or decrease. Studies of clinical samples, using hospital admission data, covering a much broader age range (usually fifteen to sixty-four years) provide less divergent data with regard to the relationship between parasuicide rates and age during the adolescent period. They also show, however, that there is a large and unexplained international variation in peak ages for parasuicide. In some countries (such as the United Kingdom and the United States) parasuicide rates peak in the late teens or early twenties. In others (such as the Netherlands and Denmark) this occurs about ten years later. Both categories of studies, however, support the existence of a dramatic puberty effect (Diekstra, Kienhorst, & De Wilde, in press; Rey & Bird, 1991; Andrus et al., 1991).

Community survey studies and studies of clinical samples both show that a considerable percentage of parasuicidal adolescents attempt repeated parasuicidal acts: between 14 percent (Hawton et al., 1982) and 51 percent (Mehr, Zeltzer, & Robinson, 1981, 1982), depending partially on length of follow-up period.

It appears that depressed mood or depressive disorder is a characteristic of a substantial proportion of, but not all, adolescent parasuicides. Rates of depressive conditions may vary depending on the population studied, with the highest rates found in psychiatric samples, much lower rates in medical units and community samples (Spirito et al., 1989). A problem here is that the assessment of depression is usually made after the parasuicidal act.

Suicide. Suicide in adolescence is a rare event, the ratio of suicide to parasuicide being about one to forty or fifty. The lifetime suicide risk among adolescents (eleven to eighteen years) varies from about 0.04 to 0.2 percent between countries that report suicide statistics to the World Health Organization (Diekstra, Kienhorst, & De Wilde, in press). There is a clear age effect, with suicide mortality increasing sharply over the adolescent age period.

A substantial proportion of adolescent suicides appear to suffer from depressive disorders, with prevalence rates of such disorders at the time of death ranging from a low of 22 percent (Runeson & Beskow, 1991) to a high of 51 percent (Marttunen et al., 1991; see also Diekstra, Kleinhorst, & De Wilde, in press).

Secular trends in depressive disorders and suicidal behavior

Depressive disorders

A number of studies point to an increasing risk for depressive disorders among successive birth cohorts over the course of this century (Hagnell et al., 1982; Klerman, 1985; Weissman et al., 1991; Robins, Locke, & Regier, 1991). The lifetime prevalence rates for depression appear to be higher for adolescents and young adults today than they were for their parents at that age, who in turn had higher rates during their adolescence or young adulthood than their parents had (see Figure 6.1).

One of the causes of this increase seems to be the lowering of the age of onset for depressive disorders, a phenomenon that has also been reported

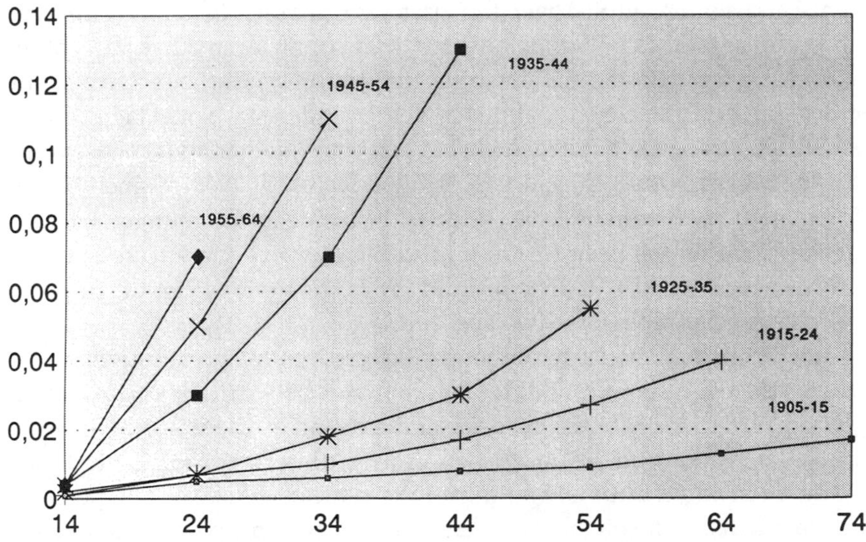

Figure 6.1. Major depression: period-cohort effects and lifetime prevalence. (From the Epidemiologic Area Catchment Study NIMH, adapted from Weissman et al., 1991)

for a number of other disorders, such as substance abuse and delinquent behavior. There is reason to assume, however, that the increase is restricted to white populations living in the highly industrialized urban areas of North America and Northern Europe, since studies of identical design on other populations have not confirmed this finding (Canino et al., 1987; Karno et al., 1987).

The same studies that show an increase in risk for depression in younger birth cohorts also suggest a closing of the classical sex gap in depression, in that the rise seems to be greater for young men than young women (Hagnell et al., 1982). In one study (Joyce et al., 1990) the prevalence rates among young men were even higher than among young women.

Suicide

As mentioned earlier, any analysis of trends in suicide risk among adolescents and young adults is hampered by the deficiencies in suicide mortality statistics on late childhood and early adolescence (WHO, 1987, 1988, 1989, 1992, for lack of adequate data on the age group below fifteen years).

If we limit ourselves to an analysis of rates for those aged fifteen to twenty-nine or thirty-four the following conclusions appear to be warranted. First, there has been a real increase in suicide risk among adolescents and young adults over the past two decades in many European countries as well as in highly industrialized countries in other parts of the world. Figures 6.2 and 6.3 illustrate this by presenting age-specific suicides for the United States and the Netherlands as a percentage of total suicides in five-year (United States) or ten-year (Netherlands) age groups, for the census years 1970 and 1987 (United States) or 1965–69 and 1985–87 (Netherlands). As can be seen, the rates of suicide in the younger age categories (roughly between fifteen and thirty to thirty-four) were substantially lower around 1970 than around 1987. The trend is just the opposite for older age groups (forty-five and over).

As Figure 6.4 shows for nineteen selected countries throughout the world, there is a significant difference in trends between the sexes over the period 1970 to 1986. In the majority of the countries there was an increase in suicide among males in all age groups, this trend being most pronounced in adolescents and young adults (a mean change of + 70 percent). Among females the picture is different. In the age group fifteen to twenty-nine years, the majority of countries still show an increase (a mean change of + 40 percent), but it is noteworthy that a number of countries with a sig-

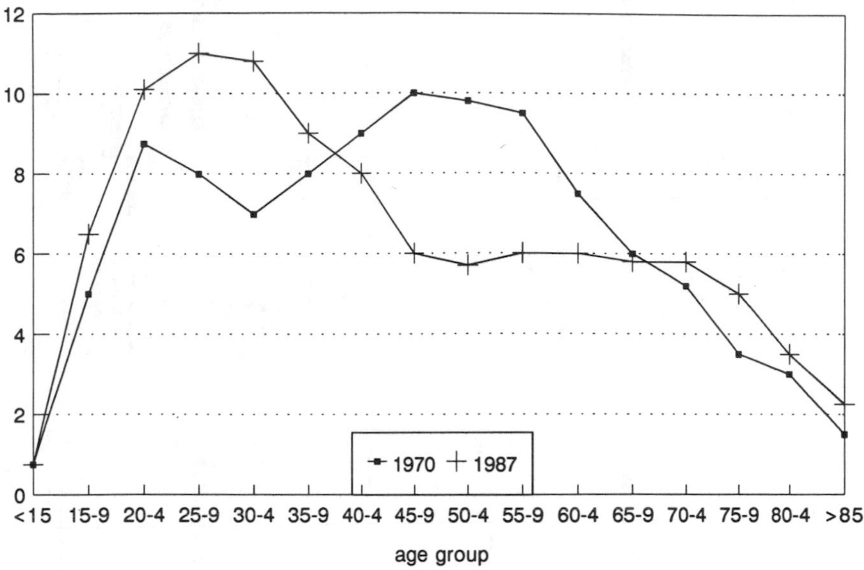

Figure 6.2. Percent of all suicides per age group: United States, 1970–87 (Data for U.S., source: Buda & Tsuang, 1990, 5-year age groups)

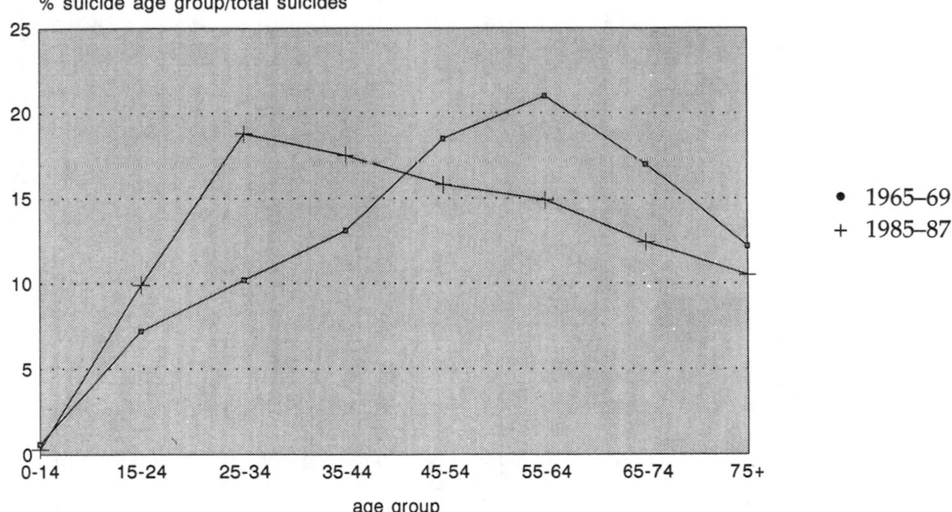

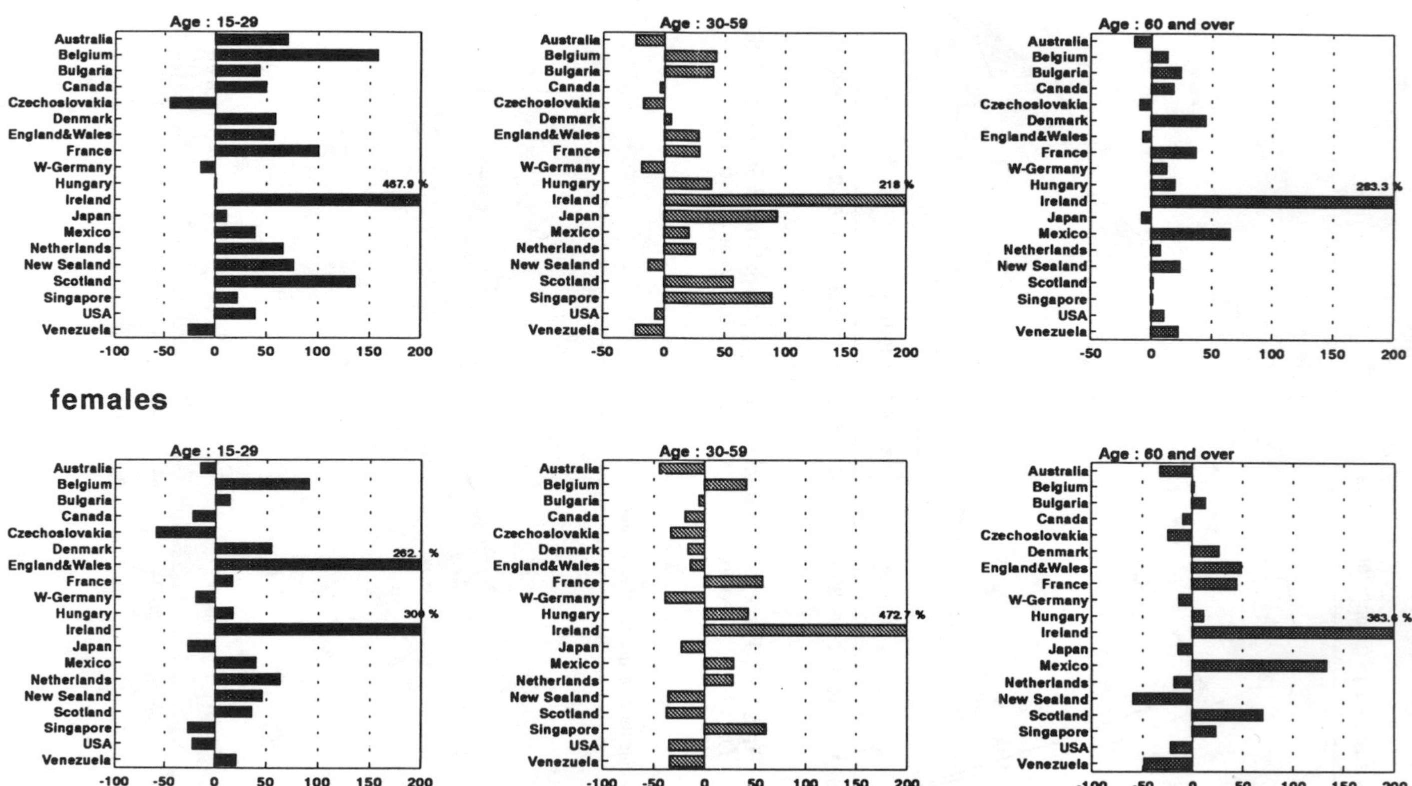

Figure 6.4. Percent of change in suicide rates, 1970–86. (Source: WHO Statistics Annual)

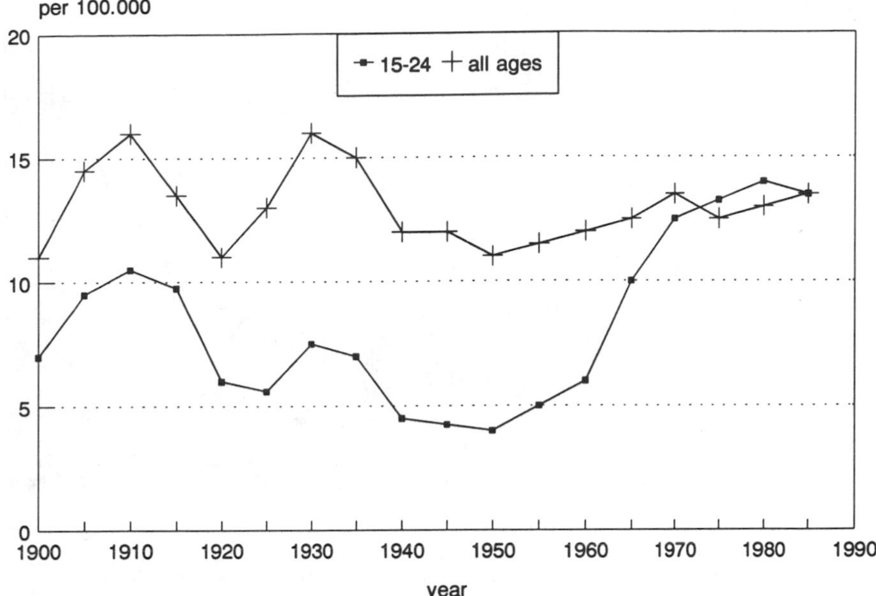

Figure 6.5. Suicide rates in the United States, 1900–87. (Source: Buda & Tsuang, 1990)

nificant increase in suicide in young males show a decrease in young females (e.g., Canada and the United States). (For the age categories thirty to fifty-nine years and sixty years and older only a minority of countries show a significant increase in suicide mortality among females.)

A number of studies of suicide trends in countries like Canada (Solomon & Hellon, 1980; Reed, Camus, & Last, 1985; Barnes, Ennis, & Schober, 1986), the United States (Murphy & Wetzel, 1980; Lester, 1984), Australia (Goldney & Katsikitis, 1983), Germany (Häfner & Schmidtke, 1985), England & Wales (Murphy, Lindesay, & Grundy, 1986), Italy (Vecchia, Bollini, & Mazio, 1986), Belgium and the Netherlands (Moens, 1990) and Sweden (Asgard, Nordström, & Rabäck, 1987), all applying birth cohort methodologies, have confirmed this picture of a shift toward younger ages over the course of this century as well as a relatively greater risk increase among young males. This is poignantly illustrated by Figures 6.5 through 6.7, presenting the suicide rates for the fifteen- to twenty-four and twenty-nine-year-olds for the years 1900 through 1987 in the United States and the Netherlands.

In both countries there are two conspicuous peak periods in youth suicide mortality over the course of this century, one around 1980 and another in the beginning of the century, around 1910. This pattern has

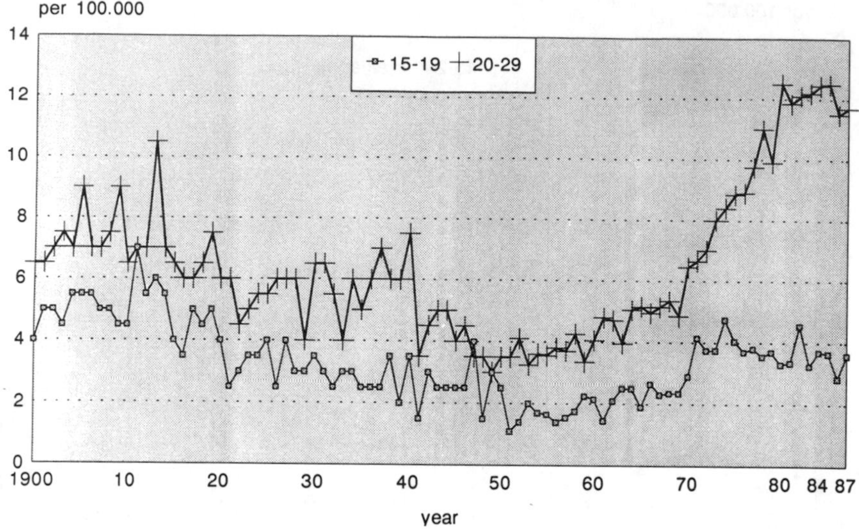

Figure 6.6. Suicide rates in the Netherlands, 1900–87. (Source: Central Bureau of Statistics of the Netherlands: WHO Statistics Annual, until 1950 age groups are 16-20 and 21-29 years)

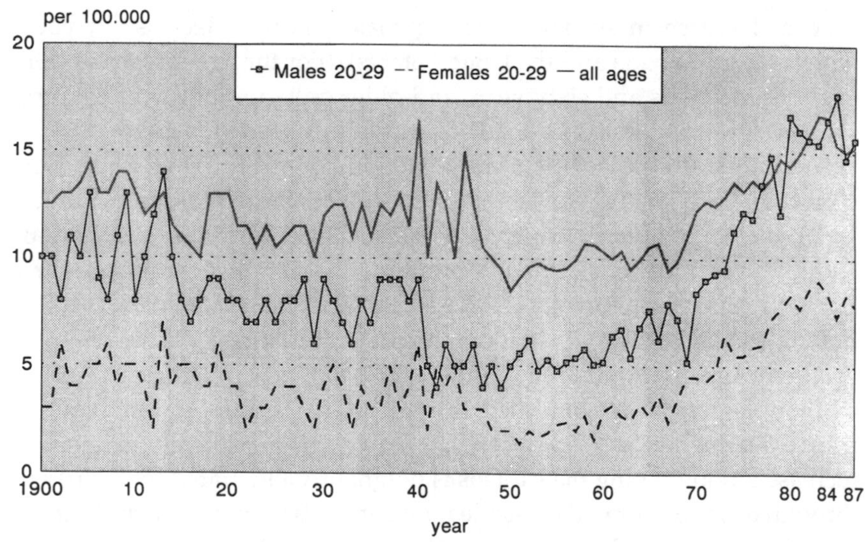

Figure 6.7. Suicide rates for the Netherlands, 1900–87. (Source: Central Bureau of Statistics of the Netherlands: WHO Statistics Annual, until 1950 age groups are 16-20 and 21-29 years)

been observed in other European countries as well. In this respect, it is of more than just historical relevance that the first scientific meeting on suicide ever held took place in Vienna in 1910. The meeting was organized by the Viennese Psychoanalytic Society and chaired by Alfred Adler. Sigmund Freud was one of the discussants. The special topic of the meeting was suicide among adolescents. Increased rates in youth suicide in Austria and other European countries, and several so-called "school epidemics" at that time, had aroused public and professional concern. Besides the similarities between the graphs for the United States and the Netherlands – after an all time low around 1950, the rates rapidly rose until around 1980 they reached the level of the 1910 period and then broke through that barrier to climb to all time highs – there are also some notable differences. For the Netherlands, in contrast to the United States, this is so only for the age group twenty to twenty-nine years old, both in males as well as in females. In the age group fifteen to nineteen the suicide rates remained below the level of the beginning of the century, although since 1950 we also observe a substantial increase in this age category.

The interaction between age and gender over time in overall suicide mortality appears to be different between the two countries. In the Netherlands the increase of young males in contrast to young females is accompanied by a decrease of this ratio for the older age groups taken together. This is not so for the United States (Diekstra, Kienhorst, & De Wilde, in press).

Secular trends in depressive disorders and suicide mortality: preliminary conclusions

The findings presented in the two preceding paragraphs on secular trends in depressive disorders as well as in suicide mortality lend support to the hypothesis that a true increase in these phenomena has occurred over the larger part of this century among the white urban adolescent and young adult populations of North America and Europe. This conclusion is corroborated by the data on depressive disorders and suicide which converge on the fact that this increase is particularly conspicuous among young males.

Of further relevance is evidence suggesting that the percentage of adolescent male suicides suffering from a depressive disorder at the time of death has increased over the past decades. In a comparison of psychological autopsies in two series of male suicides separated by twenty-five years, it was found that the prevalence of depressive disorders was higher among young males in the more recent series (Carlson et al., 1991).

It is difficult to assert whether the earlier age of onset observed for depressive disorders is also reflected in an increase of suicide mortality at a lower age, given the problems with suicide statistics for early adolescence mentioned earlier, but there is indirect evidence to suggest that this might be the case. As described earlier, there have been a number of community survey studies assembling (retrospectively) data on lifetime prevalence of parasuicide among both the general and high school student populations. Given the reasonable expectation that lifetime prevalence rates should increase with age since time augments risk, it is surprising that the lifetime parasuicide rates in general population studies do not exceed and sometimes even remain below the rates for high school students (Diekstra, Kienhorst, & De Wilde, in press). Assuming that recall of past episodes remains constant throughout the life span (an assertion still under heavy debate; see Fombonne, in press), one possible explanation for this finding is a lower age of first-ever parasuicidal acts in recent decades. Since parasuicide is an important, presumably the most important, precursor of suicide, a lower age for first-ever parasuicides can be expected to predict a lower age for suicides as well.

Secular trends in depression and suicide: The search for causal mechanisms

The plausibility of the assertion that depressive disorders and suicide mortality have been increasing among the adolescent and young adult populations over the larger part of this century, raises the question as to the possible causes of these increases. We are dealing here with a very complicated issue. Depression and suicide are descriptive or phenotypical categories and not etiological or genotypical concepts. It is highly probable that the observed secular increases can be attributed predominantly to a subgroup of the different causal pathways to, or genotypes of, depression and suicide. Research addressing this question is virtually nonexistent, however.

But even if we could identify which pathways to depression and suicide are more frequently seen today than in the past, we still would not automatically have explained secular changes. It is one thing to explain what causes a phenomenon to occur in the first place; it is quite a different thing to explain changes in that phenomenon. It may very well be, for example, that weather conditions are associated with a change in the incidence of road traffic accidents in a particular period compared to previous and following periods, but that does not imply that the weather causes road traffic accidents (nor does it necessarily mean that reduction of bad weather leads to reduction of road accidents in the long term).

In trying to explain secular trends, we must look for variables that have a known etiological and/or "control" function with regard to depression and suicide and whose changes in a specified period can be empirically related to changes in the prevalence and incidence of depression and suicide in the same or a later period. No research programs are currently addressing these two issues in conjunction. By default we must resort to the "bits and pieces" method, which can only deliver very preliminary answers.

Biological changes

In the highly industrialized countries of Europe and North America a remarkable biological-developmental change has taken place over the course of the past 150 years. Around 1850 the average age of menarche was sixteen years; in most countries today the average age is around twelve and a half years (Petersen and Leffert, this volume). A similar trend seems to apply to boys (age of spermarche) but is harder to document. A number of authors have tried to attribute secular changes in emotional disturbances in adolescence to this change (Hamburg, 1989; see also Fombonne, in press). Although earlier puberty might explain earlier onset of depressive conditions or earlier occurrence of suicidal behaviors – given the validity of the assumption that puberty contributes to risk, an issue not yet settled – it still does not automatically explain higher prevalence rates.

A more plausible explanation seems to be that the lower puberty age has caused a disjunction of biological development on the one hand and psychological and social development on the other. The brain does not reach a fully adult state of development until the end of the teenage years (Hamburg, 1989) and social changes during two centuries, particularly during the last century, have postponed the end of adolescence – and of social dependence- until much later. This phenomenon of *bio-psycho-social dysbalance* is a distinctly human evolutionary novelty (Hamburg, 1989) and might pose on many youngsters stresses and strains that overtax, at least for a number of years, their coping repertoires and those of families and educators. In most countries, too, the present average age of puberty coincides with another important developmental task for the early adolescent, the transition from elementary to secondary or high school (Petersen, Compas, & Brooks-Gunn, 1993).

Some researchers hypothesize (see Fombonne, in press) that these processes particularly affect girls. This hypothesis seems to be substantiated by the fact that depressive disorders, suicidal ideation, and parasuicide are more prevalent in girls than in boys, but it also seems to be contradicted by the fact that the rise in depressive disorders and suicides is greater among boys than among girls.

Psychological/behavioral changes

The lowering of the average age of puberty has been accompanied by the earlier use of various life- or (mental) health-threatening substances. For example, over the past thirty to fourty years increasing percentages of young people have started to drink alcoholic beverages, their alcohol consumption has increased in quantity and frequency, and the age at which drinking starts has become lower (Perry, 1989; WHO, 1989). Problem drinking and alcohol-associated morbidity and mortality rates have increased among adolescents and are higher for boys than for girls, although the rise in alcohol use appears to be as strong for girls as for boys (Perry, 1989). Chronic excessive use of alcohol among adolescents is often a reaction to social problems, such as family difficulties or failure at school, and can also aggravate these problems. Acute intoxication often removes inhibitions that would otherwise prevent risky behaviors. It is especially implicated in aggression, crime, accidents, and, of particular relevance to this chapter, suicidal behavior.

What applies to alcohol use applies, mutatis mutandis, to the use of other substances, such as tobacco, cannabis, cocaine, and psychopharmaca (prescribed or nonprescribed). The age of onset of use has lowered, and quantity and frequency of use in adolescence have generally increased. There is also growing evidence to suggest that the use of substances tends to cluster. Adolescents who are regular smokers have a higher probability of using alcohol regularly. Adolescents who drink regularly are more likely than others to use illicit drugs (WHO, 1989). Regular multiple substance use is associated with poorer performance at school, at work, at sports, and with a pessimistic future perspective.

From a sociocultural perspective it is important to note that the increase in substance use among adolescents, in particular the use of alcohol, tobacco and psychopharmaca, is associated with greater availability of those substances both in the family and at the societal level (the supermarket substance shelves) and with an increased acceptability of their use by young people as portrayed in the media, for example.

The combination of increased availability and acceptability of chemical mind and mood changing substances in highly industrialized countries (Rose, 1990) is, from a behavioral perspective, particularly relevant to suicidal behaviors. In many countries, the majority of parasuicides in men and women and the majority of suicides in women (in men a considerable minority) in many countries are by overdoses of drugs or (other) poisonous substances, often in combination with alcohol. Once people have taken to coping with life stresses and strains through the use of chemical substances, such as alcohol, there is a strong increase in the probability of the use of other chemical substances and their (combined) abuse or overdosage, often labeled parasuicide in case of a nonfatal outcome and suicide in case of a fatal outcome. If this is one of the pathways that explain (partially) the secular increases in suicidal behaviors, one would hypothesize that the incidence of both suicide and parasuicide should be high among psychoactive substance abusers and the correlation between changes in national suicide rates among adolescents and young adults and changes in national alcohol consumption should be high and positive. The available evidence lends support to both hypotheses (Miles, 1977; Kreitman, 1977; Fremouw, De Perczel, & Ellis, 1990; Diekstra, 1989).

The role of substance abuse disorders in the secular increase of suicidal behaviors may, however, be restricted to young men. In a case control study of teenage suicides it was found (Gould, Shaffer, & Davies, 1991) that of the male suicides 37 percent suffered from a substance abuse disorder (as against 7 percent of the normal group), whereas 5 percent of the female suicides had such a disorder (as against 7 percent of the normal group).

From a behavioral perspective another finding of that study is of considerable interest. Over a third of the adolescent suicides (41 percent in males and 33 percent in females) had a first- or second-degree relative who had attempted a parasuicidal act or committed suicide. This suggests that the probability of suicidal behavior is, among other things, a function of the availability of suicidal "models" in the present or past social network of the adolescent. Earlier studies (Kreitman, 1977) have demonstrated that the same relationship exists for parasuicides: Suicidal behavior was significantly more frequent among significant others (not necessarily people of kin) of parasuicidal persons than in representative samples of the general population. This imitation effect has also been observed with models not belonging to family or other immediate social networks (such as school). Public discussion (through television, radio, newsprint, and the like) of celebrities or non-celebrity young people (fictional or nonfictional) who have committed suicide often elicits an increase in suicides (Diekstra, Kienhorst, & De Wilde, in press), particularly among youth.

These findings render plausible the hypothesis that suicidal models within a society have a causative effect on the incidence of suicidal behavior among young people in that society. Although no studies have measured media coverage of (fictional or nonfictional) suicide cases over the course of this century, it seems safe to assume that an increase in coverage has occurred.

Social changes

It has been repeatedly shown that both depression and suicidal behaviors among adolescents are associated with a variety of social conditions such as unemployment and economic hardship, interpersonal difficulties such as parental discord and family conflicts, interpersonal losses (for example, through parental divorce), parental mental disorders such as depression and psychoactive substance abuse, and physical and sexual abuse during childhood and/or adolescence (Fombonne, in press; Diekstra, Kienhorst, & De Wilde, in press; Petersen, Compas, & Brooks-Gunn, 1993). A number of reports indicate that these adverse social conditions have increased over the last three to four decades (Coleman & Husen, 1985; Preston, 1984). In their report for the Organization for Economic Cooperation and Development (OECD), Coleman and Husen conclude that although "the number of social changes in the highly industrialized countries with extensive consequences for youth . . . differ in different OECD countries, the pattern is so widespread that it can be regarded as a general change" (1985: 8). If the prevalence of such social and interpersonal problems in the community in general has been rising, it may well be that the increasing rates of depression and suicidal behavior reflect in part the increasing presence of these social stressors. There are, however, very few studies carried out at an international level that shed some light on this issue (WHO, 1982; Diekstra, Kienhorst, & De Wilde, in press) and they have, for obvious reasons, focused exclusively on the relationship between secular trends in some of these social conditions and secular trends in suicide (no such studies are available for depression or parasuicide).

Sainsbury and colleagues (WHO, 1982), in cooperation with the World Health Organization, investigated the relationship between certain social conditions and changes in suicide rates in eighteen European countries after 1960. The social characteristics of countries in 1961–63 associated with a subsequent increase in rates of suicide in the period 1972–74 were (1) a high divorce rate; (2) a low percentage of the population under the age of fifteen years; (3) a high unemployment rate; (4) a high homicide rate; (5) a high proportion of women employed. Sainsbury and colleagues (WHO, 1982) also analyzed which changes in social conditions after 1960 were related to changes in national suicide rates. The results indicated similar but not identical factors associated with suicide trends. Increased suicide rates were associated with (1) a reduction in population aged fifteen and under; (2) an increase in the percentage of the population aged sixty-five and over (the age group with the relatively highest suicide rate in European countries), and (3) an increase in females in tertiary education, possibly an indicator of the changing status of women and of family structure. Sainsbury's study examined only the relationship between social factors and changes in total suicide rates and therefore did not provide information on changes in rates among adolescents and young adults. Diekstra and coworkers, within the framework of the WHO Program on Preventive Strategies on Suicide (1988), carried out a similar analysis on the fifteen- to twenty-nine-year-old age group. Changes in suicide rates for this age group for the same European countries over the period 1960–61 to 1984–85 were related to proportional changes in a number of social variables (all age groups). The extent to which the (seven) variables investigated accurately predict observed changes in national suicide rates can be deduced from the fact that the multiple correlation between those seven variables and changes in suicide rates was 0.84.

Five of these variables are identical or similar to the ones shown by Sainsbury's study to be associated with changes in national overall suicide rates. Unlike Sainsbury's findings, however, this study showed a positive relationship between the percentage of young people in the population and the suicide rate (see also Holinger, Offer, & Zola, 1988). The two other variables related to change in youth suicide rates, the change in use of liters of pure alcohol per head of population and the proportional change in church membership (nine countries only), an indicator of secularization, require some additional comments. First, the change in use of alcohol has the highest single correlation (0.70) with change in suicide rate. This seems to substantiate what we discussed in the preceding paragraph about the relationship between the increasing emergence of a pattern of behavior involving the use or abuse of psychoactive substances to cope with life problems and depressive and/or suicidal reactions.

The association between the proportional change in church membership and change in suicide rate suggests a change in moral values and hence in attitudes toward suicide and the frequency with which it occurs. It might also be seen as an indicator of decreasing social integration, since churches have for centuries also functioned as social havens.

In conclusion, the results from the two studies seem to indicate that societies, communities, or social groups increasingly and simultaneously subject to such conditions as economic instability or deprivation (unemployment), breakdown of traditional primary or family group structure, greater intragenerational pressures and competition, interpersonal violence and increase in criminal behavior, secularization and (possibly) more permissive attitudes toward suicide, and increasing substance use and abuse are at a high risk for an increase in suicide mortality.

The exact nature of the association between each of these conditions separately and suicide mortality remains, however, rather obscure. At the individual level unemployment, for example, appears to be related to depression and suicidal behavior in a number of ways (Fombonne, in press). Unemployment of a family member, particularly the father, is associated with both depressive conditions and suicidal reactions in children and adolescents, but the association is moderated by a number of other variables, such as the presence or absence of other problems in the family, for example, poverty, marital disruption, and parental mental illness (Rutter et al., 1976). Furthermore, parental unemployment appears to be a risk factor of unemployment in adolescent children, a phenomenon sometimes labeled "transgenerational problem transmission." Unemployment of the adolescent or young adult is also, independent of parental unemployment, associated with elevated risk of suicidal behavior and presumably also depression (Platt, 1984). The interpretation of this latter association is uncertain. Unemployment might be a "stadium" on a pathway leading to depression or suicidal behavior, but the reverse might also be true; depressive or suicidal reactions causing poor functioning at work, continued absence from work, and loss of job. The associations between other social problems, such as parental divorce and the risk of depression and suicidal behavior in adolescents, are of similar complexity. There appears to be growing consensus in the literature that the associations between social problems and mental ill-health are generally stronger among adolescents than among adults (Platt, 1984; Rutter, 1980); that is, adolescents are more vulnerable to social and interpersonal adversities than are adults. Illustrative of this are the results of a study on attitudes toward suicide and age (Diekstra & Kerkhof, 1989). In a factor analysis of the answers to a suicide attitude scale taken from two samples of the general population, two principal factors were found that could be interpreted as follows:

1. Respondent's ability to imagine any circumstances at all in which he or she might commit suicide
2. Estimated probability of physical and social problems as reasons or motives for committing suicide by respondent or others

Relevant for the present discussion are the findings on the relationship between age and factor scores on the second factor. The older and younger age groups showed no differences in estimated probability of suicide (by self or others) under conditions like incurable or terminal illness or chronic mental illness. They did, however, differ very strongly in estimated probability of suicide under adverse social conditions such as loss of job, breaking off of a (love) relationship, unwanted pregnancy and the like. The adolescents and young adults rated the probability that they or others would commit suicide under such circumstances much higher than the older age groups.

Conclusion

To develop oneself is to work on one's self and to be worked on by other persons and by nonpersonal processes and events. Developmental stress is, therefore, a form of work stress and vice versa. The most recent and well-substantiated models or schemes of work stress – often labeled as interactional or relational models – explain this and its emotional and physical consequences as the outcome of the interaction between five sets of factors:

1. task demands (their number, natures, and patterning)
2. the available social support (both emotional/affective, informational and behavior-regulatory) for meeting those demands
3. the available resources (material, financial, technical) for meeting those demands
4. the available personal (coping) skills and attitudes relevant to the task demands
5. the socioecological context in which demands have to be met

If one inserts the word "developmental" before the words "task demands" in (1) above, it immediately becomes clear that this scheme might be as applicable to developmental stress as to work stress in *sensu strictu*. Developmental stress and related emotional disorders can thus be seen as resulting from the discrepancies between developmental task demands on the one hand and available support, resources, coping skills, and socioecological environment on the other hand. Complex or potentially highly stressful developmental tasks need not have adverse emotional consequences if support, resources, personal skills, and environment measure up to those demands. If the assumption is valid that over the past one hundred years or so the developmental tasks of adolescence have grown not only in number but also in complexity, the key question is whether available support, resources, skills, and suitability of the developmental context have grown or changed in similar ways, or alternatively have lagged behind for certain subgroups of adolescents.

The data on secular trends in depression and suicide as presented and discussed in this chapter seem to suggest that the number of disadvantaged adolescents has grown in most industrialized countries. Despite a general rise in standard of living and physical health, it remains doubtful whether the quality of mental life and of social well-being for many adolescents has improved. It also remains doubtful whether adolescents at the lower end of the social continuum today are better off than their peers fifty or a hundred years ago.

There are no clear signs that social inequity in health, particularly in mental health, is decreasing in most countries, and it cannot be ruled out that it has instead been increasing over the past decades and that the increase will continue in the next decades (WHO, 1989).

In the opinion of the author the priorities of the future public health and research agendas, as far as adolescents are concerned, should be (1) a precise identification of the developmental tasks in contemporary adolescence; (2) a careful description of the conditions, both material and physical, psychological and social, for their successful completion in adolescence; and (3) a clear delineation of who is to be held responsible for the fulfillment of those conditions during adolescence.

Surprising as it may sound, national youth policies or research programs have not, as far as these three goals are concerned, reached adolescence in the countries of Europe and North America. They are still in the stage of early infancy.

References

Achenbach, T. M. (1991). *Manual for the Youth Self-report and 1991 Profile*. Burnton, Vermont.: University of Vermont, Department of Psychiatry. (Also: Integrative guide for the 1991 C.B.C.L./4–18, YSR, and T.R.F. profiles)

Andrews, J. A., & Lewinsohn, P. M. (1990). *The Prevalence, Lethality and Intent of Suicide Attempts among Adolescents*. Paper presented at the 98th Annual Convention of the American Psychological Association, Boston.

Andrus, J. K., Fleming, D. W., Heumann, M. A., Wassell, J. T., Hopkins, D. D., & Gordon, J. (1991). Surveillance of attempted suicide among adolescents in Oregon. *American Journal of Public Health*, 81, 1067–9.

Asgard, U., Nordström, P., & Rabäck, G. (1987). Birth cohort analysis of changing suicide risk by sex and age in Sweden 1952 to 1981. *Acta Psychiatrica Scandinavica*, 76, 456–63.

Bachman, J. G., Johnston, L. D., & O'Malley, P. M. (1986). *Monitoring the Future. Questionnaire Responses From the Nation's High-School Seniors.* Ann Arbor, Mich.: Institute for Social Research, University of Michigan.

Barnes, R. A., Ennis, J., & Schober, R. (1986). Cohort analysis of Ontario suicide 1877–1976. *Canadian Journal of Psychiatry*, 31, 208–13.

Barraclough, B. (1973). Differences between national suicide rates. *British Journal of Psychiatry*, 122, 95–6.

Beck, A.T. (1976). *Cognitive Therapy and the Emotional Disorders.* New York: International Universities Press.

Buda, M., & Tsuang, M. T. (1990). In *Suicide Over the Life Cycle*, ed. S. Blumental & D. Kupfer, pp. 17–38. Washington, DC: APA Press.

Canino, G. J., Bird, H. R., Shrout, P. E., Rubio-Stipec, M., Bravo, M., Martinez, R., Sesman, M., & Guevara, L. M. (1987). The prevalence of specific psychiatric disorders in Puerto Rico. *Archives of General Psychiatry*, 44, 727–35.

Canton, G., Gallimberti, L., Gentile, N., & Ferrare, S.D. (1989). L'ideazione di suicidio nell'adolescenza: prevalenza in un compione di studenti e relazione con i sintomi psichiatrici (Suicidal ideation during adolescence: prevalence in a student sample and its relationship with psychiatric symptoms), *Rivista di Psichiatria*, 24(3), 101–7.

Carlson, G. A., Rich, C. L., Grayson, P., & Fowler, R. C. (1991). Secular trends in psychiatric diagnoses of suicide victims. *Journal of Affective Disorders*, 21, 127–32.

CDC-Centers for Disease Control. (1991). Attempted suicide among high school students – *United States 1990, Leads from the Morbidity and Mortality Weekly Report. Journal of the American Medical Association*, 266, 14, 911.

Coleman, E. A., & Husen, T. (1985). *Becoming an Adult in a Changing Society.* Paris, OECD.

Diekstra, R. F. W. (1989a). Suicidal behavior and depressive disorders in adolescents and young adults. *Neuropsychobiology*, 22, 194–207.

(1989b). Suicidal behavior in adolescents and young adults: The international picture. *Crisis*, 10, 1, 16–35.

Diekstra, R. F. W., De Heus, P., Garnefski, N., de Zwart, R., & Van Praag, B.M.S. (1991). *Monitoring the Future: Behavior and Health Among High School Students.* The Hague: NIBUD.

Diekstra, R. F. W., & Kerkhof, A. J. F. M. (1989). Attitudes towards suicide: The development of a suicide attitude questionnaire (SUIATT). In *Suicide and Its Prevention: The Role of Attitude and Imitation*, ed. R. F. W. Diekstra, R. Maris, S. Platt, A. Schmidtke, & G. Sonneck, pp. 91–107. World Health Organization copublication). Canberra: Leinde.

Diekstra, R. F. W., Kienhorst, C., & De Wilde, E. (in press). Suicide and parasuicide. In *Psychosocial Problems of Youth in a Changing Europe*, ed. M. Rutter. Cambridge: Cambridge University Press (prepared for the Academia Europea Study Group on Youth Problems).

Douglas, J. D. (1967). *The Social Meanings of Suicide.* Princeton, N.J.: Princeton University Press.

Dubow, E. F., Kausch, D. F., Blum, M. C., Reed, J., & Bush, E. (1989). Correlates of suicidal ideation and attempts in a community sample of junior high and high school students. *Journal of Clinical Child Psychology*, 18, 158–66.

Farberow, N. L. (ed.) (1980). *The Many Faces of Suicide: Indirect Self-Destructive Behaviour*. New York: McGraw-Hill.

Fombonne, E. (in press). Secular trends in depressive disorders. In *Psychosocial Problems of Youth in a Changing Europe*, ed. M. Rutter. Cambridge: Cambridge University Press (prepared for the Academia Europea Study Group on Youth Problems).

Fremouw, W. J., De Perczel, M., & Ellis, T.E. (1990). *Suicide Risk: Assessment and Response Guidelines*. New York: Pergamon Press.

Goldney, R. D., & Katsikitis, M. (1983). Cohort analysis of suicide rates in Australia. *Archives of General Psychiatry*, 40, 71–4.

Goldney, R. D., Winefield, A. H., Tiggemann, M., Winefield, H. R., & Smith, S. (1989). Suicidal ideation in a young adult population. *Acta Psychiatrica Scandinavica*, 79, 481–9.

Gould, M. S., Shaffer, D., & Davies, M. (1991). Truncated pathways from childhood into adulthood: Attrition in follow-up studies due to death. In *Straight and Devious Pathways from Childhood into Adulthood*, ed. L. Robins & M. Rutter, pp. 3–9. New York: Cambridge University Press.

Häfner, H., & Schmidtke, A. (1985). Do cohort effects influence suicide rates? *Archives of General Psychiatry*, 42, 926–7.

Hagnell, O., Lanke, J., Rorsman, B., & Ojesjö, L. (1982). Are we entering an age of melancholy? Depressive illnesses in a prospective epidemiological study over 25 years: the Lundby study, Sweden. *Psychological Medicine*, 12, 279–89.

Hamburg, D. (1989). Preparing for life: the critical transition of adolescence. In *Preventive Interventions in Adolescence*, ed. R. W. F. Diekstra, pp. 4–15. Toronto/Bern: Hogrefe & Huber.

Harkavy Friedman, J. M., Asnis, G. M., Boeck, M., & DiFiore, J. (1987). Prevalence of specific suicidal behaviors in a high school sample. *American Journal of Psychiatry*, 144, 1203–6.

Hawton, K., O'Grady, J., Osborn, M., & Cole, D. (1982). Adolescents who take overdoses; Their characteristics, problems, and contacts with helping agencies. *British Journal of Psychiatry*, 140, 118–23.

Holinger, P. C., Offer, D., & Zola, M. (1988). A prediction model of suicide among youth. *Journal of Nervous and Mental Disease*, 176, 275–9.

Irwin, C. E., & Vaughan, E. (1988). Psychosocial context of adolescent development: study group report. *Journal of Adolescent Health Care* 9,6, 11–19.

Jobes, D. A., Berman, A. L., & Josselsen, A. R. (1986). The impact of psychosocial autopsies on medical examiners' determination of manner of death. *Journal of Forensic Science*, 31(1), 177–89.

Joyce, P. R., Oakley-Browne, M. A., Wells, J. E. Bushnell, J. A., & Hornblow, A. R. (1990). Birth cohort trends in major depression: increasing rates and earlier onset in New Zealand. *Journal of Affective Disorders*, 18, 83–9.

Karno, M., Hough, R. L., Burnam, M. A., Escobar, J. I., Timbers, D. M., Santana, F., & Boyd, J. H. (1987). Lifetime prevalence of specific psychiatric disorders among Mexican Americans and non-Hispanic whites in Los Angeles. *Archives of General Psychiatry*, 44, 695–701.

Kienhorst, C. W. M., De Wilde, E. J., Van den Bout, J., Diekstra, R. F. W., & Wolters, W. H. G. (1990a). Self-reported suicidal behavior in dutch secondary education students. *Suicide and Life Threatening Behavior*, 20, 101–12.

Kienhorst, C. W. M., De Wilde, E. J., Van den Bout, J., Diekstra, R. F. W., & Wolters, W. H. G. (1990b). Characteristics of suicide attempters in a population-based sample of Dutch adolescents. *British Journal of Psychiatry*, 156, 243–8.

Klerman, G. L. (1985). Birth cohort trends in rates in major depressive disorders among relatives of patients with affective disorders. *Archives of General Psychiatry*, 42, 689–99.

Kreitman, N. S. (1977). *Parasuicide*. Chichester: Wiley.

Lester, D. (1972). *Why People Kill Themselves: A Summary of Research Findings on Suicidal Behavior*. Springfield, Ill.: Thomas, 5–12.

(1984). Suicide risk by birth cohort. *Suicide and Life Threatening Behavior*, 14, 132–6.

Maris, R. W. (1991). Suicide. In *Encyclopedia of Human Biology*, Vol. 7, pp. 372–85. New York: Academic Press.

Marttunen, M. J., Aro, H. M, Henriksson, M. M., & Lönnqvist, J. (1991). Mental disorders in adolescent suicide. DMS-III-R axes I and II in suicides among 13 to 19 year olds in Finland. *Archives of General Psychiatry*, 48, 834–9.

McCarthy, P. D., & Walsh, D. (1975). Suicide in Dublin: I. The underreporting of suicide and the consequences for national suicide statistics. *British Journal of Psychiatry*, 126, 301–8.

Mehr, M., Zeltzer, L. K., & Robinson, R. (1981). Continued self-destructive behaviours in adolescent suicide attempters: Part I. *Journal of Adolescent Health*, 1, 269–74.

Mehr, M., Zeltzer, L. K., & Robinson, R. (1982). Continued self-destructive behaviors in adolescent suicide attempters: Part II. *Journal of Adolescent Health Care*, 2, 182–7.

Miles, C. P. (1977). Conditions predisposing to suicide: a review. *Journal of Nervous and Mental Diseases*, 16, 231–46.

Moens, G. F. G. (1990). *Aspects of the Epidemiology and Prevention of Suicide*. Leuven: Leuven University Press.

Moscicki, E. K., O'Caroll, P. W., Rae, D. S., Roy, A. G., Locke, B. Z., & Regier, D. A. (1989). Suicidal ideation and attempts: The epidemiological catchment area study. In *Report of the Secretary's Task Force on Youth Suicide. Department of Health and Human Services Publication*: Rockville-USA: Department of Health and Human Services Publication, no. (ADM) 89–1264, pp. 4–115/4–128.

Murphy, E., Lindesay, J., & Grundy, E. (1986). 60 years of suicide in England and Wales. A cohort study. *Archives of General Psychiatry*, 43, 969–76.

Murphy, G. E., & Wetzel, R. D. (1980). Suicide risk by birth cohort in the United States, 1949 to 1974. *Archives of General Psychiatry*, 37, 519–23.

Nagy, S., & Adcock, A. (1990). *The Alabama Adolescent Health Survey: Health Knowledge and Behaviors*. Summary Report II. Alabama: The University of Alabama and Troy State University.

Perry, C. L. (1989). Teacher vs Peer-led Intervention. *Crisis*, 10,1, 52–61

Petersen, A. C., Compas, B., & Brooks-Gunn, J. (1993). *Depression in Adolescence: Current Knowledge, Research Directions and Implications for Programs and Policy*. Washington, DC: Carnegie Council on Adolescent Development.

Platt, S. (1984). Unemployment and suicidal behaviour: A review of the literature. *Social Science and Medicine*, 19,2, 93–115.

(1988). Data from the Royal Infirmary Edinburgh, Scotland.

Platt, S., Bille-Brahe, U., & Kerkhof, A. J. F. M. (1992). Parasuicide in Europe: The WHO/EURO multicentre study on parasuicide I. Introduction and preliminary analysis for 1989. *Acta Psychiatrica Scandinavica*, 85, 97–104.

Preston, S. H. (1984). Children and elderly in the U.S. *Scientific American*, 251, 6, 36–41.

Pronovost, J., Cote, L., & Ross, C. (1990). Epidemiological study of suicidal behaviour among secondary-school students. *Canada's Mental Health*, 38, 9–14.

Reed, J., Camus, J., & Last, J. M. (1985). Suicide in Canada: Birth-cohort analysis. *Canadian Journal of Public Health*, 76, 43–7.

Rey, J. M., & Bird, K. D. (1991). Sex differences in suicidal behaviour of referred adolescents. *British Journal of Psychiatry*, 158, 776–81.

Robins, L. N., Locke, B. Z., & Regier, D. A. (1991). An overview of psychiatric disorders in America. In *Psychiatric Disorders in America: The Epidemiologic Catchment Area Study*, ed. L.N. Robins & D.A. Regier, pp. 328–66. New York: Free Press.

Rose, G. (1990). Doctors and the nation's health. *Annals of Medicine*, 22, 297–302.

Roy-Byrne, B. P., Post, R. N., Uhde, T. W., Borcu, T., & Davis, D. (1985). The longitudinal course of recurrent affective illness: life chart data from research patients at the NINH. *Acta Psychiatrica Scandinavica Supplementum*, 71, 3–34.

Rubenstein, J. L., Heeren, T., Housman, D., Rubin, C., & Stechler, G. (1989). Suicidal behavior in "normal" adolescents: risk and protective factors. *American Journal of Orthopsychiatry*, 59, 59–71.

Runeson, B., & Beskow, J. (1991). Borderline personality disorder in young Swedish suicides. *Journal of Nervous Mental Diseases*, 179, 153–6.

Rutter, M. (1980). *Changing Youth in a Changing Society. Patterns of Adolescent Development and Disorder*. Cambridge: Harvard University Press.

(1986). The developmental psychopathology of depression: issues and perspectives. In *Depression in Young People*, ed. M. Rutter, C. E. Izard, & P. B. Read, pp. 3–30. New York: Guilford Press.

Rutter, M., Graham, P., Chadwick, O. F. D., & Yule, W. (1976). Adolescent turmoil: fact or fiction? *Journal of Child Psychology and Psychiatry*, 17, 35–56.

Sainsbury, P. ,& Barraclough, B. M. (1968). Differences between suicide rates. *Nature*, 220, 1252.

Sainsbury, P., Jenkins, J., & Baert, A. E. (1981). Suicide trends in Europe: A study of the decline in suicide in England and Wales and the increases elsewhere. Copenhagen: *WHO/EURO document ICP/MNH 036*.

Smith, K., & Crawford, S. (1986). Suicidal behavior among "normal" high school students. *Suicide and Life Threatening Behavior*, 16, 313–25.

Solomon, M. I., & Hellon, C. P. (1980). Suicide and age in Alberta, Canada: 1951 to 1977. *Archives of General Psychiatry*, 37, 511–3.

Spirito, A., Brown, L., Overholser, J., & Fritz, G. (1989). Attempted suicide in adolescence: A review and critique of the literature. *Clinical Psychology Review*, 9, 335–63.

Strober, M., & Carlson, G. A. (1982). Bipolar illness in adolescence with major depression: clinical, genetic and psycho-pharmacologic predictors in a 3–4 year prospective follow-up investigation. *Archives of General Psychiatry*, 39, 545–55.

Vecchia, C. la, Bollini, P., & Imazio, C. (1986). Age, period of death and birth cohort effects on suicide mortality in Italy, 1955–1979. *Acta Psychiatrica Scandinavica*, 74, 137–43.

Watanabe, N., Ninomiya, M., Shukutani, K., Aizawa, S., & Hasegawa, K. (1988). Structural analysis of behavioural patterns of junior high school students. *Japanese Journal of Child and Adolescent Psychiatry*, 29,3, 160–72.

Weinstein, S. R., Noam, G. G., Grines, K., Stone, K., & Schwab-Stone, N. (1990). Convergence of DSM-III diagnoses and self-reported symptoms in child and adolescence in-patients. *Journal of the American Academy of Child and Adolescent Psychiatry*, 29, 627–34.

Weissman, M., Livingston Bruce, M., Leaf, P. J., Florio, L. P., & Hozer III, C. (1991). Affective disorders. In *Psychiatric Disorders in America: The Epidemiologic Catch-*

ment Area Study, ed. L.N. Robins & D.A. Regier, pp. 53–80. New York: Free Press.

Whitlock, F. A. (1971). Migration and suicide. *Medical Journal of Australia*, 2, 840–8.

WHO Chronicle (1975). *Suicide Statistics: The Problem of Comparability*, 29, 188–93.

WHO (1982). *Changing Patterns in Suicide Behaviour*. Copenhagen, Denmark: WHO/Euro, reports and studies, 74.

WHO (1987, 1988, 1989, 1992). *World Health Statistics Annual*. Geneva: World Health Organization.

WHO (1989). *The Health of Youth*. Geneva: World Health Organization.

II. Preventive strategies

7. Promoting successful coping during adolescence

BRUCE E. COMPAS

What are likely to be the significant sources of stress facing adolescents in the year 2000? Will they encounter threats and challenges similar to those that confront the youth of today? Or will the continuing social and political changes in our world contribute to a new set of stresses for adolescents in the near future? Whatever specific events and circumstances confront youth at the turn of the millennium, stressful events and conditions will continue to represent a significant threat to positive development and a source of risk for psychopathology. Much of the stress they encounter will be an unavoidable part of development and the nature of the times in which they achieve adolescence.

Given the inevitable nature of some sources of stress, the skills and resources that adolescents bring to bear on trying to cope with the stresses they face will be important determinants of the course of their psychological adjustment during adolescence and adulthood. Efforts to alter stressful conditions, strategies for managing negative emotions experienced under stress, and support received from family and friends will all contribute to successful resolution of stress. On the other hand, some attempts at coping and certain types of interpersonal relationships will serve to worsen the impact of stress and contribute to maladaptive development.

Consider as examples the situations faced by two adolescents, each attempting to cope with a very different type of stress. The first is a twelve-year-old boy who reports that he is teased by others at school. The teasing occurs repeatedly and is a source of considerable distress for this youth. When asked how he tries to deal with the problem, he reports three coping responses. First, he tries to ignore the boys who tease him, trying not to listen to them. Second, he tries to think about other things to get his mind off the teasing. Finally, he simply wishes that others would be nice to him. On self-report measures of symptoms of anxiety and depression, his scores were more than two standard deviations above the normative mean.

A thirteen-year-old girl faces a quite different set of circumstances. Her father was recently diagnosed with cancer and is undergoing an arduous chemotherapy procedure. She is trying to deal with this situation through the use of five coping strategies, all of which, she reports, are intended to prevent herself from thinking about her father's illness. She avoids thinking about her father's illness by riding her bicycle, reading books, watching television, playing with her pet cats, and going for walks. She suffers substantial distress, however. Her self-reported symptoms of anxiety and depression are more than three standard deviations above the normative mean.

The situations encountered by these two adolescents and the ways in which they have attempted to cope indicate the diversity of the concepts of stress and coping. Stressful events include seemingly minor occurrences that become truly problematic only through repeated exposure to them. Stress also includes events that are grave and severe in magnitude, such as a life threatening illness in a loved one. The coping responses reported by these adolescents also suggest the breadth of these concepts, including efforts to change a stressful situation directly and to manage one's emotions in response to the stressor. The high levels of depressive and anxious symptoms experienced by these two young people suggest that their coping efforts may have been ineffective in managing the stressors they are facing.

A major challenge for behavioral scientists and mental health professionals involves the prevention of maladaptive coping and promotion of effective coping in youth, regardless of the type of stress they encounter. The continued development of programs to promote effective coping in youth is dependent on answering a series of basic questions. First, what is the nature of stress during adolescence? Second, what is the natural course of the development of coping during childhood and adolescence? Third, what are the characteristics of effective coping during adolescence? Fourth, what are the attributes of programs found to be effective in promoting successful coping? And finally, what are the next steps in research and in program development in this area? These questions provide the structure for this chapter.

Coping with what? The nature of stress during adolescence

To consider the importance of coping for adolescent development, it must first be established that psychosocial stress represents a significant threat to positive development during this age period. This requires a clear understanding of what is meant by the concept of stress, empirical evidence that stress and maladjustment are related in prospective longitudinal studies, examination of subtypes of stress and of individual differences in patterns of response to stress.

Defining stress

Few constructs in research on mental health and psychopathology have been as important but at the same time as difficult to define as the concept of "stress." Numerous definitions have emerged over the years, some so broad or difficult to operationalize as to render them useless for the purpose of scientific inquiry (Lazarus, 1990). Stress nevertheless continues to be central to most models of psychopathology.

As a result of confusion surrounding the definition of stress, several different approaches to measuring child or adolescent stressful experiences have guided research in this area. One approach has focused on stress as manifested in discrete environmental events (for example, loss of a loved one, a natural disaster, a sudden economic change) that represent measurable changes (Holmes & Rahe, 1967). These so-called "major life events" are assumed to affect the individual through the disruption they cause in the person's ongoing social environment. An alternative approach is reflected in transactional models which view stress as a consequence of environmental events and circumstances as they are perceived or appraised by the individual (Lazarus & Folkman, 1984). Stress is defined as the transaction between the individual and the environment. Conceptualizations of stress have also differed in their emphasis on the occurrence of major changes in the individual's life situation that involve significant levels of social readjustment as opposed to ongoing transactions, as reflected in daily hassles, chronic strains, or small events. These various approaches to conceptualizing and measuring stress have all been represented in research on adolescent stress (Coddington, 1972; Compas, et al., 1987; Kanner & Feldman, 1991).

A comprehensive perspective on adolescent stress includes both the objective nature of environmental events and conditions as well as individuals' cognitive appraisals of the environment. That is, neither objective nor subjective elements are sufficient alone to understand individual differences in the nature of what is stressful and who is vulnerable to what types of stressful situations (Lazarus, 1990). The broad definition offered by Lazarus and Folkman (1984: 19) fulfills these criteria: "a particular relationship between the person and the environment that is appraised by the person as taxing or exceeding his or her resources and endangering his or her well-being."

Longitudinal research on adolescent stress

An important goal of research in this area has been to determine the degree to which stress functions as a cause, correlate, or consequence of emotional or behavioral problems and disorders. Cross-sectional studies are useful in establishing an association between stress and emotional and behavioral problems that is worthwhile to pursue in more costly longitudinal investigations. Cross-sectional designs cannot, however, address temporal relations between stress and emotional or behavioral difficulties. Prospective designs are essential to examine the direction of the stress-disorder association – whether stress predicts increases in symptoms of psychopathology, whether symptoms predict increases in stress, or whether stress and symptoms are reciprocally related. In spite of the hope that prospective designs can allow for the inference of causality in these associations, it is important to remember that even prospective designs fail to control for third variables that could be influencing both stress and emotional or behavioral problems. Causal inferences are limited to the interpretation that data may be consistent with a hypothesized model although not providing definitive proof of the causal relationships within the model.

Several prospective longitudinal studies with adolescents have found an association between stress and emotional and/or behavioral problems in a follow-up assessment, even after controlling for initial symptoms. Stressful events reported in a follow-up assessment predicted an increase in symptoms, syndromes, and disorders over the time between the two data collections (Allgood-Merten, Lewinsohn, & Hops, 1990; Cohen, Burt, & Bjork, 1987; Compas et al., 1989a; Hammen, Burge, & Adrian, 1991; Stanger, McConaughy, & Achenbach, 1992). Thus, recent stressful events are associated with observable increases in emotional or behavioral problems over and above the initial levels of symptoms reported by adolescents.

Several studies have also established that stressful events of both major and minor magnitude are predictive of subsequent internalizing and externalizing problems in late childhood and adolescence (Compas et al., 1989a; DuBois et al., 1992; Hammen Burge, & Adrian, 1991). These studies have shown that initial levels of stressful events and chronic strains are predictive of increases in symptoms of internalizing and externalizing problems, after controlling for initial levels of maladjustment.

Although this research has been useful in establishing stress as a predictor of psychological maladjustment in adolescence, it is important to note several limitations. First, the strongest effects have been found when adolescents' self-reports have been used to measure both stress and psychological symptoms. Thus, the association between stress and maladjustment may be influenced to some degree by measurement confounds. Second, the sources of stress in the lives of adolescents, that is, the extent to which they contribute to stress in their own lives as opposed to stress resulting from the environment, remain unclear. Third, the amount of variance in maladjustment explained by stress has been relatively small. This suggests that other factors may moderate the relation between stress and maladjustment, including differences in the effects of subtypes of stress and individual differences among adolescents in their responses to stress.

Subtypes of stress: Generic, acute, and chronic stress

Stress is not a unitary phenomenon, but rather includes a heterogeneous set of events and circumstances that vary along a number of dimensions. These dimensions include the degree to which the stressor is normative or atypical, large or small in magnitude of occurrence, and acute or chronic in nature (Compas, 1987b). Considering these dimensions, stressors can be organized into three broad categories important for understanding mental health outcomes for adolescents – generic or normative stress, severe acute stress and severe chronic stress (see Figure 7.1).

All adolescents will be exposed to some level of generic stress as an ongoing part of development. This includes normative daily stresses and hassles, as well as major events such as transition to a new school. Generic stress, most notably the accumulation of daily stresses and hassles, has been found to be related to internalizing and externalizing symptoms during adolescence (Compas et al., 1989a; DuBois et al., 1992). The association between levels of generic stress and maladjustment has typically been quite modest, however, indicating that this type of stress may not tell the whole story of the association between adolescent stress and maladjustment.

In addition to the normative stresses and strains of adolescence, a subgroup of adolescents will encounter severe acute events that are traumatic in magnitude. This category encompasses serious illness or injury, disasters, loss of a loved one through death, and parental divorce. These events are qualitatively different from normative stress processes in that they

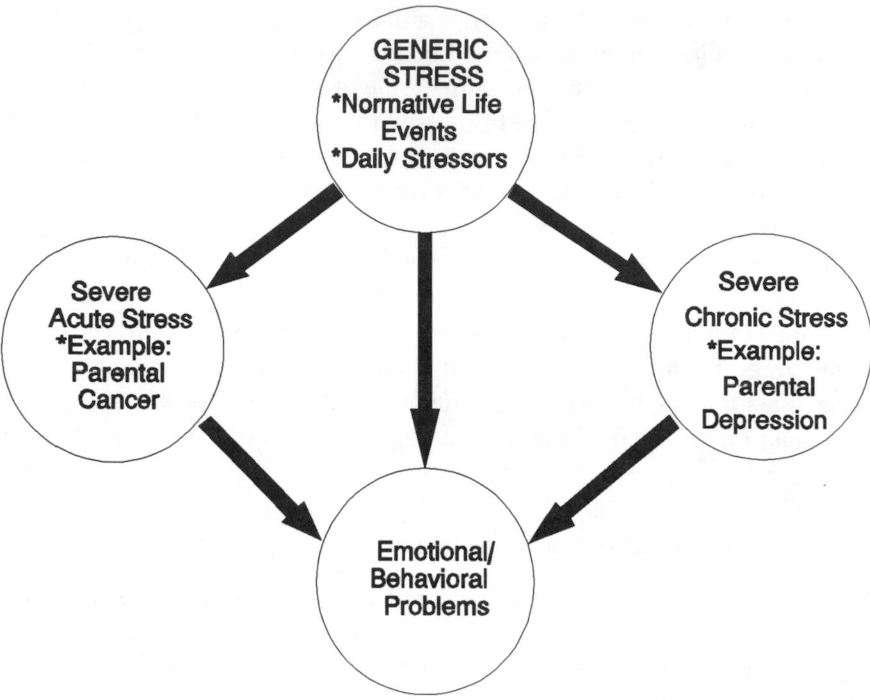

Figure 7.1. Subtypes of stress: generic stress, severe acute stress, and severe chronic stress.

have a discrete onset, affect only a small portion of adolescents, and exert an extreme level of disruption in the adolescents' ongoing world. A prototype of severe acute stress that we have pursued in our research is the diagnosis of a life threatening illness, specifically the diagnosis of cancer, in mother or father (Compas et al., in press). Adolescents appear to experience more psychological distress when their parents receive a diagnosis of cancer than do younger children, and the level of distress depends on the gender of the adolescent and whether mother or father is ill (Compas et al., in press). Adolescent daughters whose mothers are ill appear to experience the highest levels of depression and anxiety.

A subgroup of adolescents will be exposed to severe, chronic stress as an ongoing part of their environment. Chronic stress and adversity include exposure to poverty, neighborhood or familial violence, racism, sexism, and parental psychopathology. Parental psychopathology, most notably parental depression, is a prototype of severe, chronic stress in the lives of adolescents (Downey & Coyne, 1990; Hammen, 1991). Adolescents with a parent who suffers from depression are at extreme risk for a variety of adjustment problems. The increased risk for depression in adolescents in these families is not noteworthy, but these youth are also at risk for a variety of other internalizing and externalizing problems.

Generic, acute, and chronic stress are not assumed to be mutually exclusive. Adolescents may be exposed to some or all of these forms of stressful events and circumstances. Further, acute stressful events may exert some of their effects through the creation of ongoing chronic stressful circumstances in adolescents' environments. The categories are offered here as a general framework for considering the types of stress that may affect adolescent adjustment. Moreover, these three categories of stress provide a framework for organizing preventive interventions for adolescents.

Individual differences in response to stress

It appears that there are significant changes in the types of stress experienced in adolescence as compared to childhood, that these changes in stress are different for boys and girls, and that they may be related to psychological symptoms and disorder. For example, in a longitudinal study of adolescents, Petersen and colleagues (Petersen, Sarigiani, & Kennedy, 1991) found that adolescent girls experienced more challenging and stressful events than adolescent boys and that these differences in stress accounted for gender differences in depressed mood. Specifically, adolescent girls who experienced the biological changes associated with the onset of puberty in close proximity to making a transition to junior high school were at greatest risk for increases in depressed mood. Brooks-Gunn, Warren, and Rosso (1991) found that depressed mood was more likely to be reported by early maturing adolescent girls who had experienced negative family and school events than late maturing girls, providing further evidence for the adverse consequences of coinciding biological and social events.

Using a cross-sectional design, Wagner and Compas (1990) also found developmental differences during adolescence in the relation between subtypes of stress and emotional or behavioral problems. Emotional and behavioral problems were predicted most strongly by family events among young adolescents, by peer events among middle adolescents, and by academic events in a sample of older adolescents attending college (Wagner & Compas, 1990). Early adolescent girls reported more family, peer, intimacy, and social network stressors than did boys, and they perceived these events as more stressful. Middle adolescent girls reported more intimacy and network stressors and perceived these events as more stressful than did boys. It is noteworthy however, that stressful events did not statistically account for gender differences in levels of symptoms in this study. In another investigation of subtypes of adolescent stress, Aseltine, Gore, and Colten (1991) found that adolescents with a history of chronic depressed mood, as compared with those consistently asymptomatic, had a history of chronic stress within the family which led to both more depressed mood and efforts to orient away from the family and toward greater involvement with peers.

Recent evidence also suggests that there are developmental and gender differences in symptoms in response to a severe, acute stressor. As noted above, in our ongoing study of the stress associated with the diagnosis and treatment of cancer in a parent, we found that adolescents, and especially adolescent girls whose mothers are ill, reported more symptoms of depression and anxiety at the time of their parent's diagnosis and four months after the diagnosis, than did younger children (Compas et al., 1992a). Thus, a severe illness in a loved one led to greater depressive and anxious symptoms in a subgroup of adolescents girls than in adolescent boys.

Summary

Generic and atypical acute and chronic stress are all significant threats to the psychological well-being of adolescents. These three broad categories can be further delineated into subtypes of stress involving different life domains for adolescents. There appear to be substantial individual differences in vulnerability to stress as a function of the type of stress, age, gender, and other personal characteristics of adolescents. The ways in which adolescents cope with these various types of stress may be a critical individual difference factor in understanding vulnerability and resilience to stress.

What is coping? The nature of adolescent coping processes

If stressful events are a threat to the psychological well-being of adolescents, what steps can youths take to ward off these adverse consequences? Research concerned with the ways in which adolescents attempt to cope with stress may offer some answers to this question (Compas, 1987a).

At the most general level, the term coping is used to refer to all responses of individuals under stress. This definition is problematic, however, in that it includes both nonvolitional as well as intentional responses of the individual. For example, some responses to stress reflect reflexive or habitual, overlearned behaviors whereas other responses involve purposeful attempts at emotional and behavioral self-regulation (Compas, Malcarne, & Banez, 1992b). Thus, to avoid a conceptualization of coping that is overly inclusive, it is best defined as effortful or purposeful thoughts and actions undertaken in an attempt to manage or overcome stressful situations and the negative emotions associated with them (Lazarus & Folkman, 1984).

The literature on child and adolescent coping has identified some important developmental changes and stabilities in the nature of coping during adolescence. At least eight recent studies of the ways that children and adolescents cope with a wide range of stressors have examined developmental changes and stabilities in problem-focused coping (that is, attempts to act on a stressor) and emotion-focused coping (that is, attempts to manage one's emotions associated with a stressor) or in subtypes of these two categories (Altshuler & Ruble, 1989; Band, 1990; Band & Weisz, 1988; Compas, Malcarne, & Fondacaro, 1988; Curry & Russ, 1985; Kliewer, 1991; Ryan, 1989; Weigel, & Feldstein, 1987). All these studies have found at least some evidence of a positive relationship between reports of emotion-focused coping and age or some other marker of developmental level (for example, cognitive development). Evidence for this developmental change has been found in samples of children and adolescents ranging from five to seventeen years old. Increases with age in emotion-focused coping have been found in reports of coping with a variety of types of stress, including medical or dental stressors (Altshuler & Ruble, 1989; Band & Weisz, 1988; Curry & Russ, 1985) and interpersonal stressors (Compas, Malcarne, & Fondacaro, 1988).

In contrast to consistent findings of developmental increases in emotion-focused coping, no consistent developmental changes have been found in problem-focused coping, with three studies finding no change with age (Altshuler & Ruble, 1989; Compas, Malcarne, & Fondacaro, 1988; Wertlieb, Weigel, & Feldstein, 1987) and two studies finding a decrease in problem-focused coping with age (Band & Weisz, 1988; Curry & Russ, 1985). The decreases in problem-focused coping were found in reference to medical or dental stressors, whereas no changes in problem-focused coping were found in relation to a wider range of stressors.

Building on these earlier studies, Worsham, Ey, and Compas (1994) recently investigated perceptions of control and coping in children, adolescents, and young adults whose parents have cancer. This study offered an opportunity to examine cognitive appraisals and coping with a similar stressor across a wide developmental range. The findings indicate that although appraisals of control did not change with age in this sample, the use of emotion-focused and dual-focused coping (that is, strategies that accomplish both problem- and emotion-focused coping functions) increased from childhood to adolescence but not between adolescence and young adulthood. These patterns were present in comparisons between children and adolescents in analyses across age groups and in age group correlations between coping and age for children and adolescents. By examining reports of coping with a similar stressor across both age groups, these findings add to previous studies that found developmental increases in emotion-focused coping and stability in problem-focused coping with age (Altshuler & Ruble, 1989; Band & Weisz, 1988; Compas, Malcarne, & Fondacaro, 1988). Further, no changes in coping were found from adolescence to young adulthood, indicating that the use of emotion-focused coping had leveled off by early adulthood. Prior research had not compared coping of adolescents and young adults; these findings were useful in establishing a point in development at which increases in emotion-focused and dual-focused coping appear to stabilize. Finally, the increase in emotion-focused coping from childhood to adolescence was not the result of developmental changes in perceived control over the stressor, as perceptions of both personal and external control remained stable across the three age groups.

Summary

It appears that the skills to master stressful situations as well as the skills to manage one's negative emotions under stress follow predictable developmental paths during childhood and early adolescence. Less is known, however, about the ways in which skills in problem-solving and emotion management may continue to develop during adolescence. Further attention must be given to understanding the subtypes of problem-focused and emotion-focused coping during adolescence. Finally, the specific types of strategies used to cope with generic, acute, and chronic stress have not been documented. It is not clear whether these types of stress elicit similar or different coping responses from adolescents.

Does coping help? Characteristics of effective coping

Identifying the characteristics of effective ways of coping is a deceptively simple task. On the one hand, it suggests a rather straightforward goal of identifying those coping strategies associated with positive psychological outcomes. On the other hand, however, variations in the nature of stress and individual differences among adolescents suggest that successful coping may vary considerably. Both cognitive appraisals of stress and coping processes may be important factors in understanding the ways in which individuals adapt to generic stress, acute stressful events, and chronic stressful conditions in their lives.

The relation between one aspect of cognitive appraisal, namely perceptions of personal control, and coping processes has received considerable attention in stress and coping research, as well as in basic research on perceived control. Folkman (1984) outlined a complex set of relations among control beliefs, appraisals of threat and challenge, and the use of problem- and emotion-focused coping. Among these is the notion that problem-focused efforts are more adaptive when they are directed toward aspects of the person-environment relationship that are perceived as changeable, whereas emotion-focused efforts are more adaptive when a situation is recognized as uncontrollable. Along this line, Weisz (1986) suggested that a key developmental task involves learning to distinguish between situations where persistence, which can be seen as similar to the continued use of problem-focused coping efforts, pays off and situations where it does not. Perceptions of control may play a central role in this judgment process. Weisz (1986) also noted the need for research examining whether behavior that involves compliance, which may represent emotion-focused coping in that it is a form of acceptance, has different correlates depending on whether it is associated with a sense of a loss of control or a sense of secondary or vicarious control.

Although there is some evidence to support the notion that both problem- and emotion-focused coping are tied to perceptions of control (Folkman & Lazarus, 1980), other findings suggest that problem- and emotion-focused coping are matched to separate sets of cues. Problem-focused coping efforts may be regulated in conjunction with increases and decreases in perceived control over a stressful situation, whereas emotion-focused coping efforts may be linked to internal cues of emotional distress. For example, Forsythe and Compas (1987) found that college students' perceptions of control were related to their reports of greater use of problem-focused coping, whereas their reports of emotion-focused coping were unrelated to perceived control and positively related to symptoms of emotional distress. This pattern reflects the different functions served by problem- and emotion-focused coping outlined by Lazarus and Folkman (1984). Specifically, Folkman (1984) proposed that emotion-focused efforts should increase as threat appraisals and associated emotions increase; as these emotions increase more coping efforts have to be directed toward emotion regulation. In contrast, problem-focused coping efforts are directed toward those aspects of the environment perceived as controllable or changeable. Although the relations between problem-focused coping and control and between emotion-focused coping and emotional distress are most likely reciprocal in nature, longitudinal data to test this possibility have not been reported.

The few studies that have examined the relation between perceived control and coping in children and adolescents indicate that the association between control beliefs and problem-focused coping may emerge fairly early in development. With regard to coping with generic stress, problem-focused coping has been found to be positively correlated with perceived control whereas emotion-focused coping has been found unrelated to control beliefs in studies of coping with interpersonal stress (for example, conflicts or problems with peers) in young adolescents (Compas, Malcarne, & Fondacaro, 1988). Similar findings were also noted in a study of adolescents' responses to severe acute stress. An investigation of children, adolescents, and young adults coping with the diagnosis of cancer in their mother or father found that reports of problem-focused coping were related to a greater sense of personal control over the parents' illness and recovery (Worsham, Ey, & Compas, 1994). In both these studies, reports of emotion-focused coping, although unrelated to control beliefs, were related to higher levels of emotional distress.

The concept of matching one's coping efforts was also noted by Beardslee and Podorefsky (1988) in their research with adolescents who proved to be resilient in the face of depression in a parent. They noted that resilient adolescents were those who held a realistic appraisal of the stress associated with their parents' depressive disorder and acted in a manner congruent with this appraisal. Beardslee and Podorefsky (1988) observed that these youths wanted to change or cure their parents' depression but over the course of time came to recognize that they could not accomplish this goal. These adolescents then turned their attention to providing support for the depressed parent and other family members in whatever ways they could. The researchers noted that this response was more congruent with the objective demands of the parents' depression, as the adolescents came to recognize that their parents' behavior was beyond their control.

These recent studies of children's and adolescents' control beliefs and coping suggest the importance of both cognitive and emotional processes in the development of coping. Adolescents show some evidence of an association between their control beliefs and their use of problem-focused

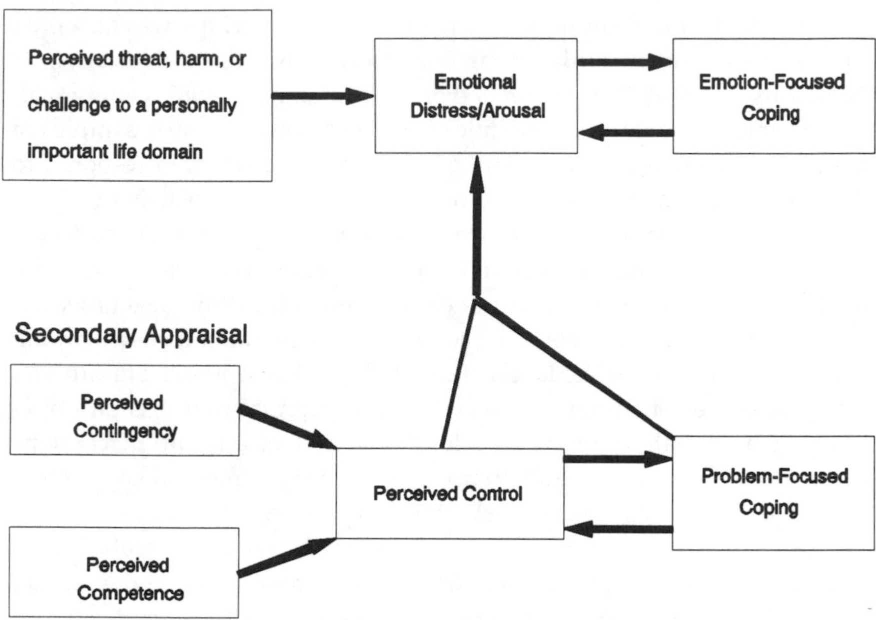

Figure 7.2. Model of control-related beliefs, coping, and emotional distress.

coping strategies. Emotion-focused coping, on the other hand, appears to be more closely tied to emotional arousal and distress than to control beliefs. Drawing on these studies and the broader literature on perceived control, a conceptualization of contingency, competence, and control beliefs, emotions, and coping is presented in Figure 7.2 (see Compas et al., 1991). First, contingency and competence beliefs contribute directly to perceptions of personal control in stressful situations (Weisz, 1986). Control beliefs and problem-focused coping are related in a reciprocal fashion; a high sense of personal control will lead to greater use of problem-focused coping, and problem-focused coping efforts may enhance feelings of control if they are effective in changing the environment. Emotion-focused coping efforts are unrelated to control beliefs, but instead are used to a greater or lesser degree in response to levels of emotional distress or arousal.

There is evidence that emotional distress or arousal is related to the interaction of control beliefs and problem-focused coping. Emotional distress has been found to be lower when problem-focused coping is used and perceived control is high (a good match between control and coping).

Elevated levels of emotional distress have been found when problem-focused coping efforts are used and perceived control is low (a poor match between control and coping). This pattern of relationships was observed in previous studies with young adolescents (Compas, Malcarne, & Fondacaro, 1988), college students (Forsythe & Compas, 1987) coping with generic interpersonal and academic stress, and nonpsychiatric samples of adults (Vitaliano et al., 1990). The picture alters, however, in response to the acute stress of the diagnosis of a parent's cancer (Worsham, Ey, & Compas, 1994). Symptoms of anxiety and depression were related to the match between control beliefs and coping in adolescents faced with the acute stress of the diagnosis of cancer in a parent. In this case however, perceptions of personal control and the use of problem-focused coping combined to predict *higher* levels of psychological symptoms. The authors interpreted these findings as indicating that parental cancer is an objectively uncontrollable stressor for adolescents and, as a result, perceptions of personal control and efforts to use active, problem-focused coping will lead to an increased sense of frustration, helplessness, and distress in trying to deal with a situation beyond the control of these adolescents. This is similar to the picture of the uncontrollable nature of parental depression described by Beardslee and Podorefsky (1988). In both instances, adolescents may have little real control over their parents' condition and efforts to alleviate their parents' distress may result in feelings of failure. Although more direct comparisons of coping with generic, acute, and chronic stress are needed, it appears that differences among these types of stress in the objective degree of control that is available may lead to differences in the efficacy of the use of active problem-solving strategies.

In addition to considering the relationship of appraisals of control with problem-focused and emotion-focused coping, it is important to examine the relative efficacy of specific subtypes of problem- and emotion-focused coping during adolescence. Research in this area has been lacking with adolescent populations, but research by Nolen-Hoeksema on coping and depressive outcomes in adults is instructive. Nolen-Hoeksema (1991) has hypothesized that two types of emotion-focused coping, rumination and distraction, play very different roles in the maintenance and exacerbation of depressed mood. Rumination involves coping responses that involve a high level of attention to one's emotional experience. In response to depressive emotions, thoughts and behaviors that focus attention on depressive emotions and symptoms as well as on the cause of the mood and its implications are hypothesized to heighten depressed affect. Further, these responses allow the depressed mood to affect thinking and can activate negative memories, thereby increasing the current depressive mood. This focus on negative emotional states can also increase negative self-evaluation and negative explanations for failures and thereby increase helplessness in future tasks. Furthermore, cognitive attention to emotional processes may interfere with concentration and initiation of instrumental behaviors that might increase chances for controlling the environment and achieving positive outcomes. Individuals who use distraction, on the other hand, may be protected from depression by their prototypical response set of emotional distraction, purposely turning their attention away from the depressive mood to more pleasant or neutral activities. This shift in focus and the initiation of instrumental behaviors may relieve the negative mood as well as increase chances for obtaining positive reinforcement and a sense of control over the environment. The effects of rumination, distraction, and other subtypes of coping warrant attention in research on adolescent coping.

Summary

Recent research has provided some guidelines for understanding the nature of effective coping with stress during adolescence. Effective coping appears to involve matching one's appraisals of stress, especially perceptions of personal control, with the relative use of active problem-focused coping strategies. Ineffective coping, on the other hand, may be characterized at least in part by the use of coping methods that focus one's attention on negative affect. Further research is needed, however, to identify similarities and differences in coping strategies effective in dealing with generic, acute, and chronic stress. Differences in the objective controllability of stress may influence the effectiveness of certain types of coping in response to these three categories of stress.

Promoting successful coping: Exemplary intervention programs for adolescents

Having outlined some of the characteristics of stress and coping during adolescence, it is now possible to consider systematic efforts designed to foster effective coping during this developmental period. Although research in this area is still in its very early stages, several exemplary programs have been developed. Existing programs will be discussed in terms of the three types of stress described above: (1) programs that facilitate the development of skills for coping with generic or normative stress, (2) programs that promote coping with severe acute stress, and (3) programs that promote positive coping with severe, chronic stress. In each case, evaluations on the efficacy of the program and the degree to which program characteristics are consistent with research on effective coping will be considered.

Coping with generic stress

The most widely used programs have been aimed at the enhancement of a set of positive outcomes variously labeled social competence, life skills, or coping skills (for reviews see Compas, Phares, & Ledoux, 1989b; Hamburg, 1990; Weissberg, Caplan, & Harwood, 1991). These programs share a common set of features centered around the development of adaptive skills of the individual adolescent. One group of these programs is broad-based in nature, typically delivered as part of the public school curriculum, and aimed at the development of a set of basic skills that enhance individuals' abilities to solve social problems and cope with life stress. A second group of programs has been designed to teach a similar set of skills with the goal of preventing specified problems such as substance abuse, teen pregnancy, or aggressive and antisocial behavior.

The primary goals of generic programs center on the development of attitudes and behaviors that foster positive feelings toward the self, mutually adaptive relations with others, and skills to solve life problems and stressors. These include, but are not limited to, a sense of self-efficacy; the ability to control one's emotions under stress; the ability to act assertively in changing one's environment in response to a problem; the ability to consider alternative solutions to a problem; the capacity to pursue goal-directed behavior; the capacity to resist pressure from others and, concomitantly, to experience a sense of autonomy and personal control over one's behavior; and the capacity to evaluate the effectiveness of one's actions and pursue alternative solutions if necessary. These goals are shared by several programs, including the Yale–New Haven Social Problem Solving Project (YNH-SPS; Weissberg, Caplan, & Bennetto, 1988) and the Comprehensive Stress Management Program for Children (CSMPC; Ledoux, 1985).

These basic skills are critical in the proactive process of developing a positive sense of oneself, a sense of subjective well-being, and a repertoire of behaviors that allows one to deal with the social environment in a manner perceived by others as socially skilled and acceptable. Further, these skills enable the individual to maintain these positive attributes in the face of normative life events and daily stress. The goal of these programs is the development of a diverse set of coping skills which can be applied to the variety of stressful events adolescents are likely to encounter. These coping skills include both active responses to change the source of stress (problem-focused coping) and responses directed to the negative emotions experienced in the face of stress (emotion-focused coping).

A commonly used protocol involves teaching youth to identify sources of stress in their lives, to recognize the physical and emotional consequences of stress, and to implement adaptive coping responses in the face of stressful events. Specific skills have included a six-step response sequence developed by Weissberg, Caplan, and Bennetto (1988) based on an information-processing model of social competence:

1. stop, calm down, and think before you act
2. articulate the problem and how you feel
3. set a positive goal
4. think of many solutions
5. think ahead to the consequences
6. try the best plan

Programs have been implemented in schools in formats varying from eight to twenty or more sessions during the school year, typically delivered on a weekly basis as part of the regular school curriculum. They have been carried out by school personnel (teachers, counselors) who received special training from mental health professionals. Many recent models have argued for a more explicitly developmental approach to the promotion of positive mental health through a series of developmentally appropriate interventions, ranging from kindergarten through the twelfth grade (Long, 1986). The YNH-SPS program is noteworthy in that it has shown sensitivity to sociocultural factors by focusing on those sources of stress of greatest concern to the inner-city population which has been served by the program. Both the YNH-SPS and CSMPC programs have addressed the developmental level of their participants by focusing on those stressors most salient to young adolescents.

Evaluation studies have focused on a variety of outcomes and have shown that these programs are quite promising in promoting various aspects of positive mental health and preventing emotional or behavioral problems. Relative to untrained controls, the YNH-SPS program participants improved their ability to effectively solve social problems; increased their peer involvement; experienced increased impulse control, sociability with peers, and improved academic performance as rated by teachers; and decreased self-reports of misbehavior, including fighting, stealing, and being sent out of the classroom (Caplan et al., 1992). Young adolescents who participated in the CSMPC, as compared with controls, have shown an increase in their ability to use emotion-focused coping skills, a decrease in their perceptions of stress, increased perceptions of personal competence, and lower rates of externalizing emotional or behavioral problems (Compas et al., 1992c).

A second set of interventions has been developed to address specific problems or types of psychopathology. An example is the Life Skills Training (LST) approach to the prevention of substance abuse (Botvin, 1983; Botvin & Dusenbury, 1989). The LST program consists of fifteen to twenty class periods with seventh graders focusing on three broad areas: (1) information and social resistance skills targeted specifically at substance abuse prevention; (2) generic personal coping skills; and (3) generic social skills. These are addressed through five components of the program whereby participants learn (Botvin & Dusenbury, 1989):

1. factual information concerning the negative consequences of substance abuse
2. self-directed behavior change
3. independent decision-making
4. skills to effectively cope with anxiety
5. interpersonal skills

Efforts have been made to make necessary changes in the program as it has been applied to inner-city minority youth.

Programs that target specific problems have documented considerable success. The LST program has proven successful in deterring substance abuse: Program participants have been found less likely than controls to begin smoking cigarettes (Botvin & Eng, 1982; Botvin, Eng, & Williams, 1980; Botvin, Renick, & Baker, 1983), to consume alcohol (Botvin et al., 1984a), or to use marijuana (Botvin et al., 1984b).

Coping with acute stress

Relatively fewer examples are available of programs designed to help adolescents cope with severe acute stress. One salient example, however, is provided by interventions to promote successful coping with the stress of divorce (see Grych & Fincham, 1992, for a review). Parental divorce is a complex stressor that entails much more than the occurrence of a discrete event involving the marital breakup. Divorce, like many acute events, is best viewed as a period of transition involving numerous discrete events and ongoing stresses and strains. It is still useful, however, to consider interventions for coping with divorce within a category of coping with acute stressors, because most interventions are still designed with exposure to the event of divorce as the identifying characteristic of youth who are included in the intervention. Further, the marital breakup still serves as the marker event around which the intervention is organized.

Several different programs have been developed to teach children and adolescents the skills to cope with divorce, all of which share several common characteristics (Kalter, Pickar, & Lesowitz, 1984; Pedro-Carroll & Cowen, 1985; Stolberg & Garrison, 1985). These programs typically attempt to affect cognitive appraisals by clarifying confusing and upsetting information about divorce, provide a supportive group context in which adolescents can cope with the emotions elicited by their parents' divorce, develop skills for coping with upsetting feelings and stressful family situations, and improve parent-child communication skills. These programs have usually been based in the public schools to maximize the availability of the intervention for those who might not otherwise have access to such services.

One of these interventions, the Children of Divorce Intervention Project (CODIP; Alpert-Gillis, Pedro-Carroll, & Cowen, 1989; Pedro-Carroll & Cowen, 1985; Pedro-Carroll et al., 1986) makes explicit reference to the concept of matching coping strategies to controllability of the situation. Participants are instructed to distinguish between those problems that are beyond the adolescent's control (for example, parental reconciliation) and those that are within their control (for example, appropriate ways of communicating feelings). Problem-focused and emotion-focused coping strategies are taught which can be used in controllable and uncontrollable situations. The degree to which participants are successful in matching coping and control and the efficacy of such matching has not been documented (Compas, Phares, & Ledoux, 1989b).

Ongoing research by Gersten, Pillow, West, and colleagues is aimed at developing theory and research-based preventive interventions for two groups of adolescents exposed to severe acute stress – children of divorce and children who have lost a parent to death (Gersten, Beals, & Kallgren, 1991; Pillow et al., 1991; West et al., 1991). This research is in the initial phase of developing models to explain the processes and mechanisms that place some children at risk when exposed to parental loss through divorce or death. Closer links among theory, research, and intervention will be important in the continued development of preventive interventions in this area (Grych & Fincham, 1992).

Interventions for other sources of severe acute stress during adolescence, including the diagnosis of a personal life threatening illness or a similar illness in a loved one, have not been reported in the literature. Programs to assist adolescents and their families in coping with acute stress should have a high priority for future research.

Coping with chronic stress

In spite of the significance of chronic stress as a risk factor for emotional or behavioral problems during adolescence, little work has been conducted on the development of interventions to help adolescents cope with it. Specifically, the development and evaluation of interventions for adolescents whose parents manifest depressive disorders or other forms of psychopathology have been rare. This is striking in light of the clear evidence for the enormous level of risk for maladjustment in these youth (Downey & Coyne, 1990; Hammen, 1991).

One notable exception has been the work of Beardslee and colleagues on the development of a preventive intervention for children of depressed parents (Beardslee, 1990; Beardslee et al., in press-a; Beardslee et al., in press-b). These researchers have developed a cognitive psychoeducational intervention to be delivered by clinicians to families of parents with depressive disorders. The four primary aspects of the intervention include careful assessment of all family members, teaching what is known about depression and its impact on families, linking knowledge about depression to the family's own experience, and focusing on the children's present needs. The overarching goal is the promotion of increased self-understanding on the part of children in these families (Beardslee, 1990). Self-understanding includes an appraisal of the stresses associated with the parent's depression, a realistic appraisal of one's capacity to act and realistic expectations regarding the consequences of one's actions, and actions that reflect these appraisals (Beardslee & Podorefsky, 1988). Thus, the intervention is designed to facilitate accurate appraisals of the stressors associated with parental depression and to facilitate the use of coping strategies that are matched to the demands of the situation. Preliminary evaluations of the intervention indicate that the intervention is feasible and safe and that participants are satisfied with the intervention as compared to a lecture intervention (Beardslee et al., in press-a, in press-b). Data on the prevention of maladjustment in adolescents in these families are not yet available.

Continued development of interventions for youth exposed to chronic stress is an important area for future research. Programs to facilitate coping with family stress such as the stress associated with a parental psychiatric disorder are greatly needed. Programs are also needed, however, to assist adolescents in coping with chronic stress outside the family, including stress in neighborhoods characterized by poverty and violence.

Toward a comprehensive model of coping interventions

The task of promoting successful coping with stress during adolescence can appear daunting in the face of the variety of different types of stress and adversity that confront youth today and are likely to face them in the future. The research reviewed above suggests that interventions for promoting coping can be organized and coordinated within a sequential and hierarchical model consisting of three levels. The first level involves the promotion of effective coping with generic or normative stress in all adolescents. The second level involves interventions for youth exposed to specific forms of severe acute stress, and is limited to those adolescents who have recently encountered such exceptional circumstances. The third level of intervention is intended for adolescents faced with severe chronic stressful conditions, with the goal of providing intervention services before exposure to chronic stress and adversity has taken a toll in the manifestation of significant psychological disorder in these youth.

Programs to promote coping with the normative stresses and strains of adolescence represent true primary prevention efforts. Services are delivered to the whole population, based on observations that all adolescents are exposed to stress as part of their daily lives, that normative or generic stress exacts a toll on the psychological adjustment of adolescents, and all can benefit from developing stronger skills in solving stressful situations and regulating their emotions under stress. These programs cannot be expected, however, to provide sufficient support and skill development for youths who are exposed to severe acute or chronic stress. The circumstances faced by some adolescents will warrant additional resources to assist them in coping with extreme forms of adversity. More specialized programs are needed for adolescents identified on the basis of their exposure to extreme levels of acute or chronic stress. These more specialized interventions would be implemented in addition to, rather than in place of, the generic programs available for all adolescents. Thus, the interventions would be sequential in that all adolescents would be exposed to generic coping skills training during late childhood or early adolescence. This first level of intervention would be supplemented by more specialized interventions for those who are exposed to conditions of high risk as manifested in either acute or chronic stress. The interventions would be hierarchical in that programs for adolescents exposed to severe acute or chronic stress would be more intensive and would deal with problems that are more severe in magnitude. It is likely that adolescents who receive these more specialized services would already be manifesting some early symptoms of distress or maladjustment, placing these programs in the role of secondary prevention efforts.

This hierarchical and sequential model of prevention raises important questions regarding the most effective distribution of human and financial resources. Careful consideration must be given to how to expend our limited resources for promoting the development of effective coping in adolescents. Is it cost effective to teach generic coping skills to all adolescents when we know that some subgroups of youth are exposed to conditions of high risk? The answer appears to be a qualified yes, in light of data indicating that normative stress is predictive of increases of psychological symptoms, especially depressive and anxious symptoms, in longitudinal analyses (Compas et al., 1989a; DuBois et al., 1992). As noted above, however, the types of skills likely to be developed in generic programs cannot be assumed to be sufficient for adolescents exposed to more extreme forms of acute or chronic stress. The skills that could be acquired in a generic intervention program can lay the foundation for additional skills that could be developed in more specialized programs for youth in high risk circumstances. This model does imply, however, an increased commitment of resources to prevention at all levels.

Programs to facilitate effective coping represent one aspect of a larger effort that is needed to promote positive mental health and development during adolescence (Compas, 1993). Coping skills are only one component of the skills and values necessary for positive psychological development. Specifically, coping skills are reactive in nature in that they involve the ability to respond to adversity. Reactive skills are complemented by more generative skills that enable adolescents to become involved in personally meaningful activities and relationships in their lives (Compas, 1993). The combination of skills to manage stress and the skills and motivation to pursue personally meaningful goals reflects a broader model of positive development and mental health.

In closing, let us consider two adolescents who have encountered stressful circumstances similar to the cases presented at the opening of this chapter. The coping efforts of these two adolescents are more reflective of the types of responses we hope to develop in the youth of tomorrow. An eleven-year-old girl reports that a significant stressor for her is being teased by classmates at school. She copes with this problem by asking the girls who tease her to go away, by reporting the girls to the teacher, by trying to ignore them, and waiting until they become involved in another activity and then leaving the situation herself. This girl reports very few symptoms of depression or anxiety, both well within the normative range. As a final case, a twelve-year-old girl is coping with the recent diagnosis of cancer in her mother. She reports taking five steps to try to cope with this crisis: She went to the physician and asked questions about things she was unsure of, she went with her mother to see where she received her radiation treatment, she asked her parents questions about the illness, she asked her mother what she could do to help, and she told herself that everything would be fine and she had nothing to worry about. This girl also reported levels of depressed and anxious symptoms that were well within the normal range.

An important goal of intervention programs is to assist adolescents in developing the type of diverse and flexible coping repertoires represented by these two individuals. Facilitating the development of a wide range of different types of coping skills that can be used flexibly in response to the diverse stressors of adolescence will play an important role in the promotion of effective coping in the youth of tomorrow.

References

Allgood-Merten, B., Lewinsohn, P. M., & Hops, H. (1990). Sex differences and adolescent depression. *Journal of Abnormal Psychology*, 99, 55–63.

Alpert-Gillis, L. J., Pedro-Carroll, J. L., & Cowen, E. L. (1989). The Children of Divorce Intervention Program: Development, implementation, and evaluation of a program for young urban children. *Journal of Consulting and Clinical Psychology*, 57, 583–9.

Altshuler, J. L., & Ruble, D. N. (1989). Developmental changes in children's awareness of strategies for coping with uncontrollable stress. *Child Development*, 60, 1337–49.

Aseltine, R. H., Jr., Gore, S., & Colten, M. E. (1991). *Alternative Pathways of Adolescent Depression*. Unpublished manuscript.

Band, E. B. (1990). Children's coping with diabetes: Understanding the role of cognitive development. *Journal of Pediatric Psychology*, 15, 27–41.

Band, E. B., & Weisz, J. R. (1988). How to feel better when it feels bad: Children's perspectives on coping with everyday stress. *Developmental Psychology*, 24, 247–53.

Beardslee, W. R. (1990). Development of a clinician-based preventive intervention for families with affective disorders. *Journal of Preventive Psychiatry and Allied Disciplines*, 4, 39–61.

Beardslee, W. R., Hoke, L., Wheelock, I., Rothberg, P. C., van de Velde, P., & Swatling, S. (in press-a). Preventive intervention for families with parental affective disorders: Initial findings. *American Journal of Psychiatry*.

Beardslee, W. R., & Podorefsky, D. (1988). Resilient adolescents whose parents have serious affective and other psychiatric disorders: Importance of self-understanding and relationships. *American Journal of Psychiatry*, 145, 63–9.

Beardslee, W. R., Salt, P., Porterfield, K., Rothberg, P. C., van de Velde, P., Swatling, S., Hoke, L., Moilanen, D. L., & Wheelock, I. (in press-b)., Comparison of preventive interventions for families with parental affective disorder. *Journal of the American Academy of Child and Adolescent Psychiatry*.

Botvin, G. J. (1983). *Life Skills Training: Teacher's Manual (Seventh Grade Curriculum)*. New York: Smithfield Press.

Botvin, G. J., Baker, E., Botvin, E. M., Filazzola, A. D., & Millman, R. B. (1984a). Alcohol abuse prevention through the development of personal and social competence: A pilot study. *Journal of Studies on Alcohol*, 45, 550–2.

Botvin, G. J., Baker, E., Renick, N. L., Filazzola, A. D., & Botvin, E. M. (1984b). A cognitive-behavioral approach to substance abuse prevention. *Addictive Behaviors*, 9, 137–47.

Botvin, G. J., & Dusenbury, L. (1989). Substance abuse prevention and the promotion of competence. In *Primary Prevention and Promotion in the Schools*, ed. L. A. Bond & B. E. Compas, pp. 146–78. Newbury Park, CA: Sage.

Botvin, G. J., & Eng, A. (1982). The efficacy of a multicomponent approach to the prevention of cigarette smoking. *Preventive Medicine*, 11, 199–211.

Botvin, G. J., Eng, A., & Williams, C. L. (1980). Preventing the onset of cigarette smoking through Life Skills Training. *Preventive Medicine*, 9, 135–43.

Botvin, G. J., Renick, N. L., & Baker, E. (1983). The effects of scheduling format and booster sessions on a broad-spectrum psychosocial approach to smoking prevention. *Journal of Behavioral Medicine*, 6, 359–79.

Brooks-Gunn, J., Warren, M. P., & Rosso, J. T. (1991). *The Impact of Pubertal and Social Events Upon Girls' Problem Behavior*. Unpublished manuscript.

Caplan, M., Weissberg, R. P., Grober, J. S., Sivo, P. J., Grady, K., & Jacoby, C. (1992). Social competence promotion with inner-city and suburban young adolescents: Effects on social adjustment and alcohol use. *Journal of Consulting and Clinical Psychology*, 60, 56–63.

Coddington, R. D. (1972). The significance of life events as etiological factors in the diseases of children: II. A study of a normal population. *Journal of Psychosomatic Research*, 16, 205–13.

Cohen, L. H., Burt, C. E., & Bjork, J. P. (1987). Life stress and adjustment: Effects of life events experienced by young adolescents and their parents. *Developmental Psychology*, 23, 583–92.

Compas, B. E. (1987a). Coping with stress during childhood and adolescence. *Psychological Bulletin*, 101, 393–403.

(1987b). Stress and life events during childhood and adolescence. *Clinical Psychology Review*, 7, 275–302.

(1993). Promoting positive mental health during adolescence. In *Adolescent Health Promotion*, ed. S. G. Millstein, A. C. Petersen, & E. O. Nightingale, pp. 159–79. New York: Oxford University Press.

Compas, B. E., Banez, G. A., Malcarne, V. L., & Worsham, N. (1991). Perceived control and coping with stress: A developmental perspective. *Journal of Social Issues*, 47, 23–34.

Compas, B. E., Davis, G. E., Forsythe, C. J., & Wagner, B. M. (1987). Assessment of major and daily stressful events during adolescence: The Adolescent Perceived Events Scale. *Journal of Consulting and Clinical Psychology*, 55, 534–41.

Compas, B. E., Howell, D. C., Phares, V., Williams, R. A., & Giunta, C. T. (1989a). Risk factors for emotional/behavioral problems in adolescence: Parent and adolescent stress and symptoms. *Journal of Consulting and Clinical Psychology*, 57, 732–40.

Compas, B. E., Ledoux, N., Howell, D. C., Phares, V., Williams, R. A., Giunta, C. T., & Banez, G. A. (1992b). *Enhancing Coping and Stress Management Skills in Children and Adolescents: Evaluation of a School-Based Intervention*. Unpublished manuscript, University of Vermont.

Compas, B. E., Malcarne, V. L., & Banez, G. A. (1992a). Coping with psychosocial stress: A developmental perspective. In *Personal Coping: Theory, Research, and Application*, ed. B. Carpenter, pp. 47–64. New York: Praeger.

Compas, B. E., Malcarne, V. L., & Fondacaro, K. M. (1988). Coping with stressful events in older children and young adolescents. *Journal of Consulting and Clinical Psychology*, 56, 405–11.

Compas, B. E., Phares, V., & Ledoux, N. (1989b). Stress and coping preventive interventions for children and adolescents. In *Primary Prevention and Promotion in the Schools*, ed. L. A. Bond & B. E. Compas, pp. 319–40. Newbury Park, CA: Sage.

Compas, B. E., Worsham, N., Epping, J. E., Grant, K. E., Mireault, G., Howell, D. C., & Malcarne, V. (in press-a). When Mom or Dad has cancer: I. Symptoms of anxiety and depression in cancer patients, their spouses and their children. *Health Psychology*.

Curry, S. L., & Russ, S. W. (1985). Identifying coping strategies in children. *Journal of Clinical Child Psychology*, 14, 61–9.

Downey, G., & Coyne, J. C. (1990). Children of depressed parents: An integrative review. *Psychological Bulletin*, 108, 50–76.

DuBois, D. L., Felner, R. D., Brand, S., Adan, A. M., & Evans, E. G. (1992). A prospective study of life stress, social support, and adaptation in early adolescence. *Child Development*, 63, 542–57.

Folkman, S. (1984). Personal control and stress and coping processes: A theoretical analysis. *Journal of Personality and Social Psychology*, 46, 839–52.

Folkman, S., & Lazarus, R. S. (1980). An analysis of coping in a middle-aged community sample. *Journal of Health and Social Behavior*, 21, 219–39.

Forsythe, C. J., & Compas, B. E. (1987). Interaction of cognitive appraisals of stressful events and coping: Testing the goodness of fit hypothesis. *Cognitive Therapy and Research*, 11, 473–85.

Gersten, J. C., Beals, J., & Kallgren, C. A. (1991). Epidemiology and preventive interventions: Parental death in childhood as a case example. *American Journal of Community Psychology*, 19, 481–500.

Grych, J. H., & Fincham, F. D. (1992). Interventions for children of divorce: Toward greater integration of research and action. *Psychological Bulletin*, 111, 434–54.

Hamburg, B. A. (1990). *Life Skills Training: Preventive Interventions for Young Adolescents*. Washington, DC: Carnegie Council on Adolescent Development.

Hammen, C. (1991). *Depression in the Family Context*. New York: Springer-Verlag.

Hammen, C., Burge, D., & Adrian, C. (1991). Timing of mother and child depression in a longitudinal study of children at risk. *Journal of Consulting and Clinical Psychology*, 59, 341–5.

Holmes, T. H., & Rahe, R. H. (1967). The Social Readjustment Rating Scale. *Journal of Psychosomatic Research*, 11, 213–18.

Kalter, N., Pickar, J., & Lesowitz, M. (1984). School-based developmental facilitation groups for children of divorce: A preventive intervention. *American Journal of Orthopsychiatry*, 54, 613–23.

Kanner, A. D., & Feldman, S. S. (1991). Control over uplifts and hassles and its relationship to adaptational outcomes. *Journal of Behavioral Medicine*, 14, 187–201.

Kliewer, W. (1991). Coping in middle childhood: Relations to competence, type A behavior, monitoring, blunting, and locus of control. *Developmental Psychology*, 27, 689–97.

Lazarus, R. S. (1990). Theory-based stress measurement. *Psychological Inquiry*, 1, 3–13.

Lazarus, R. S., & Folkman, S. (1984). *Stress, Appraisal, and Coping*. New York: Springer-Verlag.

Ledoux, N. (November, 1985). *A Comprehensive Stress Management Program for Elementary and Secondary Students and their Families*. Paper presented at the Seventh National Conference on Child Abuse and Neglect, Chicago, Ill.

Long, B. B. (1986). The prevention of mental-emotional disabilities: A report from a National Mental Health Association Commission. *American Psychologist*, 41, 825–9.

Nolen-Hoeksema, S. (1991). Responses to depression and their effects on the duration of depressive episodes. *Journal of Abnormal Psychology*, 100, 569–82.

Pedro-Carroll, J. L., & Cowen, E. L. (1985). The Children of Divorce Intervention Program: An investigation of the efficacy of a school-based prevention program. *Journal of Consulting and Clinical Psychology*, 53, 603–11.

Pedro-Carroll, J. L., Cowen, E. L., Hightower, A. D., & Guare, J. C. (1986). Preventive intervention with latency-aged children of divorce: A replication study. *American Journal of Community Psychology*, 14, 277–89.

Petersen, A. C., Sarigiani, P. A., & Kennedy, R. E. (1991). Adolescent depression: Why more girls? *Journal of Youth and Adolescence*, 20, 247–71.

Pillow, D. R., Sandler, I. N., Braver, S. L., Wolchik, S. A., & Gersten, J. C. (1991). Theory based screening for prevention: Focusing on mediating processes in children of divorce. *American Journal of Community Psychology*, 19, 809–36.

Ryan, N. M. (1989). Stress-coping strategies identified from school age children's perspective. *Research in Nursing and Health*, 12, 111–22.

Stanger, C., McConaughy, S. H., & Achenbach, T. M. (1992). Three-year course of behavioral/emotional problems in a national sample of 4- to 16-year-olds: II. Predictors of syndromes. *Journal of the American Academy of Child and Adolescent Psychiatry*, 31, 941–50.

Stolberg, A. L., & Garrison, K. M. (1985). Evaluating a primary prevention program for children of divorce: The Divorce Adjustment Project. *American Journal of Community Psychology*, 13, 111–24.

Vitaliano, P. P., DeWolfe, D. J., Maiuro, R. D., Russo, J., & Katon, W. (1990). Appraised changeability of a stressor as a modifier of the relationship between coping and depression: A test of the hypothesis of fit. *Journal of Personality and Social Psychology*, 59, 582–92.

Wagner, B. M., & Compas, B. E. (1990). Gender, instrumentality, and expressivity: Moderators of the relation between stress and psychological symptoms during adolescence. *American Journal of Community Psychology*, 18, 383–406.

Weissberg, R. P., Caplan, M. Z., & Bennetto, L. (1988). *The Yale-New Haven Social Problem-Solving Program for Young Adolescents*. New Haven, Conn.: Yale University.

Weissberg, R. P., Caplan, M., & Harwood, R. L. (1991). Promoting competent young people in competence-enhancing environments: A systems-based prospective on primary prevention. *Journal of Consulting and Clinical Psychology*, 59, 830–41.

Weisz, J. R. (1986). Understanding the developing understanding of control. In *Cognitive Perspectives on Children's Social and Behavioral Development: The Minne-*

sota Symposium on Child Psychology, ed. M. Perlmutter, Vol. 18, pp. 219–75. Hillsdale, N.J.: Erlbaum.

Wertlieb, D., Weigel, C., & Feldstein, M. (1987). Measuring children's coping. *American Journal of Orthopsychiatry*, 57, 548–60.

West, S. G., Sandler, I. N., Pillow, D. R., Baca, L., & Gersten, J. C. (1991). The use of structural equation modeling in generative research: Toward the design of a preventive intervention for bereaved children. *American Journal of Community Psychology*, 19, 459–80.

Worsham, N. L., Ey, S., & Compas, B. E. (1994). *When Mom or Dad has Cancer: II. Developmental Consistencies and Differences in Coping with Family Stress*. Manuscript submitted for publication.

8. Positive effects of participation in youth organizations

JANE QUINN

Introduction

America's youth organizations rank second only to the public schools in the number of young people reached by their services each year, yet little is known about their current activities. Few studies have attempted to describe their programs and target populations, much less analyze the effectiveness of their efforts.

This chapter will report specific findings of a three-year study of American youth organizations conducted by the Carnegie Council on Adolescent Development (1992), an operating program of the Carnegie Corporation of New York. The study, the Project on Youth Development and Community Programs, sought to document and assess the current work of a broad array of services for adolescents, with a view toward recommending constructive change in three arenas – program, funding, and policy.

The study was comprehensive in scope but this chapter focuses on just four sets of issues examined by the Carnegie staff and advisors: a brief descriptive overview of contemporary American youth organizations; a summary of what is known about the effects of participation in these organizations; an analysis, drawn from both research and practice, of the characteristics of effective programs and organizations; and the implications of these findings for the formulation of youth-friendly public and social policy.

An overview of American youth organizations in the 1990s

Collectively such organizations as Girl Scouts, Boy Scouts, Boys and Girls Clubs, Camp Fire Boys and Girls, 4-H, Girls Incorporated, the YMCA and the YWCA reach an estimated thirty million American youth per year

(National Collaboration for Youth, 1990: 1). Similar work is conducted by a vast network of other agencies – public and private, secular and religious, national and local.

Despite the extensive scope and reach of this set of organized services, despite the relatively substantial base of financial support they enjoy, and despite their apparently great potential for promoting positive youth development, little systematic analysis of their work has been undertaken. A few studies, including a book by Hanson and Carlson (1972) and a monograph by James (1979), have sought to document the current work of some of these services, and the research of sociologist Judith Erickson over the past twenty-five years has contributed greatly to our appreciation of the rich history and traditions of the country's mainline agencies (Erickson, 1986), as well as to our understanding of their basic organization, structure, and functioning (Erickson, 1991a). Three additional reports – two that examined the educational role of youth organizations (Kleinfeld & Shinkwin, 1982; LaBelle & Carroll, 1981) and one that analyzed public policy issues in relation to school-age child care (Lipsitz, 1986) – have also made valuable contributions to the literature on youth organizations. The Carnegie study builds on that small but important body of work, seeking to both broaden and deepen current knowledge in an effort to expand developmentally appropriate, community-based services for America's adolescents.

There is no one commonly accepted definition of the universe of community-based youth development organizations in the United States. Early in its work, the Task Force on Youth Development and Community Programs decided to take an inclusive approach, looking at an array of private, nonprofit as well as public sector institutions that emphasize youth development and primary prevention of youth problems. This choice was neither arbitrary nor automatic. We sought to include the current major providers of nonschool youth programs (such as national youth organizations) as well as smaller subsectors with great potential for expansion (such as intergenerational programs); and we sought to balance our desire to take a systematic look at the largely unstudied private voluntary sector with our recognition that these agencies share many goals and approaches with certain public sector institutions.

Perhaps it is equally important to note the types of youth programs excluded from our study. Because of our interest in learning about and expanding programs that seek primarily to enhance positive development or to prevent youth problems from starting, we chose not to study services that are focused principally on remediation and treatment, such as the juvenile justice, foster care, mental health, or protective service systems. Although we recognized that there is much to learn from our colleagues in other countries, and we did study the organization of services and policies in several other nations for purposes of comparison, our investigation focused on the United States.

We decided to concentrate our study on five sets of American institutions, which might be broadly defined as community-based youth development programs and services:

1. Private, nonprofit national organizations that serve youth (including organizations primarily or exclusively youth-serving in their focus as well as multiservice organizations that offer substantial service to youth)
2. Grassroots youth development organizations not affiliated with any national structures
3. Religious youth groups
4. Youth programs conducted by privately sponsored adult service clubs, sports organizations, senior citizens groups, and museums
5. Youth programs conducted by selected public sector institutions, including libraries, parks, and recreation departments.

The Carnegie study presented a description and critique of the work of each subsector of this extensive universe of programs. This chapter offers a summary analysis of current services and outreach. Since the Carnegie Task Force was concerned from the outset with young adolescents (ages ten to fifteen), particularly those living in high-risk environments, much of our analysis focused on the extent to which these young people are reached and appropriately served by current programming.

Several broad and consistent themes emerged from our examination of this universe of services. Despite the diversity of the institutions that were examined, the Task Force learned that

1. Many of these institutions find it difficult to retain the interest and participation of teenagers, with a precipitous decline in participation occurring somewhere between ages twelve and thirteen.
2. Most of the institutions find it difficult to reach and serve young people living in low-income and other high-risk environments.
3. Most cite the quality of adult leadership as the single most important variable in producing successful outcomes, although many of the adult leaders (paid and unpaid) of the programs operated by these institutions have had little or no preparation in working with youth.
4. Funding has always been relatively precarious and is a growing problem as public sector institutions (libraries, park and recreation departments) enter the competition for private dollars and as both public and private agencies cope with government cutbacks at all levels.
5. Accountability, in terms of both data about youth served and evaluation of program outcomes, appears to be quite low in most of these institutions.

From a national perspective, these programs and organizations can perhaps best be described as a nonsystem, albeit a large and significant one. Joan Lipsitz, during her tenure as Director of the Center for Early Adolescence, called this nonsystem a "crazy quilt" (Lipsitz, 1986: 31), a term that calls attention to several of its features – on the one hand, the richness and diversity of its component parts and on the other a lack of cohesiveness and the "stitched together" quality of its underlying infrastructure. The strengths that characterize the existing array of community-based youth development programs include tradition, durability, commitment, credibility, diversity, and widespread support. The extensive reach of these services is impressive.

The best single source of national information about the participation of young adolescents in community programs is the 1988 National Education Longitudinal Study (NELS), which reported 71 percent of the 25,000 eighth graders in their sample to be involved in some type of organized activity outside of school. The activities named most frequently were nonschool team sports (37 percent), religious youth groups (34 percent), summer programs (19 percent), and hobby clubs (15 percent). The single largest category of participation was in the programs of national youth organizations (Scouting, Boys or Girls Clubs, "Y" or other youth groups, 4-H), which totaled 49.5 percent. Whereas the proportion of males and females who engage in at least one activity is about the same, the survey revealed important gender differences in program selection. Males were twice as likely as females to be involved in scouting and nonschool team sports; females were more likely to participate in religious youth groups and summer programs (National Center for Education Statistics [NCES], 1990). Table 8.1 provides a further description of the NELS data on participation of young adolescents in community programs.

The study highlighted a major weakness in current services by delineating the wide disparity in participation between upper and lower income groups. As Table 8.1 indicates, only 17 percent of eighth graders from the highest income quartile reported no involvement in out-of-school activities, whereas fully 40 percent of their lower-income peers indicated no participation. In addition to the alarming inequity in current service delivery patterns, other weaknesses appear to be fragmentation of service, financial vulnerability, inadequate preparation and compensation of staff, and lack of accountability, particularly in regard to service demographics and program outcomes. These weaknesses seem to result not from a lack of ingenuity or goodwill but, rather, from the idiosyncratic history of the

Table 8.1. *Percentage of eighth graders participating in 1988 in outside school activities, by selected background characteristics*

Background Characteristics	Any Outside School Activity	Scouting	Boys or Girls Clubs	"Y" or Other Youth Group	4-H	Religious Youth Groups	Hobby Clubs	Neighborhood Clubs	Summer Program	Nonschool Team Sports
TOTAL	71.3	14.2	10.7	15.3	9.3	33.8	15.5	12.7	19.2	37.3
SEX										
Male	70.7	18.9	11.2	14.3	8.5	29.5	17.1	13.6	16.3	45.1
Female	71.8	9.8	10.2	16.2	10.0	37.9	13.9	11.7	22.0	29.9
RACE/ETHNICITY										
Asian and Pacific Islander	67.9	13.1	9.1	12.7	4.7	27.4	16.7	11.8	24.2	32.0
Hispanic	60.3	10.9	13.2	13.9	6.1	24.6	15.5	13.3	19.5	31.3
Black	65.6	20.0	23.7	23.0	13.8	30.0	22.4	23.4	29.6	33.9
White	74.4	13.7	8.1	14.3	9.1	36.6	14.1	10.7	17.1	39.1
American Indian/Native Alaskan	60.9	17.3	18.0	15.7	10.0	27.5	20.6	17.6	22.0	34.1

Table 8.1. *Continued*

Background Characteristics	Any Outside School Activity	Scouting	Boys or Girls Clubs	"Y" or Other Youth Group	4-H	Religious Youth Groups	Hobby Clubs	Neighbor-hood Clubs	Summer Program	Nonschool Team Sports
SES QUARTILE										
Lowest Quartile	60.0	12.9	14.5	14.0	11.1	22.7	16.3	14.1	16.5	29.5
25–49%	68.5	13.6	11.1	15.5	10.0	30.1	15.0	13.3	16.6	35.6
50–74%	74.2	14.4	9.5	14.8	9.4	35.9	15.1	11.6	18.7	38.4
Highest Quartile	82.6	16.0	8.0	16.7	6.7	45.6	15.5	11.7	24.7	45.2
LOCATION										
Urban	69.1	15.2	14.6	17.9	5.9	29.6	17.7	16.7	23.7	35.6
Suburban	71.5	14.0	9.1	14.2	7.1	33.3	14.9	11.3	18.5	40.0
Rural	72.8	13.9	9.9	14.8	14.9	37.9	14.7	11.2	16.7	35.1

Source: U.S. Department of Education, National Center for Education Statistics, "National Education Longitudinal Study of 1988: Base Year Student Survey."

development of the services. The absence of central coordination and support for youth development services, at both the national and local levels, lies at the heart of these current dilemmas in the United States. Since no one is in charge of worrying about these problems, no one is responsible for addressing them. And each organization – from the smallest local program to the largest national organization – is virtually on its own as it seeks to assess its current efforts and plan its future initiatives. In addition, the highly local nature of these services all but assures that young people in economically disadvantaged neighborhoods will have least access to needed programs. In determining how to address these problems of equity of access and fragmentation of service, our Task Force looked to other countries for effective models, and later in the chapter we present the results of that investigation, with an emphasis on relevant policy solutions. But first we will turn our attention to the effects of participation in American youth organizations, what is known at the present time, where the gaps in our knowledge are, and how we might fill those information voids.

Effects of participation in youth organizations

Two kinds of evidence support the rationale for expanding the role of community-based youth development programs: *theoretical* evidence, which analyzes the appropriateness of the content and approaches of these programs in contributing to positive youth development; and *empirical* evidence, which demonstrates that participation in such programs is perceived as valuable by youth and adults, and that it does have a positive and significant impact on youth needs or competencies.

There is a strong theoretical basis for the argument that positive youth development can be fostered by well planned community programs and services. Francis Ianni's work on adolescent development in an interactive framework of multiple influences builds on two decades of research on the "ecological model" of human development. This model, formulated by Urie Bronfenbrenner (1979) and applied by a host of other researchers, sees individual development as the result of a series of ongoing interactions and adaptations between the individual and a set of overlapping systems that relate both to the individual and to each other (Bronfenbrenner, 1979).

One researcher who has applied this model to early adolescent development is Peter Benson (1990), whose study entitled *The Troubled Journey* validated the basic ecological model as well as the notion of additive influences. Benson defined twenty at-risk indicators covering nine major problem areas such as alcohol, drug and tobacco use, sexual activity, school behavior, and antisocial behavior. He developed a survey instrument, which he administered to some forty-six thousand young adolescents, to determine the effects of internal and external assets (for example, parental standards, positive school climate, involvement in community organizations) and of individual deficits (for example, unsupervised time, stress, physical abuse, negative peer pressure) on at-risk behavior. Benson found that the more assets an adolescent has, the lower the likelihood of high-risk behavior. Using four key assets (positive school climate, family support, involvement in structured youth activities, and involvement in church or synagogue), Benson further found that at-risk indicators are reduced almost on a one-to-one basis as key assets are added. Sixth-through eighth-grade students with no key assets showed an average of four at-risk indicators, those with only one asset showed three at-risk indicators, those with two showed two, and those with three showed 1.4 (Benson, 1990).

A similar study by Bogenschneider, Small, and Riley used the concepts of protective factors and risk factors to analyze the positive and negative influences on high-risk behavior among their sample of adolescents (Bogenschneider, Small, & Riley, 1990). Both studies found that there are protective factors and risk factors in every system – family, peer group, school, work, and community – and that increases in protective factors or assets correlated directly with decreases in at-risk indicators.

A related body of work has investigated the development of resiliency in children, especially young people growing up in high-risk and otherwise stressful environments. Prevention expert Bonnie Benard (1991) examined the major protective factors that research had identified as contributing to the development of resiliency in young people and outlined the implications of this research for the development of effective prevention programs. Her analysis revealed four specific attributes consistently identified with resilient youth:

1. Social competence
2. Problem-solving skills
3. Autonomy (defined as a sense of one's identity and an ability to act independently and exert some control over one's environment)
4. A sense of purpose and future.

Benard concluded that "shifting the balance or tipping the scales from vulnerability to resilience" necessitates action on two levels, developing carefully designed interventions for youth that enhance these four attributes and implementing broader environmental strategies that build protection into the lives of all children and families (Benard, 1991).

In the ecological model community thus refers to much more than community programs. The term is used to describe a range of formal and informal structures that surround, and can support, individuals and families. Joan Wynn and her colleagues at the Chapin Hall Center for Children have defined community supports as follows:

> Community supports are both the informal and the organized resources within communities that contribute to the physical, emotional, cognitive, and social development of individuals. Community supports include (1) opportunities to participate in organized, ongoing groups, (2) avenues for contributing to the well-being of others, (3) sources of personal support, and (4) access to and use of community facilities and events including museums, libraries, parks, civic events, and celebrations. (Wynn et al., 1987)

Some of the most compelling theoretical evidence for strengthening community programs comes from the field of formal education. The literature on learning theory and the application of this theory to education reform suggests that learning is enhanced when it is offered in real-life settings outside the classroom (Lipsitz, 1986; Sarason, 1982), the functions and reasons for learning are clear, instruction and curriculum build on relevant experience and past knowledge, and instructors recognize that learning is not necessarily a linear process (through which simple things are learned first and complex things later) (Weinbaum, 1990). This literature strongly indicates that most people learn more effectively in their communities and workplaces than in traditional educational programs (Raizen, 1989).

Recent work on middle-grade reform also lends credibility to the methods traditionally employed by community-based youth organizations. This literature encourages the use of flexible and varied teaching techniques, active student participation in planning and decision-making, greater personal interaction between students and teachers, increased and more varied systems of feedback and recognition, and smaller, more flexible and heterogeneous student groupings (Epstein, 1988; Carnegie Council on Adolescent Development, 1989). These themes are generally quite consistent with youth organization tradition and practice.

The move from theoretical to empirical evidence that supports the rationale for expanding the role of community-based youth development programs requires an examination of a quite different body of research. First of all, this research is largely "untamed" – that is, it resides in several literatures, which have not been synthesized before; second, much of this research is "fugitive" – that is, unpublished or not accessible through traditional data bases. Further, few of these studies conform to commonly valued research standards, such as random assignment to groups. Nonetheless, this initial attempt to examine and organize the empirical evidence of the value of participation in community youth programs revealed several themes that bolster the case for such involvement and should serve as the starting point for future research.

1. *Young people, their parents and other concerned adults want such programs.* A survey of 764 Oakland sixth-graders and their parents (published in 1982) found that, regardless of income, race or ethnicity, parents believed that organized activities were an important part of their children's education. The sixth-graders themselves believed they had plenty of free time but too little to do during that time that was worthwhile or interesting; 41 percent reported being bored and at a loss for things to do (Medrich et al., 1982).

A more recent survey of third- through twelfth-graders in St. Louis revealed strong youth interest in community- and school-based programs during the nonschool hours. Asked what supports they thought would be helpful when they could not be with parents after school, these young people responded: "a safe place to go if you are afraid"; "planned activities in the school building"; "after-school programs in the neighborhood"; and "ideas about how to take care of yourself after school" (*Survey of St. Louis Kids*, 1986).

A 1986 survey in Minneapolis of more than 1,200 parents and over 1,200 students (grades four through eight) found that approximately one-third of urban children and two-thirds of suburban children participated in after-school programs. Parents definitely wanted to increase the level of participation; their children were less sure they wanted to increase their participation in organized programs, although they expressed great interest in acquiring knowledge and skills in a wide range of extracurricular activities (Hedin, Su, Saito, Goldman, & Knich, 1986).

According to a 1988 survey conducted by the National Association of Elementary School Principals, 84 percent of the 1,175 responding elementary and middle-school principals believed that children in their communities needed increased access to organized before- and after-school programs. Yet only 22 percent reported that their schools offer such services. When asked why they believed schools should provide such programs, 37 percent of proponents responded that children may perform better in school if they are not left unsupervised for long periods during nonschool hours (National Association of Elementary School Principals, 1988).

2. *Young people value and want more programming to help them build personal and social skills.* Nearly four out of ten teens polled in a 1988 survey sponsored by the American Home Economics Association felt that at best schools do only an adequate job of teaching the life skills necessary for responsible and productive adult life (American Home Economics Association, 1988).

High school students surveyed in an Indiana youth poll in 1989–90 indicated that social and personal skills were some of the most interesting things they learned in school (Erickson, 1991b).

The 1986 survey of Minneapolis parents and children cited above revealed that young people wished to participate in a wide variety of extracurricular activities in order to gain knowledge and learn new skills. Of particular interest were participation in sports and outdoor activities, acquiring personal and social skills, and (for junior high school students) learning about possible career choices (Hedin et al., 1986).

3. *Young people and adult alumni value their participation in nonschool youth programs.* Eighty-one percent of the girls surveyed in a recent Louis Harris poll commissioned by the Girl Scouts of the U.S.A. reported that Girl Scouting is either very or somewhat important to them (Brown & Conn, 1990).

Market research conducted for the Boy Scouts of America revealed that current members valued the following features of their Boy Scout experience: learning about the outdoors, having fun, learning new skills, going to new places, going to summer camps, and participating in regular weekend camping or hiking trips (Tyler, 1987).

Alumni of youth organizations reported that participation in programs during the adolescent years contributed significantly to their personal development. A 1987 survey of alumni of 4-H and other youth groups found that alumni felt participation had contributed to their personal development in eight areas: pride in accomplishment, self-confidence, ability to work with others, ability to communicate, ability to set goals, employment skills, leadership skills, and community involvement (Ladewig & Thomas, 1987).

A 1986 Harris survey commissioned by the Boys Clubs of America revealed that nine out of ten of the 1,202 responding alumni felt their Boys Club experiences had a positive effect on their lives, giving them skills for leadership, helping them get along with others, and influencing their success later in life. For a majority of former members, the Boys Club was a place they could go in the neighborhood to participate in organized activities, find refuge from the streets, and be part of a support system that offered a constructive alternative to delinquency and drug abuse (Harris, 1986).

4. *Participation in community-based youth development programs is especially valued by minority youth and young people growing up in single-parent families.* The recent Louis Harris poll commissioned by the Girl Scouts of the U.S.A. revealed that Girl Scouting is especially important to black and Hispanic girls and to girls living in urban areas. Six out of ten black Girl Scouts and more than four out of ten Hispanic and American Indian or Alaskan Native Girl Scouts reported that scouting was personally very important to them, compared to one-third of white and one-quarter of Asian members. Forty-four percent of Girl Scouts living in urban areas said Scouting was very important, compared to 33 percent in the suburbs and 27 percent in rural areas. Girl Scouting was considered important because it offered opportunities for fun, learning, making friends and meeting new people, and community service (Brown & Conn, 1990).

An outside evaluation of the Association of Junior Leagues' Teen Outreach Program found that participation in the program had the greatest impact on young people from single-parent families, "probably because these students had the greatest need for the support, companionship and inspiration the program provided" (Allen & Philliber, 1991).

5. *Participation in community-based youth development programs can promote prosocial behavior.* Several studies have confirmed that participation in extracurricular activities appears to have a positive effect on educational attainment and on subsequent involvement in voluntary organizations (Hanks & Eckland, 1978; Otto, 1975; Spady, 1970; Willits, 1988).

Similarly, participation in voluntary activities and organizations is associated with adult participation in civic and political organizations and in the political process in general (Ladewig & Thomas, 1987; Hanks, 1981).

Participation in community service programs appears to have a significant impact on a variety of youth competencies. A survey of a random sample of ACTION volunteers (ages twelve to twenty-three) in the Young Volunteers for ACTION Program found gains in such areas as understanding of community service, ability to work with others, development of career objectives, increased willingness to learn, and reduced need for supervision (ACTION, 1986).

Other studies of community service participants found similar improvements in personal and social skills, vocational skills, and appreciation and continued involvement in community service (Hamilton & Fenzel, 1987; Wolf, Leiderman, & Voith, 1987).

A 1989 follow-up survey conducted by ASPIRA staff to measure the effect of their Public Policy Leadership Program found that 32 percent of the participants were enrolled in school government, 63 percent were involved in school clubs, and more than half held school club offices. Three-quarters of those surveyed reported they felt more assertive and self-confident as a result of their participation in ASPIRA's programs and that they had improved their leadership skills (ASPIRA, 1989: 7).

An outside evaluation conducted by the Center for Informative Evaluation of the Salvation Army's Bridging the Gap Between Youth and Community Services program revealed that participants made substantial gains in knowledge about themselves, the community, and its resources, felt the program contributed to their knowledge, self-confidence, and more positive self-image, and would recommend the program to others (B. Hamburg, 1990).

6. *Participation in targeted prevention programs can lead to reduction in high-risk behaviors.* In four consecutive annual evaluations, participants in the Teen Outreach Program (TOP) sponsored by the Association of Junior Leagues International – a school-based life skills management and community service program for middle and high school students – were less likely than their nonparticipant peers to have experienced either pregnancy or school failure. In the four years ending in 1988, TOP participants had, on average, a 16 percent lower rate of school suspension, a 36 percent lower rate of school discontinuation, and a 42 percent lower rate of pregnancy than did the carefully matched comparison students (Association of Junior Leagues, 1991).

An experimental evaluation of Girls Incorporated's Friendly PEERsuasion (substance abuse prevention) program for young adolescents indicated that the program reduced the incidence of initial drinking among participants who had not previously used alcohol. The program also led girls to leave some types of situations where friends were using harmful substances and to disengage from peers who smoked or took drugs (Smith & Kennedy, 1991).

Another targeted intervention developed by Girls Incorporated, the Preventing Adolescent Pregnancy Program, has also shown positive results. A three-year study involving 750 teenage women (ages twelve to seventeen) indicated that participation in all four program components was associated with lower overall rates of pregnancy, and that participation in individual components led to specific pregnancy-related effects. For example, participants in the Growing Together (parent-daughter communication workshop series) program were less than half as likely as nonparticipants to have sexual intercourse for the first time. Young adolescents who participated in nearly the entire Will Power/Won't Power component (assertiveness training designed to help participants say "no" to early intercourse) were only half as likely as nonparticipants to become sexually active. Older teenagers who participated consistently in the Taking Care of Business and Health Bridge components were less likely to have sex without birth control, and less likely to become pregnant than were nonparticipants (Girls Incorporated, 1991).

An outside evaluation of WAVE Inc.'s dropout prevention program found that participation was associated with improved attendance, lower dropout rates, and increased scores in job readiness, math, reading, and self-esteem (WAVE, 1991).

7. *Participation in overall programming of a comprehensive youth development program can lead to reduction in high-risk behaviors and promotion of prosocial behaviors.* An outside evaluation of Boys and Girls Clubs of America's SMART Moves (substance abuse prevention) initiative revealed that a comprehensive youth development program, with or without interventions targeted toward specific risks, can both reduce problem behaviors and promote prosocial behaviors.

To evaluate five Boys and Girls Clubs that had implemented the SMART Moves intervention, each of these clubs was assigned two control sites: one public housing site with a Boys and Girls Club without SMART Moves, and one public housing site without a Boys and Girls Club. These control sites were geographically and demographically matched with the Clubs with SMART Moves. Matching criteria included the size of the public housing site, its geographic locale, and demographics of the population served.

The evaluators found that, although the differences in impact between the Clubs without SMART Moves and Clubs with SMART Moves were not great, there were substantial differences between the housing projects that had clubs and those that did not in positive outcomes for youth, for parents, and for the surrounding community. The evaluators noted: For youth who live in public housing and who have access to a Boys and Girls Club, the influence of Boys and Girls Clubs is manifest in their involvement in healthy and constructive educational, social and recreational activities. Relative to their counterparts who do not have access to a Club, these youth are less involved in unhealthy, deviant and dangerous activities.

Data from the evaluation showed that adult residents of public housing were also beneficially affected. Compared with parents in the control (no-Club) sites, adult family members in communities with Boys and Girls Clubs were more involved in youth-oriented activities and school programs. For adults and youth alike, Boys and Girls Clubs appeared to be associated with an overall reduction in alcohol and other drug use, drug trafficking, and drug-related crime (Boys Clubs of America, 1991).

8. *Sustained and comprehensive interventions stand the best chance of effecting real change in the lives of disadvantaged youth.* An outcome evaluation conducted by Public/Private Ventures (P/PV) of its Summer Training and Employment Program (STEP) showed impressive short-term effects in stemming losses in reading and math skills among economically disadvantaged urban youth, ages fourteen and fifteen, during the summer months. In this random assignment study of five thousand young people in five U.S. cities, participants also gained in knowledge and positive attitudes about sex, contraception, and adult responsibilities (although effects on their sexual behavior were inconsistent). A few years after their involvement in STEP, however, participants did not differ systematically from control group members in patterns of work, dropping out, school completion, or teenage pregnancy. P/PV investigators concluded that carefully designed programs such as STEP are an important component of a much more sustained and comprehensive set of services needed to effect change in the lives of young people who have already experienced school failure. These services, according to the investigators, must include consistent support from adults, the use of more active and interactive teaching styles, and involvement of family members. Furthermore, they must continue throughout adolescence, not just for several weeks or two summers (the duration of the STEP intervention) (Walker & Vilella-Velez, 1992).

These findings were corroborated by the twin evaluations conducted by Girls Incorporated of its Friendly PEERsuasion (substance abuse prevention) and Preventing Adolescent Pregnancy programs. The Friendly

PEERsuasion evaluation found statistically significant short-term gains for program participants over control group members, but these effects were greatly diminished over the longer term, leading investigators to conclude that some of the program elements, especially the peer leadership component, should be extended over time (Smith & Kennedy, 1991). The Preventing Adolescent Pregnancy Program evaluation found that "dosage makes a difference," in that the effectiveness of the program was associated directly with the intensity of the individual's participation (Girls Incorporated, 1991).

In summary, both theoretical and empirical evidence supports the expansion of community-based youth development programs. The theoretical case builds on a strong body of educational and human development research that points to the need of adolescents to experience more supportive environments and their need for opportunities to engage in a variety of active and prosocial experiences, and to the potential of community programs in employing methods developmentally appropriate for young adolescents and with a good likelihood of success with this population. The empirical case provides a more mixed picture, with a wealth of survey data that verify these needs and suggest positive outcomes, and a handful of promising studies that document the actual outcomes. Taken together, existing evidence appears to represent a more than sufficient base on which to build a solid rationale for strengthening and expanding the role of community-based programs in the promotion of healthy adolescent development. Additional evidence is needed to bolster that case and to deepen our understanding of what types of programs and services are most likely to be effective with individual adolescents and with particular groups of adolescents.

Characteristics of effective programs and organizations

A review of the research and practice literature on young adolescents, children at risk, adolescents at risk, and community programs reveals several common themes about the design and implementation of appealing and effective community programs for youth (Dryfoos, 1990; D. A. Hamburg, 1986; Heath & McLaughlin, 1991; Honnet & Poulsen, 1989; Lipsitz, 1986; Pittman & Wright, 1991; L. Schorr & D. Schorr, 1988; Snider & Miller, 1991; United Way of America, 1991a, 1991b; Amherst H. Wilder Foundation, 1988). The Carnegie Task Force analyzed these themes and outlined a set of principles that define the "best practice" in community-based youth development programs. This section will present these guiding principles, followed by a brief description of the meaning and application of each one.

Responsive, pro-active community programs for young adolescents should:

1. Tailor their program content and processes to the needs and interests of young adolescents
2. Recognize, value, and respond to the diversity of backgrounds and experience that exists among young adolescents
3. Specify and evaluate their outcomes
4. Work collectively as well as individually to extend their reach to underserved adolescents
5. Strengthen the quality and diversity of their adult leadership
6. Enhance the role of young people as resources to their communities
7. Serve as vigorous advocates for and with youth
8. Reach out to families, schools, and other community partners in youth development
9. Work to stabilize their funding bases
10. Establish solid organizational structures, including energetic and committed board leadership.

Principle 1: Tailor program content and processes to the needs and interests of young adolescents. Teenagers generally know what they like and what they want. As part of its research, the Carnegie Task Force conducted focus groups with young adolescents to find out how they spend their nonschool time, what their activity preferences are, what kinds of qualities they like in adult leaders of youth programs, and how they would describe an ideal youth center. They consistently stated that the center would have a staff that listened to and respected them, provide a safe environment where they can "be themselves," and offer an interesting array of programs, including organized sports and classes on a variety of subjects (S. W. Morris & Company, 1992).

People, places, and programs – these are the key ingredients of attractive and successful programs, according to young people in the Carnegie focus groups and in other youth surveys. These themes are consistent with current research knowledge as well as with the experience of seasoned practitioners in the youth development field.

The kind of program content that teenagers say they **want** often matches up nicely with what experts say they **need**. It is not surprising that experts recommend building program content around the developmental tasks of adolescence, calling for content that addresses at least one of the following needs of youth: health and physical well-being, personal and social competence, cognitive or creative competence, vocational awareness and readiness, and leadership and citizenship. Such content might include:

- Health and physical well-being: Health education, including substance abuse, sexuality, and AIDS education; health promotion; health services; sports; physical fitness; other recreation
- Personal and social competence: Life skills training; independent living skills; individual and group counseling; peer education and counseling; mentoring; interpersonal relationship skills, including conflict resolution; child and sexual abuse prevention
- Cognitive or creative competence: Academic tutoring; homework clinics; English as a second language; communications skills; computer skills; visual and performing arts; culture and heritage
- Vocational awareness and readiness: Career awareness; job readiness; job skills training; internships; summer jobs; in-house paid employment
- Leadership and citizenship: Community service; community action; leadership skills training; youth advisory boards; civics education and political involvement

Although community programs should address the serious concerns of today's young people, they should also respond to the desire of adolescents for "fun" and "friends," providing many opportunities for young people to socialize, hang out, and choose from an assortment of interesting and challenging activities.

Community programs for youth should use processes that actively engage young people by providing opportunities to practice new skills, make new friends, have new experiences, and explore new options. Such active processes include experiential (hands-on) education, cooperative learning, and peer leadership. Young people should be offered many opportunities to develop new skills through practice and reflection, and their accomplishments should be recognized frequently. Programs should foster supportive relationships with peers and adults, and provide opportunities to teach same-age or younger peers. Finally, a comfortable atmosphere and safe, predictable environment can help young adolescents feel welcome and encourage them to participate (Heath & McLaughlin, 1991).

Principle 2: Community programs should recognize, value, and respond to the diverse backgrounds and experience that exist among young adolescents. Community programs should be sensitive to the differences among young adolescents, particularly those differences based on gender, race, or ethnicity. Because the formation of a personal identity is central to the "work" of adolescence, these critical issues in personal identity must be considered by program developers.

Concerns related to gender have dominated the thinking of some youth development organizations and have been far less consciously addressed in others. New attention to gender issues has sometimes been thrust upon organizations as a result of litigation or political action designed to achieve gender equity. Current practice finds youth development organizations serving girls and boys in a variety of settings – coeducational, separately for girls and boys, and a mixture of these options – and taking a variety of perspectives on gender and its importance to program development. There is no research basis for concluding that it is preferable to offer youth development programs on a single-gender or coeducational basis. There is, however, a strong body of research that can inform decisions about how programs of either configuration can be responsive to the needs of young adolescents of both genders.

A key consideration in programs for youth is the fact that, by the time they reach early adolescence, boys and girls have had differing experiences based on their gender. A second consideration is the physical and psychological effects of puberty, particularly the fact that, during early adolescence, young people of the same chronological age may have reached quite different states of pubertal development. One overarching strategy for managing gender issues in youth development programs is to recognize that all young people need to be prepared for the adult roles of paid worker, family member, and community citizen. This is not easily accomplished because preparing young adolescents to be members of an equitable society requires attention to today's continuing inequities. Youth organizations are well positioned to provide both boys and girls with experiences that encourage the development of interests and skills associated in the past with the other gender (that is, community service and arts for boys, sports and science for girls).

America's young adolescents represent a rich array of racial, ethnic, and cultural backgrounds at the present time, and this diversity will increase in the coming decades until there will be no majority population group in the United States by the middle of the next century. This present-day reality and the demographic projections emphasize the urgency of ensuring that community programs are prepared to recognize and celebrate this diversity.

Program planners should become familiar with the family configurations of their program participants, be aware of the norms and values that undergird the culture of the program itself, and examine how these are either consonant or discordant with family values and practices. Planners should involve family and community members in program plans and activities, and support the ethnic orientation not just of teens but of the family as a whole. Planners should take the same approach in dealing with individual young people in their programs.

Youth organizations also have a crucial role to play in helping young people to learn about, understand, and appreciate people with backgrounds different from their own. Such work, although not easy, is consistent with the missions of many youth organizations, is sorely needed, and can flow directly from their regular ways of interacting with young people. Youth organizations can purposefully create environments that not only meet psychosocial needs and develop competencies but also celebrate and build on aspects of participants' races and ethnic backgrounds in the process. Young adolescents are poised to take risks, to widen their circle of relationships and affiliations, and to explore actively their worlds and themselves. Youth development programs can take advantage of these predispositions by opening new vistas for youth and by fostering the development of skills and competencies that complement and/or supplement those provided by schools and families.

Principle 3: Community programs should specify and evaluate their outcomes. Program developers should work to achieve clarity and realism when defining outcomes of their efforts. As much as possible, these outcomes should focus on the results of positive youth development rather than solely on preventing problem behaviors such as substance abuse, delinquency, and adolescent pregnancy. The outcomes should be stated in terms of behavioral functioning in the real world, and the indicators associated with each outcome should also be identified. Success is more likely to ensue if the frequency and duration of a program intervention matches well with its intended outcomes.

There is a critical need to anchor youth development programs in the best available current knowledge. Many programs are based on outmoded theory or, worse yet, no theory. It is not uncommon to find programs rooted solely in political or philosophical ideology. Effective programs follow a five step process of conceptualization, design, implementation, evaluation, and maintenance/dissemination (Weissberg, Caplan, & Sivo, 1989).

Achieving more rigorous outcome evaluation of youth development programs raises a host of general and specific problems – none insurmountable but nonetheless real. General problems in evaluating the effects of social interventions include deciding what outcome variables (knowledge, attitudes, behaviors) to measure, constructing valid and reliable instruments for determining change, building in sufficient controls to be able to prove that the intervention was responsible for causing these changes, and allowing enough time to elapse for the desired changes to occur. Specific problems in evaluating the effects of youth development programs include recruiting and retaining participants in the program and assessment (a challenge in any voluntary setting), and dealing with the issue of random assignment to treatment and control groups, which runs counter to the public service orientation of most youth organizations.

To address these challenges, youth organizations may find it useful to work with evaluation experts from other institutions, including universities and nonprofit technical assistance organizations. Outside evaluators should see themselves as equal partners with youth agency personnel in designing and implementing evaluations. And the young people themselves should be active participants in evaluations of all types. The methods used to evaluate youth development programs should be appropriate to the organizational setting and to the age of the participants as well as to the individual programs.

In a world of scarce resources, the best candidates for rigorous outcome evaluations are those programs that are carefully designed and implemented, that have shown promising results, and that have the greatest chance of being amenable to large-scale replication. In addition to their individual efforts, youth organizations should work in partnership with one another and with social science researchers to conduct longitudinal studies that document the long-term effects of participation in youth development programs (Carnegie Council on Adolescent Development, 1992).

Principle 4: Community programs should work collectively as well as individually to extend their reach to under-served adolescents. Increasing the access of young people living in low-income areas to supportive community programs will require individual and collective action at both the local and national levels. Community programs for youth should view themselves as actors in a network of services, and these networks should engage in systematic planning and coordinated decision-making. Youth needs, rather than organizational concerns, should remain at the center of these efforts from their inception. An expanded and realigned set of services should build on the strengths of current programs and organizations; but all actors in the network should anticipate that adaptation and change will be required on an ongoing basis.

Principle 5: Community programs should strengthen the quality and diversity of adult leadership. Across all subsectors of the varied universe of community programs studied by the Carnegie Task Force, the quality of adult leadership was consistently named as both vitally important and inadequately addressed (Carnegie Council on Adolescent Development, 1991). Youth-serving agencies, religious youth groups, sports programs, parks and recreation services, and libraries all report that the adults who work with young people in their systems, whether they are serving on a paid or pro bono basis are on the one hand, the most critical factor in whether or not a program succeeds and on the other, do not receive adequate training or ongoing supervision. These training and supervision problems are reported to be the result largely of resource constraints, although they may also be tied to the widely held view that work with youth is neither highly valued nor particularly complex.

Improving the quality of adult leadership involves issues of pre- and in-service training, of recruitment and retention, of paid and unpaid (or volunteer) staff at all levels. An immediate first step is for community programs greatly to expand the availability of appropriate training and other forms of staff development for all the adults who work directly with young people on either a paid or pro bono basis. The Carnegie study (1992) also outlined a set of longer-term strategies for addressing this critical issue.

Principle 6: Community programs should enhance the role of young people as resources to their communities. A good place to begin implementing this recommendation is within youth organizations themselves. Community programs should involve young people in decision-making at all levels, from choices about program activities to organizational governance. In addition to carrying out roles in organizational decision-making, young people should have opportunities to participate in all other aspects of agency life, including teaching skills to other participants, caring for the physical facility, planning special events, and representing the organization to the media and policymakers.

Community programs should also ensure that youth have opportunities to provide meaningful service to the larger communities in which they live. The program can act as a broker between youth and other community institutions, by developing and nurturing relationships with these groups and by working to publicize the good work that young people contribute. Youth should be active participants in determining which issues they wish to address through service activities and which strategies they will employ. Adult leaders may underestimate the creativity and concern for social justice that young adolescents bring to the design of such efforts. Current projects around the United States see young people involved in building neighborhood parks for younger children, planting trees and reclaiming trash-ridden streams, registering adults to vote, staffing soup kitchens, and working to end the killing of dolphins in tuna fishing.

Principle 7: Community programs should act as vigorous advocates for and with youth. All types of organizations that sponsor community programs for youth – adult service clubs, senior citizens groups, sports organizations, national and local youth agencies, churches, museums – should become advocates for youth. Staff members and volunteers (board members, fund-raising associates, and program volunteers) should consider advocacy as part of their work with the agency. The organizations themselves should join local, state, and national advocacy coalitions in an effort to elevate youth issues in public policy debates. Adults should work with young people as partners in the multiple advocacy processes of educating the public about youth needs and influencing youth-related public policy, including funding levels and mechanisms. Youth and other community organizations should educate funders that advocacy is a legitimate and ongoing part of their total work.

Principle 8: Community programs should reach out to families, schools, and other community partners in youth development. Effective community programs for youth see themselves as partners with families, schools, and other community institutions in the youth development process. They work hard to maintain solid working relationships with their partners, and to clarify how their role complements, supplements, and differs from that of others.

There are at least five constructive ways to involve parents and other family members in the work of youth organizations:

1. Keeping families informed of organizational activities
2. Inviting family members to contribute their time and energies to the agency's efforts
3. Designing programmatic activities that encourage young people to consult with and interview family members
4. Supporting families in their child-rearing responsibilities
5. Providing direct services to families.

At the simplest level, schools and community-based agencies should work together to share information about individual students and to effect appropriate referrals from one institution to another. Youth organizations should reach out to schools in publicizing their services and in eliciting suggestions from school personnel about the needs of their students. A second level of cooperation sees community agencies delivering program services in school facilities, either during the school day or on a "wraparound" basis (that is, before and after school). A third level involves joint planning that focuses not just on individual students but on the delivery of services for all students. A fourth level, one that has been realized in few American communities, is a unified system of educational and human services. This system views its role as youth development and recognizes the common goals of the schools and community agencies while respecting their inherent differences and strengths.

Principle 9: Community programs for youth should work to stabilize their funding bases. One of the most striking features of America's youth development programs is the precariousness of their funding. A few organizations enjoy regular annual surpluses and substantial bodies of assets, but most are heavily dependent on outside funding, over which they have little control. Because of this dependence, community programs for youth cannot stabilize their funding bases by themselves.

Specific actions they can take are diversifying their funding sources; making best use of existing resources; viewing themselves as having an interdependent relationship with funders, educating funders about their real needs and responding to funders' requests for greater accountability and responsiveness to community needs; continually working to develop innovative and stable sources of core support for their organizations (comparable to the sale of Girl Scout cookies, which provides some 60 percent of the core support for the work of that agency's local councils); working collectively with other youth organizations to increase the stability and total level of support for the sector's work, through action directed toward both traditional sources and innovative new mechanisms (for example, a Children's Investment Trust that would earmark public funds for youth services or a special type of postal stamp that would encourage individuals to make voluntary contributions to youth programs each time they purchased stamps through the U.S. Postal Service).

Stability of service is essential to maintaining continuity of relationships, especially for youth at critical junctures in their lives. Long-term commitment to their young constituents requires that community programs and organizational sponsors plan for lean funding years by raising unrestricted operating and endowment funds to cover gaps in restricted funding.

Principle 10: Community programs should establish solid organizational structures, including energetic and committed board leadership. Just as programs must be shaped to meet the changing needs of the youth population, so organizations that would present those programs effectively must be well structured and adequately supported. Effective programs are generally found in stable, well managed organizations. Although there are exceptions to this rule – particularly small, locally developed programs that serve young people successfully at the neighborhood level – for the most part, the connection between programs and organizations is so close that it is difficult to know exactly where one ends and the other begins. Research and experience show that effective youth organizations make a serious commitment to both their programs and their staff.

The importance of board leadership in nonprofit organizations cannot be overstated because, in carrying out its policy-setting function, an agency's board establishes its future direction and priorities. Organizations with effective programs for young adolescents have generally made a board-level commitment to such work; this commitment may involve a decision to raise new funds for expanded program activity as well as the establishment of new organizational policies on such issues as adolescent sexuality, substance use, and youth employment. Board members also play a critical role in determining where to locate agency facilities and programs, and whether or not to charge fees for program participation – decisions that determine, to a great extent, whether or not the organization will be successful in reaching out to young people living in low-income neighborhoods.

Policy implications

The ability of any individual program or organization to implement these ten principles will depend on several factors that are within its direct control as well as on larger outside forces. Public policy can either support or impede the efforts of youth organizations in their work of improving the delivery of community-based services to adolescents. Current U.S. youth policy, for the most part, ignores – and is therefore not supportive of – youth development. Rather, it is oriented toward remediation of individual difficulties, following a pathology or deficit model. In line with this orientation, public funding of U.S. youth services tends to focus on youth problems, defining these problems according to strict categories, such as substance abuse, juvenile delinquency, adolescent pregnancy, youth unemployment, and school failure.

As part of its research, the Carnegie Task Force commissioned a paper on cross-national perspectives in an effort to learn from the experience of selected other countries, focusing on the most transferable lessons and models. Researcher Michael Sherraden, an international expert on youth employment and national service, undertook the challenge of researching and analyzing how other countries approach youth development (Sherraden, 1991). One major finding was that the content of youth policies and programs in the five countries studied – the United Kingdom, Australia, Germany, Sweden, and Norway – tends to be **developmental, broadly based, inclusive, and participatory**. This orientation toward broad development and normal socialization differs markedly from current U.S. youth policy.

A second major finding was that the national government of each of these other countries has identified youth issues as a broad public responsibility, has established legal and organizational structures for shouldering that responsibility, and has appropriated funds at a significant level and on a stable basis to carry out youth policies and programs. In some of these other countries, federal funding did not provide the majority support, but it was substantial enough to leverage local and voluntary resources and to create youth service partnerships guided by national policy but adapted and implemented by local actors, both public and voluntary. The United States has a vibrant voluntary sector, but it is largely independent of the public sector in terms of overall planning and coordination. This situation poses a sharp contrast to all five of the countries studied by the Carnegie Task Force in which youth policies involve explicit public-voluntary cooperation and coordination to an extent unknown in the United States. This coordination occurs through both law and organizational structure.

In each of the five countries studied, and in many other European nations, there are local youth boards that are, in one way or another, charged with implementing or overseeing public and voluntary youth services. Generally, these local bodies also provide significant financial support. In reflecting on these differences, Sherraden observed:

> Realistically, we probably cannot expect the U.S. government, at least in the near future, to appropriate extensive new funding for

> youth policy. However, we can question whether the existing pattern of U.S. expenditures is wise. A portion of the funding that now goes to deviance and deficiencies would be better spent on general developmental youth services, making a greater effort to establish youth programs in every neighborhood and community in the country. The guiding principle should not be money for every problem, but programs for every community. (Sherraden, 1991: iii)

Another factor that differentiates the United States from other countries is its lack of a national perspective on, and system for, preparation of youth-work professionals. Sherraden described rich models for pre- and in-service education that address such issues as career ladders, adequate compensation, and other forms of professional recognition, citing in particular the efforts of Germany, the United Kingdom, and Sweden.

Research on youth issues presents another lesson the United States might learn from other countries. Research dollars in the United States are directed toward studies of youth problems, but virtually no funding – public or private – is oriented toward youth development or community-based youth organizations. Sherraden noted that "It would be difficult to overstate the problem. A researcher working in an urban area, for example, can more easily obtain a million dollars to study youth purse snatching than a thousand dollars to study youth theater and dance groups. This is a misallocation of research dollars. Unfortunately, it becomes a vicious circle – the more we study problems, the more we spend on problems; and the less we study solutions, the less we spend on solutions" (Sherraden, 1991: iv). Citing the Youth Education Studies Centre in Australia as a model, Sherraden recommended that the United States place far greater emphasis on studying ordinary youth development and successful youth services at the community level. He also noted the urgency of developing better information networks among youth work practitioners and researchers, including the need for the types of youth service magazines and journals available in several other countries.

The wide-ranging analysis offered by Sherraden in his discussion of youth development from a cross-national perspective provides many instructive lessons, but perhaps the most elucidating aspect involves what is missing from current U.S. policy. What is missing is a national policy on youth, particularly on positive youth development. One has only to read about the British Youth Service, an organized comprehensive system for delivering youth policy, built on a foundation of local youth clubs; or to learn of Australia's Office of Youth Affairs, which was established by the commonwealth government in 1977 in response to a federally sponsored study on youth issues; or to recognize that Germany's system of youth services, including its Federal Ministry of Youth, rests on national legislation (the Federal Youth Welfare Act) that was passed in 1922. The existence, the longevity, and the viability of these legislative and structural mechanisms in other developed countries make a persuasive case for what the United States currently lacks – a national youth policy, authorizing legislation, a cabinet or sub-cabinet level official who coordinates youth policy. One has only to read about Sweden's system of youth boards at the community level, which are heavily subsidized by the federal government, or to learn that the Swedish government pays about half the costs of its youth organizations, to understand that alternatives do exist to America's fragmented and highly inequitable youth development delivery system.

Sherraden noted that, "Overall, U.S. youth services are less planned, less coordinated, less public, less funded, less egalitarian, less comprehensive, and less developmental" (Sherraden, 1991: 51) than those in the other nations cited in his report. He recommended not that the United States adopt any specific model whole-cloth, but rather that we adapt pieces of existing models to meet our own particular needs.

References

ACTION. (1986). *Young Volunteers in Action (YVA) Effects Evaluation: Final Report.* Washington, DC: Author.

Allen, J. P., & Philliber S. (1991). *Process Evaluation of the Teen Outreach Program: Characteristics Related to Program Success in Preventing School Dropout and Teen Pregnancy in Year 5 (1988–89 School Year).* New York: Association of Junior Leagues International.

American Home Economics Association. (1988). *Survey of American Teens.* Alexandria, Va: Author.

Amherst H. Wilder Foundation. (1988). *Funders' Guide Manual: A Guide to Prevention Programs in Human Services – Focus on Children and Adolescents.* St. Paul, Minn.: Author.

ASPIRA Association, Inc. (1989). *National Office Annual Report,* p. 7. Washington, DC: Author.

Association of Junior Leagues International, Inc. (1991). *Teen Outreach Program: A Three-Year Proposal For Replication/Institutionalization.* New York: Author.

Benard, B. (1991). *Fostering Resiliency in Kids: Protective Factors in the Family, School and Community,* pp. 18–19. Portland, Ore.: Northwest Regional Educational Laboratories, Western Regional Center for Drug-Free Schools and Communities.

Benson, P. L. (1990). *The Troubled Journey: A Portrait of 6th–12th Grade Youth.* Minneapolis: Lutheran Brotherhood.

Bogenschneider, K., Small, S., & Riley, D. (1990). *An Ecological Risk-Focused Approach for Addressing Youth-At-Risk Issues.* Paper presented at the Youth at Risk Summit of the National Extension Service, Washington, DC.

Boys Clubs of America. (1991). *The Effects of Boys and Girls Clubs on Alcohol and Other Drug Use and Related Problems in Public Housing Projects*. New York: Author.

Bronfenbrenner, U. (1979). *The Ecology of Human Development: Experiments by Nature and Design*. Boston: Harvard University Press.

Brown, S. J., & Conn, M. (1990). *Girl Scouts: Who We Are, What We Think* (Research study conducted for the Girls Scouts of the U.S.A.). New York: Girl Scouts of the U.S.A.

Carnegie Council on Adolescent Development. (1989). *Turning Points: Preparing American Youth for the 21st Century*. Washington, DC: Author.

(1991). *Report on the Consultation on Professional Development of Youthworkers, May 13, 1991*. Washington, DC: Author.

(1992). *Report on the Consultation on Evaluation of Youth Development Programs, January 15, 1992*. Washington, DC: Author.

Dryfoos, J. (1990). *Adolescents at Risk: Prevalence and Prevention*. New York: Oxford University Press.

Epstein, J. L. (1988). Effective schools or effective students: Dealing with diversity. In *Policies for America's Public Schools*, ed. R. Haskins & D. MacRae, pp. 89–126. Norwood, N.J.: Ablex.

Erickson, J. B. (1986). Non-formal education in organizations for American youth. *Children Today*, 15, 17–25.

(1991a). *1992–1993 Directory of American Youth Organization*, 4th ed. Minneapolis: Free Spirit Publishing.

(1991b). *Indiana Youth Poll: Youths' Views of High School Life*. Indianapolis: Indiana Youth Institute.

Girls Incorporated. (1991). *Truth, Trust and Technology: New Research on Preventing Adolescent Pregnancy*. New York: Author.

Hamburg, B. (1990). *Life Skills Training: Preventive Interventions for Young Adolescents*, pp. 63–71. Working paper of the Carnegie Council on Adolescent Development, Washington, DC.

Hamburg, D. A. (1986). *Preparing for Life: The Critical Transition of Adolescence*. Reprinted from the Annual Report of the Carnegie Corporation of New York.

Hamilton, S. F., & Fenzel, L. M. (1987). *The Effect of Volunteer Experience on Early Adolescents' Social Development*. Paper presented at an American Educational Research Association Conference, Washington, DC.

Hanks, M. (1981). Youth, voluntary associations and political socialization. *Social Forces*, 1, 211–23.

Hanks, M., & Eckland, B. K. (1978). Adult voluntary associations and adolescent socialization. *The Sociological Quarterly*, 19, 481–90.

Hanson, R. G., & Carlson, R. E. (1972). *Organizations for Children and Youth*. Englewood Cliffs, N.J.: Prentice-Hall.

Harris, L. (1986). *Testimony to Boys Clubs: A Report to the Leaders of America Compiled by Boys Clubs of America* (based on independent research by Louis Harris & Associates, Inc.). New York: Boys Clubs of America.

Heath, S. B., & McLaughlin, M. W. (1991). Community organization as family: Endeavors that engage and support adolescents. *Phi Delta Kappan*, April, 623–7.

Hedin, D., Su, S., Saito, R., Goldman, A., and Knich, D. (1986). *Summary of the Family's View of After-School Time*, p. 7. Minneapolis: University of Minnesota.

Honnet, E. P., & Poulsen, S. J. (1989). *Principles of Good Practice for Combining Service and Learning* (Wingspread Special Report). Racine, Wis.: The Johnson Foundation.

James, D. (1979). *Description Study of Selected National Youth Serving Organizations.* Washington, DC: U.S. Department of Agriculture, Science and Education Administration/Extension.

Kleinfeld, J., & Shinkwin, A. (1982). *Youth Organizations as a Third Educational Environment Particularly for Minority Group Youth* (Final Report to the National Institute of Education). Washington, DC: U.S. Government Printing Office.

LaBelle, T. J., & Carroll, J. (1981). An introduction to the nonformal education of children and youth. *Comparative Education Review,* 25, 313–29.

Ladewig, H., & Thomas, J. K. (1987). *Assessing the Impact of 4-H on Former Members.* College Station, Tex.: Texas A&M University System.

Lipsitz, J. S. (1986). *After School: Young Adolescents on Their Own.* Carrboro: University of North Carolina, Center for Early Adolescence.

Medrich, E. A., Roizen, J. A., Rubin, V., & Buckley, S. (1982). *The Serious Business of Growing Up: A Study of Children's Lives Outside School.* Berkeley: University of California Press.

National Association of Elementary School Principals (1988). *NAESP Principals' Opinion Survey: Before- and After-School Child Care.* Alexandria, Va: Author.

National Center for Education Statistics. (1990). *National Education Longitudinal Study of 1988: The Profile of the American Eighth Grader.* Washington, DC: U.S. Government Printing Office.

National Collaboration for Youth. (1990). *Making the Grade: A Report Card on American Youth–Report on the Nationwide Project,* p. 1. Washington, DC: Author.

Otto, L. B. (1975). Extracurricular activities in the educational attainment process. *Rural Sociology,* 40, 162–76.

Pittman, K. J., & Wright, M. (1991). *A Rationale for Enhancing the Role of the Non-School Voluntary Sector in Youth Development.* Unpublished manuscript prepared for the Carnegie Council on Adolescent Development, Washington, DC.

Raizen, S. (1989). *Reforming Education for Work: A Cognitive Science Perspective.* Berkeley, Calif.: National Center for Research in Vocational Education.

Sarason, S. S. (1982). *The Culture of the School: The Problems of Change,* 2d ed. Boston: Allyn and Bacon.

Schorr, L., & Schorr, D. (1988). *Within Our Reach: Breaking the Cycle of Disadvantage.* New York: Doubleday.

Sherraden, M. (1991). *Community-Based Youth Services in International Perspective.* Unpublished manuscript prepared for the Carnegie Council on Adolescent Development, Washington, DC.

Smith, C., & Kennedy, S. D. (1991). *Final Impact Evaluation of the Friendly PEERsuasion Program of Girls Incorporated.* New York: Girls Incorporated.

Snider, B. A. & Miller, J. P. (1991). *Land-Grant University System and 4-H: A Mutually Beneficial Relationship of Scholars and Practitioners in Youth Development* (draft paper). College Station: The Pennsylvania State University, Department of Agricultural and Extension Education.

Spady, W. G. (1970). Lament for the letterman: Effects of peer status and extracurricular activities on goals and achievements. *American Journal of Sociology,* 75, 680–702.

Survey of St. Louis Youth. (1986). St. Louis, Missouri: East-West Gateway Coordinating Council.

S. W. Morris & Company. (1992). *What Young Adolescents Want and Need From Out-of-School Programs: A Focus Group Report.* Unpublished manuscript prepared for the Carnegie Council on Adolescent Development, Washington, DC.

Tyler, J. M. (1987). *Toward the Development of a Marketing Study Implementation Plan*, p. 4. Report prepared by SRI International for the national office of Boy Scouts of America.

United Way of America. (1991a). *Investing in Children: A Strategy to Change at-Risk Lives* (a report of the Task Force on Children at Risk). Alexandria, Va: Author.

United Way of America. (1991b). *Promising Prevention Programs for Children*. Alexandria, Va: Author.

Walker, G., & Vilella-Velez, F. (1992). *Anatomy of a Demonstration*. Philadelphia: Public/Private Ventures.

WAVE, Inc. (1991). *Summary of the First Year of WAVE*. Washington, DC: Author.

Weinbaum, S. (1990). *Center for Youth and Literacy: A Conceptual Framework*. New York: Academy for Educational Development.

Weissberg, R. P., Caplan, M. Z., & Sivo, P. J. (1989). A conceptual framework for establishing school-based social competence promotion programs. In *Primary prevention and promotion in the schools*, ed. L. A. Bond & B. E. Compas, pp. 255–96. Newbury Park, Calif.: Sage.

Willits, F. K. (1988). Adolescent behavior and adult success and well-being: A 37-year panel study. *Youth and Society*, 20, 68–87.

Wolf, W. C., Leiderman, S., & Voith, R. (1987). *The California Conservation Corps: An Analysis of Short-Term Impacts on Participants*. Philadelphia: Public/Private Ventures.

Wynn J., Richman, H., Rubenstein, R. A., & Littell, J. (1987). *Communities and Adolescents: An Exploration of Reciprocal Supports*. Chicago: University of Chicago, Chapin Hall Center for Children. Paper prepared for the William T. Grant Foundation Commission on Work, Family and Citizenship, p. 11.

9. Community influences on adolescent behavior

ALBERT J. REISS, JR.

Introduction

The objective set for this chapter was to review what we have learned about community influences on adolescent behavior. Given the many investigations on prosocial as well as antisocial behavior and conduct disorders, that seemed daunting. Fortunately the task proved less burdensome than expected because the number of studies that include measures of community in their investigation of adolescent behavior are surprisingly few. This lighter burden has the unfortunate consequence that there are more leads for investigation than solid conclusions.

The scope of this review is limited in three other respects. First, it focuses disproportionately on antisocial behavior, partly because this is my area of expertise and partly because the existing literature is especially deficient in studies of community effects on prosocial behavior. What we know about antisocial behavior in adolescence and how communities affect it is largely limited, however, to a few kinds of antisocial behaviors – principally those dealing with delinquency and the use of drugs, including alcohol, tobacco, and other drugs.

Second, the review focuses primarily on studies undertaken in the United States, partly because of my greater familiarity with them, but also because U.S. sociologists early on grounded their explanations of antisocial behavior in ecological and organizational theory.

Third, the topic is limited by the very few studies of the effects of community interventions on adolescent behavior. Most preventive programs have instead focused on either the school (see Mortimore, this volume), the young people themselves (see Compas, this volume), or their families (see Farrington, this volume).

Caveats, disclaimers, and clarifications

Explaining variation and development in antisocial behavior

There is considerable variation in antisocial behavior among societies and within them among residential communities and neighborhoods made up of diverse individuals and their families. Our understanding of individual, family, and community influences on antisocial behavior is gained primarily through cross-sectional comparisons of their effects. No study has successfully separated the effects of all these different levels in explaining antisocial behavior in longitudinal study designs (Reiss, 1986) and no individual, family, or community influences on offending have been demonstrated conclusively (Farrington, 1993).

Although the profound effect of culture and societal organization on the development and forms of antisocial behavior is recognized, this review scants these effects. Attention focuses primarily on what we know about community and neighborhood effects on individual and family development.

What is a community?

So far as we know, no form of prosocial or antisocial behavior is distributed uniformly in territorial space. There is considerable variation, for example, among places of different size and between the city and suburbs of a metropolis. A community, as that concept is used in this chapter, entails more than spatial variation; it involves social as well as ecological organization. A community is a demographic and spatially bounded collectivity characterized by dominant cultural or normative orientations, formal and informal collective controls, social cohesion, and local networks. To say that a community has these properties is not to say that all communities have them to the same degree. A community may also be made up of neighborhoods, spatial collectivities that symbolize even more local organization, participation, and control.

Like individuals, communities come, so to speak, in all sizes and shapes. They are less easily bounded in time and space than are individuals and their births and deaths, if such analogy be appropriate, are not usually recorded. Their structural and organizational properties are not easily measured. It is difficult to spatially bound neighborhoods within a community or to bound communities one from another. Moreover, communities are dynamic and can change considerably even in a brief time. The symbolic community or neighborhood changes with a person's age. These conceptual and related measurement problems make it difficult to draw generalizations about the effects of communities on the development of antisocial behavior during adolescence.[1]

Communities and locally based organizations

Communities and neighborhoods are collectivities. They are not to be confused, therefore, with ego neighborhoods, functional areas, or the decentralized territories of formal and bureaucratic organizations. An ego neighborhood is a symbolic place uniquely defined by whomever Ego considers neighbors or nigh-dwellers. By their successive overlapping, ego neighborhoods form an imbricated structure, not a collective organization. Communities are not synonymous with functional areas of places or groups, such as business or industrial zones, the turf of a delinquent gang, or the territory of syndicated crime. Moreover, they differ from the spatially bounded decentralized units of formal and bureaucratic organizations such as police precincts, school districts, religious parishes, and civil districts for housing, health, and welfare. Although localized within communities, these domains usually overlap two or more communities. The bounds of publicly supported and parochial middle and higher schools attended by adolescents, for example, usually transcend them. Privately supported schools commonly draw their student populations from different communities.

Beyond families, the three forms of organizations presumed to significantly affect adolescent development and behavior are schools, peer networks, and communities. No longitudinal study, however, has successfully separated individual, family, peer network, school, and community effects on adolescent antisocial or prosocial behavior (Farrington, 1993).

Studies of the effects of schools on human development and behavior rarely consider community effects. Community is generally treated as a structural property of schools and therefore confounded with school effects rather than treated as an independent source of variation. Schools are rarely a microcosm of the communities in which they are located. They represent only the children in attendance and their families. These families

1. Selected comparison of human development in communities that differ considerably, for example, of rural with urban communities, nevertheless can be instructive for further investigation even though hardly conclusive. An excellent example is the comparison of conduct disorder among ten-year-old children in Inner London and the Isle of Wight (Rutter, et al., 1975a; 1975b), a rural-urban comparison showing, as expected, that there were higher rates of conduct disorder among children in Inner London. The finding that these differences disappeared after controlling for adversity is intriguing since it suggests communities have no direct effects on conduct disorder, although given the considerable variation among communities it is hardly conclusive. Their finding for conduct disorder, nonetheless, is consistent with that of Robins (1966) who concluded that the neighborhood of children did not predict juvenile antisocial behavior after controlling for antisocial parents.

often do not even constitute a majority of the residents in a community. Schools lack the collective organization and formal and informal controls of communities – controls that operate beyond the hours, days, and months that children are in school or are not under the control of their families. It is at these times that adolescents are most likely to engage in deviant behavior. Moreover, the teachers, principals, and other employees of the school who exercise control over children are ordinarily not residents of the communities from which their pupils are drawn. One can therefore expect greater variation within communities than within schools, and the variations among communities should be greater than those among schools.

It should thus be evident that it is not easy to separate school from community effects. All too commonly, schools are simply equated with the communities in which they are located. A good example of this confounding is Coleman and Hoffer's (1987) study of adolescent academic achievement, which purports to investigate how the social capital of families and communities affects the achievement of students in public, private, and parochial schools in the United States. They do not, however, measure these effects independently. They are posited as a functional property of schools because of their auspices and location. There are no studies as yet that separate resource from human and social capital and none that also separates these from the moral capital of families, schools, and communities.

A more sophisticated attempt to separate school from community effects was made by Rutter and his colleagues (1979) in controlling for these effects by choosing schools from seemingly similar communities. Such controls for both school and community effects in studying internal processes in schools limits the structural explanation of both school and community variables, as Rutter and his colleagues (1979: 49–50) recognized. In their investigation, however, each school is a congeries of communities based on the proportion of children in each school coming from each type of geographical area. Consequently, youths from the same community will for various reasons be assigned to different schools, confounding community and school effects.

Despite the difficulty of separating school from community effects, it is a mistake to assume that a school is a representative slice of a community.

Separating school from community effects is also complicated by the fact that there are separable effects within schools such as classroom and teacher effects. Recent advances in the development of hierarchical modeling of school effects (Raudenbush, 1988) make it possible to separate individual, teacher, and classroom effects on academic outcomes such as academic achievement. There are substantial conceptual and operational problems, however, when other outcomes, such as antisocial behavior, are considered where the introduction of other school effects into the model is analytically and conceptually problematic.

The separation of school from community effects is further complicated by the presumed effect that adolescent peers have on behavior. Peer relationships and networks develop and have their effects in both schools and communities. And an adolescent's peer network may span a considerable age range and include persons within and without the school attended.

Because studies of adolescent behavior have not successfully separated community from peer network and school effects, conclusions in this chapter about community effects are confounded with school effects. This risk of confounding is shared with the chapter on school effects on adolescent behavior (see Mortimore, this volume).

Communities, like families and schools, organize differently for boys and girls. Yet little is known about how communities affect adolescent development of gender identities and of same and cross-sex relationships. Unfortunately, far more is known about how communities affect the antisocial behavior and development of adolescent males than females. This is partly because research on community effects on antisocial behavior has focused on delinquent offending, which is far more prevalent among males.[2] In addition, few investigations have focused on how communities affect the development and expression of prosocial behavior. Particularly striking is the relative absence of investigations of how communities affect cross-sex relationships that loom large in later adolescence, especially since there are reasons to conclude that community organization and controls have substantial effects on cross-sex behavior.[3] Because of these limitations, this review focuses disproportionately on antisocial behavior of adolescent males.

Why study adolescent development in communities?

Some years ago (Reiss, 1986: 29), I concluded that we cannot understand the respective roles of individual, family, and community in explaining

2. With the development of national crime victim surveys, increasing attention hass been paid to community variation in crime victimization rates. Yet little attention has been given to adolescent victimization, in part because of victim survey design. The sexual victimization of adolescents, both male and female, is particularly scanted in current victim surveys.

3. There is a growing literature on teenage pregnancy and sexually transmitted diseases among adolescents in the United States. Except for epidemiological studies of community variation in rates, however, the nature of these community risks is unexamined.

delinquent and criminal behavior until we develop and test "longitudinal designs that follow not only the changes in the structure, composition, and organization of communities but also the individuals who reside there so that we may partition the variation attributable to individuals and to communities" (Reiss, 1986: 29). At the same time, I drew attention to the fact that communities, like individuals (and their families) are dynamic units, changing considerably over time owing to the dynamic processes of populations, of persons, of organizations, and of communities. Accordingly, one must study individual, family, organizational (for example, schools), peer network, and community development and change in the same longitudinal design (Reiss, 1986: 29).

There are several major reasons why one should investigate human development and change in a longitudinal study of changing communities.

The first justification is that the main effects of individual and community are potentially confounded in all previous research on antisocial development. Two separate bodies of research have grown up, one attributing antisocial behavior to individual propensities and experiences and the other to differences in the normative and control organization of communities. One focuses on individual properties and the other on collective properties. Neither design has permitted the separation of these two main sources of effects.[4] There are many examples of this confounding of effects in the literature on delinquency. Sociologists conclude that living in a poor neighborhood increases one's chances of committing violent crimes whereas psychologists conclude that individuals with a propensity to aggression are more likely to commit violent crimes. How much variance is due to neighborhood effects and how much to individual differences is confounded because, for example, individuals with propensities to aggression may selectively move to such communities or such communities may socialize into aggressive behaviors.

A second reason for studying individual development in community environments is that one can expect strong interaction effects between individual or family behaviors and structural and behavioral properties of communities. William Wilson's work on poverty deals with such interaction effects. He concluded that the effects of poverty are different when the poverty is concentrated in urban ghetto neighborhoods where it creates social isolation than when the poor are not isolated from the main oppor-

4. Farrington made a related point in a recent paper (1993), concluding that no individual, family, or neighborhood effects on offending have been conclusively demonstrated because they have not been separately measured in a longitudinal design.

tunities of society. He hypothesized (1991: 10–12) that poor economic position leads to weak labor force attachment, a weak family control system, and illegal acquisition of resources only when poor people are concentrated and socially isolated in ghetto neighborhoods. When they are concentrated in neighborhoods that provide avenues to social mobility and collective controls, the poor have a greater sense of collective efficacy and their children are more likely to break the cycle of poverty.

A third reason for investigating the development of individuals in community systems is that one must expect reciprocal causal effects between community structure and delinquent behavior. Delinquency in a community can reach a threshold that leads to an exodus of stable residents and businesses, and employers from the community; the resulting instability contributes to a further increase in delinquency and a continuing downward spiral of delinquency (Bursik & Grasmick, 1992).

A fourth reason for studying communities as well as individuals is that communities, like individuals, are dynamic entities. Investigating individual development in communities with different conditions and rates of change permits, for example, an examination of the effect of stability of an environment on individual development.

A final reason for studying individual development in different communities is that it indicates where, when, and how to intervene to discourage antisocial development and behaviors and encourage prosocial development and behaviors and whether to intervene at the individual, family, or community level or in some combination of individual, family, and community levels. Current interventions deal with either individuals and their families – usually with professional technologies – or with communities on a macro-social level – usually with organizational or resource technologies. In studying the development of anti- and prosocial behavior in changing environments we should acquire better knowledge about strategic times, places, and conditions for intervention.

A major accelerated longitudinal study, designed to take these dynamic changes in individuals, families, and communities into account,[5] has been launched in the city of Chicago in the United States.

Nine cohorts of individuals ranging from the prenatal to age twenty-four will be measured for eight years in some seventy neighborhoods of the city and the dynamic changes in neighborhoods and communities will

5. The study, Project on Human Development in Chicago Neighborhoods, is co-directed by Felton Earls and Albert J. Reiss, Jr. under the Program on Human Development and Criminal Behavior, Harvard School of Public Health.

be studied as well. The design will analytically separate individual from community effects (Raudenbush, 1993).

Adolescence and adolescent transitions

One of the profound cultural and societal effects on adolescent behavior that we cannot take directly into account is the normative and collective organization of the adolescent status in our societies. Van Gennep (1909) first drew attention to the importance of ceremonies that mark an individual's transition from one status to another within a given society. He called these ceremonies rites of passage and concluded that these, like most rituals, have a tripartite sequence: separation followed by transition and then incorporation.[6] Of these, the most significant, perhaps, is the transitional or liminal[7] phase within the ceremony. He noted that when individuals or groups are in this ceremonial state of suspension where they are not as yet incorporated into a new status, they are a threat to themselves and to the larger group. In this state, they lie beyond the normal spheres of control and accordingly must be integrated into a new one, lest they disrupt the society. He observed also an internal structure to the liminal period in the ceremony with entry into the period, the period itself, and departure from the period of transition.[8]

Are we to say, by extension, that the absence of rites of passage for adolescents in our society leaves adolescents in a state of suspension? The critical periods for understanding adolescent development are thus the transitions to and from adolescence and a critical task is to understand the nature and effect of the prolonged liminal or transitional phase in which adolescents pose a threat to the larger group.

Transition to adolescence

Adolescence is a transitional status between childhood and adulthood, but it is less institutionalized in Western than in many other modern and premodern societies. Moreover, it is less institutionalized than either of the

6. Chapple and Coon (1942) distinguished rites of passage from rites of intensification. A rite of passage is a ceremony to restore the equilibrium of an individual with his system when there are changes that upset his equilibrium and that of others in the system in which he interacts. "These changes are caused by non-periodic crises which are repetitive for the group but not, as a rule, for the individual" (506). Examples are birth, puberty, marriage, and death. By contrast, a rite of intensification "restores equilibrium for the group after a disturbance affecting all or most of its members" (507).
7. Or threshold phase.
8. Van Gennep (1909) was also among the first to conclude that puberty or initiation rites do not coincide with physiological puberty. Rather, they are scheduled according to societal definitions and calendar.

two age-based status positions it borders and connects, childhood and adulthood. It is brought on by the social construction of puberty around signs that one is changing into a person with adult capacities. Yet adolescence is a marginal status in which the person no longer is accorded the privileged status of the child but yet does not enjoy the rights and responsibilities of the adult (Reiss, 1960).

Evidence of the low institutionalization of the adolescent status is the fact that most norms governing adolescent behaviors do not have specific adolescent behavior patterns as their reference point (Reiss, 1960: 309). In the United States, the status is recognized primarily by treating persons of this age who violate statutory law as wards of family or juvenile courts, the state acting in the role of *parens patriae*, legitimating state intervention for "child protection or welfare." Increasingly, too, special statutes defining juvenile offenses, so-called status offenses – running away, incorrigibility, and truancy – have been abolished and replaced with a language of children in need of supervision. This deep cultural ambivalence about whether persons of adolescent age are children or adults is also reflected in the growing tendency of U.S. courts to remand juveniles who commit more serious offenses to the criminal courts where they are tried as adults. What distinguishes them is less their age status than the seriousness of their offense.

There are few institutionalized expectations of how one is to behave as an adolescent in the sense that achieving those status expectations is a positive transitional link to adult status. This failure to deal with the transitions to and from the adolescent years appears to account for certain patterns of delinquency and antisocial behavior that we associate with these years and that have profound effects for communities in which adolescents spend most of their time. It might be said that children spend the bulk of their time in families, small play groups, and in smaller protected school environments, and adults spend their lives in child rearing, workplaces, and work associations, whereas adolescents are profoundly creatures of their residential community made up largely of their community organizations, their peer networks, and their schools.

Transition to adult status

We noted that at the transition from childhood to adolescence the community of peers and schools gradually replaced the family as the locus of socialization and control. In the transition out of adolescence and the teen years, youths are involved more and more in community life and the opportunities it affords.

Many low-income communities are characterized by a substantial proportion of youths who have dropped out of school. These communities provide relatively few legitimate opportunities for gainful employment and they lie primarily in low status and low paying jobs. The alternatives for dropouts are to migrate or to pursue a career in the illegitimate businesses endemic in these communities. Most remain. Early dropout is often linked to teenage pregnancy and cohabitation with a high rate of subsequent separation. Poverty and welfare and increasing drug use soon dominate the adolescents' lives. By contrast, transition to adult status is prolonged for middle-class adolescents.

The status consequences of lengthening the adolescent period in modern societies is a topic of much discussion. Prolonged adolescence results in greater dependency of the young on their families and expectations that they stay in school and be educated in preparation for adult roles. These normative expectations are not characteristic of all communities, however; they are generally rejected in communities with delinquent subcultures with other role models. These subcultural values and goals come into conflict with those of the surrounding society that emphasize status achievement through education and mandate that a child remain in school until legally permitted to leave and hold a regular job. In communities where adolescents reject schooling, habitual truancy is common and life becomes organized around the streets and peer networks that include older youths.

We explore below ways in which the transition to and from adolescence and the corresponding effects of the prolonged liminal state are critical, not only because of their low institutionalization but because of their links to community patterns of organization that either facilitate or exacerbate problems of growing up.

Community effects on antisocial behavior

A basic tenet of the Chicago human ecologists was that neighborhoods and communities vary considerably in their social organization. Some areas of cities, particularly those in the inner city, are socially disorganized, characterized by conflicting social values and norms and weakened formal and informal controls over the residents, a concept later designated as *differential social organization* of communities. Because the human ecologists presumed a causal relationship between weakened family and community controls, it followed that variations among neighborhoods should be reflected in variation in rates of delinquency and crime. Or, correlatively, variation in rates of delinquency and crime were an indication of weakened social organization (McKay, 1949: 34). Their studies in Chicago and more than a dozen American cities (Shaw & McKay, 1931; 1942; McKay, 1949: 34–6) led to several conclusions:

[1] delinquency rates vary considerably among areas of every city and they remain stable or increase over time;

[2] high rates in areas cannot be accounted for by nativity, nationality, or ethnic groups because the rates remain the same in high delinquency areas when there is a succession of these groups and because in the same types of areas, the different groups have approximately the same rates;

[3] the areas of highest delinquency rates in any city have external characteristics in common with areas with high rates in other cities;

[4] areas with high rates of delinquency also are characterized by other community problems, such as high morbidity and mortality, dependency, physical deterioration, and unemployment.

[5] areas of high delinquency are generally characterized by a conflict in values, largely due to the fact that it is organized around nonconventional as well as conventional institutions with which the child comes into contact.

Community variation in delinquency and crime rates characterizes cities in many different countries. But as Wikström (1991) and Wikström & Dolmén (1990: 16) pointed out, after studying variations in crime rates in Stockholm, the social problem residential areas in Stockholm are all in the outer communities of metropolitan Stockholm rather than in the inner cities as in the United States. It is there that the new immigrant groups reside (Wikström, 1991:120).

The basic paradigm of differential social organization (or social disorganization) leading to differential socialization of the young, particularly in the adolescent years, remains the basic paradigm of community effects on antisocial behavior. Colloquially phrased, the paradigm holds that bad communities produce bad kids.

This basic paradigm has been criticized on a number of grounds. A major criticism is that both individuals and communities are dynamic entities. One needs to understand how community as well as individual crime careers develop (Reiss, 1986: 26–9). Moreover, just as studies of individual development fail to take account of the dynamic nature of the community and social contexts in which individuals grow up, so studies of community development and change fail to take account of how individual development and selective migration change community structure and processes.

A second major criticism, of which Shaw and McKay were well aware, is that the basic paradigm fails to take into account the considerable variability in antisocial behavior and delinquency within as well as among communities. In some communities where predatory delinquency rates are low, some persons nonetheless become delinquent and later have criminal careers. Correlatively, even in the highest crime rate communities of a metropolis, the majority are law-abiding juveniles and adults. Their number may even vary by street or neighborhood within a larger community (Burnham & Burnham, 1970; Suttles, 1968). Moreover, Thrasher noted that even in gangland there were streets and areas where one did not find gangs and that gangs could be found in the interstitial areas bounding middle-class areas or within them (Thrasher, 1927: 19).

A third criticism is that most youths desist early on from delinquent behavior even in high crime rate communities. What needs accounting for is how and why communities vary not only in their prevalence rates but also in their persistence and desistance rates for criminal careers. This suggests the need for longitudinal studies to disentangle community from other factors in explaining variation in individual criminal careers.

Family and community

Recent investigations by Kupersmidt and her colleagues (1992) demonstrate that both families and neighborhoods influence preadolescent and adolescent children's social and behavioral adjustment (1992: 18). They tested the effect of four models of neighborhood influence and eight types of family structures on the adjustment of second through fifth grade children living in twenty-nine neighborhoods of a North Carolina city. Four types of neighborhood influence were tested: high risk of maladjustment; protective environment inhibiting maladjustment; potentiator low risk; and interactional where the interaction between individual and neighborhood risk increases the probability of maladjustment. Each child was classified into one of eight types of families based on dichotomies of race, income, and family structure (single- versus two-parent homes).

All four models of neighborhood influence were supported. Low socioeconomic status (SES) neighborhoods operated as independent additive risk factors with family type in predictions of delinquency. Middle SES neighborhoods operated as protective factors for reducing aggression among children from high risk families, interacted with family type to produce a poor fit between person and environment that increased peer rejection, and potentiated the development of home play companions for children from low risk families (Kupersmidt, 1992: 2).

Peer networks in communities

With the transition to adolescence, young people live in a society of their own, a society of peers. Coleman (1961: 312) concluded that the family no longer is "a psychological home" for adolescents, and numerous studies show that adolescents spend the large majority of their time with peers in school and away from home. Consequently, the home has less opportunity to mold them than does the school or the community. This varies by type of community as well as by social status with lower status youth living in ghetto communities spending more of their time with peers (Suttles, 1968).

The prototypic antisocial behavior of adolescents – delinquency – is committed with others. The bulk of adolescent offending is co-offending, i.e., it occurs with other adolescents. Few criminal careers are made up entirely of solo offending (Reiss, 1988).[9] The prototypic delinquent behavior has three major characteristics that are determined by the community in which the adolescent lives and which set adolescent offending apart from much postadolescent offending.

The first characteristic is that delinquent offending is localized within the neighborhood. Suttles (1968: 207) showed that in the Addams slum neighborhood he studied intensively, almost two-thirds of all the boys' offenses were committed within the local neighborhood; almost one-half of these were committed within less than a block from the home of the nearest co-offender. It was somewhat less for the London cohort but more than one-half of both the sample males and their co-offenders committed the offense within one mile of their home (Reiss & Farrington, 1991: 388).

A second characteristic is that the bulk of a delinquent's co-offenders are selected from the neighborhood network of peers. This appears to be as much the case in Sweden (Sarnecki, 1986) as in London (Reiss & Farrington, 1991: 389) and Chicago (Suttles, 1968: 207). In the London cohort, the residence of sample males was close to that of their co-offenders; in 60 percent of the cases, the two addresses were within one mile of each other and in three-fourths of the cases within two miles (Reiss & Farrington, 1991: Table 9). Some of this propinquity in selection of co-

9. There is variation by type of offense. Some contend that status offenses are least likely to involve co-offending, especially running away from home. There is little evidence on co-offending in status offending.

offenders arises from the selection of brothers as co-offenders – a family rather than a community basis of selection.[10] Propinquity in the selection of co-offenders declines with age. In the London cohort, it declined from 100 percent at ages ten to thirteen living within one mile distance to 53 percent at ages twenty-one to thirty-two (Reiss & Farrington, 1991: 389). For adolescents one's neighbors are thus both victims and co-offenders.

A third characteristic derives from the fact that most offenders and their co-offenders do not belong to organized delinquent gangs.[11] Rather, offenders are linked in a loose web of affiliations (Reiss, 1986; Sarnecki, 1982; 1986). Sarnecki (1982: 140) found that in a medium-sized Swedish city only 13 percent of the 1,162 pairings in an offense persisted beyond six months and only 4 percent of the pairs were still offending together after one and one-half years. He also identified clusters of peers and concluded that most existed for relatively short periods of time; only one, the largest of his clusters, existed for the entire six years of his study (Sarnecki, 1982: 153). Suttles (1968: 157–67) identified thirty-two street-corner groups in his Addams neighborhood in Chicago and concluded that there was considerable turnover in their membership, partly owing to residential mobility. Klein and Crawford (1967: 66) found in their study of black gangs in Los Angeles that many members affiliate for only brief periods of a few days to a few months. Klein (1969: 68) offered evidence from his study of gangs that co-offending even among persons from the same network does not in itself demonstrate that the delinquent event represents the outcome of gang group processes.

A substantial proportion of all delinquent boys in a neighborhood, moreover, do not affiliate with these network clusters (Short & Strodtbeck, 1965: 56–7; Suttles, 1968: 173). Although few boys are isolates, most do not affiliate with enduring groups that are designated delinquent gangs.

Community stability and change

Ecological models of community stability and change generally associate rapid change with destabilization of community control. Accordingly, population turnover and increasing heterogeneity in the community are

10. It is difficult to disentangle family from community residence, though in the London cohort co-offending among brothers was most likely to occur when the brothers were close in age and when the male sibship was large. Too few brothers lived away from the sample male to determine whether propinquity of residence was a factor in selecting siblings as co-offenders.

11. There is considerable controversy about the group nature of delinquency and for that reason I developed the concept of co-offending; whether or not co-offenders or those offending alone are members of organized groups or gangs is a problem of definition for which there is, as yet, no agreement. Bursik and Grasmick (1993) provided a recent excellent discussion of the pitfalls and problems in defining groups and gangs.

expected to lead to an increase in delinquency and other antisocial forms of behavior linked to weakened community controls.

The relationship of delinquency to population turnover and increasing heterogeneity in a community, with consequent weakening of community controls and a rise in delinquency, is well illustrated by Rieder's study of Canarsie (1985), a section of New York City in which neighborhoods occupied by Jews and Italians were undergoing change with an influx of black Americans. Italian neighborhoods were more tightly organized and offered far greater resistance to this influx than did the Jewish ones, although the Jews gradually offered increasing resistance. What is striking is how these neighborhoods lent support to the young people who increasingly turned to violence to resist the movement. Waves of violence toward new black neighbors were organized and condoned. Initially, violence was confined to fighting between teenage boys but gradually it encompassed bombing of houses occupied by blacks, a high school race riot, and growing private acts of vengeance among young persons. Strong support for maintaining the neighborhood and strong community controls were thus a source of increased violence by young people.

Bursik and Grasmick (1992: 250) offer evidence on the complexity of the relationship between demographic change in communities and its effect on delinquency and crime. They concluded that neighborhoods similar in composition may be characterized by significantly different trends in their delinquency rates. In their study of continuity and change in delinquency rates of seventy-seven Chicago communities over a forty-year period, they observed that the average delinquency rate is higher in neighborhoods with elevated rates of unemployment and the rate of delinquency accelerates with increasing unemployment (1992: 261). Even when the rate of unemployment slows down, the delinquency rate continues to accelerate. This ongoing effect on delinquency is consistent with the generally held view that local institutions are less controlling in neighborhoods and communities characterized by high rates of unemployment. Consequently, one should not expect that the delinquency rate in a community will respond directly to increased employment. Rather, it will depend on how rapidly changes in employment strengthen control by local institutions.

Bursik and Grasmick (1992: 261) also found that although a significant increase in the nonwhite population of Chicago communities was accompanied by a significant increase in the delinquency rate, nonwhite communities that were moving towards stability showed significant declines in delinquency rates. This finding, as they note, is consistent with McKay's observation (1949: 39; 1967: 115) that the stabilization of conventional local institutions and the elimination of conflicting illegal ones may lower delinquency rates in neighborhoods formerly characterized by traditions of illegal behavior. The strengthening of local institutions can thus decelerate or alter a community's career in crime (Reiss, 1986: 17).

Effects of community normative and control structures

Despite the fact that most delinquents are linked in only a loose web of affiliations in their neighborhood, the normative and control structure of communities can have a considerable impact on the structure and patterns of delinquency. Two of the principal ways it does so are through community subcultures of crime and delinquency and the generation of territorial gangs. Each of these is illustrated below.

Whether or not most delinquency is the result of group or gang processes, some groups are organized around conflict relations with others, a fact first noted by Thrasher (1927) in his study of 1,313 gangs in Chicago in the twenties. Thrasher designated sections of the city as gangland where gangs evolved from play groups into delinquent groups and some finally into adult criminal gangs. Conflict gangs, for Thrasher, were territorially organized and located in interstitial areas of the city. They protected their territory or turf from intrusion by other gangs by violence. Violent conflict gangs continue to exist in the largest American cities and, as in the 1920s, so in the 1990s, they often organize in the ethnic neighborhoods of the new immigrants.

Recent research on gang homicide in Chicago by Curry and Spergel (1988: 400) concluded that the community correlates of gang homicide rates and of delinquency rates differ. The principal correlates of community delinquency rates are poverty and unemployment whereas community disorganization in the immigrant areas is the principal correlate of gang homicide. Immigration and settlement in urban areas disrupts local community institutions of control, and ethnic group controls are weakened, especially for the adolescents.

Violent gangs in the United States also arise in black and Hispanic ghettos over the control of marketing specific kinds of drugs.[12] The street marketing of drugs is localized in certain neighborhoods, and gang homicides involving disputes over the territory in which drugs can be marketed are largely responsible for the rise in the young black male homicide rate in the United States.

12. The fact that arrested youths are usually processed as juveniles rather than adults creates considerable opportunity in the marketing of drugs. Moreover, the economic opportunity of the drug market makes it an especially attractive one for adolescents, even those under age twelve.

Subcultural norms and subcultural communities

The social and cultural system of lower class neighborhoods gives rise to different subcultures that shape the nature of antisocial behavior in a given neighborhood. Several such subcultures have been identified in major metropolitan communities but it is not known how extensively they replicate in other cities or whether other subcultures shape delinquent behavior.

Spergel (1964) provided the most theoretically and empirically grounded subcultural explanation of variation in delinquent patterns among neighborhoods. Building on Cloward and Ohlin's (1960) opportunity theory of delinquency, he identified three major subcultures: racket, conflict, and theft subcultures. They differ in their emphasis on legitimate and illegitimate opportunities for achieving success, the desirable role models, and their status goals. The racket subculture arises in poor communities because the illegal opportunities of rackets provide an alternative to the limited available means of occupational success in their neighborhoods. The major role models are the affluent racketeers who symbolize success (Spergel, 1964: 34–8). Conflict subcultures are built around quite different values that shape a community's delinquent patterns. Although aspiring to modest working class occupational success, the neighborhood subculture stresses that achievement in the adolescent delinquent society is based on reputation for gang fighting: Achieving a "rep" for toughness and violence is the status goal of adolescents in the conflict subcultural neighborhood. Although theft is a major delinquent activity in all the subcultural neighborhoods, it is the major means to valued material success in theft subcultures. In the theft subcultural neighborhood, material goods, including flashy cars, fine clothes, and money are the criteria of a successful status (Spergel, 1964: 48).

Although these subcultures shape the system of adolescent status achievement in some lower-class neighborhoods, Spergel was careful to emphasize that delinquents should not be regarded as limiting their behavior to these dominant value constellations because boys in all neighborhoods show versatility in their delinquent behavior. Rather, these are "constellations of delinquent behavior that differentiate delinquent subcultures" and not "behavior patterns that may be common to delinquents regardless of type of lower-class neighborhood" (Spergel, 1964: 29).

Spergel concluded that there was little evidence that the communities he studied had a retreatist subculture built around drug use and addiction. Perhaps his failure to delineate a drug subculture resulted from his focus on addiction and use rather than on drug marketing, which he regarded as one of the rackets. In the United States, many lower status urban neighborhoods and street blocks now have drug markets that dominate the social life of the neighborhood. Drug selling becomes a major means to material success and status achievement, even for very young adolescents. The drug dealer represents an alternative life style and symbol of material success to young males, especially in black ghetto communities, but also in immigrant communities where the importation of drugs is endemic.

Reciprocal causation: Individual and community

There are no studies of reciprocal causation documenting the feedback effects of the accumulation of individual delinquency on the community and of how the changed community in turn affects the likelihood of individual delinquency and types of delinquent careers. Nonetheless, cross-sectional and some longitudinal studies provide evidence to infer such relationships.

One basic model posits that predatory crime causes a deterioration in communities, the deteriorated condition in turn giving rise to further predatory crime (Di Iulio, 1989). The model posits that a high prevalence of delinquents in a community causes high victimization of local residents, industries, businesses, and other local institutions such as schools. High victimization leads to selective out-migration of the more stable residents who leave for communities with less crime. Businesses and industries with higher costs due to the destructive effects of predatory crime also leave the community and the curriculum of schools is adapted to high truancy, early dropout, and disciplining rather than teaching. These changed conditions in residents and local institutions create conditions that lead to an increase in the prevalence rate. These include a permanent underclass in which delinquency is endemic (Wilson, 1987; 1991) and low economic development which further truncates opportunities for regular employment. The high prevalence rate of delinquency coupled with high adult criminality in the community also leads to the loss of the male population to jails and prisons. Consequently, the area becomes populated by single mothers whose male children lack stable male role models. These conditions increase the prevalence rate of delinquents who further increase the crime victimization rate, which further accelerates community deterioration. These communities may also disproportionately attract delinquent and criminal persons from other neighborhoods.

Charles Murray (1990) contended that a permanent underclass exists in all major cities in the United States and that it is not uniquely a black ghetto underclass. Furthermore, it is not unique to American cities. He referred to the underclass as "a subset of poor people who chronically live off mainstream society (directly through welfare and indirectly through crime) without participating in it" (1990: 4). A permanent underclass, he concluded, has emerged in major cities in Britain and is developing in some European countries as well. One may question his argument as to the reasons for the permanent underclass and its extent in the United Kingdom, and his conclusion that we don't know how to reverse the conditions that create an underclass contrasts with the less pessimistic public policy perspective of William Wilson (1991).

Role model variation among communities

Evidence from ethnographic studies of communities shows they vary considerably in the adult role models made available to adolescents. Spergel (1964), for example, emphasized the importance of the racketeer as a role model in the racket subculture. Other studies emphasize the importance of the drug dealer as a role model in drug marketing neighborhoods.

Eli Anderson (1990: 69) emphasized the importance of role relationships in communities and their effect on antisocial behavior. He particularly emphasized the relationships between what he calls "old heads" in the traditional black community and young boys. The acknowledged role of the old head was "to teach, support, encourage, and in effect socialize young men to meet their responsibilities with regard to the work ethic, family life, the law, and decency" (Anderson, 1990: 69). Their relationship was that of mentor and protégé, the old head offering guidance and moral counseling to youth in the community. In the black community, female old heads are as important for girls as male old heads are for boys. But, Anderson contended, those patterns have changed. Old heads have lost prestige because communities no longer offer meaningful employment to young black people; many are unemployed and too demoralized to listen to the lessons of old heads (Anderson, 1990: 72). Equally important, he contended, is the effect of the rise of a black middle class that has abandoned the neighborhood to a black underclass. Anderson's work in black communities raises again the question of the role of a permanent underclass, its localization in urban ghetto neighborhoods, and its patterns of socialization into antisocial behavior of adolescents.

Little is known about how prosocial role models available to adolescents affect their prosocial development. The success of minority persons in sports and entertainment appears to influence prosocial development of minority youth, yet these appear to be more mass than local effects. Just how much influence, if any, local community elites in sports, schooling, and religion have upon individual development is unknown.

Concentration effects in communities

Growing up in a poor community

For many years investigators have pointed to a moderate relationship between poverty and antisocial behavior, especially for crime and delinquency. The links between the two have not been clearly established and the relationship leaves open the question of why so many poor people do not behave in criminal ways. Recent theorizing and research by Wilson (1991: 10–11) and others point to the importance of the concentration of poor people in ghetto neighborhoods and their social isolation from the more mobile poor as major causes in the development of antisocial behavior. Wilson's basic argument is formulated as follows:

> "Poor individuals with similar educational and occupational skills confront different risks of persistent poverty depending on the neighborhoods they reside in, as embodied in the formal and informal networks to which they have access, their prospects of marriage or remarriage to a stably employed mate, and the families or households to which they belong. Moreover, a social context that includes poor schools, inadequate job information networks, and a lack of legitimate employment opportunities not only gives rise to weak labor force attachment, but increases the probability that individuals will be constrained to seek income derived from illegal or deviant activities. This weakens their attachment to the legitimate labor market even further. (1991: 10)

Growing up in a ghetto neighborhood where there is the concentration of a more or less permanent underclass – a persistent concentration of the poor – generates both a weak labor force attachment and a moving to illegal alternatives to earn a living. Moreover, Wilson contends, in the more socially isolated ghetto neighborhoods, individuals develop a sense of low self-efficacy and doubt that they can achieve socially approved goals (Wilson, 1991: 11). A central hypothesis of this theory is that an individual's feelings of low self-efficacy grow out of weak labor force attachments that are reinforced by similarly situated persons in the neighborhood; the result is lower collective self-efficacy (Bandura, 1982) in the inner city ghetto. By contrast, growing up in a poor neighborhood where the families are employed and some individuals are upwardly mobile out of the community promotes a sense of self-efficacy and a search for legitimate opportunities to get ahead.

Growing up in a violent community

There are no longitudinal studies that specifically examine the differential effect of growing up in communities that vary in their violence rates or the effect of violent communities on an individual's rate of violent offending. Ethnographic studies of communities and macro-cross-sectional surveys provide support for the inference that communities affect individual rates of violent offending. Because many adults do not reside in the neighborhoods or communities in which they grew up, it is important that we establish this relationship for adolescents.

Growing up and residing in communities where the friendship and neighboring networks are sparse, where teenage peer groups are largely unsupervised, and where organizational networks are rare and participation in them low is associated with high crime rates. Sampson and Groves' (1989: 789) analysis of British Crime Survey data from 1982 and 1984 disclosed that the prevalence of unsupervised teenage peer groups has the most substantial effect on rates of robbery and violence by strangers. Moreover, the survey data show that the density of local friend networks, as measured by the proportion of friends living in the neighborhood, also had a significant negative effect on robbery rates. Finally, their analysis shows that the lower the organizational participation by residents, the higher the robbery and stranger violence rates. Taylor, Gottfredson, and Brewer (1984: 320) similarly found that the higher the proportion of residents in neighborhood blocks who belonged to an organization to which coresidents belong, the lower the violent crime rates for assaults, homicide, and rape.

Housing tenure, family patterns, and delinquency patterns

Communities vary considerably in their housing patterns and tenure. Some housing patterns such as public housing in the United States and housing estates in the United Kingdom often have higher delinquency rates than the surrounding community, raising the question of whether the pattern of public housing and its tenancy affects delinquency. Housing patterns are linked to the types of families who occupy them. Consequently, it is difficult to disentangle the effects of family structure from housing tenure and of either from the communities in which they are located.

Research by Bottoms and Wiles (1986) provided evidence that public housing is not in and of itself a factor in delinquency since, at least prior to the Thatcher government, a great many public housing estates were middle class with lower rates of delinquency than public housing in lower class areas (1986: 168). They also showed that although there is considerable variation in all housing sectors in Britain (1986: 123), public sector housing and privately rented housing are the two housing sectors with the highest offender rates.

To understand the variation in offender rates among housing estates bottoms and Wiles investigated the housing allocation process. What they learned is that the bureaucratic process of housing allocation accounted for differences in crime rates among similarly situated housing estates. Two patterns of housing allocation particularly resulted in high delinquency rates. One was concentrating families with young children and single mothers with children in some housing estates. When coupled with high transiency in the housing estate, this led to low community control over male youths with concomitant high rates of vandalism and high theft and burglary rates (1986: 128), a finding confirmed more generally by Sampson and Groves (1989) for American cities. The other housing pattern resulted from clearance of a slum with a notorious reputation for youth gangs, adult rackets, and violent crimes. The inhabitants were rehoused in the new housing estate and soon recreated the norms and behaviors of their slum neighborhoods (Bottoms & Wiles 1986: 127–8).

There are clearly two major implications here. The first is that housing allocation policies in a community can markedly affect the kind and rate of offending behavior in a community. The second is that the concentration of large numbers of families with young children and especially of single families with male youths in a community without strong community controls over their behavior will engender vandalism, gang violence and theft subcultures.

Moving among communities

Although there is some disagreement about the validity and reliability of self-reports of delinquent and criminal behavior, the results generally show that there is more serious crime in poor neighborhoods than in those where residents are well off. Although most explanatory theories assume that living in a poor neighborhood with high delinquency and crime rates increases the likelihood that one will become delinquent or criminal, there are no adequate tests of these hypotheses. Because there is considerable movement among residential communities that vary in their crime rates, one way to test for community effects on delinquent behavior is to determine whether movement of families and their children from poor to better off neighborhoods reduces their delinquency whereas movement from affluent to poor increases the rate. Only two studies in the United States have tested this hypothesis (Reiss & Rhodes, 1961; Johnstone, 1978). These show that delinquency rates increase for movers from low to high crime school areas and decrease for those who move from high to low crime school areas. One difficulty with such evidence is that there is a selective migration of families. Families usually move because of changed circumstances so it is difficult to determine whether change in a child's behavior after the family moves reflects the influence of the new neighborhood or the effect of factors that led to the move. Families may move to a poor neighborhood because of changed economic circumstances of the family, for example, a divorce may result in reduced income for the spouse responsible for the children and she moves to public housing in a low income area. It would be difficult in that case to determine whether an increase in delinquency was due to the disruption of the family structure and the changed income level or to increased exposure to delinquency.

Macro-social interventions: Schools and communities

Few interventions to discourage adolescent antisocial behavior or encourage prosocial behavior focus on changing some aspect of communities. Most are designed either to change adolescents and their behavior patterns directly or to affect those behaviors and patterns indirectly by changing some aspect of their internal school environment. Only in rare instances are macro-social interventions designed to affect adolescent behavior by changing systemic features of communities. We have selected examples below to illustrate the nature, significance, and limits of community interventions to affect adolescent development.

The form that interventions should take to prevent or control delinquency appears to vary with the stage of adolescence. Thornberry and colleagues (1991: 32) provided evidence that commitment to school and delinquent behavior have strong reciprocal relations. Low commitment to school leads to high delinquency which in turn further decreases school commitment. This argues for focusing on interventions in schools to raise the commitment. They contended that interventions that attempt to break this reciprocal causality should be particularly effective in the early stages of adolescence. Such interventions become less salient for later adolescence, however, because work is more salient for dropouts and for adolescents at the point of transition from school to community (Thornberry et al., 1991: 32). One option is to intervene at the individual level by increasing job skill training, but skills are often unrelated to the jobs available in a community and of little value when job opportunities are few. Accordingly, interventions to increase job opportunities for youths with on-the-job skill training seem more salient in later adolescence and early adulthood.

Another form of intervention is to affect child development by moving families from low to higher income communities where greater opportunities prevail. The Gutreaux program in Chicago which mandated by court order the removal of low income black families from public housing in the inner city to private housing in Chicago and its suburbs is an example. Beginning in 1976, some 3,900 poor families who had lived much of their lives as part of the inner city underclass and many of whom are second generation welfare recipients have been moved from public housing to private housing in better off communities (Rosenbaum & Popkin, 1990). Without any other interventions than their removal, the evaluation found that location of families in middle-class suburbs with employment opportunities substantially altered the employment patterns of families. There are clear spill-over effects for children in these families (Rosenbaum & Popkin, 1990; 1991).

Jones and Offord (1989) devised a community intervention program to reduce antisocial behavior in poor children by nonschool skill development. Dubbed PALS for "participate and learn skills," the design of the intervention called for introducing PALS into an experimental housing project. Comparisons were made with a control housing project. The basic objective of PALS was to advance children toward higher individual skill levels in recreational activities and to integrate the children into community recreational leagues. Unexpectedly, the Boys and Girls Clubs of Canada opened a large new recreational facility directly abutting the control housing project, thereby compromising the control comparison. The main difference between the two projects was that PALS recruited nonparticipant children systematically and aggressively.

Nonobtrusive measures were utilized to evaluate events such as turning in false fire alarms and the number of police charges and housing security guard reports per month. There were either no or marginal spill-over effects on school performance. Clear changes were found, however, on unobtrusive measures of antisocial behavior outside the home and school.

Program resources declined after the first year and the number of participants declined in the next two years. Effects were evaluated sixteen months following intervention. The end of intervention produced significant rebound effects specific to the changes that had occurred during the interventions. Clearly, the prosocial impact of the intervention declined without continuing reinforcement and integration into ongoing leagues that could continue skill development (Jones & Offord, 1989: 748). The effect of short-term nonschool skill development on the antisocial behavior of poor children is accordingly limited.

The major lessons to be learned from this community intervention experiment are that unanticipated social changes can interfere with a planned experimental intervention and that without continuing resources and continued reinforcement the effects of nonschool skill development on antisocial behavior are short-term.

Epilogue

Two intellectual traditions, psychology and sociology, have molded inquiry into prosocial and antisocial behavior. The emphasis in the psychological traditions has fallen more upon investigating conduct disorders and problem behaviors whereas sociology has dealt disproportionately with law violations. Neither tradition has expended as much effort on studying prosocial behavior. The two intellectual traditions bifurcate in another way. The psychological tradition has emphasized the important influence of individual factors whereas the sociologist has emphasized the importance of social environments. They converge in emphasizing the importance of family factors, though the emphasis of sociologists is more on structural than nurturing properties of families. There has also been some convergence in the study of peer relations with the psychologists focusing more on adolescent friendships and the sociologists on delinquent gangs. Only recently have both disciplines turned their attention to the investigation of peer networks.

There have been significant departures from these traditions. Psychologists have increasingly recognized the importance of the school environment for the development of children. The seminal research of Rutter and his colleagues (1979) has made significant contributions to demonstrating that structure and process in schools make an important difference in adolescent development. Sociologists early on recognized the importance of community environment in shaping behavior but their research focused on the influence of community risks of antisocial behavior with little attention to individual and family influences.

Perhaps not surprisingly, there is thus a paucity of research focusing on community and individual influences on adolescent behaviors and development. Yet, as the early section of this chapter contends, there are persuasive reasons why these influences should be measured independently in longitudinal research that captures both the dynamic features of individual and family development and change and community change.

Not surprisingly also, most interventions to discourage the development of antisocial behavior or enhance prosocial behavior of adolescents focus on individuals or schools where the intervention can be more carefully controlled. Family and community interventions are less amenable to controlled interventions, yet it seems reasonable to conclude that interventions must pay more attention to the interaction and feedback effects between individuals, families, peer networks, and school and community environments.

References

Anderson, E. (1990). *Street Wise: Race, Class, and Change in an Urban Community.* Chicago: University of Chicago Press.

Bandura, A. (1982). Self-efficacy mechanisms in human agency. *American Psychologist,* 37, 122–47.

Bottoms, A. E., & Wiles, P. (1986). Housing tenure and residential community crime careers in Britain. In *Communities and Crime,* ed. A. J. Reiss, Jr. & M. Tonry, pp. 101–62. Chicago: University of Chicago Press.

Burnham, D., & Burnham, S. (1970). El Barrio's worst block is not all that bad. In *Crime in the City,* ed. D. Glaser, pp. 154–62. New York: Harper & Row.

Bursik, R. J., Jr., & Grasmick, H. G. (1992). Longitudinal neighborhood profiles in delinquency: The decomposition of change. *Journal of Quantitative Criminology,* 8, 247–63.

Bursik, R. J., Jr., & Grasmick, H. G. (1993). *Neighborhoods and Crime: The Dimensions of Effective Community Control.* New York: Lexington Books.

Chapple, E. D., & Coon, C. S. (1942). *Principles of Anthropology.* New York: Henry Holt & Co.

Cloward, R. A., & Ohlin, L. E. (1960). *Delinquency and Opportunity.* Glencoe: Free Press.

Coleman, J. S. (1961). *The Adolescent Society: The Social Life of the Teenager and Its Impact on Education.* Glencoe: Free Press.

Coleman, J. S., & Hoffer, T. (1987). *Public and Private Schools: The Impact of Communities.* New York: Basic Books.

Curry, G. D., & Spergel, I. A. (1988). Gang homicide, delinquency, and community. *Criminology,* 26, 381–405.

Di Iulio, J, J., Jr. (1989). The impact of inner city crime. *The Public Interest,* 96, 28–46.

Farrington, D. (1993). Have any individual, family, or neighborhood influences on offending been demonstrated conclusively? In *Integrating Individual and Ecolog-*

ical Aspects on Crime, ed. D. P. Farrington, R. J. Sampson, & P-O Wikström. Stockholm: National Council on Crime Prevention, Sweden.

Johnstone, J. W. C. (1978). Social class, social areas, and delinquency. *Sociology & Social Research*, 63, 49–72.

Jones, M. B., & Offord, D. R. (1989). Reduction of antisocial behavior in poor children by non-school skill-development. *Journal of Child Psychology & Psychiatry*, 30, 737–50.

Klein, M. (1969). On group context of delinquency. *Sociology & Social Research*, 54, 63–71.

Klein, M., & Crawford, L. Y. (1967). Groups, gangs, and cohesiveness. *Journal of Research in Crime and Delinquency*, 4, 142–65.

Kupersmidt, J., Griesler, P., De Rossier, M., Patterson, C., & Davis, P. (1992). *Family and Neighborhood Influences on Children's Social and Behavioral Adjustment.* Chapel Hill: University of North Carolina, Department of Psychology.

McKay, H. D. (1949). The neighborhood and child conduct. *The Annals of the American Academy of Political and Social Science*, 261, 32–41.

(1967). A note on trends in rates of delinquency in certain areas of Chicago. In *Task Force Report: Juvenile Delinquency and Youth Crime*, The President's Commission on Law Enforcement and the Administration of Justice, pp. 114–18. Washington, DC: U.S. Government Printing Office.

Murray, C. (1990). The British underclass. *The Public Interest*, 99, 4–28.

Raudenbush, S. W. (1988). Educational applications of hierarchical linear models: A review. *Journal of Educational Statistics*, 13, 85–116.

(1993). Modeling individual and community effects of deviance over time: Multilevel statistical models. In *Integrating Individual and Ecological Aspects on Crime*, ed. D. P. Farrington, R. J. Sampson, & P.-O. Wikström. Stockholm: National Council for Crime Prevention, Sweden.

Reiss, A. J., Jr. (1960). Sex offenses: The marginal status of the adolescent. *Law and Contemporary Problems*, 25, 309–33.

(1986). Why are communities important in understanding crime? In *Communities and Crime*, ed. A. J. Reiss, Jr. & M. Tonry, pp. 1–33. Chicago: University of Chicago Press.

(1988). Co-offending and criminal careers. In *Crime and Justice: A Review of Research*, ed. M. Tonry & N. Morris, Vol. 10, pp. 117–70. Chicago: University of Chicago Press.

Reiss, A. J., Jr., & Farrington, D. (1991). Advancing knowledge about co-offending: Results from a prospective longitudinal survey of London males. *Journal of Criminal Law and Criminology*, 82, 360–95.

Reiss, A. J., Jr., & Rhodes, A. L. (1961). The distribution of juvenile delinquency in the social class structure. *American Sociological Review*, 26, 729–32.

Rieder, J. (1985). *Canarsie: The Jews and Italians of Brooklyn Against Liberalism.* Cambridge, Mass.: Harvard University Press.

Robins, J. (1966). *Deviant Children Grown Up.* Baltimore: Williams & Wilkins.

Rosenbaum, J., & Popkin, S. (1990). *Economic and Social Impacts of Housing Integration.* Northwestern University: Center for Urban Affairs and Policy Research.

Rosenbaum, J., & Popkin, S. (1991). Employment and earnings of low-income blacks who move to middle-class suburbs. In *The Urban Underclass*, ed. C. Jencke & P. Peterson. Washington, DC: The Brookings Institution.

Rutter, M., Cox, A., Tupling, C., Berger, M., & Yule, W. (1975a). Attainment and adjustment in two geographical areas: I. The prevalence of psychiatric disorder. *British Journal of Psychiatry*, 126, 453–509.

Rutter, M., Maughan, S., Mortimore, P., & Ouston, J. (1979). *Fifteen Thousand Hours: Secondary Schools and Their Effects on Children*. London: Open Books.

Rutter, M., Yule, B., Quinton, D., Rowlands, O., Yule, W., & Berger, M. (1975b). Attainment and adjustment in two geographical areas: III. Some factors accounting for area differences. *British Journal of Psychiatry*, 126, 520–33.

Sampson, R. J., & Groves, W. B. (1989). Community structure and crime: Testing social disorganization theory. *American Journal of Sociology*, 94, 774–802.

Sarnecki, J. (1982). *Brottslighet och Kamraatrelationer: Studie av ungbrottsligheten i en svensk kommun* (Criminality and friend relations: A study of juvenile criminality in a Swedish community). Stockholm: National Council for Crime Prevention, Sweden.

(1986). *Delinquent Networks*. Report No. 11986:1. Stockholm: National Council for Crime Prevention, Sweden.

Shaw, C. R., & McKay, H. D. (1931). Social factors in juvenile delinquency: A study of the community, the family, and the gang in relation to delinquent behavior. In *Report on the Causes of Crime*, Vol. 2, no. 13, National Commission on Law Observance and Enforcement. Washington, DC, U.S. Government Printing Office.

Shaw, C. R., & McKay, H. D. (1942). *Juvenile Delinquency and Urban Areas: A Study of Delinquents in Relation to Differential Characteristics of Local Communities in American Cities*. Chicago: University of Chicago Press.

Short, J. F., Jr., & Strodtbeck, F. L. (1965). *Group Processes and Delinquency*. Chicago: University of Chicago Press.

Spergel, I. (1964). *Racketville, Slumtown, Haulburg: An Exploratory Study of Delinquent Subcultures*. Chicago: The University of Chicago Press.

Suttles, G. D. (1968). *The Social Order of the Slum: Ethnicity and Territory in the Inner City*. Chicago: The University of Chicago Press.

Taylor, R. S., Gottfredson, S., & Brower, S. (1984). Block crime and fear: Defensible space, local social ties, and territorial functioning. *Journal of Research on Crime and Delinquency*, 21, 303–31.

Thornberry, T. P., Lizotte, A. J., Krohn, M. J., Farnworth, M., & Jang, S. J. (1991). Testing interactional theory: An examination of reciprocal causal relationships among family, school, and delinquency. *The Journal of Criminal Law and Criminology*, 82, 3–35.

Thrasher, F. (1927). *The Gang: A Study of 1,313 Gangs in Chicago*. Chicago: The University of Chicago Press.

van Gennep, A. (1909). *The Rites of Passage*. 1960 edition. Chicago: University of Chicago Press.

Wikström, P.-O. (1991). *Urban Crime, Criminals, and Victims: The Swedish Experience in an Anglo-American Comparative Perspective*. New York: Springer-Verlag.

Wikström, P.-0., & Dolmen, L. (1990). Crime and crime trends in different urban environments. *Journal of Quantitative Criminology*, 6, 7–30.

Wilson, W. J. (1987). *The Truly Disadvantaged: The Inner City, the Underclass, and Public Policy*. Chicago: University of Chicago Press.

(1991). Studying inner city social dislocations: the challenge of public agenda research. *American Sociological Review*, 56, 1–14.

10. The positive effects of schooling

PETER MORTIMORE

Introduction

In almost all societies, attendance at school is considered essential for children between the ages of six and sixteen. In some countries, high proportions of students start school earlier and finish later. There is a widespread presumption that schooling must have a positive effect (see, e.g., the six ideal types of schools recently specified by European educationalists Husen, Tuijnman, & Halls, 1992) although, for some children and young people, there is evidence that schooling has had a negative impact on their development. This question of the impact of school has been explored over the last twenty or so years by a series of specialist research studies. These have shown that the effects of schooling are differential: Some schools promote positive effects, others negative ones. Furthermore, some researchers have found evidence that the same school can impact differentially on groups of students according to their gender, social class, or perceived ability.

Although the circumstances and contexts of schooling differ widely across the world, there is a fairly common view – held by governments at least – that schooling, in general, is increasing in cost and decreasing in quality. Although it is often difficult to investigate empirically the truth of these claims, they are constantly stressed by the popular media with the result that reforms are introduced based more on ideological commitment than on research evidence. Findings from scientifically sound studies (especially where these are replicated) about the power of individual schools to promote or reduce their positive impacts are, therefore, of critical importance.

This chapter will present some of the available evidence on variations between schools with regard to four sets of outcomes: attendance, student attitudes, student behavior and scholastic attainment. The mechanisms

The author wishes to acknowledge the helpful comments on an earlier version of this chapter by Michael Rutter and the participants of the Marbach Castle Seminar, 1992.

identified by researchers as being implicated in the differential impacts of schools will also be discussed and differences between schools in terms of their effectiveness for different groups will be considered. Knowing what makes one school more effective than another (for all or some of its students), however, is not the same as knowing how to change a less effective school into a more effective one. For this reason we will comment on the efficacy of various interventions undertaken in a number of different countries. Finally, we will consider the implications for policymakers and practitioners of the evidence that has emerged from studies of school effectiveness and school improvement.

A major difficulty of writing a chapter like this is deciding what should and should not be included. Given the extent of the relevant literature, it will be impossible to be exhaustive. Studies have been selected, therefore, on the basis of their relevance to the argument being undertaken. Inevitably, both relevant individual works and whole categories of studies have been omitted. One example of this general omission is the category of Social Policy Research, thus excluding from the United States the study of "High School Achievement," focusing on public and private differences, by Coleman, Hoffer, and Kilgore (1982); from the United Kingdom, "The Comprehensive Experiment" by Reynolds, Sullivan, and Murgatroyd (1987); and from Germany, the study of "The Management of Individual Differences in Single Classrooms" by Roeder and Sang (1991).

A model of school effectiveness

Studies of variations between schools exist in both simple and more sophisticated forms. The simpler studies take little or no account of differences in the characteristics of students entering and attending the schools. They also tend to focus on only one outcome measure: student scholastic achievement. The difficulties of this simple approach, as experienced teachers will recognize, is that schools do not receive uniform intakes of students. Some take high proportions of relatively advantaged ones likely to do well in examinations; others (on the whole) receive high proportions of disadvantaged students who, all things considered, are less likely to do well. To compare the results of scholastic achievement tests or examinations, without taking into account these differences in the students when they enter the school and to attribute good results to the influence of the school, may therefore be quite misleading.

The more sophisticated form of research endeavors to overcome the problem of differential student intake by using a statistical technique to equate, as far as possible, for these differences. Ideally, the statistical technique would be replaced by a random allocation of students to schools but, in most countries, this would be considered an unacceptable infringement of the parental right to choose schools. Accordingly various definitions of effectiveness have been formulated. One definition of an "effective" school that has been used is "one in which students progress further than might be expected from consideration of its intake" (Mortimore, 1991: 9).

Note that this definition does not assume that all students from disadvantaged backgrounds are likely to do badly in tests of scholastic attainment. Some individual students from disadvantaged backgrounds will undoubtedly do well; they will buck the trend. What the definition implies is that, all things being equal, disadvantaged students are less likely to do as well as those from advantaged backgrounds in any assessment which is highly competitive. Accordingly, measures of progress are needed that can take account of the students' initial starting points.

Various methods have been developed by researchers to deal with the problem of intake differences, and various statistical methods, ranging from simple standardization through multiple regression techniques to the latest multilevel modeling, have been employed to equate for the initial differences. Regardless of the technique used, however, most approaches have been based on an underlying model of school effectiveness.

In this model, a series of outcomes suitable for the type of school must be identified. For an elementary school, these might include basic skills of literacy and numeracy, as well as other measures to do with the students' personal and social development. For a secondary school, the outcomes are likely to be based on achievement but may also include attendance, attitudes, and behavior.

The second stage of the usual procedure is to relate these chosen outcomes to available data on the characteristics of the students as they entered the school. Such characteristics can include earlier reading levels, former attendance rates, behavior ratings completed by teachers in the previous phase of schooling and any available information on home background, including the occupation of the parents. Using the most sophisticated mathematical techniques available, researchers attempt to take account of this intake variation, and to adjust the outcome measures accordingly to provide what is increasingly known as a value-added component. An attempt is thus made to see how the outcomes would look if all schools had received a similar intake. To use the research terminology: like is being compared with like.

At the third stage, researchers usually seek to relate the adjusted outcomes to whatever information has been collected about the life and functioning of the school. Researchers sometimes call this "backward mapping" of outcomes to process measures. To avoid a mismatch, these previous measures must have been collected as the particular students were passing through the school.

In essence, this is the model that school effectiveness researchers have been refining over the last twenty or so years as they have investigated the differential effects of schools.

Methodological issues

Like so many other research topics, studies of the effects of schooling vary a great deal in the scope of their designs and in their chosen methodologies. Some of the problems of interpretation of a number of the earlier studies have already been discussed by Rutter (1983) and by Purkey and Smith (1983). More recently, a number of articles in a special edition of the *International Journal of Educational Research* addressed this topic (Scheerens & Creemers, 1989; Raudenbush, 1989; Bosker & Scheerens, 1989) as does a series of papers in Reynolds and Cuttance (1992). The types of issues that have been raised include:

- the need for clearer conceptualization and theory development
- the use of more sophisticated statistical techniques (such as multilevel modeling)
- the inadequacy of current sampling techniques
- the choice of appropriate outcome measures
- the methods of relating outcome to process data.

On the whole, the later studies have used more sophisticated methods than the earlier ones. The improvement in methodology, however, has not been matched by similar advances in the development of theory. The need for better theory has been recognized and a number of research teams working in this area are addressing the issue.

What are the findings of studies into variations between schools?

As noted earlier, the most common outcomes chosen by researchers have been the attendance patterns of students, their attitudes toward schooling, their behavior, and their scholastic attainment. We will discuss each of these in turn and refer to a selection of the research studies that have been carried out.

Attendance at school

Attendance data have been collected by many researchers. Attendance can be defined as an outcome of schooling as well as being used as a measure of students' attitudes toward school. It can also be seen as a process variable: schools with high attendance rates are better able to secure scholastic achievement for their pupils than those with poorer attendance rates, all things being equal. Various measures of attendance have been used in studies, including one-day surveys and whole-year individual student data sets.

A number of studies of the elementary years of schooling have also used this measure. In Mortimore and colleagues (1988), for instance, attendance data were collected for each student. When these were aggregated, it was found that there were systematic differences between schools. When the proportion of variance between students in their attendance was divided, however, it was found that the contribution of the school was relatively small, possibly because the overall level was so high (92 percent), thus leaving little scope for school variation.

At secondary level, measures of attendance were used by Reynolds, Jones, and St. Leger (1976) in a study of nine schools in a mining community of South Wales. The researchers found that attendance data varied from a school average of 77.2 percent to 89.1 percent. In a study by Rutter and colleagues (1979) data on individual students of three separate age groups were collected in each of the twelve schools in the sample. The whole-school figures revealed considerable differences. For example, out of a possible maximum of twenty attendances, the average for sixteen-year-old students varied from 12.8 in one school to 17.3 in another. Furthermore, the proportion of poor attenders in each school varied between 6 and 26 percent.

Attendance was also addressed by Galloway, Martin, and Wilcox (1985) in a study of schools in the Sheffield area of England. They found clear evidence of school effects on the attendance rates. Smith and Tomlinson (1989) collected statistics of attendance in research which followed the careers of students transferring to twenty multiethnic secondary schools at the age of eleven, through to the end of compulsory schooling. Using a measure of the number of half-days a pupil was absent from school, they drew up a series of outcomes for each school. This measure was repeated in each of four years. On average, researchers found students to be absent about 7 percent of the time. They found no differences between boys and girls but they did find some between students from different ethnic groups. In general, those from Caribbean ethnic backgrounds had better attendance than their British counterparts, whereas those from Asia had poorer attendance records.

Attitudes towards schools

Only a few studies have used systematic measurements of attitudes to school. This is partly because the measurement of attitudes is complex and partly because the attitudes of young people tend to be less stable than those of their older counterparts. Measures have been used in three studies, however. Mortimore and colleagues (1988) developed a set of measures to capture the feelings of young students towards their schools. A series of "smiley" faces was used so members of the sample were able to indicate their overall approval or disapproval of any particular aspect of school life. The results showed considerable variation between schools on a range of activities. Overall, the most effective school had an average of 4 points and the least effective had an average of 2.7, out of a scale of 5. The school appeared to be a more important influence on attitudes than were the student background factors.

The same measure was adopted by Tizard and colleagues (1988) in their study of infant schools. The researchers interviewed their sample of elementary school students at the age of seven and also used the "smiley" method to elicit feelings about mathematics, reading to the teacher, reading to themselves, writing, and going to school.

Pupil attitudes were examined in relation to secondary school students by Smith and Tomlinson (1989). They sought to investigate pupils' enthusiasm for school, as well as participation in activities within the school or organized by it. A different approach toward student attitudes was adopted by Ainley and Sheret (1992) in their Australian study of twenty-two secondary schools. These researchers sought to investigate the effectiveness of schools in their "holding power" over students. They found that some schools retained a higher percentage of students in the senior year than others, even after they had allowed for differences in the social background of students, but not necessarily a link to achievement.

Behavior of students

Like attendance and attitudes, behavior can be viewed as an outcome of a school. The rationale for such a view is that the specific experiences at the school, or the particular group of pupils attending it, lead to a collective style of behavior, both within and beyond the school. Like the other variables, however, behavior can also be viewed as part of the school processes. Other outcome measures can be influenced by the behavior experienced within the school.

Overall, seven studies using behavior as an outcome will be noted here. The study of student behavior is problematic. Taking account of the impact of different teachers on different sets of students, and vice versa, is difficult. Bennett (1976) studied the relationship between teaching style and pupil progress. As part of his study, he sought to measure the on- and off-task behavior in a sample of over one hundred students. He also collected measures of the level of student and teacher interactions for the same sample. In the second study, Mortimore and colleagues (1988) developed a behavior scale which was completed by teachers. One advantage of this scale was that good as well as bad behavior could be recorded. The results showed that the average behavior score for a school ranged from 48 to 76 on a scale with a maximum of 135 points.

Heal (1978) studied a random sample of pupils in both elementary and secondary schools. Data from the elementary schools were used to assess their influence on subsequent behavior of students. The measure included petty misdemeanors and more serious activities, both in and outside of school. Rutter and colleagues (1979) used a scale compiled from items from a self-report student survey, teachers' interviews, and researchers' in-school observations. In all, twenty-five items were aggregated together. Some were minor (not having a pen or pencil with which to write) but others were more important and included the serious interruption of the lesson by aggressive behavior. The twenty-five items revealed a highly significant pattern of intercorrelations. Overall, some schools had up to five times as much good (or bad) behavior as others. Intake differences were taken into account using the results of the "Rutter B" behavior scale, collected on a sample of the students during their elementary schooling.

Although the study of Reynolds, Jones, and St. Leger (1976) did not deal directly with in-school behavior, it included a measure of delinquency. This showed that the school average ranged between 4 and 10 percent. Delinquency data have also been used by Power and colleagues (1967) and by Cannan (1970). They used police data to examine school differences and reported considerable differences in the average delinquency rates of schools. In a study carried out in Scotland (Gray, McPherson, & Raffe, 1983), over twenty thousand students were tracked through the secondary school system and clear evidence of school differences were revealed.

Scholastic attainment of students

A great number of studies have been carried out in the United States focusing on the scholastic attainments of students (witness the 750 references in the register of the North-West Regional Educational Laboratory synthesis; NREL, 1990). One of the first major studies was conducted in the late 1960s by Weber (1971). Four schools, considered to be "institutionally effective," were selected for study. It was found that scholastic attainment (measured by reading levels) was markedly above the average for the school neighborhood. A second study was carried out in 1974 by the New York Department of Education. Two schools, with contrasting levels of average attainment but with similar intake characteristics, were identified and studied (Edmonds, 1979).

Further studies focusing on student scholastic attainment by Madden (1976), Brookover and Lezotte (1977) and Edmonds and Frederiksen (1979) reinforced the conclusion that some schools were more effective in promoting achievement than others. As a result of these pioneering studies, a number of intervention projects were inaugurated (Clark & McCarthy, 1983; McCormack-Larkin & Kritek, 1982; Murphy et al., 1982).

A long-term empirical investigation has been started and its early results reported (Teddlie et al., 1984; Teddlie, Kirby, & Stringfield, 1989). A relatively new strand of work concerns what is known as "self-efficacy" (Wood & Bandura, 1989). In this work the learners' beliefs in themselves are reinforced or reduced and the effects on achievement noted. In general, the stronger the feeling of "self-efficacy" the better the level of achievement. Moreover, the individual's feeling is affected by the school attended. If the teachers hold positive views about ability and about their teaching skills they are more likely to produce academic learning in their classrooms (Bandura, 1992).

In elementary schools in the United Kingdom, Bennett (1976) studied reading, writing and mathematics progress and attainment. Galton and Simon (1980) also studied reading attainment and progress. In addition to reading and mathematics, Mortimore and colleagues (1988) studied writing and speaking skills and, where possible, included measures of progress as well as attainment in their study of school differences. Tizard and colleagues (1988) included measures of reading, writing, mathematics attainment and progress in their study of early student attainment.

In a study of Welsh secondary schools, Reynolds, Jones, and St. Leger (1976) found a range of over 40 percentage points between the school with the highest and the one with the lowest academic attainment. Brimer and colleagues (1978) worked with a sample of forty-four secondary schools and used information on parental background to control for differences in intake in their study of examination results. Rutter and colleagues (1979) found systematic large-scale differences between school averages when examination results were collated.

Gray, Jesson, and Sime (1990), drawing on a sample of over twenty thousand Scottish students' records, found evidence of both social class and school influence on academic attainment. In their study – again focusing on examination results – Smith and Tomlinson (1989) found that school differences were stronger than differences in the ethnic background of students. Daly (1991) studied examination results in a sample of thirty secondary schools in Northern Ireland and found a complicated pattern of school differences, made more difficult to interpret by the selective school system.

Nuttall and colleagues (1989) studied the examination performance of over thirty thousand students taking British school examinations over several years. They found clear evidence of school differences, as well as differences related to family background and ethnic group. Blakey and Heath (1992) have recently released preliminary findings from the Oxford University School Effectiveness Project. These findings show that, in their schools, the proportion of students obtaining high levels in five subjects in public examinations varies from 1 to 19 percent.

Attention so far has focused on a selection of research studies carried out in the United States or in the United Kingdom. Similar studies have also been undertaken in many other parts of the world, however. See, for instance, Fraser (1989) in Australia, Brandsma and Knuver (1989) and Creemers and Lugthart (1989) in the Netherlands, Dalin (1989) in Norway, and Bashi and colleagues (1990) in Israel.

Although the studies cited vary considerably in rigor, scope, and methodologies, their findings are fairly uniform: that individual schools can promote positive or negative student outcomes; that those outcomes can include both cognitive and social behaviors; and that they are not dependent on the school receiving a favored student intake. The fact that the studies have taken place in different phases of students' schooling and in different parts of the developed world, adds considerable strength to the interpretation that schools can make a difference to the lives of their students. Although in some cases, the range of attainment outcomes that can be traced directly to the influence of the school might be relatively small, it can be the difference between academic success and failure, and so can have a long-term effect on students' life chances.

It has also become apparent from these studies that there are likely to be differences in the average progress achieved by students from different schools, and that this variation is less susceptible to factors of home background than are the more usual measures of attainment at any time.

Because there have been more studies of scholastic attainment than of attendance, attitudes, or behavior (which have largely been confined to the U.K. work), measures and instruments are more likely to be available for this outcome than for the others. As a result, differential effectiveness in cognitive areas is more widely understood, but the scope for further development of sensitive measures of behavior and attitudes and the opportunities for studies to use noncognitive measures are considerable. This is especially important in view of the lack of perfect agreement between outcomes reported by Reynolds, Jones, and St. Leger (1976), Rutter and colleagues (1979), and Mortimore and colleagues (1988).

The studies cited here have been criticized and their methodologies dissected. See reviews by Clark, Lotto, and Astuto, 1984; Rutter, 1983; Purkey and Smith, 1983; and Good and Brophy, 1986. For a detailed description of the processes involved in the public discussion of two British studies, see Mortimore (1990).

Do the positive effects of schooling vary according to time?

The evidence on whether positive effects of schooling vary over time is mixed. The earliest British studies (Reynolds, Jones, & St. Leger, 1976; Rutter et al., 1979) drew on student outcomes for different years and found that, in general, there was consistency over time. Two large-scale analyses – one from the Scottish data set (Willms & Raudenbush, 1989) and one from the work carried out in inner London (Nuttall et al., 1989) revealed, however, large-scale differences in student academic outcomes over time. Unfortunately, the other large-scale London-based study, by Mortimore and colleagues (1988), studied only one cohort of students over a four-year period and thus cannot contribute to this interesting debate.

The possibility of change over time should not be surprising. After all, schools take in different groups of students each year and, in some cases, change staff regularly. The question is whether the ethos of a school, once it has been established, is strong enough to resist that change. There is also the question of how rapid change is likely to be. Gradual change in outcomes is likely if the particular ethos changes and staff are replaced. A faster rate of change would be likely if, for instance, the intake to the school varied considerably from one year to another, in terms of its social class background or its earlier performance in other phases of schooling. The school is also likely to change more rapidly as a result of some outside intervention (if a new principal is appointed or an inspection by outside experts takes place). Finally, and not surprisingly, rapid change can be expected as a result of a particular crisis in the life of the school, such as the threat of closure due to lack of students. Schools can also be conservative places, however, which seek to resist change (as the later section on interventions will demonstrate). Further work is needed to identify the most potent mechanisms for change and to investigate under what conditions they are likely to be most successfully introduced.

Do the positive effects of schooling vary according to school membership?

To answer this question, it is first necessary to ask a series of related questions. First, do students with different levels of ability or with different gender, class, and ethnic characteristics achieve different outcomes from the same school processes? The British evidence on this question is mixed. A large number of publications emanating from the Scottish study (Gray, Jesson, & Sime, 1990; Cuttance, 1985; Willms & Cuttance, 1985; MacPherson & Willms, 1987) all suggest that schools can have differential effects according to the characteristics of their students. This actuarial approach suggests that, given the students' gender, age, and social class, the likely academic outcomes can be predicted for particular schools. Further supporting evidence comes from a methodological study by Aitken and Longford (1986), which found that schools did have differential effects on the progress made by particular groups.

Against this view of differential student effect can be set the evidence from the early studies (Reynolds, Jones, & St. Leger, 1976; Rutter et al., 1979) that schools that were positive were likely to have a consistent effect on all groups of students. Furthermore, Gray, Jesson, and Sime (1990) reported little evidence of varied outcomes for different kinds of students.

The findings from Mortimore and colleagues (1988), were also positive on this question: in general it was found that schools that had positive effects for one group were likely to have similar positive effects for others although these could be more or less pronounced. For example, some schools had positive effects in promoting reading progress for girls but not for boys. It is interesting, however, that in their sample of fifty schools the research team found no case where students whose parents had manual occupations performed markedly better, on average, than those from nonmanual groups. Schools were not able to overcome these powerful social class effects. Students from manual groups in the most effective schools, however, sometimes outperformed those from nonmanual groups in the least effective schools. The school was the unit of change rather than the class group within it. A re-analysis of the data of the London School Study shows that the regression line slopes are similar for all groups of students (Sammons & Nuttall, 1992). The data collected by Smith and Tomlinson (1989) showed that, although differences between ethnic groups varied between schools, much larger variations could be found in general school differences: "The ones that are good for white people tend to be about equally good for black people" (305).

The U.S. studies (Hallinger & Murphy, 1987; Teddlie, Kirby, & Stringfield, 1989) have investigated this problem in a different way. By focusing on schools which, by chance, attracted different intakes and could be classified as serving low-, middle- or upper-middle-income communities, the researchers were able to investigate whether schools that were unusually effective were similar or different in how they related to their students. They report that, in general, schools had similar characteristics regardless of the intake of students. Commonly cited correlates include

> a safe and orderly environment; a clear mission; capable instructional leadership; high expectations; a well co-ordinated curriculum; monitoring of student progress; and structured staff development. (Hallinger & Murphy, 1986, cited in Levine & Lezotte, 1990: 65)

The researchers also found differences, however. In the low socioeconomic status (SES) schools, there was a tendency for the curriculum to focus on basic skills, and principals in low SES schools tended to be more forceful in asserting themselves and intervening in classes. The researchers found that in the high SES schools principals tended to use a more collaborative style of decision-making (Hallinger & Murphy, 1986).

The second related question concerns whether – if schools have different outcomes for different groups of students – this is due to policy differences in the way the students have been treated, or to differences in the reactions they have elicited from those who work in the schools. It is quite possible that a school, or an individual teacher, may have a policy of treating students equitably in terms of adult time and encouragement, and yet may end up responding to some groups of students differentially. In the London study (Mortimore et al., 1988), for example, classroom observations showed no evidence of inequitable attention or any obvious signs of bias. Yet the same study produced evidence of lower expectations for certain groups of students – in the main those from Carribbean family backgrounds, or those who were chronologically young for the school year. It was not possible to explain these differences satisfactorily, but it can be speculated that a mixture of unconscious prejudice – against groups of students from a different cultural background or against children who appeared immature – and of successful student strategies involving the elicitation of positive responses by other groups, was responsible. Those students with advantaged backgrounds, perhaps, used their advantages to get more out of their schooling experience.

In other cases, it is likely that schools will target those groups that teachers believe most likely to benefit. Evidence shows that in "tracked" selective schools, the premier group of students received a greater share of attention and resources than others and that this had a deleterious effect on all but this group (Lacey, 1975). At the other extreme, Athey (1990) has shown how preschool programs can be targeted on the most disadvantaged students to lessen the gap between their achievements and those of other children. This evidence is in line with a series of studies based on other kinds of institutions, such as the work in mental hospitals which shows that differential efforts can be targeted to considerable effect (Brown & Wing, 1962).

The answer to the key question of whether the positive effects of schooling vary according to school membership is, therefore, complex. The evidence suggests that at the secondary stage at least, different subgroups of students may or may not benefit and, furthermore, that schools can choose to target certain groups. At the elementary stage, the evidence points to a more uniform effect. Schools that are effective are likely to be positive for all subgroups of students although some groups may benefit to a greater extent than others. There is no evidence in either sector of schools, however, to suggest that different factors are responsible for differential effects. It is a question of which subgroup is affected, for which group are high expectations held, who is likely to be rewarded, and so forth.

Do the positive effects of schooling vary according to the particular strengths and weaknesses of schools?

It appears that even though schools that are generally effective in one area are usually reasonably effective in others, some variation is possible. In the London study of fifty primary schools fourteen were uniformly effective, seven were uniformly ineffective, and the rest had mixed profiles (Mortimore et al., 1988). The extent of this within-school variation is important and will be further investigated in a new British study of secondary schools (Nuttall et al., personal communication).

What are the mechanisms associated with differential school effectiveness?

It is seldom possible for educational researchers to impose experimental conditions on their subjects. They are generally welcomed into schools and classes, but they usually have to observe things as they are. This helps them to gain a realistic picture of school life but means that they are rarely able directly to trace causal relationships. All too frequently, researchers are limited to tracing patterns of association and the use of correlations.

Nevertheless, even with such methodological limitations, researchers from different countries have reached a number of conclusions about the variables commonly associated with the functioning of more effective schools. The plausibility of these variables operating as mechanisms of school effectiveness has been increased by the frequency with which they have been replicated.

The following list of mechanisms is not intended to be comprehensive or exhaustive. It has been culled from a sample of ten reviews or studies drawn from different countries, selected because of their use of different methodologies. Because of different wording and a lack of scientifically precise language, it is not possible to compare in a highly accurate way findings from so many different studies, many of which are composite reviews of a number of individual research projects. It is possible, however, broadly to collate variables to ascertain the most common mechanisms found by researchers to be associated with effectiveness. The following list is the result of this exercise.

Strong positive leadership of schools

Although a few studies (notably, Van de Grift, 1990) have claimed that the principal has little impact or that the leadership of the school can be provided by somebody else, almost universally this mechanism was found to be important.

Different studies have drawn attention to different aspects of principals' roles, but Levine and Lezotte (1990) have provided a clear analysis of how strong leadership can provide mechanisms to aid effectiveness. In their view, this occurs through the rigorous selection and replacement of teachers; "buffering" the school from unhelpful external agents; frequent personal monitoring of school achievements; high expenditure of time and energy for school improvement actions; supporting teachers; and acquiring extra resources for their schools.

The British studies support this analysis but perhaps add a further subtle task: that of understanding when – and when not – to involve other staff in decision-making. The British studies have found evidence that both autocratic and overdemocratic styles of leadership are less effective than a balanced style which depends on the crucial judgment of when, and when not, to act as decision-maker. Fullan (1992) has argued that strong leadership, by itself, is not sufficient in a complex, postmodern society. Instead, he argued that heads (principals) have to find appropriate leadership roles for teachers.

High expectations: An appropriate challenge for students' thinking

This mechanism was commonly cited by researchers. Despite the limitations of the original experimental work (Rosenthal & Jacobson, 1968), the concept of expectations and the way these can affect the behavior of both teachers and students have been well assimilated. Dorr-Bremme (1990), for instance, drew attention to the differing mind sets of two groups of teachers from more, and less, effective schools. Members of the less effective group see their work one way:

> We are educators who work hard to take our students' needs into account. This means considering their total life situations and not expecting more of them than they can do.

In contrast, those in the more effective group saw their similar task in a quite different way:

> We are people who take our students' needs into account as we teach. This means that we challenge our students, make them work hard and do the very best that they can. (Quoted in Levine & Lezotte, 1990: 35)

The one group chose a passive role, affected by forces (the students' problems) over which they could have little control. The other group, although recognizing that problems existed, adopted a more active stance and sought to challenge the difficulties through challenging the students' thinking.

Mortimore and colleagues (1988) looked at ways in which expectations could be transmitted in the classroom. The researchers found that teachers had lower expectations for students who, for instance, were young in their year group (those with summer birthdays) or who came from lower social classes. They found that low expectations were not held in any simple way for either girls or boys per se, despite the fact that boys received more critical comments and girls more praise. These data were difficult to interpret and the research team drew on the findings of Dweck and Repucci (1973) to help explain them. (Dweck and Repucci found that greater praise from male teachers to female students for less adequate work was linked to stereotyped views of female performance.)

Monitoring student progress

Although monitoring, by itself, changes little, the majority of the studies found it to be a vital procedure, as a prelude to planning instructional tactics, altering pedagogy, or increasing or decreasing workloads. They also saw it as a key message to students that the teacher was interested in their progress. Whether it is more effective for the monitoring to be carried out formally or informally cannot yet be answered and further work on the way this mechanism operates may be worthwhile.

Student responsibilities and involvement in the life of the school

The mechanism – in its various forms – of ensuring that students adopt an active role in the life of the school was also commonly found to be important. By seeking to involve students in school-oriented activities, or by allocating responsibilities to elicit a positive response from them, teachers have endeavored to provide a sense of ownership in the school and in the students' own learning.

Although examples of talented, but alienated, students can frequently be found in literature, the general rule appears to be that learning is most likely when the students hold a positive view of the school and of their own role within it. The attitudes of students toward themselves as learners was used as a school outcome by Mortimore and colleagues (1988). The outcome consisted of a specially designed measure of self-concept. This was the mirror image of the behavior scale completed by teachers and by students themselves. The measure revealed clear school differences: Some schools produced students who – regardless of their actual ability – felt reasonably positive about themselves; others produced students who were negative about themselves even when, in the judgment of the research team and according to their progress, they were performing well.

Rewards and incentives

Unlike punishments, rewards and incentives appear to act as mechanisms for eliciting positive behaviors and, in some cases, for changing students' (and at times teachers') behavior. Thus, Purkey and Smith (1983) noted that a key cultural characteristic of effective schools is a

> school-wide recognition of academic success: publicly honouring academic achievement and stressing its importance encourages students to adopt similar norms and values. (183)

Levine and Lezotte (1990) made two further points. First, that the use of rewards extends beyond academic outcomes and applies to other aspects of school life – a point supported by the British research. Second, that school-wide recognition of positive performance may be more important in urban schools, and especially those in inner cities where, because of the correlation with disadvantage, there are low achieving students. Levine and Lezotte cited Hallinger and Murphy's (1985) study to support this argument. Hallinger and Murphy argued that one of the roles of principals in advantaged schools was to

> sustain existing norms, rather than create new ones . . . In low SES (disadvantaged) schools the principal must ensure that the school overcomes societal and school norms that communicate low expectations to the students . . . (whereas in higher SES schools) school disciplinary and academic reward systems need not focus as much on short-term accomplishments, rely heavily on tangible reinforcers or develop elaborate linkages between the classroom and the school. (3)

Finally, in one of the British studies, Mortimore and colleagues (1988) found that rewards could be given in a variety of ways, if the policy of the school was positive. In some schools, the policy was to reward individuals for good work or behavior, whereas in others it was to focus on sport and social factors. Schools experienced the problem of trying to create a common system of incentives. This was a particular problem for schools where the age range was wide: rewards that appealed to younger pupils sometimes lost their enchantment for older students.

Parental involvement in the life of the school

Parental involvement is possibly one of the most important issues in the current educational debate. The idea is not new and has been pioneered by a number of educational researchers in the United Kingdom and in the United States. There is also a large and rapidly growing literature on the topic. In the United Kingdom, much of the debate has been about the gains to be made from developing contact between homes and schools with regard to children's learning, as well as about ways to increase the accountability of schools to parents.

The vital role that parents can play in the intellectual development of their children has long been known, but experiments to use this resource more effectively have met with varied success. One pioneering British study (Tizard, Schofield, & Hewison, 1982), however, demonstrated that parental involvement in reading more than equalled the benefits from the use of an extra teacher in schools.

The Head Start programs in the United States (Lazar & Darlington, 1982) have also provided evidence that the involvement of parents is an important aspect of the programs' success. Similar programs in England show that the gap between the achievement levels of advantaged and disadvantaged can be reduced (Athey, 1990). In another British study, Mortimore and colleagues (1988) found that schools varied a great deal in their attitudes toward parents. Some schools kept parents out; others used parents as cheap labor. A few schools involved parents in school planning and sought to use their talents and abilities in both the classroom and at home. The researchers found, however, that some principals appeared to be insufficiently confident in their relationships with parents, especially in more socially advantaged areas. They found, though, that when the energy and talents of parents were harnessed, the rewards for the school were high. It is interesting that they also found Parent-Teacher Associations were not necessarily positive, in that they could form a "clique" for particular groups of parents and thus present a barrier to the involvement of others. The range of parental involvement programs in both elementary and secondary schooling in the United Kingdom has been summarized by Jowett and Baginsky (1991).

The ways in which parents act as a mechanism for effectiveness are not well understood. It is possible to speculate that where both long-term and short-term objectives are shared by teachers and parents, where parents are able to offer considerable help through coaching, and where ideas generated in one area of a child's life can be rehearsed and expanded in another, learning will be helped. Stevenson and Shin-Ying's (1990) study of three cities (Taipei, Taiwan; Sendai, Japan; Minneapolis, United States) illustrates the lengths to which oriental families will go to involve not just parents, but other relations, in the coaching of children. Stevenson and Shin-ying showed that a belief in the supremacy of hard work over natural ability and the willingness to be critical, when combined with high expectations, can provide powerful support for learning. Parental involvement, however, is not without difficulties and those responsible for school programs need to have clear policies in place before embarking on this potentially valuable strategy (Mortimore & Mortimore, 1984).

The use of joint planning and consistent approaches toward students

The efficacy of joint planning and consistent approaches have been clearly recognized by many research studies. Levine and Lezotte (1990) argued

> almost by definition, faculty members committed to a school-wide mission focusing on academic improvement for all students tend to exemplify greater cohesiveness and consensus regarding central organisational goals than do faculty at less effective schools. (12)

Levine and Lezotte maintained that cohesion and consensus are especially important to schools (rather than other institutions) because schools set teachers a number of difficult and sometimes conflicting goals. Teachers must respond to the individual needs of students while emphasizing the requirements of the whole class. They have to be fair to the group but take account of individual circumstances. It is thus easy for what Levine and Lezotte call "goal clarity" to be reduced and for improvement efforts to be fragmented.

Where students are subject to conflicting expectations and demands and, as a result, become less confident, they often take time to learn the ways of each new teacher. This exercise may provide a helpful pointer to the ways of adults, but it is clearly not a useful mechanism for a school.

The involvement of faculty members in joint decisions relates to the strength of leadership of the institution. There is clear evidence that when teachers and others in authority (including the assistant principal) are given a role to play, they – in the best management tradition – will be far more likely to feel ownership of the institution and, as a result, offer greater commitment to it.

Academic emphasis and a focus on learning

There has been much research on this topic. Some of it has been concerned with the question of time-on-task (see, e.g., Sizemore, 1987). A number of research studies have drawn attention to the waste of time in the school day, particularly at the start of classes, through poor administration and lack of preparation (Blum, 1984). Rutter and colleagues (1979) found evidence of time wasted at the end of classes. The researchers described the chaotic situation that could develop when a high proportion of classes in the school finished before the scheduled time. The problem, therefore, is not simply about time: It is about the use of time. Mortimore and colleagues (1988) noted that although some schools in their sample programmed extra time (some twenty minutes per day) for classes, a straightforward correlation with effectiveness was not found. The value of time appeared to depend greatly on how it was used.

Emphasizing the learning of core skills has also been cited as an important aspect of this mechanism. In the United States, this has sometimes been associated with experiments in mastery learning (Gregory & Mueller, 1980). Levine and Lezotte (1990) argued, however, that in some cases the original concept of Bloom-type mastery learning has been misimplemented and cannot fairly be judged. In Britain a Department of Education and Science (DES) discussion paper (Alexander, Rose, & Woodhead, 1992) has drawn attention to the danger that elementary schools can lose sight of the central focus on student learning and dissipate the energies of teachers in an unproductive way.

These were the most commonly cited mechanisms arising from the research literature. As noted earlier, however, other factors have frequently been studied and may also be of considerable importance for particular schools at particular times. Thus, if schools receive students of a certain background, if the community is subject to particular experiences, or if the school authorities invoke a specific series of reforms, other mechanisms for coping with change will come into play. These may act as mediating influences and, as a result, distract the attention of teachers and principals; they should never supplant the prime focus of school – the learning of pupils.

How successful have preventative interventions been?

This question is difficult to answer. It requires a clear definition of preventative interventions and in view of the most recent history of schooling in many parts of the world such a definition is not easy to formulate. Straightforward application of the knowledge and understanding of, for instance, school effectiveness, by those involved in school improvement programs, represents one kind of intervention. Complex governmental initiatives, for what have previously been considered fairly autonomous school systems, is another. Both may be found in some school systems.

In reality, school effectiveness and school improvement are very different phenomena. As Clark, Lotto, and Astuto (1984) have argued so clearly, researchers pursuing these two lines of enquiry pursue different questions (what affects student outcomes, and how schools change) and use different outcome measures (student achievement and the level of innovation). What the two approaches share is their interest in schools. The contrast between school effectiveness and school improvement is illustrated by a comparison of the work of Rutter and colleagues (1979), seeking explanations for poor student outcomes in one geographical area, with the International School Improvement Study's (ISIS) endeavors, operating in fourteen countries to describe and, where appropriate, to change various school processes (Bollen & Hopkins, 1987).

A different kind of initiative is a government-sponsored project such as that on the school development plans of the (then) English Department of Education and Science (now the Department for Education). This project was designed to promote concepts, culled from research, on the necessity of systematic planning (Hargreaves & Hopkins, 1989; DES, 1991).

Different still are the programs of school restructuring and school reforms that have been introduced in the United States and the United Kingdom. In the case of school restructuring, a variety of different interest groups have expressed their fears about aspects of American schooling and, in line with political policy, have been encouraged to put thinking into practice (Murphy, 1991). In Chicago, for instance, a parents' collective alliance has been established to oversee the restructuring of the city's education system (Hess, 1992). In New York, critics such as Domanico and Genn (1992) have argued that curtailment of the city's power over education is essential to enable parents and others – using public money – to run their own schools.

In the United Kingdom, a series of legislative changes have dominated recent educational events. Among other actions, the 1988 Education Reform Act established a National Curriculum and its associated testing at the ages of seven, eleven, fourteen, and sixteen; introduced a system of parental choice based on open enrollment; and delegated financial decision-making to the school principal and the governors (a small group representing the interests of teachers, the local education authority – where appropriate – and the wider community).

The 1992 Education Act created a new form of privatized school inspections, whereby appropriately qualified and trained inspectors can compete for contracts to inspect schools as part of a four-year cycle. Among the proposals of recent British legislation are the establishment of "Education Associations" to take over the management of failing schools and a further loosening of local government powers over schooling.

These developments in the United States and the United Kingdom have led to different kinds of interventions designed by researchers and practitioners with different patterns of outcomes. The American situation has been summarized in a briefing report to the House of Representatives by the United States General Accounting Office (GAO, 1989). This shows that, in the last year for which full data were available, approximately 41 percent (6,500) of U.S. districts representing over 38,000 schools were involved in various forms of interventions and that a further 17 percent of the districts were planning to implement such programs during the next couple of years. Based on published accounts, Levine and Lezotte (1990) have drawn up a list of the most promising interventions. Practices studied by researchers include the following 14 types of interventions:

- Establishment and facilitation of an informal group of participating principals who regularly meet and work together
- Provision of parallel and coordinated training for administrators
- Sponsorship of individual schools' audits
- Establishment of principals' academies
- Redesign and utilization of personnel evaluation instruments
- Assignment of new principals to a program of shadowing
- Selection of faculty at poorly functioning schools for a tailored program of improvement
- Training of future administrators
- Establishment of a central office intervention team to work with schools
- Establishment of paid link teachers between individual schools and central office
- Assignment of former principals to serve as mentors
- Accelerated learning programs for students
- Development of auditing and other technical assistance teams
- Establishment of mentor teachers to staff other than the principal

The United Kingdom has had fewer interventions by researchers and practitioners, but more governmentally generated initiatives. Reynolds (1992) has summarized those that have taken place. In particular, he has drawn attention to the following developments.

- Teacher-researcher movement's focus on improvement in the 1970s
- Self-evaluation and review programs of the 1980s
- Local Education Authorities own initiatives (such as the Hargreaves and the Thomas Reports, Inner London Education Authority (ILEA), 1984 and 1985 respectively)
- Schools' Council's Guidelines for Review and Institutional Development (GRIDs) scheme

To this list should be added the recent work on school development planning (Beresford et al., 1992) and government-sponsored activities. The work on school planning shows that almost all LEAs have encouraged their schools to adopt School Development Plans and that many Authorities are now using these as a basis for their own support and interventions in schools. As already noted, the government initiatives stem from recent legislation.

By seeking to create a market in which parents can choose schools to suit their children, the U.K. government has striven to induce competitive conditions which, it hopes, will improve the effectiveness of schools. In particular, by enabling school communities to opt out of their school districts and to manage themselves, it has sought to encourage principals to take initiatives otherwise denied them. It is as yet too early to report systematically on the outcome of this experiment, but it is already possible to see both encouraging and worrying signs in those schools that have taken advantage of opting out. Encouraging signs can be detected in the increasing self-confidence of staff and in the benefits of local, rather than area-based, decision-making mechanisms. (The schools have also benefited from increased funding.) The worrying signs are that, rather than parents choosing schools, the schools appear to be choosing the students and – because of a legislative requirement to publish examination results – those with special needs, or those who are likely to be low-achieving, are much less likely to be chosen than are their more able, less problematic, peers. If this trend develops, the low achievers will be clustered in those schools (with less resources) that have not opted out, and the vital ingredient of effectiveness – a balanced intake – identified by Rutter and colleagues (1979) will be stymied. This situation needs to be monitored closely.

Table 10.1 shows the range of interventions that take place. This list is not intended to be exhaustive: Interventions have been included simply to illustrate the available range of activities. Two dimensions have been identified, focus and scope. Focus varies from specific to general. Scope includes single schools, groups of schools, the local system, and national categories.

In terms of success, most of the preventative interventions cited have achieved something. None, however, has been hailed as a panacea for all the ills of schooling; each will have a range of costs and benefits.

Some initiatives, such as the Reading Recovery Project (Clay, 1985), are still the subject of critical evaluations (see, e.g., Glyn et al., 1989) but have been hailed as being of direct value in other countries and other systems. Others, such as the Comer Program (Comer, 1991) and the Olweus (1991) projects, have been recognized nationally as being capable of supporting young people and their schools, particularly in urban areas. Yet others, such as the London Study (Maughan et al., 1990; Ouston, Maughan & Rutter, 1991), revealed much information about whether – and how – schools can change their practices and their outcomes, although the changes were

Table 10.1 *Interventions classified according to their focus (column 1) and scope (columns 2–5)*

Focus	Single School	Group of Schools	Local System	National
Specific	US High School Academies of enriched schooling (Archer & Montesano, 1990) Changing an English Disruptive School (Badger, 1992)	The Comer New Haven Program (Comer, 1991) Cognitive interactions in primary schooling in Germany (Einsiedler, 1992)	The Sheffield Early Literacy Programme (Hannon et al., 1991) Academic feedback at school level in Northern England (Fitz-Gibbon, 1991)	Norwegian Ministry of Education Anti-bullying Program (Olweus, 1991) Reading Recovery in New Zealand, U.S. and the U.K. (Clay, 1985)
General	The Baz Attack – Canada (Toews & Murray-Barker, 1985) Enrichment for preschool students (Athey, 1990)	The London Study (Maughan et al., 1990) The Israeli Study (Bashi et al., 1990)	The Halton Canadian Growth Plan (Stoll & Fink, 1989) The Calgary Plan (Waldron, 1983)	What works (U.S. Dept. of Education, 1987) The Australian Exercise (McGaw et al., 1991)

not brought about as a direct result of the intervention. Much more work needs to be done in order to exploit fully the knowledge that now exists about the potential positive effects of schools.

The Olweus intervention is interesting in view of its long time scale and its complex research design. Its major goals were to limit, as much as possible, the number of incidents of bullying and to prevent development of new bully and victim problems. The intervention program included the development of better information for teachers and administrators of schools about bullying and what they could do to counteract it. Information about bullying was also provided to parents of all children in the Norwegian school system. A cassette showing episodes of bullying was produced and made available for schools to rent or borrow. Finally, a questionnaire was designed to elicit information about all aspects of the bully and victim problem in schools. This was completed anonymously by individual students in school time.

About 2,500 students drawn from forty-two schools in Bergen were followed up over a period of two and a half years. This student sample was divided into four cohorts and a series of measurements were collected from before the initiation of the antibullying program until several years after it had been completed. The research team used time-lagged contrasts between different cohorts to investigate whether there were genuine changes in behavior over this period. A series of outcome variables based on the reported accounts of being bullied or of taking part in bullying incidents were developed from a questionnaire completed by the students. The research team concluded that reductions in bully and victim problems had taken place and that these were likely to be the result of the intervention program rather than other factors.

What are the implications of this work for policy and practice?

There are numerous possible implications stemming from the work carried out over the last twenty or so years on the positive effects of schooling. Perhaps the most important is an implication for those involved closely with schools. This is the confirmation of the potential power of schools to affect the life chances of their students. Although the difference in scholastic attainment likely to be achieved by the same student in contrasting schools is unlikely to be great, in many instances it represents the difference between success and failure and operates as a facilitating or inhibiting factor in higher education. When coupled with the promotion of other prosocial attitudes and behaviors, and the inculcation of a positive self-image, the potential of the school to improve the life chances of students is considerable.

The second major implication of this work relates to governments. Legislation can provide a helpful framework for achieving an education system of high quality, but this can only be guaranteed by the conscious strategies of teachers and administrators, and the purposeful commitment of students. Excellence cannot be mandated by politicians or bureaucrats. Governments, central or local, would do well to realize this and ensure that any legislative framework that is created is likely to stimulate and elicit from those most involved ownership, commitment, and dedication rather than learned helplessness and resentment.

The third major implication relates to practitioners. It is that a critical body of knowledge – replicated, in many cases, over time and in many different settings – has been established. This knowledge needs to be drawn upon more frequently in the quest for better schools. Some practitioners complain that information drawn from research studies is seldom made accessible or disseminated widely. This criticism undoubtedly has some validity: research journals seldom make compulsive reading for busy practitioners. It is not true, however, that efforts to disseminate widely the findings reported here have been half-hearted. Many conferences and meetings of principals' associations in many different countries have featured presentations on this topic. The work needs to continue. All those involved in trying to improve schools need to recognize the potential – not just in terms of specific actions by principals or teachers that may or may not be related to the rest of their way of working – for describing, analyzing, and evaluating effectiveness.

The fourth and final implication concerns the work of researchers. The literature on school effectiveness is now enormous. There are vast numbers of books, journal articles, chapters in edited collections, and conference papers on this topic. There are, however, relatively fewer detailed empirical studies than there are critiques and commentaries. If the field is to flourish, more empirical work is needed. Further studies extending the focus from schools to other educational institutions would help to broaden still further the knowledge base. Possibly even more important is the need for careful experimental work that tests the mainly correlational findings of the early studies. This, coupled with a compilation of an adequate theory both of what makes schools effective and of how to make them more so, would be of great value to the educational community. Some work on the theoretical underpinning of the topic has been undertaken, as the very careful synthesis of research on educational change illustrates (Fullan, 1991), but more is needed.

In conclusion, therefore, it can be stated that the positive effects of schooling have been well documented by a number of research studies carried out in different countries at different times. The mechanisms associated with these effects are also well known and are to a large extent common to the studies. The effects vary, however, according to a number of different variables and more work is needed, especially to disentangle the influence of student characteristics from school effects. On the basis of this research, a number of intervention studies have been carried out but the outcomes of such work have, in general, proved less than hoped for. The difficulties of integrating such interventions – based on sound research findings – with those dictated by the political concerns of governments, remain. Finally, a number of implications for different groups, stemming from this work, need to be addressed.

References

Ainley, J., & Sheret, M. (1992). *Effectiveness of High Schools in Australia: Holding Power and Achievement*. Paper presented to the International Congress for

School Effectiveness and Improvement, Victoria, British Columbia, January, 1992.

Aitken, M., & Longford, N. (1986). Statistical modelling issues in school effectiveness studies. *Journal of the Royal Statistical Society*, Series A, 149, 1, 1–43.

Alexander, R., Rose, J., & Woodhead, C. (1992). *Curriculum Organisation and Classroom Practice in Primary Schools: A Discussion Paper*. London: Department of Education and Science.

Archer, E., & Montesano, P. (1990). High school academies: Engaging students in school and work. *Equity and Choice*. Special Report, Winter, 16–17.

Athey, C. (1990). *Extending Thought in Young Children*. London: Paul Chapman Publishing.

Badger, B. (1992). Changing a destructive school. In *School Effectiveness: Research, Policy and Practice*, eds. D. Reynolds & P. Cuttance, pp. 134–53. London: Cassell.

Bandura, A. (1992). *Perceived Self-efficacy in Cognitive Development and Functioning*. Paper presented to the American Educational Research Association, San Francisco, April.

Bashi, J., Sass, K., Katzir, R., & Margolin, I. (1990). *Effective Schools – From Theory to Practice: An Implementation Model and Its Outcomes*. Jerusalem: Van Leer Institute.

Bennett, N. (1976). *Teaching Styles and Pupil Progress*. London: Open Books.

Beresford, C., Mortimore, P., MacGilchrist, B., & Savage, J. (1992). School development planning matters in the UK. *Unicorn*, 18, 12–16.

Blakey, L., & Heath, A. (1992). Differences between comprehensive schools: Some preliminary findings. In *School Effectiveness: Research, Policy and Practice*, ed. D. Reynolds & P. Cuttance, pp. 121–33. London: Cassell.

Blum, R. (1984). *Onward to Excellence: Making Schools More Effective*. Portland, Ore.: North West Regional Educational Laboratory.

Bollen, R., & Hopkins, D. (1987). *School Based Research: Towards a Praxis*. Leuven (Belgium): Academic Publishing Company (ACCO).

Bosker, R., & Scheerens, J. (1989). Issues and interpretations of the results of school effectiveness research. *International Journal of Educational Research*, 13, 7, 741–52.

Bransdma, H., & Knuver, J. (1989). Effects of school and classroom characteristics on pupil progress in language and arithmetic. *International Journal of Educational Research*, 13, 7, 777–88.

Brimer, A., Madaus, G., Chapman, B., Kellaghan, T., & Wood, D. (1978). *Sources of Difference in School Achievement*. Slough, Buckinghamshire: National Foundation for Educational Research.

Brookover, W., & Lezotte, L. (1977). *Changes in School Characteristics Co-incident with Changes in Student Achievement*. East Lansing Institute for Research on Teaching: Michigan State University.

Brown, G., & Wing, J. (1962). A comparative clinical and social survey of three mental hospitals. *Sociological Review Monograph*, 5, 145–71.

Cannan, C. (1970). Schools for delinquency. *New Society*, 427, 1004.

Clark, D., Lotto, L., & Astuto, T. (1984). Effective schools and school improvement: a comparative analysis of two lines of enquiry. *Educational Administration Quarterly*, 20,3, 41–68.

Clark, T., & McCarthy, D. (1983). School improvement in New York: The evolution of a project. *Educational Researcher*, 12, 17–24.

Clay, M. (1985). *The Early Detection of Reading Difficulties*. London: Heinemann.

Coleman, J., Hoffer, T., & Kilgore, S. (1982). *High School Achievement*. New York: Basic Books.

Comer, J. (1991). The Comer school development program. *Urban Education*, 26, 1, 56–82.

Creemers, B., & Lugthart, E. (1989). School effectiveness and improvement in the Netherlands. *In School Effectiveness and Improvement, Proceedings of the First International Congress, London 1988*, ed. D. Reynolds, B. Creemers, & T. Peters, pp. 89–103. Groningen, RION Institute for Educational Research/School of Education, University of Wales College of Cardiff.

Cuttance, P. (1985). Methodological issues in the statistical analysis of data on the effectiveness of schooling. *British Educational Research Journal*, 11, 2, 163–79.

Dalin, P. (1989). Reconceptualising the school improvement process: Charting a paradigm shift. In *School Effectiveness and Improvement, Proceedings of the First International Congress, London, 1988*, ed. D. Reynolds, B. Creemers, & T. Peters, pp. 30–45. Groningen, RION Institute for Educational Research/School of Education, University of Wales College of Cardiff.

Daly, P. (1991). *How Large Are Secondary School Effects in Northern Ireland?* Belfast: School of Education, Queens University.

Department of Education and Science (1991). *School Development Plans Project. 2. Development Planning: A Practical Guide*. London: Department of Education and Science.

Domanico, R., & Genn, C. (1992). *Creating the Context for Improvement in New York City's Public Schools*. Paper presented to the Quality of Life in London/New York Conference, March 26–27, London.

Dorr-Bremme, D. (1990). Culture, practice and change: School effectiveness reconsidered. In *Unusually Effective Schools: A Review of Research and Practice*, ed. D. Levine & L. Lezotte. Madison, Wis.: National Center for Effective Schools' Research and Development.

Dweck, C., & Repucci, N. (1973). Learned helplessness and reinforcement responsibility in children. *Journal of Personality and Social Psychology*, 25, 109–16.

Edmonds, R. (1979). Effective schools for the urban poor. *Educational Leadership*, 37, 1, 15–27.

Edmonds, R., & Frederiksen, J. (1979). *Search for Effective Schools: The Identification and Analysis of City Schools that are Instructionally Effective for Poor Children*. Eric Document Reproduction Service number ED179–396. Cambridge, Mass.: Harvard Graduate School of Education Center for Urban Studies.

Einsiedler, W. (1992). *The Effects of Teaching Methods, Class Methods and Patterns of Cognitive Teacher Pupil Interactions in an Experimental Study in Primary School Classes*. Paper presented to the International Congress for School Effectiveness and School Improvement, Victoria, British Columbia, January.

Fitz-Gibbon, C. (1991). A-levels: corrective comparisons. *Managing Schools Today*, 1, 2, 44–5.

Fraser, B. (1989). Research synthesis on school and instructional effectiveness. *International Journal of Educational Research*, 13, 7, 707–20.

Fullan, M. (1991). *The New Meaning of Educational Change*. London: Cassell.

(1992). *The Evolution of Change and the New Work of the Educational Leader*. Paper presented to the Regional Conference of the Commonwealth Council for Educational Administration, Hong Kong, August.

Galloway, D., Martin, R., & Willcox, B. (1985). Persistent absence from school and exclusions from school. *British Educational Research Journal*, 11, 2, 51–61.

Galton, M., & Simon, B. (1980). *Progress and Performance in the Primary Classroom*. London: Routledge & Kegan Paul.

General Accounting Office of the United States (GAO) (1989). *Effective School Programs: Their Extent and Characteristics*. Washington, DC: General Accounting Office.

Glyn, T., Crooks, T., Bethune, N., Ballard, K., & Smith, J, (1989). *Reading Recovery in Context*. Wellington, New Zealand: Department of Education.

Good, J., & Brophy, J. (1986). Social and institutional context of teaching: School effects. *Third Handbook of Research on Teaching*. New York: Macmillan.

Gray, J., Jesson, D., & Sime, N. (1990). Estimating differences in the examination performance of secondary schools in six LEAs. *Oxford Review of Education*, 16, 2, 137–58.

Gray. J., McPherson, A., & Raffe, D. (1983). *Reconstructions of Secondary Education: Theory, Myth and Practice since the War*. London: Routledge & Kegan Paul.

Gregory, K., & Mueller, S. (1980). Leif Ericson Elementary School Chicago. In *Why Do Some Urban Schools Succeed?* ed. W Duckett, pp. 60–74. Bloomington, Indiana: Phi Delta Kappa.

Hallinger, P., & Murphy, J. (1985). Instructional leadership and school socio-economic status: A preliminary investigation. *Administrator's Notebook*, 31,5, 1–4.

Hallinger, P., & Murphy, J. (1986). The social context of effective schools. *American Journal of Education*, 94, 3, 328–54.

Hallinger, P., & Murphy, J. (1987). Instructional leadership in the school context. In *Instructional Leadership*, ed. W. Greenfield, pp. 179–202. Boston, Mass.: Allyn & Bacon.

Hannon, P., Weinberger, J., & Nutbrown, C. (1991). A study of work with parents to promote early literacy development. *Research Papers in Education*, 6, 2, 77–98.

Hargreaves, D., & Hopkins, D. (1989). *School Development Plans Project. 1. Planning for School Development*. London: Department for Education and Science.

Heal, K. (1978). Misbehaviour among school children. *Policy and Politics*, 6, 321–32.

Hess, J. (1992). *School Restructuring, Chicago Style: A Midway Report*. Chicago, Ill.: The Chicago Panel on Public School Policy and Finance.

Husen, T., Tuijnman, A., & Halls, W. (1992). *Schooling in Modern European Society*. Oxford: Pergamon.

Inner London Education Authority (ILEA) (1984). *Improving Secondary Schools* (The Hargreaves Report). London: ILEA.

Inner London Education Authority (ILEA) (1985). *Improving Primary Schools* (The Thomas Report). London: ILEA.

Jowett, S., & Baginsky, M., with MacDonald, M. (1991). *Building Bridges: Parental Involvement in Schools*. Windsor, Berkshire: NFER Nelson.

Lacey, C. (1975). Destreaming in a "pressurised" academic environment. In *Contemporary Research in the Sociology of Education*, ed. J. Eggleston, pp.148–66. London: Methuen.

Lazar, I., & Darlington, R. (1982). Lasting effects of early education: A report from the consortium for longitudinal studies. *Monographs of the Society for Research in Child Development*, serial number 195, 47.

Levine, D., & Lezotte, L. (1990). *Unusually Effective Schools: A Review of Research and Practice*. Madison, Wis.: National Center for Effective Schools Research and Development.

MacPherson, A., & Willms, D. (1987). *Equalisation and Improvement: Some Effects of Comprehensive Reorganisation in Scotland*. Paper presented to the meeting of the American Educational Research Association, May.

Madden, J. (1976). Cited in R. Edmonds, Effective schools for the urban poor, *Educational Leadership*, 37, 1, 15–27.

Maughan, B., Pickles, A., Rutter, M., & Ouston, J. (1990). Can schools change? I. outcomes at six London secondary schools. *School Effectiveness and School Improvement*, 1,3, 188–210.

McCormack-Larkin, M., & Kritek, W. (1982). Milwaukee's Project RISE. *Educational Leadership*, 40, 3, 16–21.

McGaw, B., Banks, D., & Piper, K. (1991). *Effective Schools: Schools That Make a Difference*. Hawthorn, Victoria: Australian Council for Educational Research.

Mortimore, J., & Mortimore, P. (1984). Parents and schools. *Education*, 164, Special Report. October 5.

Mortimore, P. (1990). The front page or yesterday's news: The reception of educational research. In *Doing Educational Research*, ed. G. Walford, pp.210–33. London: Routledge.

(1991). The nature and findings of research on school effectiveness in the primary sector. In *School Effectiveness Research: Its Messages for School Improvement*, ed. S. Riddell & S. Brown, pp. 9–19. Edinburgh: Her Majesty's Stationery Office.

Mortimore, P., Sammons, P., Stoll, L., Lewis, D., & Ecob, R. (1988). *School Matters*. London: Paul Chapman Publishing.

Murphy, J. (1991). *Restructuring Schools: Capturing and Assessing the Phenomena*. New York: Teachers' College Press.

Murphy, J., Weil, M., Hallinger, P., & Mitman, A. (1982). Academic Press: Translating high expectations into school policies and classroom practices. *Educational Leadership*, 40, 3, 22–6.

Northwest Regional Educational Laboratory (NREL) (1990). *Effective Schooling Practices Update*. Portland, Ore.: NREL.

Nuttall, D., Goldstein, H., Prosser, R., & Rashbash, J. (1989). Differential school effectiveness. *International Journal of Educational Research*, 13,7, 769–76.

Nuttall, D., Sammons, P., Thomas, S., & Mortimore, P. (personal communication, August 1993).

Olweus, D. (1991). Bully/victim problems among school children: Basic facts and effects of a school-based intervention programme. In *The Development and Treatment of Childhood Aggression*, ed. D. Pepler & K. Rubin, pp. 411–88. Hove and London: Erlbaum.

Ouston, J., Maughan, B., & Rutter, M. (1991). Can schools change? II. Practice in six London secondary schools. *School Effectiveness and School Improvement*, 2, 1, 3–13.

Power, M., Alderson, M., Phillipson, C., Schoenberg, E., & Morris, J. (1967). Delinquent schools. *New Society*, 10, 542–3 .

Purkey, S., & Smith, M. (1983). Effective schools: A review. *Elementary School Journal*, 83,4, 427–52.

Raudenbush, S. (1989). The analysis of longitudinal multilevel data. *International Journal of Educational Research*, 13, 7, 721–40.

Reynolds, D. (1992). School effectiveness and school improvement: An updated review of the British literature. In *School Effectiveness: Research, Policy and Practice*, ed. D. Reynolds & P. Cuttance, pp. 1–24. London: Cassell.

Reynolds, D., & Cuttance, P. (eds) (1992). *School Effectiveness: Research, Policy and Practice*. London: Cassell.

Reynolds, D., Jones, D., & St. Leger, S. (1976). Schools do make a difference. *New Society*, 37, 321.

Reynolds, D., Sullivan, M., & Murgatroyd, S. (1987). *The Comprehensive Experiment*. Lewes: Falmer Press.

Roeder, P., & Sang, F. (1991). Über die Institutionelle Verarbeitung von Leistungsunterschieden. *Zeitschrift f. Entwicklungspsychologie u. Pädagogische Psychologie*, 23, 2, 159–70.

Rosenthal, R., & Jacobson, L. (1968). *Pygmalion in the Classroom: Teacher Expectations and Pupils' Intellectual Development*. New York: Holt Rinehart & Winston.

Rutter, M. (1983). School effects on pupil progress: Research findings and policy implications. *Child Development*, 54, 1, 1–29.

Rutter, M., Maughan, B., Mortimore, P., & Ouston, J. (1979). *Fifteen Thousand Hours: Secondary Schools and Their Effects on Children*. London: Open Books.

Sammons, P., & Nuttall, D. (1992). *Differential School Effectiveness*. Paper presented to the British Educational Research Association Conference, Stirling, August.

Scheerens, J., & Creemers, B. (1989) (Guest editors). Developments i*n School Effectiveness Research. International Journal of Educational Research*, 13, 7.

Sizemore, B. (1987). The effective African American elementary school. In *Schooling in Social Context: Qualitative Studies*, ed. G. Noblit & W. Pink, pp. 175–202. Norwood, N.J.: Ablex.

Smith, D., & Tomlinson, S. (1989). *The School Effect*. London: Policy Studies Institute.

Stevenson, H., & Shin-Ying, L. (1990). Contexts of Achievement: A Study of American, Chinese and Japanese Children. *Monographs of the Society for Research in Child Development*, serial number 221, 55.

Stoll, L., & Fink, D. (1989). An effective schools project – The Halton approach. In *School Effectiveness and Improvement: Proceedings of the First International Congress, London 1988*, ed. D. Reynolds, B. Creemers, & T. Peters, pp. 286–99. Groningen, RION Institute for Educational Research/School of Education, University of Wales College of Cardiff.

Teddlie, C., Falkowski, C., Stringfield, S., Deselle, S., & Garvue, R. (1984). *The Louisiana School Effectiveness Study Phase 2*. Louisiana State Department of Education.

Teddlie, C., Kirby, P., & Stringfield, S. (1989). Effective versus ineffective schools: Observable differences in the classroom, *American Journal of Education*, 97,3, 221–36.

Tizard, B., Blatchford, P., Burke, J., Farquhar, C., & Plewis, I. (1988). *Young Children at School in the Inner City*. Hove and London: Erlbaum.

Tizard, J., Schofield, W., & Hewison, J. (1982). Symposium: Reading–Collaboration between teachers and parents in assisting children's reading. *British Journal of Educational Psychology*, 52,1, 1–15.

Toews, J., & Murray-Barker, D. (1985). *The Baz Attack: The School Improvement Experience Utilising Effective Schools Research 1981/85*. Calgary, Alberta: Bazalgette Junior High School.

U.S. Department of Education (1987). *What Works?* Washington, DC.

Van de Grift, W. (1990). Educational leadership and academic achievement in elementary education. *School Effectiveness and School Improvement*, 1,1, 26–40.

Waldron, P. (1983). *Towards a More Effective School*. Canadian Education Association Short Course, Alberta: Banff.

Weber, G. (1971). *Inner City Children Can be Taught to Read: Four Successful Schools*. Washington, DC: Council for Basic Education.

Willms, J., & Cuttance, P. (1985). School effects in Scottish secondary schools. *British Journal of Sociology of Education*, 6,3, 287–306.

Willms, J., & Raudenbush, S. (1989). A longitudinal hierarchical linear model for estimating school effects and their stability. *The Journal of Educational Measurement*, 26, 3, 209–32.

Wood, R., & Bandura, A. (1989). Impact of conceptions of ability on self-regulating mechanisms and complex decision-making. *Journal of Personality and Social Psychology*, 56, 407–15.

III. Conclusions

11. Sociocultural trends affecting the prevalence of adolescent problems

LEE N. ROBINS

The chapters in this volume ask what is unique about the period of youth, are there discrepancies between what we know and prevailing views that suggest the public has a biased view of the status of youth, what explains whether an individual adolescent will experience a troubled or a successful phase of life, and what research issues are urgent for the near future. Haunting these chapters is the feeling that the status of youth is changing in the direction of greater stress and less confidence in the future. This chapter attempts to link these concerns to evidence that there have indeed been secular and sociocultural changes in the place of youth in modern society that give substance to the concerns.

Adolescence is not synonymous with difficulty

But first a word of caution. The view that youngsters in this generation are having a particularly difficult time should not be overdrawn. Several chapters, including in particular Petersen and Leffert's, note that the intrinsic social and biological transitions that define adolescence make it a distinctive period in the life course during which the same challenges must be met generation after generation. As Petersen and Leffert note, not only is puberty being completed, but the brain is undergoing its final developmental phase. These biological changes may have important implications for the tasks of adolescence. In particular, deferring learning and tasks typical of this period may result in permanent disability, because the biological window of opportunity may be missed as plasticity diminishes with maturation.

The tasks specific to adolescence include consolidating one's sexual identity and entering into sexual relationships, forming close, long lasting relationships with peers, setting educational goals and forming at least general ideas about occupational goals, separating oneself from one's parents by learning to take responsibility for one's own schedule and behavior, learning to postpone the satisfaction of immediate needs in favor of long-term planning and goals, and for the first time, taking on at least partial responsibility for the welfare of others. Most adolescents perform these tasks effectively and feel satisfied with themselves and their world. Yet these demands do have the potential for producing strains that are reflected in problems for a substantial minority.

Research has focused more on problems of adolescence than on its successes. The public, too, perceives adolescence as a troubled time, and tends to stereotype adolescents as loud, inconsiderate, dangerous, and selfish. One contribution that social research can make is to underscore the fact that most adolescents do their tasks well. If adults change their image of adolescents, it will improve the youngsters' self-esteem, and enable them to view their peers as members of a valuable and admirable age group.

Problems typical of adolescence

Although most young people move successfully through adolescence, there are problems that typically arise in this period. These are the years in which delinquency, both minor and serious, is at its height (see Farrington, this volume), and in which the abuse of tobacco, alcohol, and illicit drugs begins, if it ever will. A substantial proportion of adolescents begin to fail at school as they lose interest in education or have severe disciplinary problems with school authority figures. With each year past puberty, the proportion of adolescent girls becoming pregnant increases. Adolescent delinquency, substance abuse, school failure, and pregnancy can each have long lasting impacts by severely limiting later occupational and marital opportunities.

The adolescent years are also the period in which a first episode of adult psychiatric disorder is likely to make its appearance. A substantial proportion of those who will ever suffer from a major depressive disorder, panic attacks, mania, or schizophrenia experience their initial symptoms in adolescence, and the risk rises as they move from early to late adolescence. Adolescence and young adulthood are also the ages when risk of death by accident, homicide, and AIDS is highest.

Rising rates of difficulties

The prominence of each of these traditionally adolescent problems appears to have increased in recent years. Adolescents have also become vulnerable to one major problem from which they used to be relatively protected – suicide, although their rates are still below those of older persons. Some of this increase for adolescents was expectable, given the increase in the total population's rates of homicide and substance abuse, but adolescents have suffered a rise disproportionate to that of the total population. For example, the age of onset of major disorders, such as depression, appears to have dropped from a mean age of forty to about twenty-five, and cases of major depression have been increasingly recognized among adolescents, as Merikangas and Angst (this volume) note. The age of first illicit drug use also dropped as the drug epidemic progressed, sufficiently lengthening the exposure to drugs within the adolescent period for some to begin to show drug-related problems, problems that used to be delayed until the twenties.

Possible explanations for the increase in adolescent problems

The reasons for an apparent increase in the pathology of adolescence are not well established. A rise in the proportion of the adolescent population found to have problems could be explained in several ways: a true increase in such problems, longer endurance of the problems when they occur, or elongation of the period defined as adolescence resulting in more years during which problems are defined as the problems of adolescence. The elongation of adolescence has occurred at both ends of the period. Adolescence appears to begin at a younger age because the age at puberty has been dropping, and because of changes in the organization of schools, with the invention of the junior high school in the United States, which segregates those from eleven to thirteen from children in elementary school. Adolescence lasts longer as the rites of entry into adulthood, such as departure from school, beginning a full-time job, and marriage have become increasingly delayed. The duration of problems is also an important consideration in explaining their current frequency. At any moment in time, long-lasting problems are more likely to be observed as present than more transient ones.

When we address possible explanations for the increase in adolescent problems, we will consider through which of these routes they are most likely to have increased.

1. *The decline of occupational opportunities.* An important factor in the increase in adolescent problems is probably changes in the world's economic structure.

The unskilled factory jobs and entry level white collar jobs that were the mainstay of young workers have been disappearing; at the same time the supply of labor has greatly increased with the much greater participation of women in the labor force and the continuation in the labor market of the enormous now middle-aged cohort of "baby boomers." This oversupply of labor relative to job demand has brought about an increase in job applicants' minimum acceptable educational levels, keeping those with little aptitude for school in the classroom longer than they wish, with expectable declines in the average academic achievement and morale of high school and early college attenders.

As the educational credentials required have escalated, college tuitions in some countries have risen extraordinarily. Not long ago in the United States, any secondary school student in the top ranks academically had an excellent chance for college, but college is no longer financially feasible for many. As tuitions rise and entry level white collar jobs become scarcer, youngsters understandably question whether going to college is worth the effort, particularly if they have doubts about their chances for academic success.

Even those who complete college are no longer guaranteed an occupational niche. At the Harvard graduation of 1992, the message of the valedictorian speech was a humorous, but deeply serious, lament over the fact that most of the graduating seniors had still not found a job. This situation makes it apparent to adolescents that advanced education is serving not so much to prepare them for good jobs as to delay their entry into the job market, and so diminish society's unemployment level.

The disappearance of many entry level jobs elongates adolescence not only by requiring more student years, but also by keeping young people dependent on their parents and unable to afford marriage or an independent household. Those who remain in school may be there unwillingly, and those who leave but cannot find a job suffer from having no discernible function in society.

2. *Rising levels of material "needs."* The shrinking of the market for unskilled labor and other entry level jobs has unfortunately occurred at the same time that living standards have risen. Near universal access to television and the cinema awakens desires of adolescents (and their parents), desires for consumer goods and life-styles they cannot easily afford. These desires have pushed large numbers of students into part-time jobs to fund their purchases of cars and stylish clothes. These jobs can be the viaduct through which schooling is abandoned; the job takes up time that

should be spent doing homework, and if the boss offers them a full-time job, it may look more attractive than waiting to take one's chances at graduation time. In inner city areas, where even low level jobs are scarce, youth are pushed by these desires into illegal occupations.

3. *Stagnation or decline of adolescents' health.* An interesting hypothesis has been advanced by Easterlin (1968) about the "baby boom" generation. He argued that their large numbers led to disadvantage in the job market compared with the situation their parents had experienced at the same age, and despair of being able to maintain the living standard their parents enjoyed. Today's adolescents have reason to feel disadvantaged even relative to their baby boom parents. Young people are both the authors and victims of a homicide rate higher than the one their parents experienced. They also observe their peers dying by suicide, AIDS, and drug overdose. In the epochs in which adolescents' parents and grandparents grew up, life expectancy was dramatically increasing with the discovery of antibiotics and new vaccines, and the major strides being made in public hygiene. At that time, adolescents shared the experience of a decline in deaths among their peers, until deaths from natural causes became very rare for adolescents. Today, deaths from natural causes continue to decline for infants, with medicine's improved ability to keep small newborns alive, and for older adults, with improved prevention and treatment of heart disease and cancer, but medical advances can do little to prevent deaths of adolescents, which are now primarily nonnatural.

It has been noted that adolescents have failed to adopt the health promoting and disease preventing activities of diet, exercise, refraining from smoking, seat belt use, and regular checkups that seem to have improved the health and survival of their elders. This has been attributed to a sense of invulnerability; it may also reflect loss of expectation of a long life.

Physicians responded to the changing relative status of adolescents by developing a specialty area of adolescent medicine. As this specialty area grows, questions arise as to whether adolescents should be offered the increasing rights to make personal treatment decisions that adults have begun to insist on, rather than remain in their traditional status as wards of parental guardians. At present, the right of adolescents to receive care for pregnancy or sexually transmitted disease independently of their parents' consent is a controversial issue.

4. *Urbanization of society.* The rapid urbanization that has taken place in many countries may also have contributed to youngsters' problems.

David Smith (this volume) notes that crime rates tend to be positively correlated with the proportion of a country's population with urban residence. Urbanization is clearly not the only factor, however, because adolescent crime rates have increased even in countries where there has been diffusion of urban populations, rather than increasing concentration into central cities.

There are several routes through which urbanization may affect adolescents adversely. Urbanization is associated with an increased differential between living standards of the well-to-do and the poor, and increased residential segregation by class and minority group. These changes deprive poor youngsters of middle class models of behavior, enterprise, and expectation in their schools and neighborhoods. Urbanization has also led to larger schools and bigger classes, particularly where the rate of moving to urban centers outstripped the receiving cities' ability to build and staff schools. Large classes mean less personalized education and a delay in the identification of those children with special educational needs.

These are negative effects. Urbanization also has positive effects, by greatly expanding the diversity of educational and recreational opportunities for young people.

5. *Changing family structures.* The major changes in family structure over the last twenty years may in part be attributed to the effects of rapid urbanization, which disrupts extended family networks that formerly assisted in the socialization of children and turns parents into emigrants from rural settings. Like emigrants from abroad, these parents lack familiarity with being adolescent in a strange setting, and their lack of personal experience can threaten their authority over their children.

Other important changes in family structures are the great increases in mothers working outside the home, in divorce and remarriage, and in children born out of wedlock. These changes bring others with them. Not only do single parents more often work, they also go out on dates, remarry and take on care of stepchildren. Fewer young people thus have regular access to both natural parents, and the resident parent becomes less available. Because adolescents typically have no voice in these family realignments, they have a particularly hard time adjusting to them.

The increases in adult life expectancy noted above also result in encroachment on the availability of parents to their teenagers in both intact and broken families. Parents must care for their own parents, who live longer even after their health becomes irreversibly poor.

Today's families are in particularly sharp contrast to the families in which parents of today's adolescents grew up. *Their* parents had borne them in early adulthood and survived into their offspring's adolescence and young adulthood in good health, thanks to the discovery of antibiotics. Their parents were either healthy or died rapidly if they developed a terminal illness. This combination of circumstances allowed them to be readily available as mentors to their children. Yet these "normal," vigorous, intact families we look back on nostalgically may have been the norm in no other cohort in history. Earlier, high risk of death at childbirth and in mid-life meant that many adolescents grew up in broken and reconstructed families.

Each of these changes in families suggests an increase in at least one of the aspects of poor parenting found by a meta-analysis of many studies to be predictive of delinquency: marital discord, lack of supervision of and involvement with the adolescent, and inadequate disciplinary practices (Loeber and Stouthamer-Loeber, 1986).

6. *The drug epidemic.* The drug epidemic that began in the 1960s is a historical event that has almost certainly contributed to the problems of youths by turning them into both users and sellers of drugs. The market for illicit drugs became a part of the underground economy. The scarcity of entry level legal jobs and their poor financial rewards compared with the rewards for selling drugs made this illegal occupation an attractive option for poorly educated young people, albeit a very dangerous one because its contracts can be enforced only by violence, not through the courts.

The increase in drug and alcohol use has also been associated with adolescent death and morbidity from traffic accidents and overdose, and with substantial psychiatric comorbidity. The illegality of drugs makes procuring them time-consuming, expensive, and grounds for arrest; taking them interferes with concentration. Thus their use should be associated with absenteeism from school and work and decreased efficiency when present. The frequent onset of depressive symptoms in substance abusers suggests that drugs may also directly cause psychological problems. Thus the great drug epidemic, accompanied as it has been by increasing use of alcohol, has had a variety of deleterious effects on young people. There are signs that the number of young people using drugs occasionally has declined over the last ten years in the United States (Johnston et al., 1992). It is not known how worldwide this change is, or whether even in the United States it has been accompanied by a parallel reduction in use at levels heavy enough to cause deleterious effects.

7. *Decline in pubertal age.* Over the last generation, the age at puberty has dropped, presumably because of better nutrition but some suggest also because children are increasingly exposed to sexually stimulating material in conversation, television, and movies as their elders experience a decrease in inhibition about sexual matters. With puberty earlier and decreasing sexual inhibition, youngsters have become sexually active at earlier ages, exposing them to risks of pregnancy and sexually transmitted diseases. AIDS is only the newest of these.

The drop in the age at puberty may lead to a lengthening of the period considered as adolescence, as ten- and eleven-year-olds develop obvious secondary sexual characteristics. Since onset of puberty is the defining biological change of adolescence, one might expect a clear impact of the earlier appearance of secondary sex characteristics on the definition of adolescence. Perhaps surprisingly, no such consistent results have been found across studies, as Alsaker's review (this volume) notes. It appears that it is the interpretation of these changes rather than their occurrence that is determining.

8. *Ambiguity of expectations and responsibilities.* Adolescents throughout history have had difficulties in defining their roles and finding scope for contributing to society, and ambiguities with respect to the proper role for those who are neither child nor adult appear greater today than in the past. Reiss (this volume) notes that modern Western society has fewer rites of passage between childhood and adolescence than other societies, leaving adolescents in more ambiguous situations. The near-universal access to American television and movies introduces and seems to endorse adolescent behaviors not in synchrony with the values of many societies or even subcultures in America itself. Thus, adolescents often experience contradictory expectations from parents, schools, employers, the government, and the media with respect to their duties and options.

Determinants of differential risks for adolescent problems

A great variety of historical changes may contribute to what appears to be a rising incidence or duration of problems for today's adolescents, but the uniqueness of historical events makes it difficult to test which are truly causes of a change in the overall level of adolescent problems and which only plausible explanations. There is much more substantial evidence concerning which adolescents are currently at special risk.

The factors discussed above as possibly accounting for a general increase in problems should, if correct, serve also to identify individuals at special risk. These would be youngsters who lack credentials for obtaining rewarding jobs, those in large cities, those from one-parent homes, with working mothers or living away from both parents, those who try illicit drugs, and those with especially early puberty.

Studies of risk factors for adolescent problems do support findings of an elevation in the level of problems in youngsters with little education and living in inner cities, where jobs are particularly scarce and association with delinquent peers is easy. Nonetheless, many youngsters who do not attend college and live in inner cities function well, and neither develop drug problems nor have other serious problems. The other hypotheses were supported less strongly, though there are suggestive findings with respect to broken homes and early puberty, particularly for girls (Magnusson, 1988). One possible mechanism through which girls are affected by early puberty is that, looking older than their years, they are invited to associate with others older than themselves, and share in activities that are age-inappropriate.

In contrast to these modest findings, studies of individual differences in children prior to adolescence reveal striking agreement about warning signs that adolescence will be troubled. The signs lie in early personal characteristics, in the peer group, in the family, in schools, and in neighborhoods. Children with somewhat low IQs who are aggressive, truant, dishonest, and low in academic achievement, who associate with delinquents and drug users, and who use psychoactive substances heavily are at higher risk of adolescent delinquency, substance abuse, and suicide than their age mates. Adolescents reared by parents who are psychiatrically ill, criminal, aggressive, or substance abusers, who neglect or mistreat their children or are erratic in their supervision and discipline of the children also have an increased risk for these adverse outcomes (McCord, 1979). Schools in which teachers are demoralized have more delinquent students and more dropouts. Disorganized neighborhoods, defined as places where neighbors take no responsibility for children outside their own families, where crime and drug trafficking are common, and where there are few recreational facilities for teenagers, also have more troubled adolescents. As noted by Reiss (this volume), disorganized neighborhoods cause delinquency, which in turn forces law-abiding citizens and victimized businesses to move away, leaving the neighborhood increasingly disorganized and criminogenic. He also cites studies showing that neighborhoods made up largely of single-parent families are not able to control the vandalism and violence of their adolescent boys.

This agreement across studies about the factors correlated with a variety of forms of adolescent maladjustment is particularly well founded for juvenile delinquency, as noted by David Smith (this volume), but it also applies to substance abuse and poor school success. This similarity in predictors does not necessarily mean that delinquency, substance abuse (Robins & McEvoy, 1990), and school failure have exactly the same set of multiple causes. Most of these predictors are highly intercorrelated among themselves (e.g., parents who are psychiatrically ill or abuse substances are much more likely than others to mistreat or neglect their children, to produce children who are truant and dishonest, and to find housing in disorganized neighborhoods where delinquent peers are readily available to their children), and it may be the case that a different set of these correlated precursors constitutes the cause of each of these three adolescent problems. These three adolescent problems are highly intercorrelated as well, making each inevitably statistically associated with the cause of another. The direction of influence may often be reciprocal rather than entirely in the environment-to-adolescent-problem direction (e.g., teachers may become demoralized when dealing with aggressive and disrespectful teenagers; parents may give up trying to supervise children who are secretive about their whereabouts; antisocial adolescents no doubt select or are selected by antisocial peers as companions).

Analysis aimed at identifying the mechanisms through which these precursors affect adolescent problems has succeeded to some extent in resolving these uncertainties, although mechanisms are still not entirely understood.

We know, for example, that childhood conduct problems and early substance abuse are associated with a greater likelihood that mental disorders will begin in adolescence rather than later. But we do not know whether the total burden of mental illness is thus increased, or only its timing altered. Studying the time sequences among the appearance of phenomena such as puberty, conduct problems, substance use, and mental illness from the childhood years through the end of their ages of risk is beginning to reduce the confusion between events that are causes rather than effects of specific adolescent problems. Thus, conduct problems usually precede delinquency and substance use, while psychiatric problems are usually last in the sequence (Kandel, 1980; Robins and Wish, 1977).

Protective factors

A few factors have been identified which might protect adolescents from difficulty. By protective factors, we mean factors which make it possible for adolescents to avoid developing problems even when they have many of the typical precursors. As noted above, even those from poor, disorganized neighborhoods often turn out well. The same can be said for children reared by inadequate parents.

Children with high IQs and special skills appear to have some protection against the effects of poor environments (see Farrington, this volume). The presence of some supportive, loving, and conforming adult role model is another asset that may cancel out much of the impact of having inadequate parents (McCord, 1990).

Efforts to increase the protective factors, for example, by providing a concerned adult (Powers & Witmer, 1951; Tait & Hodges, 1962) have not been very successful, as measured by criminal records. Perhaps these interventions were too little or too late. Or perhaps the problem was in the narrowness of the outcome measured. Although ineffective in preventing delinquency, they may have succeeded in areas more likely to be affected by a relationship with an older caring person, such as improving interpersonal skills. Another possibility is that they were redundant with what was already being offered by private and public youth groups, where adult leaders attempt to prevent the development of adolescent problems. As noted by Jane Quinn (this volume), surveys of participants in community organized after-school activities find a considerable satisfaction with their effects on learning and development of leadership skills, and participants generally have better school records and less deviant behavior than nonparticipants. As well as being consistent with program effectiveness, the greater success of youngsters in rather than out of such programs is also consistent with the greater ability of the programs to reach youngsters destined to be successful than those headed for serious problems. Quinn notes that these groups, perhaps in part because they often lack trained leaders and are poorly funded, have difficulty in enrolling the highest risk young people. Some appeal more to girls than boys, and thus do not reach a proportionate number of the potential delinquents.

Exceptional school quality is not often listed among the protective factors that may modify outcomes of disadvantaged children. Yet, as Mortimore points out (this volume), a number of studies of school effectiveness indicate substantial differences in student achievement and attitudes even when students' liabilities at school entry are taken into account. The successful schools would seem to be acting as protective factors for high risk students. Although the positive effects of the exceptional school may be smaller than the negative effects of extreme poverty or parental failure to support educational achievement, if schools can be modified so that most have the same small effect that the best ones now have, because all children are exposed to schools, this would have very important consequences for both individuals and society as a whole.

Predictors of duration and severity

Most research relating age of onset to duration of delinquency (Loeber & Stouthamer-Loeber, 1986) shows that early onset is associated with a prolonged duration and greater severity. Early onset of drug use (Robins & Przybeck, 1985) similarly predicts developing serious drug problems, alcoholism, and antisocial personality. These observations would not be very useful in planning interventions, if they only mean that adolescents destined to have more severe problems showed the earlier signs, but they become meaningful in the context of the drop over time in the age of onset of substance abuse and depression. Such a long-term shift cannot be explained by a sufficient growth in the proportion of youngsters with an in-born liability to serious problems. This drop must be largely explained by social factors, and can potentially be manipulated. It also gives warning that a lower proportion of this generation of problem adolescents will recover on reaching adulthood than was true in the past.

Time of termination

Most adolescents who commit delinquent acts and abuse substances begin to refrain from these behaviors by early adulthood. Psychiatric problems such as depression and schizophrenia that begin in adolescence are generally more enduring, but even these sometimes end without any adult recurrence.

At present we know little about predictors of when or if adolescents will recover from their problems, other than age of onset. As Farrington notes (this volume), there is considerable evidence that the factors that predict that adolescent difficulties will occur are not effective predictors that they will persist into adult life. It would obviously be very useful to be able to know which variables identify the subgroup of affected adolescents most likely to continue problems into adulthood. This is the group for which intervention is most urgently needed. One promising research route might be to compare factors affecting continuity in adolescents whose problems began in early, middle, or late adolescence, thereby avoiding confounding them with age of onset, since we know that early onset is itself an important predict of greater continuity.

The stability of individual predictors over time

The studies reviewed here concerning factors influencing which adolescents will develop difficulties were carried out over some forty-five years. Yet all tell the same story. Observations of the predictors of adolescent problems have been extremely stable over these years, whereas the prevalence has shown striking increase. One might have expected that as the behaviors initially considered very deviant for youngsters became commonplace, different factors would determine who would participate in them. A number of studies have shown, however, that this is not the case (Robins, 1978; 1993). Instead, when behavior problems are rare, one notes that the only adolescents who exhibit them have a large number of the predictive factors. When the same behaviors are common, the only adolescents who do not exhibit them lack virtually all of the same set of predictive factors. This association between prevalence and predictors holds not only for prevalence changes over time, but also for contemporaneous differences in prevalence between males and females and between advantaged and disadvantaged groups. Thus, antisocial girls come from more disturbed families than do delinquent boys, and white prisoners display more psychopathology than black prisoners (Robins, Tipp, & Przybeck, 1991).

Experiments in preventing adolescent problems

1. *Experiments as tests of causal hypotheses.* We have discovered a variety of correlates of adolescent problems. It is important that these be separated into factors that are plausible causes of adolescent problems and those that are not. Multivariate analyses help in achieving this when the order of appearance of these various factors is known, so that causes are not confused with consequences of the problems, and no cause is discarded because an intervening mechanism through which it affects the outcome is included in the analysis. Because ascertaining order is important, these analyses are more successful when used in connection with longitudinal study designs, which measure these factors before and after the onset of the problems of adolescence. When these more sophisticated analyses have been carried out for childhood behaviors and parental characteristics, they have shown that childhood behavior, parental characteristics, peers, school, and neighborhood are each independent precursors of adolescent problems. They are still not necessarily its causes.

The most critical test of causality is the preventive experiment; if changing a precursor experimentally reduces the rate of an outcome, its role as a cause is supported. (Unfortunately, negative results of experiments rarely provide substantial evidence that the precursor is not a cause, because of the limitations that may exist in the experimenter's ability to change the precursor of interest, to keep the experimental and control groups intact and well matched throughout the experiment, and to finance a sufficiently large experiment to allow assuming that lack of statistical significance was not due only to an inadequate sample size.)

Experiments in reducing or removing precursors of adolescent problems to prevent their onset have had mixed success. The experimental studies offering after-school programs cited by Quinn (this volume) generally show small short-term gains in school performance, the avoidance of early sex and pregnancy, and abstaining from drug use. These gains disappear within a few years, however. Thus the after-school programs can be seen as useful at least in delaying the onset of problems, not a trivial achievement. Perhaps continuing the programs for longer might have enhanced their effectiveness.

Like the studies of after-school programs, most prevention experiments have shown results that are not very impressive. One difficulty may be that the studies had good effects that were not measured. Because problems tend to be intercorrelated, and so are their precursors, it would be surprising if modifying a precursor had effects exclusive to a single one of the problem behaviors of adolescence. No matter the goal that motivated an experimental program, it is worth determining whether it had any unexpected benefits. And unexpected adverse effects should be evaluated as well. The best known example of such unanticipated effects on nontarget problems is the Head Start experiment (Schweinhart & Weikart, 1980). This program was intended to raise IQ through an enriched program at age four. It had only transient effects on IQ, but years later it was discovered to have been helpful in fostering adolescent school attachment and in reducing delinquency. Once considered a failure because its impact on IQ was transient, this experiment is now been considered a success, given the broader range of outcomes examined.

2. *Experiments in coping.* Prevention can be achieved by methods other than eradicating causes of adverse outcomes. As prophylactic antibiotics can be used to prevent infection in persons at risk, even though infection is not caused by an "antibiotic deficiency," it is plausible that teaching adolescents how to cope with unavoidable stress might prevent their developing psychiatric symptoms when stressed. Compas (this volume)

reviews school programs designed to accomplish this by preparing all children to cope with common sources of stress. A variety of good outcomes have been reported for some programs. Programs aimed at children undergoing severe stress, such as parental divorce or depression, have not yet been evaluated for effectiveness.

3. *Preventing rare events.* When an adolescent problem is rare, prevention experiments are not very useful either for proving causal hypotheses or for proving the effectiveness of interventions. Such is the case of suicide. Suicide is increasing among adolescents, but it is still a very rare occurrence, and the readiness to commit suicide is often transient. As Diekstra points out in this volume, suicide's rarity in adolescence and the differences between countries in how it is ascertained makes comparing prevalence across countries difficult, but there is persuasive evidence that overall the adolescent male suicide rate has been increasing over the last twenty years. Effective prevention would require either reducing its risk factors or so precisely anticipating when it was likely to occur that a youngster could be institutionalized until the period of high predisposition had passed. Neither has yet been shown to be feasible.

Damage control during self-limited adolescent difficulties

Because delinquency and substance abuse typically arise in adolescence and then abate in young adulthood, we should be concerned with how to protect those troubled adolescents who are likely to recover from incurring irreparable damage during their period of delinquency or substance abuse. Drug use and crime carry with them the risk of receiving a label that may follow the recovered adolescent for life, the risk of rupturing relationships with the family, and a risk to health and life, as youngsters risk overdosing, motor accidents, suicide, AIDS and hepatitis, and being victims of violence. Participation in crime and drugs also preempts time and opportunities to learn the skills and amass the credentials necessary for successful adulthood.

Little has been done to identify ways of protecting adolescents in trouble from suffering such long-term consequences. Most studies of forced removal into institutions show this to be harmful rather than helpful. Thus, minimizing the level of official intervention seems helpful in protecting youngsters from long-term adverse consequences of their behavior. It seems reasonable that environments could be designed that would effectively keep youngsters from injuring themselves or others until they pass through the adolescent problem phase, but their sufficient elements have not yet been well described.

When troubled adolescents do recover, many are without the skills that other youngsters have developed, and never make up for the loss. Whether or not this reflects their having missed a vital biologically fixed period of plasticity, ways need to be explored that could overcome the interference with learning that occurs with adolescent drug use, antisocial behavior, and psychiatric disorder. Areas of deficit include interpersonal behavior relevant to job performance, relating to family members, and parenting, as well as the technical knowledge and skills needed to hold jobs. Since confinement has been shown not to be helpful, programs focusing on these developmental tasks should be made available in the community, and outside of school and employment settings so out-of-school and unemployed youths are not excluded.

Also worthy of study would be programs designed to give youth help in breaking away from gangs and association with criminals when they are ready to do so, since rejecting such companions is one of the hallmarks of recovery in those who do give up adolescent criminality. Programs might be modeled after the "witness protection system," which provides new residences and identities to those who cooperate with the police, or a national service program that would allow youngsters to move to a new area and establish new friendships and skills. Without such help, youngsters eager to disentangle themselves may not do so because of fear of reprisals from the former companions.

Families and teachers of troubled adolescents are often unaware that most antisocial youth recover in time, and may regard them as hopeless cases, destined to have problems for life. Since family support seems to be an important factor in encouraging rapid termination of adolescent problem behavior, programs should be developed and evaluated that teach parents and teachers what to expect in the natural history of these adolescent problems.

Involving young people in charting their own futures

This volume reviews what the major issues are in understanding the assets and problems of young people. It reviews prior research about this age period, and points out gaps in our knowledge about it. The authors note some directions in which services for young people should move in order to improve their chances of surviving into adulthood in good physical and psychological health, and to give them a greater sense of control over their lives, a better ability to contribute to their societies, and a better understanding of the difficulties they face in accomplishing the goal of preparing for adulthood.

In working out the details of recommended programs, it will be important to invite young people to participate in the decision-making and to serve as experts on the kinds of messages likely to have the greatest impact on their age group. Adolescents can and should have a voice in decisions that affect their own age group. They can also contribute to planning for other age groups – children, adults, and the elderly – who constitute the society in which they must live. They should also participate in decisions that affect the society as a whole. Of special importance to them should be issues of international peacekeeping, since they are or soon will be in the age range from which soldiers are recruited, and of protecting the environment, without which any solutions specific to youth will be futile.

Youth should be included in reaching solutions not only because they have so much at stake in the outcome and can contribute fresh ideas, but because their inclusion would address one of the major difficulties they face: lack of control over their own lives and lack of opportunities to feel they can contribute to their societies. In participating, they would also learn more about the very real difficulties they face in preparing for adulthood in a world in which job opportunities appear to be declining and family structures are increasingly unspecified.

Young people will welcome having a role in facing problems that concern the whole of society as well as themselves. But the argument for their inclusion is by no means only that it would be good for them psychologically and that they have the right to participate in making decisions that will affect their lives directly. Society must rely on its young people to act as a constructive force for social change. Their fresh and innovative points of view can make a very positive contribution to solutions and recommendations.

References

Easterlin, R. A. (1968). *Population, Labor Force, and Long Swings in Economic Growth: The American Experience*. New York: National Bureau of Economic Research.

Johnston, L., O'Malley, P., & Bachman, J. (1992). *Smoking, Drinking, and Illicit Drug Use among American Secondary School Students, College Students, and Young Adults, 1975–1991, Vol. I, Secondary School Students*. Washington, DC: National Institute on Drug Abuse.

Kandel, D. B. (1980). Developmental stages in adolescent drug involvement. In *Theories on Drug Abuse*, ed. D. Letrieri, M. Sayers, & H. W. Pearson, pp. 120–7. Rockville, Md.: National Institute on Drug Abuse

Loeber, R., & Stouthamer-Loeber, M. (1986). Family factors as correlates and predictors of juvenile conduct problems and delinquency. In *Crime and Justice: An Annual Review of Research*, Vol. 7, ed. M. Tonry & N. Morris, pp. 29–149. Chicago: University of Chicago Press.

Magnusson, D. (1988). *Individual Development from an Interactional Perspective*. Hillsdale, N.J.: Erlbaum.

McCord, J. (1979). Some child-rearing antecedents of criminal behavior in adult men. *Journal of Personality and Social Psychology*, 37, 1477–86.

(1990). Long-term perspectives on parental absence. In *Straight and Devious Pathways from Childhood to Adulthood*, ed. L. N. Robins & M. Rutter. Cambridge and New York: Cambridge University Press.

Powers, E., & Witmer, H. (1951). *An Experiment in the Prevention of Delinquency*. New York: Columbia University Press.

Robins, L. N. (1978). Sturdy childhood predictors of adult outcomes: Replications from longitudinal studies. *Psychological Medicine*, 8, 611–22.

(1993). Vietnam veterans' rapid recovery from heroin addiction: A fluke or normal expectation? *Addiction*, 58, 1037–50.

Robins, L. N., & McEvoy, L. T. (1990). Conduct problems as predictors of substance abuse. In *Straight and Devious Pathways from Childhood to Adulthood*, ed. L. N. Robins & M. R. Rutter, pp. 182–204. New York and Cambridge: Cambridge University Press.

Robins, L. N., & Przybeck, T. R. (1985). Age of onset of drug use as a factor in drug and other disorders. In *Etiology of Drug Abuse: Implications for Prevention*, ed. C. L. Jones & R. J. Battjes, pp. 178–92. Washington, DC: NIDA Research Monograph 56, DHHS Pub. No. (ADM)85–1335.

Robins, L. N., Tipp, J., & Przybeck, T. R. (1991). Antisocial personality. In *Psychiatric Disorders in America*, ed. L. N. Robins & D. Regier, pp. 258–90. New York: The Free Press.

Robins, L. N., & Wish, E. (1977). Childhood deviance as a developmental process: A study of 223 urban black men from birth to 18. *Social Forces*, 56, 448–73.

Schweinhart, L. J., & Weikart, D. P. (1980). *Young Children Grow Up*, Ypsilanti, Mich.: High/Scope.

Tait, C. D., Jr., & Hodges, E. F, Jr. (1962). *Delinquents, Their Families, and the Community*. Springfield, Ill.: Charles C Thomas.

Name index

Subject index